ISBN 0-7414-5019-4

Published by:

INFINITY
PUBLISHING.COM

1094 New DeHaven Street, Suite 100
West Conshohocken, PA 19428-2713
Info@buybooksontheweb.com
www.buybooksontheweb.com
Toll-free (877) BUY BOOK
Local Phone (610) 941-9999
Fax (610) 941-9959

Printed in the United States of America

Printed on Recycled Paper

Published January 2009

Confessions of a
Not-So-Good Catholic Girl

Deanna R. Adams

This book is rated PG-13 for inappropriate language, and other un-Catholic-like behavior that may be offensive to those who always listened to their mother, got along with their school mates, and had aspirations of becoming a nun. Though, in the author's defense, she redeems herself in the end.

This is a work of creative nonfiction. Some names have been changed for the individual's privacy. And some names—and other tell-tale signs that point directly to the guilty party—have been altered to save the author from receiving nasty letters and electronic missives from the easily offended, with no sense of humor.

Still, you know who you are.

To my first family:

My grandparents, Ralph and Viola (Gee Gee) Jenkins, who provided me with love, shelter, and several good stories. And many great memories. And my mother, Ginnie, who taught me more than she realized, like toughening it out, making peace, and dancing in the end.

You each taught me about faith more through your actions than your words.

I really miss you guys.

Acknowledgments

It takes a village to raise a book. Every writer who's been there will testify to that. No matter what kind of book you write, you simply can't do it by yourself. You need those who believe in your talent (because you so often do not). You need those who keep asking you when it's going to be finished (or it may never be). You need those who give you the okay to use them as your muse (fiction or nonfiction). And you need those who tell you when your work is great, and when it's crap, as my dear mentor, Lea Leever Oldham, used to say. For it is that honesty that keeps a writer working toward perfection. And it is honesty that brings the writing itself to the real heart of the story.

Of course, honesty has a price. This book will reveal to my children that their mother isn't perfect, after all. (Though, I believe they've suspected for some time). And it's something my husband of a quarter of a century has long suspected. But he loves me anyway.

So to Jeff, the true love of my life, who is always there—in the beginning, middle, and end of everything I do: You know I couldn't do this without you—for a number of reasons. Beginning with support.

To our daughters, Danielle and Tiffany, who have grown to be smart, good women, with the sense of humor so necessary in life. I give you all my love and heartfelt thanks for being who you are, and helping me learn a few things, too.

To my best friend, and best sister I never had, Nina M. Cetner, who always told me I had more stories than anyone she ever knew. Now, after nearly three decades of an amazing friendship, she'll realize there are still a few she hasn't yet heard. To Lynne Bryant, who, with her medical knowledge, explained things, in lay terms, about my mother's last days, and so helped with some medical details in this book. And my brother, Dennis, who, like me, was lucky enough to be part of a family of such great characters, with good hearts and steadfast faith.

To my awesome writing group members - The Writers of the Western Reserve: Karen Fergus, Aileen Gilmour, Cheryl Laufer, Nancy Piazza, Diane Taylor, Jan Thompson, Bill Warnock. And the "Ah-Roma Mamas": Geri Bryan, Carole Calladine, Barbara McDowell, Anne McFarland, Jan Snow. Thank you all for your help, input, and support. With special thanks to my in-depth readers, Carole Calladine and Erin O'Brien, who took extra time to guide me and pull me out of those dreaded trenches of doubt—a common writers' affliction—and get me back on course. And to Joe Tomaro, one of the Euclid Beach Boys, for allowing me to use that great photo of Laughing Sal.

Finally, to my treasured friends who have been along for the ride—past, present and future. (You all know who you are.)

Thank you all for being my personal village keepers.

Contents

Prologue

Part One: Life, Etc.

Part Three: Legacies

Epilogue

Prologue

Close Calls

*W*hen I was five I almost drowned. Even at that age, you'd think I would have had some kind of divine near-death experience—say, a bright light at the end of a tunnel, a chorus of singing angels, or visions of my short-lived life flashing before me. The drama of it all certainly warranted some kind of grand illusion. But no. What happened that day in the lake at Munroe Falls, Ohio, gave way to more practical impressions. It was my first real encounter with guilt. And regret. And thankfulness. And that was even before I ended up Catholic.

But it wasn't before I'd acquired the Ruth family gene—an inherited characteristic that runs smoothly through my grandmother's side like fine whiskey. The independent, don't-care-what-you-told-me-not-to-do-I'm-gonna-go-right-ahead-and-do-it-anyway trait. (Similarly played out in infamous fashion by George Herman Ruth, aka Babe, who our family believes is an ancestor—story in Part Two.) That same trait runs stubbornly through my oldest daughter, and in some cases, can be a good thing.

But that day, it nearly got me killed. Charlotte, my twenty-one-year-old babysitter, a responsible neighbor who'd been watching me since I was six months old, took me, along with her girlfriend and three kids, for a day of sun and fun. It was a man-made lake, and I remember those little orange balls bobbing in the water, dividing the shallow part from the deep. And the rule was: Don't go past those little balls. Stay in the designated area . . .

My Ruth side had already declared that rules can be broken. And it wasn't that Charlotte hadn't been watching me. But I specifically waited until she wasn't looking, then took off toward the diving area. Where everyone else seemed to be having a lot more fun. That little voice that lives inside us all warned me, in a forceful whisper, *Do Not Go In*. But as I said, I have this independent streak. So I compromised.

I'll just stick my foot in and see how far down the water

goes, I told my young self, not realizing there was slippery cement underneath that inviting water. With no traction, my small wet body slid in quickly, like quicksand.

How could I have known how incredibly bad my timing was? That the lifeguard had just walked away for her break?

I'm sinking. A stiffening fear grips me and I respond by thrashing wildly, trying to pull, or will, my body above the water. It doesn't help. I'm going down, farther and farther. I instinctively know not to breathe or open my mouth. But I can't hold it in any longer and try taking a quick breath, just enough to loosen the force. A gulp of nasty-tasting water rushes into me, forcing me to choke and convulse.

I know I am dying, though too young to fully understand the concept. I begin fighting and kicking harder for this life of mine. I want to see my brother Dennis again—pain in the neck though he is—and even in this heavy watery tomb, I feel remorse for disobeying my favorite sitter. I'm really, really regretting my stupid behavior. But dizziness takes over all thought. I'm getting weak, and finally, I stop kicking. Just then, an arm grabs me and wraps itself around my waist. The arm pulls me up. We are rising! I feel a surge of hope in my waning state.

The arm is attached to a woman who's now gasping for breath as she flops me onto the wet sand. My memory bank skips over the CPR part, though I'm sure that happened, and next thing I recall, I'm lying there looking up through blurry eyes at these worried faces staring down at me. Including Charlotte's—who looks startled and scared—sending burning waves of shame that rush in me as the water spurts out. I can now see that my guardian angel wears a colorful one-piece floral bathing suit and a rubber-like cap with large, floppy yellow-and-pink synthetic daisies clasped to her head. I never see her again, and don't recall my saying one word of thanks. But if we meet in heaven, I'll bow down to her because she allowed me to live out the rest of my life.

On the way home, I sit quietly in disgrace in the back seat of Charlotte's car. Her anxious expression has switched to anger, and I know I'm going to hear about this one. And surely, it comes.

"I can't believe you did that, Dee Dee," she says as she stops for a red light. I see her dark, squinty, disapproving eyes glaring at me through the rearview mirror. I don't look away from them. I fully accept the sufficient reaming I'm getting. I'm just happy to be going home. I'm happy I'm not dead.

After the stern lecture and the "you're just lucky that woman was there," her eyes begin to soften.

"Just please, *please* don't tell your mother about this or she'll never let me take you anywhere again."

Enough said.

I love going places with Charlotte. She expands my little world in Lakeline, Ohio, where I live with my divorced mother, older brother, and grandparents. She takes me swimming and bowling and teaches me games, like Badminton and Croquet. One time she took me to the Cleveland Zoo, which I really liked. The little monkeys were my favorite. They were so funny, though their obsession with their own hairy butts kind of grossed me out . . .

I welcomed all those adventures with her. Save for this last one, of course.

Although I was not yet a church-going Catholic, I'd already had some perception of a Supreme Being: a know-all, see-all, can-make-anything-happen kind of guy. Like Santa or the Easter Bunny. Some mystical being who'd be my invisible friend. Who'd save me from making bad decisions (or save me *after* I made them), and—if I asked nicely—might even come up with gifts. While this all-powerful, surreal presence didn't always save me from myself, He often provided the wisdom and sense of humor to realize the necessity of His occasional inactions.

And He did, on a continual basis, present me with immeasurable and priceless gifts that in my God-given wisdom, I fully recognize as such. Like putting that lady in the water. At just the right moment. In just the right spot. . . .

Memories and Mysteries

I have another vivid long-ago memory. One that makes people look at me skeptically, even my own mother. Well, least at first. So when asked, "What is your first childhood memory?" I usually go with that drowning incident. Or the time I learned to tie my shoes (a difficult task made worse by my being left-handed): I'd sit on the red corduroy "davenport"—as folks called it then—with my other sitter, Mrs. Freeman, a Mrs. Doubtfire look alike, for what seemed like hours, perfecting this precise art of shoe-tying until we'd both gladly settle on a game of Candy Land.

But it is my first genuine memory that invaded my thoughts throughout my childhood. And it's a doozy.

I'm in a bubble. Or maybe a cocoon. Engulfed in moist, smooth warmth. Calm. Content. Then suddenly, a blinding illumination occurs, fused with roaring, disturbing noises. Commotion. Then, cold. Fear. That is all. The memory is only that. A disturbing sensation that, throughout my childhood, haunted me. Whenever I'd close my eyes to concentrate on this mirage—in hopes of remembering more—I'd feel myself squinting to block out the brightness. I'd feel my hands rush up to cup my ears in an attempt to stifle the racket. I'd feel a wave of confusion.

In those early years, I couldn't understand why the sensation would replay in my mind over and over, particularly when I was bored. I'd lie in my little bed staring up at that wallpapered ceiling with those large, abstract-looking sunflowers varying in shades: sunshine yellow, burnt orange, sky blue. Their green leafy stems entwining through their blooms. (Nowadays one might call this pattern, *Loud*.) Least that's my memory of it. The thing is, most of my recollections of these early days, and all my dreams thereafter, play out in black and white. Or a dreary grey. The images, people, places, things . . . they're like television in the 1950s.

And yet those vivid Van Gogh-like flowers that hovered over my head I recall in Technicolor.

What is it in our brains that cause us to remember some things and not others? Some in color, some in black and white. Or grey? Why do people doubt what they can't explain, such as this first memory of mine that no one else I know has experienced? One might assume that it's merely a figment of my imagination. And perhaps it is. But then, why?

I still wonder a half-century later. What exactly is this unexplained, evasive mirage so ingrained in my psyche? And why do I remember it so?

Growing up Catholic did not solve the mystery. Yet, it did provide me with the means, and the faith, to accept enigmatic possibilities . . .

JamesT Harris. com.

fireplace screeen

---

drugstore
hairnet
zyrtec d
eye drops.

hilltopwatergardens.com
Classic urn fountain
$490. 15"x16"d 26 lbs.

islandnet.com (aquascape)
leaping frog spitter
$239.98 part #99694
12"h. 7 lbs.

And vindication was near. One night, when I was seven or eight, I overheard my mother talking at our family's Saturday night poker party (eavesdropping was my forte) about how chaotic my birth was. This is the story according to Mom: The doctor hadn't yet arrived at the hospital when I was ready to be born, and this being the 1950s, nurses were considered merely assistants, and thus not "allowed" to deliver the babies. So before my mother was knocked out with the requisite ether, the frantic nurses began pushing against her lower abdomen to hold me back until Doctor Dayton's arrival.

"They kept pushing down, hard, on my stomach," I heard her tell a captive audience. "I remember screaming three times to stop. But they wouldn't. And after she was born, wouldn't you know, she had three marks on her head – the exact size and shape of fingertips!"

When I overheard Mom tell this story, I recognized it immediately. The loud and frantic noises. The blaring lights. The drama. It was what took place in the operating room at St. Ann's Hospital in Cleveland, Ohio in 1954.

The vision that had haunted my childhood . . .

A few years ago, I was reading "Zen in the Art of Writing," by Ray Bradbury, and learned that I'm not alone in having a birth memory. Bradbury writes:

"For I am that special freak, the man with the child inside who remembers all. I remember the day and hour I was born. I remember being circumcised on the fourth day after my birth . . . "

Imagine my thrill at reading this! Minus, the "freak" reference, of course. This famous author goes on to tell of his mother's shock at his recollection because his circumcision had not, as he correctly recalled, taken place in a hospital, but rather in a doctor's office. A doctor who Bradbury vividly recalls.

***

When I was in my late twenties, I finally told my mother that I remembered being born. We were having drinks— Gin & Squirt for her, Southern Comfort & Coke for me (this being the late '70s, I was still heavily influenced by Janis Joplin). We had reached a stage in our often-difficult relationship where we could actually talk to one another like two mature adults, at least when alcohol was involved. She didn't believe me, of course. So I then proceeded to tell her about another memory. How I remember her and my father, as they looked in 1954.

"You were both standing side by side gazing over my crib with wide, proud smiles," I began. What I didn't mention was that it was one of the few times I remember feeling happy with how she looked at me. How I felt her approval.

"You can't possibly remember that," she said, looking into her glass. "Your father (she always referred to the man as "your father" in a tone of voice others used when speaking of slum landlords) was only there a few times."

"But I do remember," I said firmly. I then repeated the recollection in detail. Dad in a military uniform, Mom, her dark curly hair worn longer, her face, thinner. I described the exact location of the crib—against the wall, the white door with a clear glass knob, to the right. My brother's little bed directly across from me, where I could watch him through the wooden bars, painted white.

Mom promptly ordered another drink.

"Well, I can't believe you can remember that," she said, shaking her head. "That crib was only in that corner a short time before we moved it."

She also confirmed that this was indeed in the summer of '54 when my father had come for a visit while on leave from his short stint in the Marines (well "on leave," as in AWOL, it was later discovered). I was six months old.

Keeping the Faith

So there it is. Scientists, psychologists, and Dr. Phil dispute the possibility of anyone recalling anything before age three—particularly one's own birth. My response to that is, there's a lot we can't justify about unexplainable "coincidences." How some people experience strange premonitions. Or can feel the distinct aura of loved ones long gone. Or witness unearthly events that remain "a mystery." All fall into the realm of "coincidences." Yet we've all had them. And perhaps we're not supposed to always understand. What egos we doubting humans possess to think there must be a clear and precise explanation for everything in life.

I was in church one day, long after I became a Catholic (again), and as I was flipping through the missal, I came across the Letter to the Hebrews that says: "Brothers and Sisters: Faith is the realization of what is hoped for, and evidence of things not seen." Those early memories of mine, I believe, are my own personal proof that there is more to life than we know. That God plants us here just as He planted the trees, the flowers, and the soil from which they feed.

Like most Christians, I've had my share of doubts, questions, and momentary loss of faith. And I think we're supposed to have them. I believe life is a test, the multiple choice kind. Like when Dorothy and the Scarecrow in *The Wizard of Oz* must decide which direction to take at the four-way crossroad. The fearful ones choose to turn around and go back. The doubtful ones choose not to choose and stay stuck in neutral. The brave ones make a decision and venture on.

Perhaps we're given these tests to see what we do with our dilemmas. How we handle our relationships with the people in our lives. We're not supposed to have all the answers. It's the process, the journey, as they say, that provides the best memories—and some of the best stories. The ones in this book are mine, from a baby boomers landscape in Midwest USA.

This book is separated into three parts—what I feel are the three phases of life: Childhood and Adolescence. Young Adult and Parenthood. Middle Age and Last Call. If you're lucky, you get to live long enough to experience each stage. By the time you enter phase three, my oh my, you've got some stories to tell. . . .

I'd been planning to write a novel when my mother died in 2004. I enjoyed the thought of playing God, a chance to make up characters and situations and kill off the bad guys (or girls) at will. But then, I had to clear out Mom's little condo. The woman was a "saver" (the term "pack rat" is a bit harsh, don't you think?). Like the one who came before her, and the one who came after. I found box after box of photographs, letters, mementos (an interesting variety of matchboxes from beloved taverns, several drink chips, too), and closets filled with hidden—or otherwise not talked about—history. All documented life moments spanning generations, with varying degrees of experiences in life, love, and the legacies we ultimately leave. I decided then, why make stuff up when I have so many authentic stories and interesting characters all around me?

Of course, in the telling of these stories, I reveal actions that are oftentimes not my most shining moments. Yet those are typically the ones we learn from best. And they are experiences most of us can identify with, no matter where we come from.

This book is not merely about me, it's about all of us. My stories are your stories, too.

Being Catholic, or a woman, is not a requirement for reading this book.

Just being human is enough.

Part One

Life, Etc.

1. Child Development

Lakeline, Ohio, 1956 . . .

*T*hat's me—on the end. The chubby one. The one who looks like she's deep in thought—even at two years of age. It's the look of a writer. Writers often wear faraway gazes. They are observers. Thinkers. They find life and people fascinating. And complex. And they're usually in their "own world," as my mother often said.

Though in all likelihood, I was probably just watching a squirrel scurry across the yard. . . .

The photograph was taken in our neighbor's yard in Lakeline, a little known village in Ohio—eighteen miles east of Cleveland—so small-town that if you drive through it along Lakeshore Boulevard, you *can* nearly miss it if you blink. Although the boulevard, surrounded by trees, flowerbeds and gravel driveways, stretches more than thirty miles from Cleveland to Mentor, the land of Lakeline is only three-quarters of a mile long, sandwiched between Woodstock Road and Willowick Drive. For years, the village wasn't even recognized by the postmaster general—our mailing address was Willoughby, a city of far more miles and people.

In any case, it's no exaggeration when I say everyone knew everyone in this small township that runs along the Lake Erie shore. Today, there are a grand total of one hundred and sixty-five residents. Back in the 1950s, the estimated number was more like seventy, not counting my family's wandering cats.

I visited nearly all these folks on a regular basis. Others, I'd see only on Halloween when I—dressed as a black cat each

11

year—showed up at their front door begging for Tootsie Rolls. My brother (in the photograph, gazing admiringly at the little neighbor girl, Betty Jean) and I could hit every house in the entire community that costume night and still make it home in time for our favorite TV shows, like *Ozzie & Harriet, Make Room for Daddy,* or *Leave it to Beaver,* depending on which night the holiday fell. Even when it wasn't a special day, there'd be a slow-but-steady stream of neighbor ladies passing through the yards each afternoon sharing baked goods, gardening tips and the latest episode of *Queen for a Day.* There were no fences lining the yards, no lawn fertilizers, and no one locked their front doors at night (our house didn't even have locks).

This is where I became a writer. Where I was given all the stories and people and situations needed to weave a few good tales. Because sleepy as it was, life was never boring here. And it's where I learned a few good truths.

"Things will go smoother, and a lot faster, if you make a game out of it," Mrs. Wolff tells me as we rock back and forth on her wooden bench swing. "Tell your grandmother to set a timer for you and see how quickly you can get your work done."

As a six year old, I don't believe I should have to get any work done. I'm just a kid whose sole purpose in life is to have fun. Which is why I'm complaining to the nice neighbor lady, who wears an apron stained with dried condiments, about having to help with the supper dishes.

"You'll be amazed how much fun you can make anything, even when you don't want to do it," she says, as she distributes bird seed from her seated perch, "And you'll feel good, too, about what you've accomplished in the end."

Life Lesson, Number One.

There were more of these truths to come out of Lakeline, courtesy of not just the grown-ups, but the neighborhood kids (who often provided the toughest ones of all). With no fences to hide behind, people talked to each other here. It was not a gated community, but a bedroom one. A warm, cozy environment. An ideal place to grow up. So even if you didn't like a certain person, or disagreed with someone, you learned to be tolerant. Lakeline people, like Mayberry people in the *Andy Griffith Show,* were laid-back. And the large front yards and deep, open backyards were considered free domain. The neighbors were kind and didn't complain or holler when we kids would dart across one yard to another. Or bother them as they tried to get their gardening done, or hang their clothes on the line, or change the bird bath. Well, okay, I may have been the only one who over-welcomed her stay, but the adults seemed to take my frequent visits and constant chattering in stride. Or least appeared to.

My favorite hangout was the Pertz's house. I was practically a member of the family. Mrs. Pertz kept decorative tin containers of freshly-baked cookies—that never seemed to empty—on the kitchen countertop. She always had baked goods and took pleasure in offering them to me, so long as it wasn't too close to supper time. Treats like sweet banana cake with buttery-smooth cream frosting I'd enjoy with a cup of coffee (mixed with Half and Half), which Mrs. Pertz first introduced me to when I was ten, simply because I was curious.

The first wedding I went to was their daughter Donna's, whose hour-and-a-half long Catholic mass I thought would never end. Charlotte, her older sister, was sixteen when she began babysitting me as an infant, and somehow tolerated this kid who stuck to her like Polygrip for years after. Every Saturday, I'd go over and help her clean her bedroom, while my own remained a mess. It was more fun cleaning someone else's, especially because Charlotte had tons of old *Glamour* magazines I could flip through during my self-imposed "breaks" while she continued to dust or vacuum. I'd then chat with Mr. Pertz, who'd had a stroke years before. I'd watch him struggle in and out of his wheelchair, and was always amazed he never complained. William Pertz was quieter than the women in this family, much like my grandfather, and watched a lot of TV. So our conversations were mostly about what he was watching, which could be anything from *The Real McCoys* to Groucho Marx's *You Bet Your Life*.

While Mrs. Pertz cooked in the kitchen, she'd often ask me for a favor. "Dee Dee, can you give Mr. Pertz his *TV Guide*?" or "Could you hand Mr. Pertz his pack of Winstons, over there on the table?" Sometimes they'd let me wheel him down the narrow hallway for suppertime, and we'd talk along the way about things like who had guessed Groucho's "Secret Word."

The Pertz family was first to give me spiritual guidance. God was like another presence in that household. Jesus, Mary and Joseph statues adorned every room, and in the kitchen, Jesus and his apostles gazed down at us like true pontiffs from the large

13

portrait of the Last Supper on the wall above the dining table. Guests here had to say grace before each meal, and speak nothing but nice things about your neighbors. Even when a certain boy next door spit in your hair when you and his sister had a fight. "Forgive them for they know not what they do," was the apparent lesson. I therefore remained silent with increasingly unkind thoughts because the disgusting brat knew exactly what he did and *DAMN* if I was going to forgive the dumb jerk.

I wondered at times if the Pertz family welcomed me into their fold so easily because I was from a "broken" home and needed a prayer book full of Christian fixin'. This thought was confirmed one day, years later, as Charlotte and I sat in my adult kitchen discussing my childhood. "My mother felt sorry for you kids, with your mother being divorced and all," she stated matter-of-factly. She then added. "Plus, you know, your grandparents went out and drank a lot, so she worried you weren't being brought up right."

Although she meant no harm, I took offense to this. While the facts may have been true, for a dysfunctional family, ours functioned quite nicely, to be honest. And for the most part, I had a happy childhood, despite how things may have looked to the neighbors. I hate to think they were all being nice to me merely out of pity.

While I was clueless about the closed-door discussions they may have had about my brother's and my welfare, I loved chatting with these people. Like that day I sat with Mrs. Wolff on her backyard swing. I acquired ample bits of knowledge from these housewives and grandmothers who never seemed to go anywhere, yet always offered interesting, worldly clichés about life that sounded nothing like those dire ones I'd hear at home such as, "Do as I say, not as I do," "Two wrongs don't make a right," and "The world doesn't revolve around *you*, you know." And of course, what every kid living near the Great Lakes heard whenever they wanted to do what "everyone else is doing."

"If so-and-so jumped in the lake, would you do it, too?"

We'd all answered in the affirmative on that one. Which would then bring out The Paddle. My mother found it convenient that Dennis and I had a toy called the Paddle Ball, a red rubber ball the size of a golf ball, with a string threaded through the hole of a hard wooden paddle. One day she figured out that if you ripped out the string and ball, the paddle was the perfect weapon in which to punish bad behavior. Later, when I became Catholic, I worried that Mom would go to hell for using a child's favorite toy against him. Or her, as in most cases.

I delighted in listening to the neighbor ladies' words of wisdom. Theirs were more positive, thought-provoking. Phrases like, "Good people get rewarded in heaven." And "If you can count your true friends on one hand, you are truly blessed." And "Be nice to others and they'll be nice to you." Though I'd come to find out that last one didn't always pan out.

On the occasions when all the neighbors were too busy to visit with me (or led me to believe they were), and my little friends couldn't come out and play, I'd talk to the trees. Lakeline was surrounded by them, all sizes, shapes, and heights. I loved their powerful presence, the sharp, crisp solidness of their bark (and yes, learned to hug them). Still today, they serve as a humbling reminder how minuscule we are in this world. The statuesque leafy giants graced our yards, framed our driveways, and hovered over our houses. Every one of them, big, tall, and strong. Wonderment is a big part of being a child. When I wasn't digging the ground looking for a glimpse into China, I was lying on the ground staring up at the trees, wondering how God could've possibly created those big, beautiful branches of life. In addition, their full leaves came in handy during hot, muggy summers in a time and place when no one owned an air conditioner.

The few sweltering months we had in Northeast Ohio was tolerated well, thanks to those trees and the cooling effects of the nearby lake. Though the "Lake Effect"—as our weathermen like to call it—also produces unexpected whipping winds, and dark ominous clouds that can cause hazardous conditions on both land, and in the lake. One particular storm was ill-timed and forever known in these parts as the "Fourth of July Storm of 1969," where everyone who lived through it now relate their personal stories of where they were back then. It was so forceful that it ripped big old trees right from their roots like an excavator. The greatest damage was on the west side of Cleveland, most notably Edgewater Park where it claimed several lives. Once it was over, I didn't think it had affected me much, having rode it out in the safety of my grandparents' home. But the next day, on the front page of *The Cleveland Press*, I'd find a photo of a girl I knew, who'd just graduated from the all-girls school we both attended. She was one of the truly nice ones, and had been looking forward to college and a wedding to her high school sweetheart. They'd been at the park, and were making a mad dash from the storm when a huge tree fell on both of them. At the funeral, she was laid out in her wedding dress, alongside her suited fiancé. It was all so sad, and I had to wonder why this could happen to someone with so much promise. One of those questions atheists love.

Throughout the '60s, and much of the '70s, Lake Erie's reputation was nearly as bad as that storm. The shallowest of the Great Lakes was a murky mess. Talks of dangerous bacteria and warnings of deadly viruses filled the nightly news, though I don't recall a single North Coast swimmer dying as a direct result.

And kids don't care about the nightly news. We loved romping through its cool mucky waters, and walking along its rough—and smelly—sand. The foul odor of fish carcass was simply a part of going down to the lake. Boys loved chasing girls there to see how fast they could run while dodging the swarms of dead, disgusting—and very sharp—fish bones that littered the beach. We all had our moments of limping home with cuts on the bloody soles of our bare feet. Yet it never dissuaded me from eating a good Fish Fry.

The lake was always accessible. Every neighbor with beachfront property had metal stairs leading down to it and not one sign that read: "Keep Out." It was understood that the lake was for everyone to enjoy. Nowadays, *No Trespassing* signs are posted on trees and fences in front of nearly every property along its shores, where the privileged feel it necessary to keep others from basking in what they've paid good money for. I suppose given changing times, I can't totally blame them.

My family rarely traveled, and didn't need to. We had plenty of things to see and do, in and around our own home. And many visitors. Our family doctor lived a block away and would make house calls whenever my mother or grandmother—neither drove—couldn't make it to his office. I liked him okay, until the day he announced I had the Measles and quarantined me in my room for a week in the dark (it was believed, back then, that bright light to the afflicted could cause blindness). Every few months, Mr. Williams, the friendly insurance man who looked like Robert Young from *Father Knows Best*, would come calling to collect payment or give advice on changing rates. And nearly every day, an apron clad lady would show up at our back door to borrow a cup of sugar or milk, share a slice of just-baked coffee cake (along with the recipe), or to just spread the latest hometown gossip. All the while a stream of cats and kids would drift in and out of our house like Eagle Stamp Day at the May Company.

Our most lively visitors, however, came on Saturday nights—Poker Night at our house. The relatives would stream through the front door with arms full of penny jars and brown paper sacks of long-necked beer bottles and mason jars of caramel-colored liquor. They'd camp around the long dining room table till the wee hours of the morning. The stories I'd overhear and the observations I'd make at these parties were gourmet banquets for any aspiring writer. And rich in life lessons—ones I only came to understand much later.

Small as it was, Lakeline did have a corner store. Gruden's, with its squeaky floorboards and silver bell hanging loosely above the front door, was the size of a farmer's shed, yet had plenty of room for essential grocery items, penny candy, and paper doll books (like cardboard Lennon sisters from *The Lawrence Welk* show—complete with paper outfits). My brother and I were regulars there, even after the day that I, a six year old, decided to race him home (I figured with all the Bazookas in his pocket weighing him down, I was a shoo-in) and slipped in a driveway just as a car was backing out. In one fell swoop, I laid there like a doomed pig at a rib roast as the oncoming vehicle grew monumental in size. I squeezed my eyes shut to avoid witnessing my own demise, when suddenly the black tires screeched to an ear-splitting halt—so close I could inhale the Firestone rubber. I, scared shitless, rolled out from underneath that ominous vehicle, and squealed all the way home—alternately rubbing my scraped knees and bruised buttocks while screaming, "DENNIS! You made me do that – WAIT UP!!"

Gruden's is also where I picked up a stray cat one day that looked amazingly like our Tippy. (The only one of our usual seven or eight allowed to stay indoors since Grandpa—who always denied being a cat lover—had taken a liking to her.) At eight years old, I didn't see stealing a cat as a crime. The poor thing didn't have a collar, so therefore *had* to be homeless, and I just knew the little calico would be overjoyed living at our house, which could be likened to a cat commune. But this one was a bit more scruffy (actually, a lot more) than its look-a-like. Still, I succeeded in fooling the folks (who were distracted by company) until the next day when Grandpa looked more closely as the cat rubbed against his leg.

"Hey, that's not our cat! Dee Dee, go take that mangy thing back where you got it from!" (Somehow he knew right off I was the culprit.)

The only lady in the neighborhood who I never saw in an apron (she preferred rolled up jeans and oversized shirts) lived on the street next to Gruden's. I don't recall how our family came to know Jeanne and her husband, Jim, but the childless couple (by choice or fate, I never knew) seemed to enjoy my presence. After school, through fifth and sixth grade, I'd make my usual stop at Gruden's for a Creamsicle, then head over to their house to play Gin Rummy with Jeanne until supper time. Jim, when not at work, lived in his garage with his beloved canary yellow 1960 Chevy Impala, but always greeted me with a "How ya doin' young lady?" when he'd come into the kitchen for another beer.

With so many neighbors to choose from, I often forgot to report my whereabouts to my mother, who'd get frustrated when she didn't know where I was. I had a habit of roaming, like our cats. Many times, she'd stand out in the backyard calling out my name until someone shouted, "Ginnie, she's over here, at our house." This was back when parents encouraged kids to "go out and play" and no one feared for their safety because a child's guardian was every homeowner in the village.

My first friend, Jackie, lived conveniently next door, and also conveniently, was a year younger than me, enabling me to use this happenstance as clout. Whenever we played together, I had to go first. After all, I was the oldest. We never ran out of games to play, making stuff up as we went. Taking turns being "the mommy" to our dolls, tasting—then spewing out—handmade mud pies, or pushing high as we could on her swing set while singing "Itsy, Bitsy, Teeny Weeny, Yellow Polka-Dot Bikini" at the top of our lungs.

Entertainment came easily in Lakeline, Ohio.

It was here I learned to climb a tree, ride a bike, even feed a kitten—the one I named Frisky because she slept in a *Frisky Shoes* box—with my doll's miniature baby bottle. It's where curiosity—another trait I'd developed with so many cats around—got the best of me one day when I, merely out of this inquisitiveness, sampled a heaping spoonful of *Puss in Boots* canned cat food, which forever purged me from that characteristic often said to kill a cat.

It's where I thought it commonplace that a household consist of two grandparents, a mother, brother, and a father who appeared only at Christmastime, like Santa Claus. (That is until I started school and learned otherwise.) It's where I'd find joy in simple things, like the blossoming of our pussy-willow tree each spring. And not-so-simple things, like witnessing live births, thanks to our family of highly fertile felines. It's where I felt always welcomed by a neighbor's smile, even if my timing was bad. And where I learned what happens when someone rams a car into a tree, like the man—who they said had been drinking—did to the big oak across the street one night. And how to cope with stark and gruesome reality after finding our missing cat, Suntan, who'd disappeared one winter, and whose corpse I discovered that spring, lying on the side of the road after the melted snow revealed its stiff orange remains.

It's where I felt the pain of loss when Number One, the matriarch of our cat dynasty, was hit by a car. And how to pay tribute to a loved one when Grandpa buried her in our back woods and my twelve-year-old brother, taking long sticks, made a cross that stood high among the bushes until one day as an adult I looked for it and it was gone.

It was here, in this minuscule village of simple Midwesterners, that one little house meant the universe to me. A house I'd be forced to leave at twelve when my thirty-seven-year-old mother—in her desperate need to be free from an overbearing mother—finally won her independence. A house which I'd run back to every time I—in my own desperate need for independence from an overbearing mother—sought solace as a teenager. That same house would once again become my refuge as a twenty-five-year-old divorcee. And yet, a few years later when its last owner would die, nobody would want it anymore . . .

It was here, in Lakeline, Ohio, I learned that nothing remains the same, and isn't supposed to. And that our childhood remains in our psyche long after most of the people from that time have left us for good.

It's where I learned that a small house can hold as much life, and love, as a big one. And where I learned how to play well with others.

Well, okay, most of the time.

Little Me Too

*W*hen I was a baby, my brother would throw all his toys into my crib and Mom would screech in fear that I'd sample the pieces and parts as taste-testing morsels to savor while kept behind bars. I suppose he did this because I looked lonely, or bored, and he, as the kind older sibling, wished to entertain me. This mission was ultimately achieved when he'd run around the bedroom making funny faces and loud, strange alien noises while bouncing alternately against the edge of his bed and my crib. The finale of the show often resulted in a huge, throbbing, soon-to-be-discolored knob on his forehead, accompanied by a tomato-tinged face and louder, stranger, alien noises emitting from his wide-open mouth.

Yep, my big brother could be quite entertaining.

And truth be told, as brothers go, Dennis wasn't all that bad growing up with. Our three-year difference didn't present a problem until he turned thirteen. An age when kids realize they are, in fact, the smartest in the family. An age when they suddenly notice how distinctly uncool their younger siblings are and wonder why they hadn't noticed it before. This acute self-awareness lasts, unnervingly, for several years. Case in point:

"Are you watching The *Monkees* show?" fifteen-year-old Dennis asks in his nastiest mocking tone.

"Yeah, they're cool." I say in my most defensive tone.

"Are you *kidding* me? They don't even play their own

instruments!" (I suppose because we used to pretend to be musical prodigies—starring on *Polka Varieties* each week with our mini-accordions—he was a self-appointed expert.)

"They *do, too!* See?" I point to the TV. Then try to educate him. "Peter and Mike play guitar and there's Mickey on the drums. And Davy Jones is the singer, *Dummy.*"

"They're *fakin' it*, stupid. Sheesh, what a *Teenybopper.*"

"I told you not to call me that! *Mom!* He's calling me names again!"

Until that most difficult period, we were buddies. Our mother loved telling the story of when she went to the hospital to have me, and little Dennis ran around the neighborhood announcing to all the world that he was getting a baby sister. Although in those pre-ultrasound days, you never really knew what you were getting until the actual birth. This lucky case of accuracy seemed to confirm Dennis's early belief that he is always right. (This air of supremacy is common among older siblings, particularly males, what with that *Y* chromosome and all.)

When I'd grown too big for the crib, my mother purchased bunk beds, the perfect answer for children living in cramped quarters. Naturally, I fought Mom's notion that my brother should have the top bunk, which launched the beginning of a phrase I'd hear repeatedly throughout my childhood and, especially, in adolescence.

"But your brother is older," Mom would say whenever I'd cry, "Me, too!"

She'd then add an explanation point. "And besides, he's a boy and you're a girl!"

This logic confused me as a moppet, and angered the women's libber in me as I matured. "That shouldn't make any difference!" I'd reply with a scowl. Unfortunately, I'd come to learn the sad truth that it did make a difference. And all too often, still does.

Priding himself as my best buddy, Dennis often went to bat for me, resulting in occasionally breaking Mom's diehard rules. The bunk rule was, "Don't let your sister up there." But soon as all authority was out of range, he'd entice me.

"Ok, they're busy doin' stuff. Come on up," he'd urge when feeling big-brother friendly. As I stood on the stepladder, my helpful sibling would hoist my chubby three-year-old body up onto the top bed. Then—having a sudden change of heart—he'd promptly escape out the back door to play outside, leaving me held captive by the very privilege I'd wanted so badly. Now I badly wanted *down* but was too paralyzed to move. Leaning forward to see whether I could perhaps jump might cause me to topple over onto my head. Even at three, I was aware that this could produce great pain. I was also aware that if I cried or screamed, we'd both get a lickin' for breaking the bunk rule. While I didn't care if Dennis got whopped, I never much liked it myself.

So there I'd sit and stew, fiercely holding back my terror tears until my mean, stinkin', poo-poo-head brother returned. After repeated episodes of this—three-year-olds have terrible memories—I became quite satisfied with the bottom bunk. It took a few years to totally trust Dennis the Menace after that. But time heals and by five years old, I was back to looking up to my big brother. Especially as he sat ever-so regally in his new tree house.

"Come *on*, Dennis, lemme up." I pleaded, gazing up at him with a mixture of hopefulness and contempt. Too scared to make the journey solo, I was forced to rely on him to get down and help me up. Knowing this, he seemed to enjoy his newfound status.

"Nope, you'll fall down and break your head."

"No, I won't."

"Yes, you will."

That's when Willy, the neighbor boy, came over, climbed right up and joined Dennis in his little taunting game. This was the last straw. With "I'll show *them*!" determination, I grabbed onto the coarse bark and carefully began my ascent. I tested one branch for sturdiness before griping it so hard the bark punctured my palm. I ignored the pain as I warily placed one foot in the limb's groove and pulled myself up as hard as I could. I repeated the challenge until I could smell the dirt on their Red Ball Jet sneakers, my pride building like Lincoln Logs. I was almost there.

"**Dennis!** What did I *tell* you?!" Mom seemed to appear out of nowhere, screaming for the entire neighborhood to hear. "You *know* you're not supposed to let your sister up there!" The sound of her high-pitched shriek, accompanied by my own fear of breaking my head, and the absolute promise of a rule-breaking spanking, caused me to lose my footing and I tumbled to the cold, hard ground. And lo and behold, my head didn't break. Though my spanking prediction was right on the money.

"I *told* you you're too young to do everything Dennis does," Spank one.

"Besides, he's older, and you're a *girl*!" Spank two.

"When are you ever gonna start *listening* to me?" Spank three. To which the answer was, not anytime soon.

From that day forward, whenever I mimicked my older brother's actions, Grandpa dubbed me, "Little Me Too." A title no younger sibling would dare boast about.

Dennis the Menace and Little Me Too. That was us.

But one of us possessed no *Y* chromosome. In turn, my double-*X* gene supplied me with the just right amount of ammunition to get back when necessary. In my brother's case, I knew his biggest weakness. Dennis was prone to nose bleeds. A fact I found joyously convenient whenever he ticked me off. One quick flip with the back of my hand and whatever argument we were having was abruptly over.

"Mom! Dee Dee hit me . . . (pause to sniffle) . . . in the nose again!" he'd manage to yell before the bloody discharge started gushing from his nostrils. While he lay in bed with an ice pack, I was sent to the corner. After the ritual spanking, of course. (These were the pre-Catholic days, before I learned about mercy.)

Yet despite the taunting, bashing, and "I can do anything you can" bouts, most times we got along. My older brother especially enjoyed his role as great protector, from neighborhood bullies or from one of our own—usually Mom—since our grandparents were soft on discipline. Grandpa never raised his voice at us, and Gee Gee (our grandmother) only yelled if we were running around the house when she had a cake in the oven. So it was no surprise when Big Brother came to my rescue the time he broke the "your-sister's-too-young-to-have-bubble-gum" rule, resulting in a sticky wad of pink goo in one side of my hair.

Like most Saturday mornings, all was quiet on the home front. We sneaked behind the living room couch between episodes of *Casper* and *Quick Draw McGraw* in a vain attempt to save my soul, or at least my derriere. Efforts to pull out the stringy mess resulted in more of it sticking to our fingers, creating a new problem. We almost wiped it on the back of the couch, but then thought better of it. So we stuck it all back in where it was in my hair, best we could. My redeemer then retrieved the rusty old scissors from the kitchen drawer Gee Gee used to cut Kroger coupons, and was ready, willing and dumb enough for surgery.

It's important to note that this was to be my first haircut. Having never been the victim of cutting sheers, I, not quite six years old, possessed light brown tresses that fell like a blanket over my shoulders and down to the waist of my three-foot frame. I hadn't realized how fond I was of my lengthy locks until it was too late. One quick snip to my beloved mane and Dennis's career as a hairdresser was, definitively, cut short as well. He tried repeatedly—and in desperate fashion—to correct and re-correct the lop-sided mess he created, as tears of great loss ran down my flushed cheeks. But that only made matters worse.

There was no hiding the fact that one night their little girl had lovely long hair and the next morning, my mother and grandparents awoke to a despondent, asymmetrical Buster Brown-coiffed child they did not recognize.

Spankings, this time for both of us, and my debut trip to the beauty shop commenced.

When Dennis was six and I was three, we got a dog. Well, it wasn't really *our* dog, our family was just "watching" the little boxer while their owners—friends of my grandparents—took an extended vacation. From the moment Rocky entered our front door, there was constant pandemonium. My brother and I were thrilled with this new addition to our household. Our menagerie of cats? Not so much.

There was so much hissing and growling and claw sprouting, that we kids began inserting these daily rituals into our playtime activities and at the dinner table.

"Stop hissing at your brother, you're not a cat," my mother reprimanded.

"But he was growling at me under his breath!" I countered.

"Two wrongs don't make a right," Grandpa interjected with his famous saying, and of course added the dreaded, "Little Me Too."

Things came to a climax one day when Rocky was getting ceaselessly agitated by the fact the cats had access to the back porch and he was restricted to the "utility room." The animals were separated by a door, with lots of little window panes, enabling Rocky to see their taunting little tails swaying back and forth as if singing in unison, "*Nah, Nah, Nah-Nah, Nah.*"

Finally, he'd had enough. He backed up his stocky little

body, far as he could go, then made a dash for it and pushed himself right through one of the glass window panes.

Dennis and I were in the kitchen, saw the act from the beginning, but it all happened so fast, we were too stunned to do anything by way of stopping him. The rest of our family were at various places in the house, but the shattering of glass accompanied by the ferocious barking and shrill meowing sent us all running to the backyard to save our scurrying cats. That was the last time we saw Rocky. I believe my grandparents found a new sitter for him.

But the lesson had been learned. On how to get back at the enemy.

The very next day, I made use of this new knowledge.

First, a little explanation. Although our house was small and not the least bit fancy, the builder saw to it to give the little bungalow a hint of class. French doors separated the tiny living room to the back bedroom and bathroom. These doors, like the one dividing the utility room and back porch, had a number of square window panes. So when my brother began chasing me around the house, as he was prone to do, I headed straight toward the back bedroom and seized my opportunity. I slammed the French doors behind me, giggling evilly, and watched Dennis, as momentum would have it, crash into the doors like a bird in mid-flight, his right hand simultaneously passing through the window square.

Screams let out (from both of us, after all, I wasn't totally lacking in compassion) as blood began to spurt, and my mother, as usual, came flying.

"I *told* you two to *stop* running around the house, or someone'll get hurt and *now look* what happened!"

As Mom held his hand under cold running water in the bathroom sink, I knew soon as the blood stopped oozing, that I was in for it.

Between spankings, I tried making light of the situation. "He only cut his hand, Mom, least his nose isn't bleeding. Geeeeze . . . "

Which earned me a few extra "lickins."

Numerous events, the good, the bad, and the ugly played out in semi-normal fashion, until the aforementioned teen years left me with only one good advantage of having an older brother.

Dennis would, with some regularity, bring home cute guys. That lone compensation was worth all the hassles a younger sister must endure during sibling rivalry and adolescence, and once that benefit was no longer applicable upon my marrying, I was forced to revert back to our former bond as siblings. And accept the notion that you can choose your friends, but not your family. And that blood is thicker than water. And that you can call your siblings all kinds of nasty names—like poo-poo head—but if someone else does, they're asking for trouble.

Poker Night at Ralph and Vi's

*E*veryday life with my Midwest family wasn't terribly exciting most days. Through my early years, give or take unusual events, our basic routine went something like this:

Like the calendar, our week began on Sunday. Gee Gee would rise at 5 a.m. to begin cooking a feast that would last well into the week. While she created a five-course dinner—with, always, two homemade pies—Grandpa, Mom, Dennis and I would do our standard, boring chores before turning on the "boob tube" to watch our favorite local programs, *The Gene Carroll Show* and *Polka Varieties*. The 12-inch black-and-white television sat atop an old Victrola, which, after two hours of craning our necks upward (a shortage of furniture often forced Dennis and me to sit on the floor), always resulted in leg cramps, stiff necks, and—annoying even to us—perpetual whining. Our reward came in Gee Gee's magical meals.

You could set a clock by Sunday dinner. At the sound of the last polka note, the TV was clicked off and we'd take our rightful place at the long mahogany table at precisely two o'clock. Dishes were washed by two-thirty, and naps commenced at the stroke of three. Feeding time resumed at six (usually a sandwich from the main course), and by seven, we were all settled in the living room for an evening of *Lassie, Mr. Ed*, and, of course, *The Ed Sullivan Show*. Eating pie and ice cream.

Through the week, Gee Gee continued her cuisine routine (lest the Great Depression made a comeback). Mom went to work at the Cleveland Trust Bank. Grandpa alternated shifts at the loading dock. And Dennis and I filled our time at school, playing outside, or watching *Captain Kangaroo, Barnaby, Woodrow the Woodsman* or, during Christmas break, *Mr. Jingeling.* (Ask any kid from Northeast Ohio about the theme song and they won't skip a beat: *"Mis-ter Jing-a-ling, how you ting-a-ling, keeper of the keys. On Halle's seventh floor, we'll be looking for, you to turn the keeey.")*

After supper, we'd take our customary places in front of the box that amused us so. Mondays were Mom's ironing nights, at least during the school season. She'd stand there for hours in the corner of the archway that separated the tiny kitchen and equally tiny dining room. She'd sprinkle our clothes with water from an old beer bottle (usually POC, an abbreviation for Pride of Cleveland, though some called it Piss of Cleveland, which I thought wasn't very nice), pressed out all the wrinkles, then hung them up neatly on wire hangers. Finally, the lining up of our Buster Browns directly below each outfit declared it a night, usually just in time for *The Andy Griffith Show.*

Come summertime, though, all routine bets were off. Particularly on Saturday nights. That was Poker Night. And that was entertainment.

The guests began arriving at eight. Relatives filed through our doorway in sequence, like they'd just stepped off a bus. With penny jars in hand, they'd come here to the small two-bedroom bungalow of my grandparents, Ralph and Vi (short for Viola). They were mostly relatives from Grandpa's side since nearly everyone from Gee Gee's family still resided in her hometown of Fostoria, a small town near Findley, Ohio, a day's long drive before the Turnpike was built.

Dorothy and Eddie—who became my godparents upon my baptism at eight years old—always entered first. Followed by the elegant and statuesque Skeet, who'd come with her equally attractive husband, Jeff. Skeet—her longer Cherokee name no one ever used—reminded me of Elizabeth Taylor with her black velvet hair, jangling sparkly jewelry, and aromatic essence of Channel No. 5. The royal pair rarely participated in the card game, preferring to sit on the sidelines smoking and drinking as if their sole purpose was to simply dress up the place.

Grandma Carter—Grandpa's snowbird mother from Miami who rented a summer cottage at Euclid Beach Park—often brought along her sisters Helen, Evelyn, and Grace. Aunt Grace resembled Ethel Merman, the robust singer from the *Ed Sullivan* show. A jolly old broad with a sarcastic charming wit, the eight-times married Grace was the comedian of the group, keeping players in high spirits (helped, of course, by other spirits). Her sense of humor, however, would elude her one night in 1963 after her last marital union went bust and she decided to stick her head in the gas oven, leaving a kitchen full of empty Pabst bottles and snuffed-out cigarette butts for Grandpa, who found her, to remember her by.

Everyone had their place at Ralph and Vi's table, and each had their favorite game played with Bicycle Playing Cards. I always knew whose turn it was when I'd hear the call of the hand. It was Grandma Carter's turn when I'd hear, "Okay, time for Baseball, nine's are wild." But sometimes she'd opt for another version called Blind Baseball. The deck would then pass to Vi, who preferred Penny Ante. Grace liked "Follow the Queen." Dorothy went for "Draw Poker." And Mom often chose "Acey-Deucy" (I always thought because of the funny name). But other times she'd just announce a wild card.

"Okay, gang, aces are wild now," she'd call out with authority. My easygoing Grandpa always opted for whatever they hadn't played yet. Those nights when I'd finally turn in after everyone had left, terms like "Jacks are better," "Your deal" and the endless shuffling of cards and giggles, would resonate in my head. It became one of my favorite childhood memories because I felt oddly safe and secure during those times. Like, if it was Poker Night, all was right with the world.

Dennis and I gladly forfeited episodes of *Perry Mason* in favor of these gaming competitions that were wholly more captivating. There were the excitable shrieks that accompanied the scooping of the copper pennies and Indian head nickels by the winners of the hand. The rattling of the penny jars. The "oooohhh" squeals that echoed from Grandma Carter whenever she'd claim a particularly high pile of coins. Secondhand smoke was never a concern back then as stifling clouds of tobacco puffs swirled around us like ghosts of the long-gone relatives often mentioned during the sessions.

"Oh, remember when Uncle Charlie and his buddy . . . Johnny, I think it was, went down to the lake . . . and they'd . . . oh, such trouble!"

I often missed the complete stories, what with the clinking of glasses, the calling out of "I'll raise you," and "I'll call ya," and the clanging of loose change thrown with abandon into the pot. Snacks, usually pretzels and peanuts, served in decorative Fostoria Glass bowls, were always available, as were the bottles of liquor that fueled the activities. And "Who's ready for another one?" was the theme of the night. Longnecks of Black Label, Rolling Rock, and P.O.C. were regularly swigged and shots of Kessler whiskey swilled. (The evening always began with the celebratory opening of a bottle of Mogan David for Grandma Carter. I like to think her fondness for this sweet concord wine, known for its high-alcohol content, contributed to her living into her 90s.)

Sometimes they'd take a break and sit around just to chit chat. That's when Gee Gee would bring out a few of her interesting gags she kept for precisely this purpose. Like the round tin can that was labeled, The Best Peanut Brittle.

"How 'bout some good peanut brittle?" she'd offer an unsuspecting visitor, poker face in place.

"Don't mind if I do," the guest would say, grabbing the can. Those who knew what was coming, held in their bursts of laughter till just the right moment when the victim opened the lid, and out sprung a spotted felt "snake" that would scare the living beejeebers out of the unsuspecting soul. The table would shake with laughter, and once the hearty echo finally died down, the card game would resume.

The best part came near evening's end when the frequent consumption of spirits brought loose and lively conversations. They'd all forget my brother and I were memorizing all the swear words as we'd wedge ourselves underneath the table, salvaging the harvest of fallen coins surrounding their inebriated feet. Sometimes we'd be there for what seemed like forever, waiting for one of them to change foot positions to be first to snatch a nickel held captive by a shoe. At times, there'd be a sudden sharp hiss and angry meow, when one of our cats got in the way and we inadvertently kneeled on its tail.

As the humid night wore on, we'd get earfuls of gossip about neighbors and friends, and boisterous opinions about politicians—some whom they weren't so fond of, made clear by the resounding cussing a certain name would produce (*"That Stupid Son-of-a-Bitch*," the most common). Occasionally, the mood grew less jovial when my partying family members became sentimental, or felt a sudden urge to recount their blessings.

Grandpa, who worked hard on the night shift, was a man of few words, and loved simple pleasures: Summers on the backyard picnic table listening to the Indians games on his transistor radio. Drinking with friends at Wally's Bar. Or moments like these, playing poker with his family. But sometimes free-flowing ales and a stack of old Indian heads brought thoughts of mortality and the meaning of life, even for someone like him. One particularly muggy night as Grandpa wiped his sweating brow with the white handkerchief he kept in his back pocket, he disclosed what sounded to me like prophetic words.

"If I died tomorrow . . . that's the way it goes. I've had a full life." I heard him say, before taking another puff from his Lucky Strike. He was sitting in his regular place at the head of the table, cards face down in front of him. I stood behind him looking at his sparse grey hair, and—perhaps for the first time—noticed his bald spot and protruding beer belly and became frightened that he knew something we all didn't. Faced with the possibility of my grandfather's death, I had a fitful sleep that night, and waited in fear all the next day for him to keel over. When he didn't by that Sunday night, I silently thanked God for sparing my dear, sweet grandpa.

Then came the night the card game broke up early in favor of nostalgia. Since some relatives only visited in summer months, Gee Gee decided to bring out old photographs that had been stashed, and mostly forgotten, in a dresser drawer. In the collection was my mother's wedding album. I was intrigued. I was seven years old and had never been privy to these pictures of my parents, together—nor the topic that had always been off-limits. Mom, appearing youthful and chatty after several rounds of Black Label, flipped open the book. As the crowd gathered around, this woman I suddenly didn't recognize began to narrate.

"I had a rainbow wedding before anyone ever heard of it," she boasted, pointing out whose dress was which color in the black-and-white portraits.

"And Helen, my maid of honor, wore lavender. I wonder whatever happened to her . . ." Her voice trailed off just then, in a way that made me realize my mother had a life before me. And friends. While she often talked of co-workers, I never knew her to have "girlfriends." I merely assumed women didn't have them once they became mothers. But there was more to this story, as I sensed that night.

My mother was in her seventies, before she revealed the mystery behind Helen, my brother's godmother. We were bonding over drinks, a Friday night tradition established once time had made us friends. Something had sparked Mom's memory of the girl she once knew.

"Helen would call me on occasion, wanting me to go out with her, but you kids were little," she began. (My mother seemed to feel that having a good time would make her an unfit parent.)

"One night Gee Gee [even Mom called her that] talked me into meeting up with her." Mom's faraway stare held me captive to her story. "I had to take two busses to get to this one bar she was at. We were having a good time at first, but she kept making trips to the bathroom. And each time she'd come out, she'd act crazier than before. At the time, I just thought it was her drinking, and eventually I got disgusted and left.

"I learned later she'd been shooting up heroin."

This was no more shocking to me than realizing that Mom actually knew what that was back then. I'd thought she only learned of such things after she retired and began watching Jerry Springer.

"You'd have never believed she'd end up like that," she added, shaking her head, the shock still fresh after all the years. "I never saw her again after that."

"OH, and there's Judy, my flower girl." Mom was now telling the poker crowd, her index finger pressed on the image of a dressed-up blonde in curls.

"That one turned into a real beauty," Vi replied. "So who's ready for another?"

I was leaning into the glossy photographs trying to envision my often-melancholy mother young, carefree, and happy, when she suddenly put her arm around me and kissed me on the cheek.

"Least I got these two out of it," she said to no one in particular, closing up the photo album.

My mother was rarely demonstrative. With the exception of those spankings when I was sure I'd been adopted ("My *real* mother would never do such a thing" I always reasoned) there was little touching between us. I later realized I wasn't alone. The lack of hugging and kissing your children was fairly common with parents in the '50s and '60s. The belief was that if they showed too much affection, their kids would grow up to be spoiled and "rotten." They'd justify this withdrawal of affection, and the spanking rituals, by quoting a well-known excerpt in the Bible. "Spare the rod, spoil the child." I could honestly say that I was not spanked a lot. Just enough to ensure I didn't become spoiled. Or rotten.

Although stunned by this rare display of maternal love, I managed to look at my mother. Her eyes were red and moist. In all my seven years, my mother never let me see her cry. I stood there, stiff and uncomfortable. And silent. I realized in that moment that my mother, who tried hard never to talk badly about her ex in front of her children (though she'd be unable to control the leak of conversations I'd overhear through the years, or my witnessing of the scowl that crinkled her face whenever *his* name was mentioned), had actually loved my alcoholic father. Despite her tight-lipped demeanor.

Memories of those poker nights faded as I grew up. The games came to an abrupt end with Grandpa's death in 1969. After that, Gee Gee spent most of her nights alone, sitting at that large dining room table playing solitaire, the old jars of Indian head pennies and nickels holding court on a top shelf, like an urn of a dead loved one. That is, until the day two juvenile delinquents—having heard the old widow was in the hospital—ransacked her home and stole them, along with other items worth much more to us than to them.

I was fifty years old when I became reacquainted with Mom's wedding album. I was cleaning out her apartment after she died and found it tucked under some clothes in a dresser drawer. I sat on her stripped-down bed and flipped through those celluloid snapshots that kept my parents youthful, lighthearted, and in love for more than half a century. I didn't have to wonder what would've happened had my parents stayed together "for the children's sake." I knew my childhood would not have been so pleasant.

Decades have passed since Ralph and Vi's poker nights, and so have all those colorful relatives of my youth. Gone are their revealing stories, their boisterous laughter, that snake in the peanut brittle can. . . .

After reliving those days one last time, I rose and placed Mom's wedding album in the box labeled "Keep," and headed toward the kitchen. It may have been my imagination, but for a brief moment I thought I smelled the sweet aroma of Chanel No. 5. And over there on the table, lined up like soldiers, stood empty Black Label, Pabst Blue Ribbon, and POC bottles. Each one with squashed cigarette butts inside, lying at the bottom like snuffed-out memories.

Choosing a Beatle

"Our theater's been jammed with newspapermen and hundreds of photographers from all over the nation. These veterans agree with me that the city never has witnessed the excitement stirred by these youngsters from Liverpool who call themselves the Beatles. Now tonight you're going to be twice entertained by them. Right now, and again in the second half of our show. Ladies and gentlemen, the Beatles!" - Ed Sullivan, 1964

Americans were still reeling from the shock of President John F. Kennedy's death three months earlier. The assassination shook the foundation of our national existence, both privately and politically. And like any stark reality moment, we remember where we were on such days.

And sometimes two memories merge together, particularly when their timing is close, and the mood they unearth is on opposite sides of the spectrum. One black, the other white.

On Friday, November 22, 1963, I was a fourth grader at Thomas Jefferson Elementary School in Eastlake, Ohio, and our class was making rice pudding. I happened to be standing next to my teacher so when the announcement came over the old scratchy speakers, Mrs. Prunty, grabbed a hold of me and began sobbing on my shoulder. I stood there, stiffly, as I felt the wetness of her tears

35

dampen the ugly plaid blouse my mother had made me wear (complete with matching bow she'd tied around my neck like a prize-winning calf). The teacher's sudden, impulsive act, right after my having screwed up the pudding recipe, caused me further horror in front of my peers. I couldn't pull away from the woman in her grief so I was forced to stand there like a department store mannequin as her heavy makeup (she looked eerily like Bette Davis in "Whatever Happened to Baby Jane"—coal black eyeliner, sharp pencil-thin eyebrows, blood-red lipstick—yet her sweet manner was more like Donna Reed, all-in-all an unsettling combo) created a freshly checkered design on the shoulder of my already hideous outfit.

As memory often does, the recollection of this day then switches scenes, and the curtain opens as I'm sitting on the school bus listening to all the kids relate their own personal stories of the dramatic afternoon. No one else had experienced their teacher sniveling on them, nor wore the proof right there for all to see.

"What happened to your blouse?" asked the girl next to me.

"Mrs. Prunty was crying on my shoulder."

"Oh," she said, leaning slightly away now. Fortunately, mine was the next stop.

It was the beginning of a strange, surreal weekend. Soon as I got off the bus, I ran into the house broadcasting the terrible news—complete with thespian-worthy overtones, as I'd seen in movies like *East of Eden* and *Days of Wine and Roses*. My grandparents at first didn't believe me. Until Gee Gee flicked on the TV.

The next four long days, our lives revolved around that television set. The recollections, again, blur into spotted segments: the five of us sitting, eating, taking bathroom breaks, all mesmerized in front of the "tube" watching the somber news reports "With Walter Cronkite." It was a weird kind of family togetherness, and was getting pretty boring until late that Sunday morning when we witnessed a live killing, thanks to the magic of television, when a man Cronkite called Jack Ruby suddenly came into our viewing screen, pointed a gun at Lee Harvey Oswald, the would-be assassin, and pulled the trigger. This was indeed more disturbing than the news of a president's murder in that we were accustomed to our television shows broadcasting *fictional* violence. The most popular ones were *Gunsmoke*, *Bonanza*, and

Have Gun, Will Travel. In these cowboy shows, the men all carried guns and played shoot 'em up, but even at a young age, we kids knew it wasn't real. We understood these scenes were all figments of someone's imagination.

After the play-by-play of the funeral procession, newsreel flashbacks on Kennedy's career, and debates on what will happen to America now, no one—adults or kids—could shake the ominous feeling of doom and gloom, making even the wonder of television a lot less fun.

Then came February 9, 1964. I don't know what television event finally brought our parents out of their funk (perhaps the soothing regularity of offbeat sitcoms like the *Beverly Hillbillies*, *Gomer Pyle,* and *Bewitched,* or maybe the reliable comfort of *I Love Lucy*), but for us baby boomers, the sky opened up that night in front of our 10-inch black-and-whites, and a beam of light shone down right there in front of us in our living rooms like some cosmic entity.

Miraculously, for one brief shining moment, old Ed Sullivan was suddenly very cool. He'd brought us a savior. Or rather, four of them.

Prior to this, kids didn't have much in the way of enjoying our kind of music on TV. Mostly, we were forced to watch Lawrence Welk and his sea of bubbles, or Mr. Sing-Along himself, Mitch Miller (and that bouncing ball dancing merrily atop musical notes). Or our local music programs, the *Gene Carroll Show* (an amateur hour featuring hometown musical acts that often resulted in embarrassing yet wholly entertaining live screw-ups) and *Polka Varieties* (targeted for viewers of ethnic persuasion, but usually minus the amusing screw-ups).

In 1964, most middle-class families had but one television set and the choice of three local stations, ours being channels 3, 5, and 8. The programming was targeted for adults, or small children (like *Romper Room,* which I grew to hate because Miss Barbara *never, ever* called my name). The preteen and adolescent audience was not even a consideration. Sunday night, especially, was out of the question. We couldn't get away from Sullivan, who, until that fateful night, offered little for us by way of amusement, unless you count Topo Gigio, the quirky little Mexican mouse puppet. Or, I suppose, those periodically intriguing circus acts.

But upon the overwhelming reaction to these four

Liverpool lads' performance, Sullivan realized he was on to something. Thus came the televised appearance of every notable rock 'n' roll band in England as well as the States. But this being the '60s, bands had to comply with censor regulations, and those who refused—like Jim Morrison, who used the forbidden words "get high"—were not asked back. (This would not be the case with Mick Jagger, despite his pissing off the network by at first agreeing to change the wording of his Rolling Stone song, "Let's Spend the Night Together," to "Let's spend *some time* together" then reneged on it once the *On Air* light came on.)

The Beatles changed my generation forever. God knows what would have become of us had they not appeared in our lives. Sure, we had Elvis, Jerry Lee Lewis, and Buddy Holly. But by now, Elvis was considered old, and making ridiculously corny B movies. And most radio stations no longer played Jerry's records since he'd up and married his thirteen-year-old cousin. And Buddy Holly, the coolest of them all, was dead.

After the Beatles appeared in our lives through that living room box, I, along with every kid in America, clamored for anything "Beatles." We all fought to be first to buy new packets of bubble gum that boasted "Collectable" Beatles cards (with photos and revealing data of their lives, including their "secret" likes and dislikes). Our days were measured in songs—from "I Want to Hold Your Hand," to "A Hard Day's Night"—and we lived solely for those AM deejays to bring us "Beatles' World Exclusives" and to buy their next record.

And as would happen more than once in my life, I was forced to choose between guys. Maybe it was because I had an older brother, but I always preferred the company of males. They were entertaining and appealing to me, either by good looks, or the fact they made me laugh. And when push came to shove, I'd choose the latter. Now, due to some odd competition, I had to pick just one of my beloved Beatles as my unending favorite in order to answer the perennial query from girls, "Which one do you like?" As if we could actually have our pick. Like we were curvy, bubble-head bachelorettes forced to choose who'd be the next lucky bachelor on the *Dating Game*. Fat chance. Yet, after that Sullivan appearance, this monumental decision became a required part of the process of being a Beatle lover, and it took me weeks to decide.

Every girl in school swooned over the obvious. Paul

McCartney was instantly labeled the "cute one," which for me, eliminated him right there. While I certainly appreciated cute every bit as the next girl, I wasn't about to be like everyone else. It wasn't my nature. On the other hand, Paul was left-handed like me, which certainly added points in his favor. Then again, my personal view of myself as an independent thinker would have none of that. So that brought it down to three.

John Lennon attracted me because he was the songwriter (his writing partner now removed from the list). I, already a hopeful writer, bumped him straight into first place. Plus, I liked his attitude. He had that certain something that separated him from the rest of the band—even demonstrated his distinctiveness on stage, as he always stood a bit further apart from his musical colleagues. He would've been my ultimate choice had he not been married, which made him ineligible with all the girls who felt a moral obligation to honor his vows. Particularly if you were Catholic. It definitely had to be some kind of a sin to be a John girl.

Two to go.

I loved Ringo Starr's sense of humor. Everything that came out of his mouth was funny and I found him charming in a Barney Rubble sort of way. He also shook his "mop-top" better than any of the others. Plus, I was drawn to drummers. Whereas most females tend to swoon over lead singers and guitar players, for me, there's always been something about drummers (maybe it's those muscular arms needed to pound those skins, or how their head bops to the music) that quicken my beating heart. So Ringo soon jumped into first place. That is, until shallowness got in the way. My measure of worthiness was still superficial when it came to beauty, and the fact that I found him not at all good looking (how could I'd have known how attractive he'd become in his later years? That somehow time and maturity—be it his or mine—would transform that nose into an asset rather than a liability). I had to, sadly, give him a pass. However, the shame at letting such as petty trait as looks get in my way of choice continued to nag me. So a few guilt-ridden months later, I honored the world-famous drummer by naming my new cat after him.

This left George Harrison.

George was perfect as my definitive choice. First of all, he was cute. Really cute. He, too, had that great British humor we American girls found so thrilling. And the fact that he was quiet (which normally would've wiped him out in my book since I liked the talkers) made him seem sophisticated, intelligent, and absolutely mysterious - three big bonus points with any hormonal male-loving girl. It was clear I'd made the right choice when he began contributing his own songs to the band, and I fell even harder after he took up with the Maharishi, started playing the sitar, and wore those cool-looking clothes. That new phase ultimately made me—having chosen him long before—appear wise and amazingly perceptive beyond my years to all those Pauly girls.

Having experienced two of the most prominent moments in 20th century history in a span of a few months, I grew up with the notion that even the most horrendous of events can be followed by the most profound and enlightening ones. Which came in handy during a few of my own life traumas.

When the Beatles bought us boomers out of our black-and-white existence, television—now airing music/dance shows like *Hullabaloo, Shindig,* and *The Midnight Special*— joined the radio jocks in providing us with a musical buffet, thus enabling my generation to inexplicitly separate ourselves from our Frank Sinatra/Lawrence Welk/Polka-loving parents. The Fab Four gifted us with the blessing of cherished childhood and adolescent memories, even for those who had few to go on. It wasn't merely their shaggy heads, but their music—those love songs with the boy/girl hooks, and rock star fantasies. Their "long-hair" and Beatle boots' appearance gave us license to rebel, with a new, albeit kooky, sense of fashion. They made us feel good, no matter what our pubescent angst. Giving us a new attitude. A new excitement. A new lifestyle that was our very own.

Moreover, The Beatles gave parents something to complain about, siblings something in common, and made even the underdogs feel triumphant. In turn, thanks to our adoration, these "exciting lads from Liverpool" became the most prominent, influential, and beloved entertainers in music history.

And more than forty years later, I can now admit, that to be perfectly honest, I secretly loved John, Paul, George, and Ringo the best.

Euclid Beach Park

ℐt wasn't officially summer until Grandma Carter arrived from Miami to reclaim her rented cottage at Euclid Beach Park. How lucky we were to have an "in" at the most popular amusement park in Northeast Ohio. The seventy-five acres along the shores of Lake Erie boasted long stretches of beach and sand with an illuminating fountain and eight hundred-ft. fishing pier (used also for leisurely strolls), and tons of rides—big and small, fast and slow. It was our own version of Coney Island, perhaps even more beautiful, with its forest of statuesque Sycamore trees, whose leafy limbs hung over the jade-green park benches like protective canopies. And against the backdrop of mobile homes and sturdy summer cottages, there was a sense of home. Particularly if you were one of the lucky ones, like us, whose great-grandmother rented a cottage there each year.

Euclid Beach had something for everyone, but we kids owned the large concrete building called The Colonnade, where "Kiddie Land" offered miniature versions of the bigger, more adult rides.

And Mini Helicopters.

"Hey, let's go on *those!*" Dennis yelled, so loud it hurt my ears. It was one of my earliest trips to the park and we'd already run around the entire building, for what seemed like a million times—hopping from the Kiddie Carousel to the Kiddie Whip to the Kiddie Circle Swing—while managing to down a Frozen Custard ice cream cone in between. Upon eyeing these colorful flying objects, my brother screeched to a halt. I watched with great suspicion as the dangerous-looking little "airplanes" danced before me, bouncing up to the ceiling, then down again, nearly scraping the floor before bobbing their way back up toward the cement sky. I gave my trusted older sibling a wary look.

"Ah, *come on*, there's nothing to be afraid of," Dennis the Menace urged.

At first I stood my ground. "No."

"Don't be a chicken. It'll be fun. Really, really fun."

"No."

His former angelic expression turned menacing.

"Dee Dee, if you don't go on this ride with me, I'll *never* play anything with you again. Not Tinker Toys, or Old Maid, or even Mr. Potato Head."

This was serious. "Never" was the operative word, as I knew that it was for a very long time. I kept my head down so as to not face the object of my fear and considered the ramifications of my brother's threat. Tears welled up as he pulled me into the line full of excited kids. Not one of them looked scared, so I tried to feel, or least act, brave. As we inched closer to the tall man with the tooth-gapped smile and hairy arms, I gave my brother my best little-sister pleading, mouth-quivering look.

In big-brother fashion, he threw his skinny arm around me.

"Awww, don't be scared," his voice smooth as the custard we'd just consumed. "It'll be okay, I wouldn't let anything happen to you. Come on!"

The minute the flying machine began its assent upwards, I screamed for my all-too-short life. The flow of tears traveled into my open mouth, making the experience all the worse by the terrible salty taste that clashed with that wonderful left-over ice cream flavor. The ride lasted *forever* and I didn't stop making terrifying noises until the ride came, mercifully, to a halt.

"Ok, kids, everybody out now," Hairy Arms said, and I

was first to comply.

After giving my big brother a hateful look.

The older kids gravitated toward the big roller coasters, like the Thriller, or the Flying Turns. Although there were other favorites as well: the Scooters, Tilt-A-Whirl, Scrambler, and the Dodgem. And there was more than rides to amuse us. For me, the Surprise House held the greatest fascination because that's where Laughing Sal was. Sal was an eight-ft. tall automaton encased in glass outside the "Laff in the Dark" ride. She wore a brown fright wig, and a "house dress," complete with little apron, on her stiff, rotund body, reminiscent of a middle-aged housewife who likes to cook. Her fat, wide feet were stuffed into black Mary-Janes, and her face flashed a permanent smile, revealing a few gaping holes where teeth should have been.

Yet with all this going for her, it was her haunting, cackling laugh echoing throughout the park that mesmerized me the most. I'd sit on that green park bench in front of her for hours cackling along with her, until a relative, usually Mom, would grab my arm, and drag me away.

"She reminds me of Aunt Grace," I said one day fighting Mom's effort to pull me off the bench and take me away from my jolly, and downright ugly, obsession.

"Shush, that's not a nice thing to say," Mom whispered, giving me *that look,* as we joined Grandma Carter, Aunt Grace's sister.

I ignored the glare. "Why? "It's true. She really does look like Aunt Grace."

Realizing you can't argue the truth with an eight-year-old, Mom, death grip on my arm, pointed ahead with her free hand, and said, "Oh, look, let's have some Frozen Custard," knowing that would shut me up. But even I wasn't fooled by her all-too-obvious attempt at changing the subject.

From May, until the brisk October winds sent our family snowbird back home again, many summer nights were spent at Grandma Carter's cottage. It was a lively place to be. There was a steady stream of guests swinging open the squeaky screen door, mostly relatives and "Euclid Beach" folks. There were Happy Hour cocktails on the screened-in porch, followed by a hearty dinner of roast beef, mashed potatoes, and Grandma's famous tomato-and-Hellman's mayonnaise salad. After supper, the women prepared for an evening at the park by hovering around the little mirror that hung outside Grandma's bathroom. There they'd dust caked powder on their faces, comb defined waves into the hair, and paint their protruding lips with tubes of Ruby Red, or Crimson Coral, finally smacking them together, almost in unison.

When I turned twelve, Mom began allowing me to stay with Grandma Carter for two whole weeks—the highlight of my summers. Realizing an almost-teenager needs some time to herself, Grandma gave me my first real taste of freedom when she'd fold a bunch of tickets in my hand and send me off myself. I'd gotten braver through the years and readily took off toward the racing coasters the minute I ventured past the grand archway entrance. Grandma never worried about giving me such free reign, in part I think because she was friends with every park security guard in the place, who would assuredly watch over me. Unaware of this, I often wondered, years later, if they'd seen things I wouldn't have wanted them to. Like lighting up a smoke between rides, or that summer after seventh grade, my first year as a teenager, when I received my first stolen kiss inside, and outside, the Surprise House. Right there in front of Laughing Sal, who seemed in full support of my carnal desires.

Thursday Nights at Grandma Carter's were equally engaging, when her little old lady friends would arrive for Poker Night. Grandma's cottage had just four small rooms. The main area—what nowadays would be called the "Great Room," though it wasn't at all large or great—served as living room, dining room and, in one corner, guest bedroom. There was the tiny bathroom (shower, no tub), kitchen (with the smallest gas stove and "icebox" I've ever seen) and Grandma's bedroom (which she always kept closed). So I slept in the guest bed up front. Within easy hearing distance of the chatty women. With the radio playing Glenn Miller, Tony Bennett, or Perry Como in the background, I'd hear talk about the weather ("It's suppose to get hotter and even muggy tomorrow . . . Oh, how long is this going to *last*?"), sale items at Krogers ("Did ya hear? Coffee prices are going up, better stock up on Maxwell House"), and of course, the grandchildren ("Timmy's just a whiz at math, Suzie's taken up ballet, seems to love it . . . ").

With one open ear on the kitchen klatch, I'd occupy myself with Grandma's *Movie Screen* magazines, reading the latest on stars like *77 Sunset Strip*'s, Efrem Zimbalist Jr. and Edd

Byrnes, who played Kookie (my first secret crush). Or the scandalous activities of *Peyton Place*'s former stars Ryan O'Neal, whose innumerable dalliances with beautiful starlets were legendary, and Mia Farrow, whose May-December affair with Frank Sinatra provided the best in tabloid journalism.

Just as I'd read the last of these gossip rags, the little old ladies, their stomachs full of cheese and crackers and Mogan David wine—thinking I was asleep— would then get to the good stuff.

"Say, did you hear about Bob and Loretta?" One blue-haired lady would begin as she shuffled the cards. She always paused then, for dramatic effect. I didn't have to see to know that all eyes were on her. She'd then continue. "Well, *they say* . . . he's having an affair with . . . oooh, you'll never believe this one . . . the divorced woman down the street from where they live! Can you imagine? Right in their own neighborhood! And with such small children and all . . .

"That cad!" another would tsk.

There'd be lots of gossipy oohhs and aahhhs and "How could theys?" until I'd eventually fall asleep, only to dream of sinister-looking Ryan O'Neals with paper-thin mustaches and sorrowful, neglected Donna Reeds with spit-up on their aprons.

Euclid Beach was also known for some historic events in its seventy-four history. The WWII days when the Lawrence Welk Orchestra played regularly in the Dance Pavilion. The frequent appearances of celebrities, such as former Clevelander Bob Hope. And political rallies, like the still-talked-about Democratic Steer Roast in September 1960, with the young and handsome presidential candidate, Senator John F. Kennedy.

To me, of course, those happenings weren't half as momentous as when I attended my first rock concert there. Seems everyone remembers, in vivid detail, their first rock concert. Where they were. Who they saw. Who they went with. The attendance of that first concert was a rite of passage.

In the 1960s, amusement parks often hosted shows by popular acts of the day. And thanks to Grandma Carter, Dennis and I had a backstage pass. Well, sort of. The Lovin' Spoonful was performing there the summer of '67, on the heels of their big hit, "Summer in the City." I was a thirteen-year-old "teeny-bopper" (oh, how I hated that term), a *16 Magazine* subscriber, and an enthusiastic Spoonful fan. So when word leaked that the group was performing in a concert at Euclid Beach Park, my really great, great-Grandma—who had connections—informed us that she could get tickets.

She left out the fact that the actual band members were going to be using the vacant cottage right next door to hers, as a dressing room. That is, until we arrived that blissful, memorable, gloriously historic day.

"How would you like to actually meet those young musicians?" she asked me and Dennis as the squeaky screen door slammed behind us. She then revealed news about her new, albeit temporary, neighbors.

"But you're not to tell a soul that they're there," she warned, "Or the place will be mobbed and you won't get through to talk to them."

Talk to them?

"If you stand outside, maybe one of them will give you an autograph." She stated nonchalantly.

I squealed in spite of myself. Suddenly I had a whole new respect for this seventy-something woman, who could pull off something like this. It couldn't get any better—not even if the Beatles themselves were right there next door – *right next door*. Visions of a tete-a-tete with my heartthrob swirled in my head. Although I liked the whole group, my heart belonged to Joe Butler, the band's drummer.

When the time came, Dennis and I politely stood outside that cottage, an attentive audience of two, waiting patiently for them to appear before us like some magic trick. Just as I was about to give up hope, thinking it really was too good to be true, one by one they stepped out, smiling, ready for this impromptu meet-and-greet. Dennis, an aspiring guitarist, began talking to singer and guitarist, John Sebastian, about their favorite instrument, while I stood there rigid and numb. It was perhaps the first time I wasn't living up to my new and horrible moniker, "Mouth"—cruelly coined by my nasty brother—I was suddenly struck dumb by celebrity.

As they all stood there chatting amiably, I gazed at each one of them, up and down. And as I did, I was surprised to feel—much as I tried to stifle it—a regretful sting of disappointment.

These four hippies standing before me, talking away casually, were just plain guys. Just regular older teenagers. With long, shaggy hair and regular one-pocket tie-dyed T-shirts and fringed jeans (a couple with fringed vests as well), they looked no different than my own brother's high school friends! I couldn't get over it. These pop idols of mine were standing right in front of me—the famous Lovin' Spoonful, whose 45s I'd play over and over on my record player in my bedroom for hours on end. "Do You Believe in Magic," "Did You Ever Have to Make Up Your Mind?" "Rain on the Roof," and of course my favorite one, their latest hit, "Hot Town, Summer in the City." Here I was, living out a teenage girl's fantasy. *Here* I was, *in their company*, and yet, yet . . . there they were . . . disappointingly, disturbingly, disgracefully . . . normal.

I had expected four sophisticated, full-grown gentlemen whose demure was suave, cool, and ever-so-mature. Like rock versions of Ryan O'Neals. But these guys weren't much taller than my own sixteen-year-old brother, for heaven's sakes. They didn't *look* like rock stars. They didn't *act* like rock stars. They didn't even have British accents!

"And how are you, young lady?" Joe Butler interrupted my disenchanted thoughts. He was smiling at me. *My Joe*, who, close up, may have looked younger than I'd expected, but now that he was giving me his undivided attention, and . . . oh, that cute smile . . . directed at nobody else but me . . .

He was endearing. He was charming. He was beautiful! He looked even better than any of those photos I had clipped in *16 Magazine*. With hands in pockets, *My Joe* was looking right through my pupils into my soul with his beguiling grin, his dark, Valentino eyes sucking me into his tunnel of love. My fantasy, now supremely resurrected.

I attempted to smile back but my face felt odd, tight, twisted. So that what actually appeared must've looked more like an ugly, cockeyed smirk.

I managed a mumbled "Hi," then handed him the piece of paper Grandma had given me.

"You want me to sign that for you?" he asked the deaf-and-dumb mute.

Scribbling his name across the white tablet paper, *My Joe* was saying something to me, but I was distracted by visions of the two of us lying together on the sandy beach, arms linked tightly around each other, lips pressed together—hard—as waves crashed passionately against the rocky Lake Erie shore.

Just then, a black limousine pulled up.

"Time to go, guys, let's hit it," John Sebastian called out. They all started toward the shiny car as I, and a growing crowd of bystanders (where'd *they* come from? And how long had they been there?) stood waving. The young rock stars returned the gesture.

"Hope you enjoy the show," *My Joe* called out, turning to look at me—me!—smiling that smile, which I took to mean that he really liked me, maybe even in a Sonny/Cher kind of way, before disappearing into the back of the limo, where he left my life forever. . . .

Postscript: Well, turns out, it wasn't forever. In March of 2008—forty-two years later—I would be a presenter on a "Rock 'n' Roll Cruise" where I would meet the current members of the Lovin' Spoonful. Then my husband, Jeff, and I would end up sitting at the airport bar with Joe Butler as we all waited for our respective flights home, where, over drinks, I related to Joe the story of "our past." Alas, he didn't remember me. But now in his sixties, he's still as charming as I remember.

That does my heart good. . . .

It seemed fitting somehow that the demise of my wonder years and the closing of Euclid Beach Park in 1969 ended simultaneously. As Bob Dylan so famously wrote, the times, they were a'changin'. Times that fueled civil unrest, racial tensions, and of course, the Vietnam War.

For this beloved amusement park, the last few years showed declining interest amid park goers. Some blamed "the economy," others blamed "the blacks, who invaded *our* park," while others simply found newer, more exciting places to vacation, such as nearby Sandusky's Cedar Point. Depending on who you talked to, any one of those issues were the cause for the park's closing.

None of that mattered to this fifteen year old. My last summer there, I was still handed as many free tickets as I wanted. Still sat on the bench chuckling at Laughing Sal. Still eavesdropped as giggly old ladies under the influence of Mogan David slapped down cards, and spread gossip across the kitchen table.

And still blissfully unaware that not only were the times a'changin,' but so was I.

2. Fits & Starts

Girl Trouble

ℐ always had to jump a puddle to get to Jackie's house. Well I didn't *have* to, after all, there were no fences. But I liked the challenge. The open spot between my backyard and her's was a small ditch behind our garage that was continually filled with rain water or, in winter, frozen ice. It became my first game, to see if I could hop across without stepping in it. I don't recall ever losing.

Not so with my early relationship with other girls. It took me years to develop a talent in the art of making friends. As a young child, this wasn't an issue. I had a playmate in my brother who, like me, took great pleasure in running around the house for no particular reason. Who taught me how to climb trees, put electric train sets together, and run blindly into furniture by throwing a blanket over my head. And I had Jackie, a built-in friend next door. She served her purpose well whenever I needed someone to play house with (my brother drew a line at this). And she came complete with readily available miniature household appliances—like pretend refrigerator and stove—along with dainty little tea sets, and matching pots and pans. She also had a gleaming new swing set, so I spent a lot of time in her yard. Another bonus was that Jackie was a full year younger than me, thus appealing to my imaginary sense of supremacy. And when she couldn't come out and play, I was perfectly content playing with our menagerie of outdoor cats, or visiting the adults in the neighborhood. Who often gave me treats.

Things changed in elementary school.

That's when I learned about competition, popularity, and mean girls. Having no experience in these matters, I wrongly assumed that being friendly with other girls was all that was needed to gain new pals. That theory went out the classroom window by second grade. Vying to be one of the popular girls quickly became complicated and frustrating. It seemed like an awful lot of work that often resulted in my losing. It reminded me a lot like playing games.

"This is stupid, I'm not playing anymore," I'd screech at my brother smack in the middle of a game of Checkers or Tiddly Winks, thus dampening his enthusiasm over his inevitable triumph.

"But you have to finish the game!" he'd screech back.

"No I don't."

"Yes, you DO!"

"NO . . . I . . . DON'T!" I'd exclaim, proving it by throwing the pieces at him and stomping off with a righteous *humph*.

You can't act like that in school. So you try your best to win. But first, you have to know how to play the game. You have to hang around the winners. And in my fourth grade class, that was Kathie. From the first day out, she was a winner in every sense— the most popular girl in Mrs. Prunty's class, *and* the "teacher's pet." I instantly saw the potential in such a status, and wanted to be just like her. So every day, I sat with her at lunch (on a very crowded bench since *everyone* wanted to sit by her), in the library (she was well read, too, of course), even followed her into the girls' lavatory. The pretext was that if you were seen with popular Kathie, you must be cool, too.

Kathie possessed qualities that I lacked, but that I hoped might be contagious. For starters, she was pretty, with a round cherub face, aquamarine eyes, and blonde hair the color of butter. She was like Janet Lennon, the youngest, cutest, and perkiest of the popular Lennon Sisters singing group—my only reason for watching the *Lawrence Welk Show*. But that wasn't all. Kathie was skinny. And smart—straight A's smart. And her penmanship was flawless, with letter-perfect loops and curves (for a time I was lucky enough to be seated next to her in class and would watch in amazement as she guided her perfectly sharp number 2 pencil just so).

Even how she spelled her name—*ie* instead of *y*—seemed

to denote a kind of soft, feminine virtue. And, for an eight year old, she sure had interesting things to talk about, and ways of describing things. Really imaginative ways. Like one day in a burst of excitement over God knows what, she squealed, "It feels like I'm having a birthday party in my stomach!" I mean, who thinks of stuff like that?? This remark irked me as much as it awed me since I couldn't come up with a simile like that if my creative life depended on it. So naturally all the girls gravitated to her, and no way could I compete.

By now, I knew there were rules to schoolyard allure. You had to be pretty. And not at all on the chubby side. And you had to be smart, and witty. And if you were really good at it, you could be the teacher's pet (normally not a good thing) and *still* be Miss Congeniality. I hated her. And hated myself for liking her so much. After awhile, I concluded I was never going to be like her, and gave up. I acquired new friends, ones more like me, who were not so pretty, or smart. But who taught me a basic rule of thumb in successful girl relationships. You had to be adept at talking about other girls when they weren't in hearing distance. Except for Kathie, of course. Her golden status, and the fact there was nothing bad to say about her, made her exempt from this particular standard. The bitch.

I soon discovered I got on better with the boys. Boys were simpler creatures. They preferred dissecting frogs to dissecting people. They thought everything was funny. And they always just wanted to have a good time.

My kind of people.

I think back now and wonder why so many of us who were the last ones to be chosen for team games became writers. Guess it's our way of getting (or giving) back. (And although we writers need to occasionally change names to prevent law suits, there is still a lot of satisfaction in knowing that the culprits, and those who know them, are left to wonder.)

This early bonding with the male gender (I even had a first grade "boyfriend") provoked an unspoken betrayal of sisterhood, thus sparking jealousy that fueled the embers of meanness. Or more often, being simply ignored. Oblivious I, of course, was clueless to all this. I blithely went about my days blinded by the clouds of resentful smoke swirling around me.

Throughout grade school, I shifted from one friend to another, few who remained long enough to leave an impression in my memory bank. By the summer after sixth grade, I thought I'd finally surpassed the girlfriend dilemma when I began hanging out with girls who lived within walking distance from my house.

Gina was my favorite. Like Kathie, she was pretty and popular, and seemed to genuinely like me. We shared a tap-and-ballet class together, and hung out at her house on weekends where we'd sneak into her fifteen-year-old sister's bedroom to steal her Beach Boy records, spray her Ambush perfume all over our budding breasts, and rifle through her dresser drawers for anything Gina could later use against her older sibling. With my modest experience with girlfriends, I took these entertaining episodes to mean we were best of friends. That first week of summer, 1966, offered the promise of a sunny season of friendship, sneaky moments, and good times.

One hot boring day, we were sitting across each other against the sturdy branches of the old oak in Gina's backyard. This was how we passed time, relating stories about school days, mean teachers, and girls we didn't like. That's when Gina invited me to her upcoming sleepover.

"Yeah, my dad said we can all sleep in the garage, it'll be so cool," was all she had to say. I was in.

In anticipation of my first cool garage party, I begged Mom for a new outfit, an attempt that rarely did any good. My divorced mother worked at the Cleveland Trust Bank, and although the sound of it made me think she must be making good money to work at a place where they *gave* people money, whenever I asked her for anything with a price tag on it, she'd say she couldn't afford it. So I usually went to a more reliable source. My grandmother was more than happy to oblige. The very next Saturday, Gee Gee took me to Robert Hall's (conveniently located near one of my grandparent's favorite bar), and where I found the perfect powder-pink baby doll blouse with gathering across the top— just the thing to make a pubescence girl feel busty and beautiful. With hot pink (I'm afraid so) cutoffs to match, I was ready for my first pre-teen party.

The excitement rose to great heights by the time the big day came. As Gina had promised, the eight of us girls had the large, detached (read: no adult supervision) garage to ourselves. We played records and danced and giggled. As time wore on, we got bored. We tried lying in our slumber bags to sleep, but couldn't. That's when one of the girls—most likely Sharon, the mean girl of the group—decided it was time to gang up on someone. Of course, I, with my all-too-nice, always accommodating, naturally positive nature—and brand new fancy blouse—was the perfect target.

They pounced on me like barn cats skirmishing for that one stray field mouse. I'd been lying there quiet, seriously attempting to sleep, when the pack of girls attacked. They caught me off guard, and I couldn't comprehend why they were holding me down with such force, until the others came at me, bright red lipstick in hands. Each one took turns marking me with streaks of crimson. Shouting in bursts of laughter, they assaulted my face, my arms, and my beloved, perfect, bust-enhancing blouse Gee Gee had so generously bought me for this special occasion. As I squirmed and struggled and screamed in hopes that Gina's distant parents would hear, the echoes of their snide laughter resonated in my ears long after they'd all finally stopped, and succumbed to sleep.

The rest of the night I lied there sobbing quietly into my pillow, wondering what makes people so cruel, and questioning what I may have done to cause these girls, whom I thought were friends—including my best one—to turn so vicious against me. I also had to dream up some stupid excuse to explain to my family why my clothes were covered with dark red lipstick and how I could've been so thoughtless and careless to get something as hard to get out as lipstick on my brand new blouse.

The truth was too humiliating.

The next day as I prepared to leave, Gina said, "I hope you're not mad about last night. We were just having fun. Still friends, right?"

In my all-too-nice, accommodating way, I replied, "Sure, don't worry about it."

It was a sign of things to come.

I knew I was in trouble that first day at my new junior high school. As the pink summer outfit already confirmed, I had no flair for style. My mother always picked out my clothes, never once asking me what I liked.

"Here," she'd say, shoving the bundle of granny looking, calf-hugging garments into my unwelcoming arms. "Try these on." It wasn't a question, but a command. She always made it clear that if she was spending her hard-earned money to clothe me,

I was to wear what she chose. The dressing room routine was to ensure the outfits were bulky enough to last through the year (after all, money was tight and clothes—and shoes—had to last). Plus, my mother had a perplexing affinity for plaid. And blouses with ribbon bows attached to the collar (See photo: And keep in mind that you always wear your very best outfit for the all-important school picture. Which gives you an idea how hideous my other fashion statements were). And pleaded skirts with elastic waists. And of course, the all-purpose elastic head band, for total humiliation. These repugnant shopping trips added fuel to my growing disdain for her.

However, for my entrance into this new academic phase in my life, Mom made a conscience effort to compensate, somewhat, and allowed me the luxury to have some say-so in choosing an outfit. But when you're twelve and finally given the opportunity of choice with no past experience, the result can be tragic.

Green was my mother's favorite color, not mine. So perhaps it was a subconscious gesture of gratitude, or stab at gaining her approval, that I settled on an all-green outfit (an appropriate shade given my unworldly judgment) and proudly hopped on the school bus that first day clad in my pale green blouse, sea-green pleaded [!] skirt and jade-green knee-high socks slid into brown penny loafers (complete with new copper for luck, which I'd desperately need). In my misguided pride at having hand-selected this ensemble, I gave no thought to how I appeared to others. That is, until I walked into my classroom and noticed I was the only girl who wasn't wearing panty hose. (Well, okay, with the exception of those two girls in the back whose fashion tastes were worse than mine—one of them decked out in a plaid blouse with matching bowtie, causing me to suspect that my mother must have some long-lost twin my grandmother hadn't told me about.) With this emerald city outfit, I looked like a leprechaun on steroids, or perhaps the Lollipop kid, minus the pop. From that poor decision on, I was labeled uncool throughout seventh grade.

Because I hated riding the noisy school bus, I decided to be a walker. Walking suited me. There's a certain rhythm you pick up that prompts you to move forward at a nice clip and helps you dismiss all that's behind you. The action of moving forward seems to kick in some part of the brain that allows great thoughts to emerge. This I would learn later. At thirteen, all I knew was that I loved the walking process, which gave me peaceful, independent moments with no one else around. And I could daydream to my heart's content. But as an after-school activity, there'd be none of that. There were always the other walkers surrounding me. An unhappy circumstance for the uncool people.

"Hey, you!" they'd call out behind me. "Did your mommy pick out that outfit?"

Giggle, giggle.

It went from there, often followed by one male or female tormentor, always older, who'd bang into me, doing whatever it took to get a reaction. The bullies ran in packs and verbally abused until I'd shamefully take off running, books in hand, amid hordes of evil laughter. A few times I couldn't run fast enough which resulted in extensive scratches and bruised arms as I struggled to get free from their grip.

Even school couldn't protect me. Cat fights among girls were a popular pastime at Kennedy Junior High. Though I never understood the appeal, nor learned the art of it all. So it was only a matter of time that I'd get beat up.

"Greasers ruled" in my middle-class school and I tried to adjust. The rolling up of the skirts soon as I left the house was easy with elastic waist bands. And so was the smacking of Bazooka. And applying the coal-black eyeliner. But I couldn't for the rattail life of me tease my hair high and wide enough. An ironic fact considering I later became a hairdresser. Each morning in the school "lav," I'd watch popular Bonnie Bentley and the other greaser girls rat up their hair that the night before had been Dippity-Doo-ed and rolled smoothly with sixteen-ounce orange juice cans. Once they got it ceiling-high and flipped up—just right at the ends—out came the Aqua-net where upon they'd spray the Bouffant Do until it was stiff as Plaster of Paris.

I was a total washout as a Greaser girl.

So when Paul Fusco, who sat behind me in eighth grade math, told me about his new "Mod" lifestyle, where all I had to do was wear bell-bottomed jeans and T-shirts, comb my hair straight against my face, and "just be yourself," I quickly changed loyalties. My transformation came in Nehru or tie-dyed shirts, corduroy Beatles cap, Beatle boots, or weather permitting, "Jesus" sandals, and hip-huggers (except in school where, this being the 1960s, dress codes demanded that girls wear skirts or dresses).

And I did learn a fine art. The knack of ironing one's own

hair to smooth out unwanted waves:

Place towel on ironing board. Comb out all snarls in hair. Lay tresses out on board. Cover with thin cotton towel and proceed to iron smooth and straight. Voila!

Now looking more like a slick Morticia Addams than a bouffant Barbara Streisand, I proudly proclaimed myself a Mod.

I may as well have added a sign, "Let the Beatings Begin" on my back in the halls of Kennedy Junior High where Greaser boys and girls outnumbered Mods two to nearly none.

"Hey, so you think you're not good enough for us anymore?" Betty, a ninth-grade female Mohammed Ali, addressed me one morning in the girl's lav. Her question suggested that I'd once been one of them, which was puzzling considering we'd never actually had a conversation before. But alert to the obvious warning sign, I bolted for the door. I wasn't quick enough. She grabbed my arm.

"You ain't goin' nowhere, hippie girl. We got things to work out, huh, girls?" she said this without actually looking at the other girls, her pack of Greaser comrades. She glared at me with menacing green eyes, all the while digging her long, sharp, Pink Passion-frosted fingernails into my beige Nehru blouse.

"Aren't you gonna say somethin' Bitch?"

The school bell saved me, but not before her solid grip ripped the sleeve of my now deflowered Mod shirt as I tried pulling away.

"Don't worry, hippie girl, I'm not done with you yet. I'll get you," the high-haired wicked witch concluded as she whizzed down the hall. Had she added "my pretty," at the end, or was it just my imagination?

"You're gonna have to fight her, ya know," my neighbor and eighth-grade classmate, Sherry, informed me after school. We were sitting in her living room as I related the day's event.

"I know," I said, though none too happy about it. I'd already endured weeks of torment and knew there was no getting away from Mohammed Betty. I knew that when someone challenges you to a fight, you look cowardly if you try getting out of it, and ultimately become more vulnerable to the next challenger. And there'll always be a next one.

"Tell her you'll fight her tomorrow, after school in The

Path," Sherry said, in a nonchalant tone. Sure, she wasn't the one that was going to get the shit beat out of her.

"The Path" was the infamous short cut to Kennedy, where smoking cigarettes and fighting (and probably adolescent sex, though it's just a guess) took place almost on a daily basis to and from school. Sherry, who I was fairly certain had never been in a fight in her life, demonstrated what to do—providing me with possibly the worst advice I'd ever been given.

"Just make sure you get the first hit in. But *tell* her to go first—to fake her out—so you can get your hit in before she hits you. And make sure it's a good one, in case ya don't get another chance."

How reassuring.

The Fight took place the next day but a revved up, tough-looking, tough-talking Betty wasn't about to wait till after school. She cornered me in the girl's lav first thing that morning.

"Okay," I said, trying to look all bad. "Let's get this over with. Go 'head, you first."

She looked at me in surprise. I took this to mean she was shocked at my sudden willingness to fight her. In hindsight, it was more likely she couldn't believe her luck in picking someone that stupid. Her quizzical look still intact, I thought I'd caught her off-guard with my "You first" command, and quickly cupped my favored left hand in a fist and went to swing. But as I leaned down to punch her in the stomach, I allowed the perfect opening for her claw-like hands to grab hold of my hair, and drag me across the floor by my freshly ironed locks. She proceeded to yank me against the sink pipes, punched me repeatedly with her free hand as she kicked me into the stalls: Punch. Kick. Punch. Punch. Slap. Kick. Kick. Slap. Punch. It was almost musical, like the theme song from *Rocky*. For the grand finale, Mohammed Betty slammed my head against the porcelain bowl. Then, suddenly, mercifully, she stopped.

It was all over in probably 6.9 seconds. I believe her all-time record.

"Now, don't fuck with me," I barely heard her say as she headed toward the door. She may have added something else, but I was too busy dragging myself up while desperately trying to keep the dripping blood from flowing and staining my new hippie clothing. I did notice, however, that the bathroom was eerily quiet. I was alone. I faintly recalled, while this was all going on, hearing an echo of encouraging shouts as I tried warding off the rapid-fire blows, but the crowd that had swirled around us was gone at the ringing of the first period bell. The coast now clear, I stumbled out of the stall, grabbed my over-thrown purse from the corner, washed the blood from my face, reapplied my midnight blue eye shadow and liner, brushed through my disheveled hair, then bravely headed to my morning class where I was immediately written up for being late.

Word-of-mouth is paramount in junior high, and by lunchtime, the entire building was privy to our little restroom rendezvous. Including, of course, the administration. At 2:55 p.m., a half-hour before school was to let out, I was summoned to the office.

"So what happened?" Mrs. Bowman said, her Joan Crawford eyes gazing at me over black-rimmed bifocals. This was the guidance teacher who, until my grades slipped a few months into seventh grade, I had been a goody-two-shoes aide for.

"I understand you started the fight?"

"What?" I said, completely forgetting for a second that upon my friend's advice, I indeed *had* hit first. Or rather, tried.

"Betty told me all about it," the woman's knowing look dared me to deny it. Seems my shrewd opponent had ratted on me soon as she learned the school authorities were hip to the main event, so she would appear as the persecuted one. It was clear that I was combating a true pro, and losing. Again. I was now forced— for once in my teenaged delinquent life— to tell the truth.

I spilled my guts. I relayed the weeks of harassment leading up to the final round of confrontations. I told her I'd done everything I could to avoid the girl, including not riding on the school bus. I confessed to old lady Bowman, most honestly, that I really didn't believe in fighting (basically because I was so bad at it), and how "a friend" had given me the advice that I, having no other choice, should try and hit her first.

By the time I finished, I was embarrassingly, shamefully, in tears. Which sparked no sympathy from this authoritative, unsympathetic witch.

"So you *did* fight her?"

That's not exactly how I'd describe it. "Well, I really didn't have a choice, she was . . . "

"Yes, you *did* have a choice, and now I'm going to have to call your mother and suspend you for three days."

This experience confirmed what I'd been saying for years as a child—that life really *isn't* fair. I'd been bullied, harassed, threatened for weeks, beaten up *in front of* my peers, suspended from school, and subsequently grounded "for life," all for trying to be what I was most comfortable with.

Funny, in childhood, we impulsively act on emotion. We feel like skipping, we skip. Feel like jumping, we jump. We take off running whenever the mood strikes. We make funny noises, yell at the top of our lungs, and bounce against furniture until our heads hurt. We squeal with joy when we feel like a party's going on in our tummies. But once puberty hits, we are suddenly ordered to act "more mature," which often means disguising who we really are in order to be accepted by the majority. We learn we must be a certain kind of person in certain surroundings. We must be one way around our parents, another around our peers. We must say and do what's expected of us, and oftentimes, lose ourselves in the process. The child, and that freedom, is gone. Usually never to return.

If we're lucky, though, we come to realize that to be truly happy we have to be who we are, and true to our spirit—the authentic person inside us. Somewhere around middle age (though, for some, this wisdom doesn't take quite that long), we discover that when we're comfortable in our own skin, we're free to once again act as we truly feel, say what we truly think. We are reunited with that liberated child who allows us to expand our horizons, and grants us permission to be ourselves.

I was yet to learn all this as a naïve, badly behaved, and confused fourteen-year-old Catholic hippie girl living in a Greaser world. Yet, through events such as these, I came to understand, and have compassion for, those leading alternative lifestyles. And those of a different race. Or religious belief. Those who often feel forced to camouflage who they are from the rest of the world they live in.

And who would have guessed that the compassion I learned to feel for all those unfairly judged would eventually extend to my former nemesis, Betty, who years later, I learned died in a car crash at the age of thirty-six.

Smoking Hazards

The first time I drew a cigarette to my twelve-year-old lips I coughed and gagged and nearly threw up.

But eventually I got it right.

I'd made a new friend in seventh grade. Susie was worlds ahead of me in the wayward acts of juveniles. She was my inauguration to junior high life of misdeeds, bad choices, and all things delinquent.

"I'm having a birthday party at my house Saturday night and you're invited," Susie said as we sat in the lunchroom eating peanut-butter-and-jelly sandwiches my second week at John F. Kennedy Junior High. We'd become fast friends and she'd already made a keen impression on me, having informed me the day before on how babies are made.

"No fuckin' way!" I said, using the new word she'd taught me the day before. This unspeakably gross information now confirmed my earlier belief that I must have, oh, most assuredly, been adopted.

"You don't know my mother," I said, pushing away my half-eaten sandwich. "There is *no way* my mother would ever do something like that. No way in *hell*!"

"Well, it's true," she said, matter-of-factly chewing away. "That's how it's done. That's how babies are made."

She couldn't have shocked me more than if her ironed-straight, chestnut-brown hair had suddenly been whipped up in a cyclone and started twirling around her pear-shaped face like a runaway Medusa.

Susie was uninhibited and sophisticated, compared to my own mundane and unworldly self. I was continually fascinated by the things she knew. While I chose not to think anymore about this unappetizing description of the birds-and-the-bees by my enlightened informant, I was willing to accept its possibility and move on to more appealing activities. Her highly-anticipated party fit the bill.

"So who's all comin'?" I asked, every bit as nonchalantly as she would have.

"Everyone, of course."

"Everyone" was her way of saying "the ones that mattered," which I happily discovered included boys.

By the time we all congregated in Susie's basement that exciting evening, I'd already gone through "liking" several of the boys invited, making the party that much more interesting. I put myself in charge of stacking the chosen records on the turntable spindle, alternating 45s of the Beatles, Rolling Stones, the Lovin' Spoonful, Herman's Hermits, the Byrds, and this new band called The Monkees, which I liked, despite my brother calling me a teeny-bopper because of it.

We were all in the middle of the floor doing "The Freddie" (a new dance made popular by the group, Freddie and the Dreamers, where you bounce around flailing your arms and legs) and singing their hit song, "I'm Telling You Now" when Billy McIntyre lit up a cigarette. Within minutes everyone followed suit. And I was a follower. The record player had already dropped down the next record, "Last Train to Clarksville," when cute, blonde-haired, blue-eyed Billy began losing his cool patience.

"No, not like that," he said, grabbing the Winston out of my terribly inexperienced fingers. "Here. This is how it's done. You go like this."

He proceeded to demonstrate by placing the lit cigarette between the tips of his index and middle finger (which, thanks to Susie, I'd learned yet another use for), put the filter end in his mouth, and sucked in like a straw. He then withdrew it, puckering his fine moist lips into a circle and exhaled. The rings of smoke that blew from his mouth puffed out into the shape of a donut, and he continued his presentation several times before having to recharge.

Now it was my turn. I did exactly as Billy showed me, but as soon as the smoke hit my lungs, I coughed so hard and so long I thought I'd never stop, and that once I did, I'd be dead.

"Don't worry," Karen, one of the popular girls, said as she led me to the bathroom (conveniently located downstairs so we weren't subjected to parental questioning). "We all do that at first."

As I leaned over the sink frantically scooping up water to swish the god-awful tobacco taste out of my mouth, she added, "After a couple of times, you stop."

"Breathing?" I mumbled, trying to be funny between spits. My new smoking buddy apparently didn't share my sense of humor.

"Huh?" her eyes squinted in puzzlement causing her midnight blue mascara-ladened lashes to stick together, and while attempting to separate them with the balls of her two fingertips, answered, "Uh, no. You stop coughing."

Somewhere in the recess of my vulnerable, naïve, pre-teen mind, I questioned that if one felt in this experience that she might choke to death, then perhaps it was a faint hint that maybe, just maybe, this act wasn't all that good for you.

However, once the coughing fit subsided, I experienced this strange, yet appealing, sense of light-headedness. Remembering Karen's assurance that I could get past the initial side effects, and with the encouragement of watching the pros puffing away to the music, I decided to try again. With no further assistance, I expertly lit up another "cig" as Bob Dylan's "Rainy Day Women" plopped down, *They stone you when you're trying to be so good . . .*" prompting us all to sing in unison. At this point, I had no clue Dylan was singing about marijuana, which I'd yet to discover. I took "stoned" to mean drinking. An assumption Susie would later correct me on. Of course.

When it came time to leave the party, we were careful to dispose all evidence, politely bid goodbye to Susie's all-too-trusting parents as they sat in their living room watching *Lawrence Welk*, and headed to the corner store where a few certified veterans with older siblings' IDs, and thirty-five cents, purchased a new pack of Winstons for the way home.

It's hard being a juvenile delinquent when you're surrounded by adults. The unwelcome presence of parents and teachers got much in the way of our daily lives, so we had no choice but to go behind their backs whenever possible. I managed to sneak in two to three cigarettes a day. One on the way to school, one on the way home, and if circumstances were right, one—split in morning and afternoon shifts—in the girls' lav. The student lavatory, turns out, was perfect for smoking. Unless teachers had good reason to go there, they stayed out.

The minute we'd enter school in the morning, we'd all head to the girls' room where we fought for mirror space. The ninth graders, with their short, clinging skirts, ruffled blouses and stacked hair, always had first dibs, so we were forced to wait our turns. When the last of the older girls pulled the door handle to leave, we'd all rush to the front of the mirror to line our eyes with coal black pencils, tease our hair high and wide, and aerosol it to a floor-waxed shine in an attempt to imitate our fifteen-year-old idols. Then, finally, it was time to smoke. We often had to wait in line for that as well, since it was best to use a stall underneath a ceiling vent. When one became available, we'd hop up on the toilet seat, light up, and with every puff exhaled, carefully blew it out through the vent. This worked fine, but we were also mindful to wait for some of the smoke to clear before opening the bathroom door, lest the grey, hazy evidence billowed out.

Looking back, I doubt we fooled anyone. It's likely we "got away with it" because teachers had more to do than bust a kid for smoking in the bathroom. After all, that would be a daily annoyance. Besides, they had their own smoking area in the teacher's lounge, a place we deemed quite mysterious, watching them moseying in and out every chance they got. We always wondered what, exactly, went on behind those doors.

But sometimes the powers-that-be were forced to deal with the student-smoking issue. Leave it to me to be the chosen one to be made the example. . . .

By eighth grade, I'd become quite competent at both smoking and not getting caught. This proud record was about to break. In an ugly and exceedingly public fashion.

One thing about smoking in school was that you had to bring your cigarettes with you. Aspiring to be adult women, teen girls always carry purses. Mostly containing makeup and neatly folded triangular-shaped notes full of bad words, boys' names, and glorified braggings of things we usually weren't guilty of. The purses in vogue in the late 1960s were Carnaby Street-inspired—as were most things post-Beatles—made of macramé with coiled handles and a single snap in the middle. There lay the problem.

Snaps generally snap open easily, making them impractical for devious teenage girls. Especially if the purse's contents were suspect, and it happened to accidentally fall from a school desk during class.

"Oh, wow, sorry," the boy walking past that desk whispered after knocking my handbag to the floor. His sorrow turned to true remorse when he looked down and saw what had spilled out. He knew I was now going to be in big, big, trouble. They all did. The event seemed to happen in slow motion: The accidental bump of the purse. My ever-so-desperate and unsuccessful attempt to grab it in mid-fall. The great scattering of illegal evidence. The audible gasp from my classmates. Then, the unified intake of breath that reverberated throughout the academic walls of the classroom.

Our science teacher, Mr. Winthrop, who reminded me of Uncle Martin from TV's *My Favorite Martian*, but with nerdy, square black-rimmed glasses, was in the middle of writing something on the blackboard. But the loud thump of the landed purse accompanied by the spurt of loud intakes of breaths, caused the instinctive red-flag alert to sound—an all-points bulletin to teachers that's something is amiss behind their back. He whipped around.

I had managed to scoop up the crumpled pack and may have been able to get away with it, had it not been that cigarettes have a nasty tendency to shed their cancer-causing stuffing.

Winthrop walked slowly down the aisle, an I've-got-you-now gaze in his muddy brown eyes. My heart pounded in rhythm to the sounds of his heavy dogged footsteps. He halted when he reached my side, his right brown shoe in direct path of the crime scene. The spread of tobacco bits dotted the scuffed vinyl tile like flakes of rat droppings.

"Miss Fedorko, did that come out of *your* purse?"

He wasn't a terribly bright person, even for a science teacher. Still, I suspected he already knew the answer to his stupid question.

Everyone has a "most embarrassing moment." This would be my first of many to come. The timing of this incident was particularly dreadful. It was just days after the assassination of Senator Robert F. Kennedy and adults were just in no mood.

"See me after class," he said, sauntering back to his chalk and board to complete his lecture on the nucleus of an atom.

I sat at my desk for the next twenty oppressive minutes, stiff with dread, horrified for my future. I had a great fear of my mother—who I had not earned points with since I was nine. Her greatest talent was making my life miserable, despite the fact I was perfectly capable of doing a fine job of that myself.

When Winthrop called me up front after class and told me that he had "no choice but to call your parents." I began with begging. Mercifully. That being unsuccessful, I started sobbing. Hard and loud. All to deaf ears.

"I'm sorry, but it's my job to report this . . . "

"You can't do that!" I yelled. Then went back to begging. Pitifully. "*Please* don't call my mother! *I'll do anything*!"

This final act of mortification was heard by at least three ninth graders who'd just entered the room for the next class. Soon the whole school knew of my *Blackboard Jungle* episode. I was suspended for three days, but somehow, someway, convinced my mother that in an act of kindness, I'd innocently been holding the cigarettes for a friend, who was already in trouble. I guess it's what she chose to believe.

After this pathetic display of public humiliation, I made a serious attempt to try the straight and narrow path. I figured I'd had enough drama for the year.

But I was fourteen. And the year was long. And I seemed to have an uncanny knack for drama. Clearly, there'd be more theatrics to come.

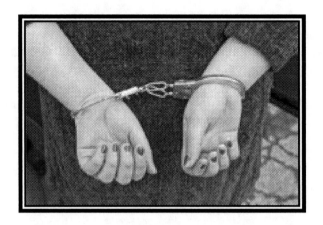

Crime & Punishment

People steal for various reasons. Attention. Poverty. Thrills.

I could, and probably did, use each one of these excuses: No one understood me. My mother wouldn't buy me anything (the fact she couldn't *afford* anything, was inconsequential). And I was captivated by the seduction and sinister pleasure of taking something and getting away with it.

Well, maybe at first.

As an adult, I not only detest the thought of people taking what isn't theirs—be it from a store, or person—I harbor a particular loathing toward those who use their deprived childhood or traumatic adolescence to explain away felony behavior. Give me a break. No matter how we grow up or what we have to endure, God gives each one of us something called free will. It's a wonderful thing. So is staying out of jail.

As a juvenile hell-bent on delinquency, I gave little thought to any of that. Teenagers rarely give much thought to anything except what's happening in their own lives, particularly on a social level. Of course, there are exceptions. I wasn't one of them.

If I could blame anyone for my short, shameful life as a thief, it would be my aforementioned friend, Susie. The one who told me where babies come from. Who encouraged sinful behavior (not being Catholic obviously kept her from that silly little gnawing guilt complex), such as swearing, smoking, and lying. (I marveled at how, one Friday night, Susie talked her mother into driving us to the movies to see Clint Eastwood's *Hang'em High*—a film we obviously wouldn't be interested in—thus allowing us a full two hours to make out with our big city boyfriends and smoke behind the theater. Then, when her mother asked about the movie on the way home, Susie further amazed me by describing the plot and characters at length. When I later asked her how she did that, she'd said she'd simply read the newspaper review.)

Turns out, stealing was another one of her notable talents.

I began this fine new skill in small ways, as most criminals do. A box of Red Hots here, pack of Bazooka there—quick and easy grabs for beginner thieves. I soon moved up to Cover Girl makeup (pink-frosted lipstick a must-have), easy-to-roll-up magazines (like my faves, *Tiger Beat, 16 Magazine,* and *True Confessions*)—pretty much anything that could fit snugly into a jacket pocket or macramé sack purse. Whether I could actually use the item or not wasn't the point. It was the art of it. I'd then report my minor successes to Susie, who'd then say something like, "Next time try for a small bottle of that Yardley of London stuff. And 45s are easy, too, so long as you don't break them. And hey, have you tried headbands, or jewelry, yet?"

She was my most supportive friend.

Soon I was ready for the Big Time. Choosing a time and place was easy. Shoregate Shopping Center was a strip mall, before we knew to call it that, and before they began building those spacious, stately-looking shopping malls we know today. It was centrally located, where all the kids could easily walk to, the jaunt being half the fun. And it offered everything: discount stores, shoes stores, clothing stores, a five-and-dime, a bowling alley, and best of all, a great record store. So, just like our future children, we teens were "mall rats," and this was our Saturday afternoon ritual. It's where we hung out with school friends, or met new ones. Where we could walk around smoking (cigarettes, and later, pot), eat those tasty hot dogs at Woolworth's Department Store's luncheon diner (and where we'd pass time getting high from spinning on the round silver stools until we got dizzy). But our sole mission was the extra-curricular activity of shoplifting.

"Now, listen," Susie said one day, taking me by the shoulders before we walked into Petries Department Store. There were four of us girls, and like all good criminals who case their target beforehand, we'd been in the store earlier that day. And we'd spotted the perfect item. A stretchy, hip-clinging, short-short, ever-so-cute, navy-blue striped dress we were sure was something the famous British model, Twiggy, would wear.

"We'll casually look around at all the items," she explained, priming me for another crucial lesson in the art of thieving. "Then we take several outfits into the dressing room. Take two sizes of the same dress, and pile one on top of the other so only one shows. This way, if they happen to see you walk in with a particular dress, they won't get suspicious when they see you walk out with it. Then put on the dress, tuck it into your jeans, and make sure it doesn't stick out of your top. Then walk out with the other clothes and remark to the salesgirl—casually—that nothing seems to fit. Then come over by me, where I'll be buying a pair of earrings—ya gotta buy something or they *will* get suspicious—then we'll all meet at the front door and walk, *casually,* out. Then go straight home before they discover them missing and call the cops and start looking for us. Got it?"

"Sure," I said, in my fake confident voice.

Yet I couldn't stifle the quiet roar in my head, *Oh my God, I can't do this. This is too big. **Too Big**! What if I blow it and get caught? My mom'll kill me. I don't want to go to jail. This is too much. It isn't worth it. Nope, I can't do it. I just can't.*

"Ready?" Susie asked.

"Ready!" I said.

When you make the wrong decision in your human right to assume free will, God has a way of letting you know how wrong you are. It begins with a rapid, pounding, chest-clenching heartbeat. From the time I entered the store until the time I—*casually*—walked out, my heart felt like it was going to explode in my chest. The steady thumping coursing through my body was distracting, but I soon ignored it in my quest to follow directions exactly as given. It helped to know that Susie and the other girls had done this before (I was new to the clique) and must know what they're doing. My faith in this knowledge got me through. Before I knew it, I was sporting my new Twiggy dress as underwear until I arrived home where I ran directly to my room and promptly tucked it in underneath other clothes in my drawer. It would be a dress my all-your-skirts-must cover-your-knees mother would know nothing about.

But God persists, albeit quietly, and always gives us an opportunity for redemption. A call I didn't heed.

That Monday, in a further act of great defiance, I wore my new dress to school (fortunately for me, a child of a working mom, she'd leave before me, and returned after). But unfortunately, none of us were too bright. All four of us wore our stolen goods that day. What are the odds?

Pretty good when you're thirteen.

"Why'd you wear *that* dress today?"

"Well, you didn't mention *you* were going to wear it!"

"Well you *shoulda* told me you were wearing it, ya jerk."

"Hey, *you* didn't mentioned it, either, bitch, so I thought it was okay."

"Well, I thought you'd *know*, stupid."

And so went the conversations throughout the morning.

Clearly, we hadn't discussed the obvious possibility. We looked like a singing sisters group from the hit dance show, *Shindig*, as we walked through the halls getting stares wherever we went. By noon that day, everyone was discussing it. Including the teachers. Who sent us all to the office.

Rule No.1 in Successful Acts of Stealing: Don't call attention to yourself in any way. If you're driving away from a bank you just robbed, make sure you're not missing a taillight, speeding down the highway, or throwing your wig out the window. If you're wearing a stolen dress, at least make sure it's dress-code acceptable.

And . . .

Rule No.2 in Successful Acts of Stealing: Do not show off your pilfered merchandise in public. Particularly when you steal the same things your partners-in-crime do. The fact that four of us in the seventh grade, who all hung out together, were wearing the exact same outfit, tended to lend itself toward suspicion. Not to mention that, in the world of fashion, it is a definite faux pas.

Our teachers had been giving us wary looks before ultimately sending us to the office, but there was no proof of any wrongdoing, other than our navy-blue fishnet stockings revealing a whole lot of leg. None of us had been in trouble before (or at least hadn't been caught) so it was determined a warning had to suffice.

"Our school policy clearly states no mini-skirts," said the guidance counselor who's idea of true fashion was Mary Poppins in Mamie Eisenhower bangs. "Don't let this happen again or there *will* be consequences."

Gee, that wasn't so bad, we thought. But then, we hadn't taken into account, *Rule Number 3:*
Don't write about your criminal accomplishments.

A few weeks later, Linda mentioned the shoplifting spree in a note she'd passed to an up-and-coming juvenile. Our English teacher, Mrs. B, of course caught the act in progress, confiscated the note, read the note, and sent her straight to the principal's office. Soon, the other accomplices—except for me who, for some providential reason Linda hadn't named in her damning letter, and for once I was all too happy to have been left out—were suspended and promptly hauled off to the police department.

"Oh my God, it was sooo scary," Linda tells me on the phone that night. "They made me sit in a small empty room and asked me all kinds of questions, wanting to know exactly how we did it and all. They said we could go to *prison* for that, or at least DH and they'll be keeping an eye on me."

"You didn't mention my name, did you?" I asked with baited breath.

"No, but I think they know another girl was involved."

Perhaps because I was a Catholic girl, I was divinely never caught. I took that as my one-and-only "get out of jail free" card, and determined that I'd better quit while ahead.

That decision lasted until a few weeks later when temptation, once again, got the better of me.

Every Saturday, my grandparents went to Wally's Bar on Vine Street, the main artery of Willowick and Eastlake's business district. Since my mother worked at the bank until afternoon, Gee Gee and Grandpa always took me with them to Wally's. As a youngster, this was great fun. I was treated to all the chips and pretzels I could eat. I was given quarters by all the bar patrons to pick out new songs, and took great pleasure in dropping them into the jukebox like a slot machine. When I was eight, Grandpa taught me how to shoot pool, and by ten, I could beat anyone on the bowling machine. It was a wonderful life. When I was twelve and no longer lived with Gee Gee and Grandpa, I'd welcome these Saturday outings with my favorite adults. Plus, it was a lot more appealing than sitting around watching *Bowling for Dollars* on TV in our small apartment, and a fine excuse for getting out of housework.

"But Mom, I really want to see Gee Gee and Grandpa!" was my mantra whenever she'd complained I hadn't done "a thing around here!" I knew Mom felt guilty about moving me away from them, so the statement always shut her up.

But this day, I'd played all my favorite songs on the jukebox: "You Were on My Mind," by the We Five. "Indian Lake," by the Cowsills. "Mrs. Brown, You've Got a Lovely Daughter" by Herman's Hermits. And of course, "I'm a Believer," by my faves, the Monkees. I'd beaten everyone who'd challenged me on the bowling machine. And I had listened to too many boring discussions on politics, television and Cleveland weather to the tune of empty beer bottles hitting the bar top and calls for, "One more before I go."

"Can I go across the street and buy a magazine?" I asked Grandpa. He rarely said no to me, so after he handed me the dollar, I jumped off the barstool and headed to the little grocery store to purchase the latest copy of *Tiger Beat*. That was my intention. That's not what I did.

The little silver bell hooked on the entrance door sounded out as I entered, but no one came to the register. The place was empty. I walked around to the back and saw, and heard, no one. I flipped through a few other magazines before clutching the one with David Cassidy on the cover, rolled it up, and headed toward the counter. And waited patiently.

As I stood there looking around, I surveyed the packs of cigarettes stacked neatly on the shelves across the counter: Marlboro, Tareyton, Pall Mall, Salem, Lucky Strike (Grandpa's brand), Chesterfield King (Mom's brand), Winstons (my brand). They all began taunting me. "*Psst, hey, you, yeah, **you**. Look! There's not a soul around, and isn't it about time for a good smoke?*" They then began fighting to be the chosen one. "*Come on home to Marlboro Country*" . . . "*NO, over here! Have a **real** cigarette, have a Camel*" "*WAIT, Lucky Strike means fine tobacco.*" "*HEY, hold it! Only **I** taste good like a cigarette should!*" But John Wayne had the last word, "*Now don't ya listen to 'em, cowgirl. Tareyton smokers would rather fight than switch.*"

They had me where they wanted me. Before giving it much thought, or rather, any, I glanced quickly around the empty store, jumped up, leaned my upper torso over the counter, and stretched as far as I could to snatch my preferred brand. With fumbling fingers, I managed to grab the end of the pretty red cellophane pack in my hot little hands. But in doing so, I'd pulled the whole stack out just enough to see them all begin tipping over the edge. As I hopped down, David Cassidy's face fell to the floor, along with a mountain of Winston packs that came tumbling down like a stack of Dominos—one after another—until they all lay on the floor like a game of 52 Pick-up.

"Oh, *shit*," I muttered, and made a run for it. The tiny bell tinkled loud and clear as I fled out the door. I ran as fast as I could, not looking back, and darted into the busy street. The dark blue Mercury with the little man at the wheel had to swerve to miss the panicked figure that was escaping back to Wally's Bar. I pushed open the door to the sounds of pool balls cracking and old folks laughing, and hopped on the bar stool next to Grandpa. "Can you take me home?" I breathlessly begged. Now. Please.

"Don't ya wanna to go across the street for a foot-long hotdog?" Gee Gee piped in to sway me to stay longer and relieve Grandpa from the burden of making an extra trip. The ice cream stand, next to the convenience store I'd just robbed, had wonderfully delicious hot dogs the size of horse tails and I'd been known to scarf down one, and occasionally two, of those babies— with all the fixings. Today, however, I'd lost my normally healthy appetite the minute I'd tucked the stolen pack of smokes into the front of my jean pockets (easier to disguise under my long tie-dyed T-shirt) while making my escape. Still shaking, all I could do was wobble my head in negative response.

"Okay, okay," my sweet, clueless grandpa said, "we'll go soon as I finish this drink." I looked intently at his brown bottle of P.O.C. and saw that it wasn't even down half-way. I'd seen him chug a beer before, and now was the most opportune time for him to display that skill. "*Please, Grandpa?*" Like I said, he rarely said no to me, so my pleading look managed to convince him to take me home right then and there. He sucked down his beer in record time, probably figuring I'd just gotten my period. And with another, "Okay, okay," he turned to Gee Gee. "I'll take her home and be right back."

As we headed toward the car, I saw the owner of the store standing on the sidewalk, hands on hips, looking all around him for the clumsy thief. I saw his eyes dart in my direction, so soon as I got in the passenger seat, I sunk down low. Disgrace overwhelmed me, eliminating my former urge for a smoke—good like a cigarette should or otherwise.

At fourteen, I had experienced the feeling of shame a time or two in my relatively short life. And I don't know what feeling—aside from fear and heartache—that could feel much worse. And while there are varying degrees of shame, this one was a humdinger. I suddenly realized my stupid adolescent behavior could have involved my grandfather, who was so accommodating, so totally unaware. And who was now, technically, an accomplice, as he drove me away from the scene of my crime.

As he tried making small talk on the way home, I was busy internally damning myself, and questioning why I did the things I did. I realized that my bad behavior was no longer about my relationship with my mother. It was solely about me. And I knew then that, after a succession of stupid teen tricks, I was heading toward disaster. A week before, I'd been sent to the office for writing a boy's name on the cafeteria table. The lunch lady hadn't seen me do it, but the handwriting, in ink, was angled in a way that it left no doubt that the destruction of property was caused by a southpaw. I might as well stamped a big **L** on my forehead, since I was the only left-handed person who'd been sitting at that table. This, coupled with an ever-growing list of unlawful juvenile stunts, proved beyond a reasonable doubt that when it came to crime, I wasn't the brightest crayon in the Crayola box.

And so, shame won. Because sometimes mental and emotional punishment hurts deeper than physical incarceration for your criminal acts. Because there is no hope of being free from yourself. And there is next to nothing that makes you feel worse than weaving innocent people into the web of your evil doings. Particularly if that someone is under the delusion that you are just one great kid.

We arrived home safely and without incident, and as I leaned over and quickly kissed my grandpa goodbye, I silently vowed right then and there to never, "So help me, God" steal another thing again.

Because it makes you feel like a real shit.

All Girls' School Blues

"If you don't straighten up, so help me you're going to Andrews!" was my mother's mantra throughout my seventh and eighth grade years.

By the end of eighth grade, I hadn't straightened up and my mother made good on her promise.

This came as a surprise to me. My mother didn't make a lot of money as a bookkeeper, and she'd always led me to believe we were one week's pay from sleeping in the car. That is if we'd had one, which we didn't, because Mom never learned to drive. Andrews School for Girls served as the greatest threat parents of wayward daughters could use in Northeast Ohio. There was also Villa Angela, another private all-girls school in Cleveland, which was even worse because it was a Catholic school where students had to wear thoroughly unattractive uniforms. But Andrews, a boarding school that boasted "where young women learn independent skills" (which I'd already had a handle on), was geographically closer to us 'burb kids, so it effectively sufficed.

"My mother can't afford to send me there," I'd cockily tell my friends upon each wayward incident.

By the age of fourteen, however, I'd finally proved myself too hard to handle for a divorced, single mother. I couldn't tell you what the last straw was. The time I skipped school with some friends who decided to camp out at another friend's house—who unfortunately wasn't with us at the time—thus adding breaking & entering to my truancy charge. Or when she discovered that I hadn't actually been at the Rollerdrome those Friday nights when I said I was. Or maybe it was during that heated argument when I screamed "I hate you!"—which was merely an outlet of my frustrations, but once articulated, sounded downright cruel.

Of course it was likely a combination of all the above. For weeks that turned into months, my long-suffering mother, who didn't know what else to do with me, sat at the kitchen table at night with her bills, pen and paper. She'd have her country music station on low, so that all I could hear as I'd lie awake in my room down the hall was of her tap-tap-tapping her unfiltered Chesterfields before lighting up. Smoking, she always said, helped her to think. She was on a mission to save her wayward daughter.

And just in time for registration, she finagled a way. If she cut corners in every aspect of her already tight budget, Mom could afford at least one year of the "good girls' school." When she finally disclosed these plans to me, she tried making it sound like I was going away to camp.

"You'll *get to* stay in a house with other girls your age [apparently she wasn't aware of my lack of social skills] with a *nice* housemother, and maybe even *get to* go horseback riding."

This last bit of fun was purely fictional when I discovered the cost of such an activity. After struggling to pay the tuition, I knew my mother *really* couldn't afford that.

The night before the big day, I threw the ugly boarding school-approval clothes into my mother's old suitcase, doing my damnedest to keep the tears from releasing my overwhelming anxiety. There was no way I'd give her the satisfaction of seeing my angst. But it was hard. Fear, sorrow, regret at my bad behavior, and a heavy feeling of abandonment wrapped around me like a blanket of darkness. My mother was sending me away. Even though I myself couldn't much blame her, I blamed her. How could she do such a thing to her own daughter?

She had told me, repeatedly, that it was for "my own good." But I knew she was also doing it for hers. . . .

Welcome to Andrews School for Girls. September 1968.

We enter the doorway of the "Mentor Avenue House" across from the school. We're greeted by a plump grey-haired grandmotherly looking lady with rimless glasses and a dubious smile. This is my punishment for skipping school, for failing school, for smarting back once too often. For wanting boys I couldn't have, and claiming friends I shouldn't have. I feel disconnected. An all-girls boarding school was never in my plans. I can actually feel my former life whooshing out at the shut of that front door, vanishing through the walls of this captivity, as I stand looking at this odd woman with the German accent.

"Hello, so nice to meet you both," she says, with what looks to me like an honestly fake greeting. "I'm the housemother, Mrs. Reuter." She is standing in the hallway welcoming all the parents and their daughters. None of which, with their neatly combed hair, long dreadful skirts, and smiles—smiles!—look all that wayward to me. I glance past Reuter, and notice the shiny wooden banister leading up the stairs and my first thought is how cool it'll be to slide down it.

The interior of the house is straight out of the Victorian age. The living room to my left has a 12-inch television atop a 1940-era strand, surrounded by three old style high-back chairs with blood red velour upholstery and curved wooden legs with balls on the bottom like a steer's. Straight ahead there's the dining room, with a long cherry wood table, properly dollied, that looks like it could seat a small army. (I've yet to read Dicken's *Oliver!* but when I see the movie a month later, the lunch scene for some reason reminds me of my first meal here). My eyes then return to the stairway and travel up to the top in time to see Rebecca of Sunnybrook Farm gleefully discovering her room.

"Mom, here it is - Dorm 4!"

My increasingly anxious thoughts are interrupted just then as the housemother discloses the "house rules" and I have to pay particular attention to ensure I break every one.

"Each girl is assigned a daily chore, which rotates on a weekly basis," Ma Reuter is telling us, but looking at Mom as if to impress upon her how structured the household will be.

"We rise <u>promptly</u> at 6:00 a.m., except for the girl on breakfast duty, who must awake at 5:30 to help prepare the meal. Breakfast is served <u>promptly</u> at 6:30. Afterward, those who aren't on the morning chores list—where they must do vacuuming, polish furniture, or breakfast dishes—go right upstairs to wash up, and dress for school. Then off they go (she, too, talks as if we're at Camp Joyful).

"After school," she continues, "they are treated to a healthy snack of fruits or nuts [*I'm sure*], then allowed one hour of free time where they can watch TV or spend time reading, or socializing, in their dorm rooms. Dinner is served <u>promptly</u> at 5:30 p.m. and then, if they don't have an after-dinner chore, they can relax before study hour, which is 7 p.m. until 8:45. Then fifteen minutes to wash up and get ready for bed, with lights out <u>promptly</u>

at 9 p.m."

This is to be my life.

My mother has sent me to prison. Life as I know it will cease to exist. I have entered the bowels of hell. Oh my God, what's going to happen to me? I'm surely going to die here in this horrible, horrible place . . .

The thoughts swirl inside my head like demons in a playground, scattering to and fro like a swarm of mazes, occasionally bumping into each other whereas two or three thoughts collide at the same time and I literally have to shake my head to rattle them out.

A girl now approaches. She has brown knee-high socks to offset the brown lines in her plaid mid-calf skirt. Her mousy brown hair, with perfectly straight part to the side, is clasped tight with matching brown clip lest an unruly strand escapes. She looks absolutely studious in her square black-framed glasses.

And she . . . is . . . *smiling.*

Of course. The thought has now occurred to me that perhaps they give these girls happy pills.

Oh, sign me up. Please.

"This is Anne," Reuter says. "She's been at Andrews since seventh grade, so she knows the ropes. Deanna, you can say goodbye to your mother now and Anne'll take you to your room. Dorm 6," she says to Anne.

I have suddenly become deaf and mute. I don't know how to act. For the first time since I can remember, I don't want my mother to leave me. I am terrified by these very strange strangers. Even the banister no longer appeals to me.

We've never been a demonstrative family, yet I feel a desperate urge to cling to my mother, then run out to the car where my grandfather—who safely stayed put in the car—and beg them to take me home with them. *I'll be good. I promise.* And I would mean it.

"Bye, Honey, I'm sure you'll like it here," my mother says to me.

Are you fuckin' kiddin' me??

I cannot believe my mother believes what she just said. And yet something inside tells me (maybe it was her calling me Honey, a definite first) that somewhere in her controlled stance, she shares my uncertain feelings. We hug, quickly, and my mother effectively closes the door on my freedom.

She wins.

"Deanna, you'll be sharing the room with two other girls," Reuter says, not quite as friendly as before. I correct her at once.

"I don't go by that name," I tell her. "Everyone calls me Dee Dee." She seems uncertain that this is allowed (I discover later this is her first year, too) but smiles a crooked smile and says, "Well, I suppose that'll be alright."

"Oh, here's one of your roommates, now," she says as another girl approaches. I now feel I really am in Oz. The girl is a munchkin. Her curly, chestnut-haired head is level to my waist. She hobbles over to us because her one leg is shorter than the other. And her back is hunched over like a ninety-year-old woman. *Oh, that's just great*, I think to myself. Once I knew my stay here was inevitable, I'd envisioned at least having a cool, rebel-like-me roommate who would share forbidden cigarettes with me, compete to be first at disobeying the "house rules," even sneak out with me on occasion for some real life adventures. This circus act was not her. Another daydream shot to hell.

"Hi, I'm Eliza." I'm taken aback. The voice doesn't match this petite deformed figure. It's weirder than that. Like Truman Capote's, including the lisp.

Anne disappeared upon Elizabeth's arrival, so I've no choice but to follow the dwarf upstairs. One small step at a time, like a death toll. As we slowly make our way up to the room—which I will see is not much bigger than a closet—Eliza says nothing. Francine, my other prized roomie, joins us later that day, and she is worse than the other one. Tall, frizzy blonde hair, teeth so crooked her braces probably won't help, face smothered in acne. Thoroughly unattractive. Okay, let's be honest here. Thoroughly ugly. I don't want to go anywhere near her things, and quickly choose the bed next to Eliza rather than sleep two feet away from this one. The little Catholic voice inside chides me for being so cruel with my first impressions of these two. It whispers that I should understand and accept that they are simply different. And try and be nice. But the ear-splitting *"I CAN'T FUCKIN' BELIEVE THIS IS FOR REAL! IT HAS TO BE A NIGHTMARE! SOMEBODY, WAKE ME UP. PLEEEEAASSSE! WAKE. ME. UP!!"* drowns out all good Christian sense like a tidal wave.

What were the odds that I'd be given the absolute worst roommates feasibly possible? I had to wonder if my mother had had it all arranged. No, even she couldn't be that merciless.

Everyday after school, the girls all hover around the black-and-white television set to watch *Dark Shadows*, a soap opera about vampires. I don't need to watch this, I think, I'm living it. But I try to be like the others and watch, but can't believe how dumb it is, and five minutes later, head to my room. By the third night, I can't take anymore. I sit up in my bed after "Lights Out" and cry.

My sobs stop short when I hear the sound of a train rushing by. I press my head against the window sill (I'd wisely chosen the bed next to the window) and realize the train tracks are right down the hill behind this house (Note to self: Must investigate later). But I can't see it for the trees. But I like the sound. The steady rumbling is oddly comforting, like music. I listen to the echo of this symbol of freedom and excitement as it roars down the tracks. Then I gaze up at the stars and think about my life.

I review my actions of the past few years, and some of it embarrasses me, though I'd never admit it to anyone. I wonder what happened? How did I go from a happy little girl who laughingly danced outside in the rain, chatted amiably with neighbors, and best loved being alone in my room with a good book, to an angry, deceitful, defiant young woman who, truth be told, didn't even like herself?

I'm crying again and can feel the heated flush of my soaked cheeks as my cotton nightgown clings to my chest from the sweat I've built up. Now I'm pissed. I don't think I hate anything more than crying. Who said a good cry makes you feel better? Whoever it was, was an idiot.

I force myself out of bed, tiptoe down the empty hall while the goblins sleep, and slip quietly into the bathroom. I grab handfuls of toilet paper, roll it around my hand like a bandage, and creep back to my room where I put it all to good use, then tuck the sopping mess under my pillow.

After a month of pity parties, and of trying to adjust, I begin to accept my fate. The extremely peculiar Francine is gone, having suffered an asthma attack that first week and citing "stress," her parents take her home. She never returns. This leaves me and Eliza, who actually proves to be quite the Chatty Kathy. I eventually forgive her for being a goody-two shoes—doing her homework on time (always with extra credit) and getting straight A's—because she makes me laugh, and Lord knows, I need that. With my encouragement, this munchkin, who usually acts like she's forty years old, begins to rediscover her inner child. I get her to loosen up, and give her permission to act silly, even goofy at times. I like to believe that I give her this gift. That I help release her from those rigid restraints. To set her free from her restrictive, all-too-serious persona, her dullness.

She, in turns, teaches me something about compassion, self-acceptance, and the true meaning of friendship. I am constantly amazed how comfortable she is in her crooked little body. At fourteen, she's more confident than I ever hope to be. She knows who she is (wise beyond her years, self-assured, hardworking), and who she isn't (pretty, popular, young-at-heart) and she doesn't seem to have a problem with any of it. Even when other people do. I'm sure her feelings are hurt numerous times, but she somehow shrugs it off, and promptly digs back inside her books.

I learn from Eliza to never again judge "a book by its cover." But most importantly, I learn through her example that it doesn't matter so much what happens to you, as how you deal with it. She tells me one night she almost died at birth, though refrains from morbid details. She says she will suffer back pain the rest of her life, and realizes that it's highly unlikely she'll ever marry or bear children. I now understand that there was one moment long ago when she decided to compensate by taking advantage of her high IQ and defy the gods that afflicted her and become an academic success.

I find her plight incredibly sad, particularly as I grow to like her more and more. We soon become the odd couple at this boarding house. After all, we couldn't be more different. And yet we enjoy each other's company and ultimately become confidants. We giggle at night, share our family histories, and past social blunders. Many nights, when I steal oranges from the wicker basket above the fridge and stuff them into my bathrobe— which conveniently has big pockets—I share them with her after lights out. The peels, like the tissues, go promptly under my pillow.

We also develop a nightly routine.

"Goodnight David," Eliza says, her signal that she's had enough fooling around for the evening.

"Goodnight Chet," I answer, knowing it's now time to

shut up.

The banter refers to David Brinkley and Chet Huntley, the newsmen who always uses the send-off at the end of their nightly broadcast. One night, nosy Reuter—who must've been eavesdropping outside the door—bursts into the room and accuses me of swearing.

"I heard you say that foul word," she sneers, all puffed up with pride at catching my evil-doing.

"That's not what I said," I insist, "I said *Chet*, you know, like the news guy . . . "

My denials only seem to convince her more ("doth protest too much"), and she assigns me extra duties all the next week for my "insolence." From then on, her new mission in life is to catch any wrongdoing on my part, and she pays particular attention to me thereafter. But I am now on to her. One night she pokes a broom handle loudly on her ceiling (our room happens to be directly above her living quarters) which is supposed to be the last straw before she makes her way upstairs. Which is my cue.

I listen for her heavy, black Footglove wide-fits to thump up the stairs. And finally, they come. As the last heel stomps onto the top step, I assume my position. I drop to my knees beside the bed and fold my hands in prayer. When she throws open the door, there I am, angel-like. A good Catholic girl who is merely misunderstood.

"Oh, sorry," she says, unsure how else to respond to this holy sight. "Uh, just go right to sleep when you've finished."

She softly closes the door.

I feel a hint of shame at my deception, but it doesn't last long. Especially because after that, she seems to lighten up on me a bit, and I become more adept at the fine art of sneakiness.

Throughout the school year, I merely tolerate the other sixteen boarders, though a few I do rather like. But as always, I'm never the popular one. In this case, that would be "New York," who is also different, but her difference is embraced. It's not merely her outgoing personality that sways the vote, it's the cool East Coast accent that sparks her nickname that first night when everyone gathers around the living room floor to "get to know each other." I don't stay long for this. I've no desire to befriend these privileged girls from well-to-do families. (Turns out, I'm the only one whose mother stayed up late for months playing with numbers.)

But because I actually begin to like New York, I pop in her room every now and then and sit on her bed to talk. We all want to make friends with the popular ones.

One morning, I'm running late and give New York a note to give to one of my only girlfriends, with whom I discuss the hippie life, smoking pot, and boys I now only see my every-third-weekend home. But on the walk to school, she opens it and reads it aloud in its entirety to the other Mentor House girls accompanying her, and the rest of the evening I'm subsequently mocked for its contents. I make a mental note never to trust anyone here again. Except for Eliza. After all, she's been there. She knows.

I hate every moment spent in this prison of a house. When I'm finally let out for my once-a-month home visits, I don't tell people I meet where I attend school. Tell people you go to an all-girls school and they tag you a lesbian or a whore. I am neither. Truth be told, I'm still a virgin and contrary to popular all-girls' school misconceptions, so are most of the girls here.

Somehow I do manage to make a few friends in this school—ones like me who were sent here as punishment—and we bask together in our shared misery. I find solace in the basement of the house, where the "rec" room is, and where I spend playing records by myself during our "free time." Occasionally, one or two girls come down for awhile, but most of them aren't into music like I am. They haven't learned how it can save you. Or don't require the need. When Kathryn brings down the soundtrack to "West Side Story," it becomes one of my favorites. Though I don't dare mention this to my cool friends.

I have a few records of my own down here in this dungeon. I listen to songs that make me feel less alone. Less abnormal. Like Jefferson Airplane's "Go Ask Alice." Blood, Sweat & Tears "When I Die" (for my real depressed times). And Big Brother & the Holding Company songs with Janis Joplin (whose poster I no longer have since Mom ripped it off my wall during a fight about my "awful" room). All my beloved Stones albums. And Jim Morrison and the Doors. I especially like "People Are Strange" because it's so appropriate to my surroundings. When their "Waiting for the Sun" album comes out, I figure an ingenious way to make the three dollars needed to buy it on my next trip home. I hold a Book Sale in my dorm. But this only seems to convince these girls from "good" families with assessable funds that I really am the peculiar one, after all. Though I do sell one paperback, *"Valley of the Dolls,"* I'm just as convinced it's purely out of pity. Then again, it's the only risqué one in the bunch, and even good, straight teen girls have their smut moments.

The after-dinner "Study Hour" is lost on me. Instead of doing homework, I sit at my designated corner feeling sorry for myself. I miss my brother, who dropped out of school and fled to Boston with his girlfriend, so I no longer see him on my weekends home. I miss my old friends—who've moved on and stopped calling and don't write. I miss my grandmother's home-cooked meals. And my grandfather's smile.

I miss my home. And, even, my Mom.

I miss my former life.

That's when, sitting at a wobbly card table staring at the wooden banister I'd just shined up that morning, this miserable, wayward Catholic girl begins to write.

Confessions of a Not-So-Good Catholic Girl

"Bless me, Father, for I have sinned. It's been, uh . . . um . . . I think . . . no . . . I guess . . . well, maybe . . . uh, probably about . . . four months? . . . since my last confession."

I have always found this holy practice quite bizarre. There you are, kneeling on hard padded wood in a pitch-black closet, confessing all your ungodly behavior to an authoritative voice that will judge you without even knowing that you're really not all that bad a person. This, after actually having waited in line to totally rat yourself out. This, after having memorized your sins because you can't bring the long list into the confessional since it's too damned (oops, sorry God, I'll add that to the list) dark in there. Still, you're supposed to keep track of each and every trespass because the numbers are important to measure out the penance. You are then forced to underplay your crimes—slyly altering possible mortal sins to venial—because you don't want this Man of God thinking poorly of you.

Finally, the grey-suited man who stood in front of you in line surfaces from the closet looking like a beaten rat (boy, he must've been really bad), and now it's your turn to talk to the black curtain.

"Okay, let's see. I smacked my brother and made his nose bleed three . . . well, just a couple times. But really Father, those were extenuating (*perhaps I could sway him with big words*) circumstances. He really did deserve it (*and so, maybe he'd let it slide*). And uh, let's see, I lied to my mother, three, well maybe four, times. I took the Lord's name in vain, but just that once (*Surely, he'd see reason*). And well, I did cheat at Monopoly when my brother got up to go to the bathroom, but that's just because I wanted to get it over with. After all, Father, as you know, it's a really, really long game (*Who could blame me there?*).

You then ask for forgiveness and hope The Voice bestows a light sentence. (You've already increased those odds by going to Father A, the kind one, rather than Father B, who'd make his own mother say the entire rosary. Twice. And with feeling.)

A few Our Father's and Hail Mary's later, you walk out with a newly cleansed soul, which lasts until that evening when you tell your mother you're going to study with a friend, and you turn in the opposite direction. . . .

Ironically, it was my father, who, far as I know, never set foot in a church once he reached adulthood, is the reason I ended up Catholic. My mother's family only went to church for weddings and funerals, and I don't recall any hint of my maternal grandmother belonging to a religious order. And although Grandpa's mother was a dedicated church-goer, whenever Grandpa was asked his faith, he'd state simply that he wasn't a "practicing Catholic," which ended all further discussion toward religion.

But love changes certain dynamics. When my mother met my father (whose large Slovenian family consisted of devout Catholics), she decided to officially join the ranks of the Roman Catholic church. She went through the required steps to become a confirmed Catholic, enabling them to marry in a Cleveland cathedral on June 4, 1949. I believe it was their only attendance.

When their divorce became final some years later, and perhaps in an attempt to smooth our way into heaven, my mother vowed to raise good Catholic children. Thus ruining our beloved Sunday routine of sleeping late, enjoying a leisurely breakfast with my grandparents, and watching television until the traditional two o'clock Sunday dinner. We now had to go to church. Every Sunday morning. And Catechism classes. Every Saturday afternoon. Which wasn't at all to my liking.

The first thing I learned as an emerging Catholic girl was that those who aren't baptized are not children of God. Which meant me. So when I came home and announced to my mother that God did not love me, that I was in fact not going to heaven, and that I, at seven years old, was doomed to end up "down there," she immediately arranged for my baptism.

"There was never any time to do that when you were a baby," she explained in a it's-not-my-fault tone. I read between her lines. By then I knew (through my habit of eavesdropping) that her life had been full of upheaval since my birth—what with her moving back to her parent's house while trying to keep her ex, who couldn't hold a job, from visiting her children drunk, all the while working banker's hours to eventually free her from her parents reign, helpful though it was. Now, there was the added pressure of making us *real* children of God.

The irony of it all is that the paper designating her a true Catholic had not even yellowed before it was rendered useless. Once she won her divorce, my now disgraced mother, the only divorcee in town, was immediately "excommunicated" from the church and subsequently banned from the honor of partaking of the sacraments. Every Sunday, as fancily dressed folks lined up for Communion, my scarf-wearing mother would remain seated, cloaked in shame. These circumstances, together with the embarrassment of divorce itself (this being the early '60s, when women endured alcoholic, or worse, husbands for the "children's sake," because then they'd grow up in a "broken home") cast a dark shroud over my mother and left her a bitter, disheartened woman for years.

And so I became part of her redemption. In no time at all, I was baptized, made my First Communion, my Confirmation, and ate fish sticks every Friday during Lent. And was reminded, repeatedly, by Mom and the church, that I must— at all times—be a good Catholic girl if I wanted to get to heaven.

Easier said than done.

First off, I hated going to church. While I was a bit intrigued by the whole pomp and circumstances connected to this religious order, I had no clue what it all meant. Mass involved an awful lot of standing, sitting, and kneeling. Though I did enjoy seeing the ladies' assorted outfits, a virtual fashion show of matching hats, gloves and shiny shoes. And the act of people-watching at least helped wile away the hour. But no one ever smiled here, they all looked so serious. Seemed to me, the time would go a lot faster—like old neighbor Mrs. Wolff always said— if they'd make this Christian duty fun. Like when I saw once on

TV how the black people do it, with all that hoopin' and hollerin' and singin' the Lord praises, and I'd think, *Now alrighty then, that's what I'm talking about! Make it a party.*

But no. In this church, all these white folks were solemn and sorrowful. Making the experience long. And dreadful. Worse yet, we had to walk to get there. More than a mile each way, regardless of the season, since my mother didn't drive. Occasionally, Grandpa would take us there or pick us up, but only if it was raining in torrents or cold enough to freeze our holy faces. Other than that, we walked—at mother's insistence not to "bother Grandpa to drive us." I was convinced that this was not so much due to that reasoning, than it was some kind of punishment because our birth and her bad choice in men had doomed her to a life I'm sure at times felt hardly worth living. Yet these were the times I had any semblance of a conversation with her. Though that usually ended poorly. Like the time I spotted a little grey kitten on our way home.

"Here pussy, pussy, come here." I called, stooping down to pet it. I looked up in time to see my mother's look of horror. At eight years old, I was well acquainted with that look.

"Don't say that word," she scowled.

"What word?" I asked with utter confusion. "You mean pussy? What's wrong with *that* word?" I was already convinced my mother was the prude of all prudes, whereas she'd find something scornful in most anything that hinted at fun, or funny, or fanciful. Yet she had me baffled on this one. I couldn't for the short life of me figure out why suddenly the name of a pussycat could bring such disgust from my mother. After all, our backyard was full of them.

She evaded my question, so I pondered it the rest of the quiet way home and finally came to the conclusion that it was all Tom Jones fault. He'd just come out with the record, "What's New, Pussycat?" and I faintly recalled rumblings that this song, and the way he performed it, triggered unCatholic-like behavior among women, with talk of his "sex appeal" and sinful gyrations. I figured that had to be it, for sure. It would be a few years before I learned otherwise.

By 1966, my mother had saved up enough money to rent her own apartment and moved me and my brother to a two-bedroom dwelling several miles away from my grandparents. Where I was now forced to share a bedroom with her. At twelve.

The summer before junior high. When no one wants to share a bedroom with a parent—or anyone else, for that matter.

Thus the beginning of my rebel phase.

Among the many changes that took place during this transition was that my mother stopped going to church. Though, she always made my brother and me go. A Catholic church was conveniently located within walking distance of our new residence, and Mom woke us up every Sunday morning to ensure our presence at 10 a.m. Mass. Soon as I left the house, of course, I chose to abstain from the sacred routine. My girlfriend Linda and I would instead meet at our own house of worship—"St. Isley's"—an ice cream parlor just down the street that, lucky for us, was open early on Sundays. We'd hang out there, chatting with the cute guy behind the soda counter while puffing away on our Winstons, until we'd see the churchgoers pass by, which was our cue.

"Wow, that time already," Linda would say, looking up at the wall clock.

"Okay, gotta go," I'd reply, smashing out what would be my last cigarette of the day.

We'd wave goodbye to cute soda boy and dutifully walk to our respective homes.

The few times we didn't go to Isley's, Linda and I would camp in the church bathroom through the length of the service. We'd sit on the window sill and talk about boys we loved, girls we hated, and teachers we despised, as we puffed away, making sure to blow the smoke out the window or the ceiling vents, until we heard the priest say, "The mass is ended, go in peace." And so we would.

Then Father J arrived. He became pastor of our church soon after I hit puberty and word soon spread that this new priest was someone you had to check out. To my pleasant surprise, I found he was actually cool and unlike any priest I ever saw, that is, under the age of "old." I immediately developed a crush on him—yet another holy hurtle I'd be faced with. A crush on a *priest*? This could not be good. In fact, I was pretty sure it condemned me to a life of damnation. His interesting liturgies about the apostles made you feel as if you were sitting around a campfire roasting marshmallows, hearing stories of *real* people and their adventures—so unlike the dismal preaching of my previous Catholic experience. I got to chat with him nearly every week when he'd stop by our confraternity classes, which in my mind was equivalent to a meet-and-greet with a rock star. And except for the telltale collar, he resembled one. He was tall, nice looking, and had Beatle-like "long hair." Well, not too long, just enough to prove that he, too, had some rebel in him. A James Dean in priest's clothing. I was now a dedicated church-going Catholic.

While the action may look good on paper, or at least in my surprised mother's eyes, the reason for my sudden enthusiasm and regular Sunday attendance, wasn't exactly what the church would want to base its collection basket on. In my own defense, I wasn't the only one enthralled with this new priest. The whole somber congregation was soon uplifted, and it was apparent that they joined me in a renewed zeal over church-going. Including my mother, who, after hearing me chatter on and on about this cool new priest, went to see for herself, and once again became a regular member, despite her deprived sacramental status.

Still in his twenties, Father J quickly won over the Catholic neighborhood flock with his youthfulness, exuberance, and lively homilies. We'd all wait with baited breath to see what he would talk about this week because he somehow managed to get away with discussing taboo subjects of the day, such as the horrors of Vietnam, the unjust acts of racism, and the flight of the homeless and depraved. All without offending even the greatest of Christian bigots. His parishioners appeared to give him special dispensation for this "long hair," which normally targeted a man as a no-good—evidence by the growing mass of kids getting kicked out of school for wearing hair that "feel below the collar." Father J's naturally wavy locks curled over his, yet no one complained about it. His hair merely grew along with his popularity. He was soon affectionately referred to as the "Hippie Priest," as one newspaper article christened him, and the church delighted in its overflowing Sunday collections and increased membership.

Best of all, we kids finally had an adult who talked to us as equals. During Father J's regular visits to the confraternity classes, he'd listen eagerly to what we had to say, and many of us stayed after to discuss what we'd just studied; the commandments, the war and the prejudices, and even the angst of being a teenager. Few adults understood that kids just want to be heard and treated with respect, but Father J did. He appeared genuinely interested in our opinions and comments. One day after class, he actually permitted me, a budding cosmetologist, to cut (well, trim), his beautiful twirled tresses when I voiced (on purpose) the need to practice cutting hair. With all this going for him, who could blame me for my sinful crush?

"How would you like to help me out?" he asked me one day in my junior year.

Is the Pope Catholic? was my first thought.

"Sure," was all I could get out once I found my voice.

"We're short on second grade teachers and I need someone to take over a class and get the kids ready for First Communion."

It was good as done. Despite the very real fact that I was in no way qualified for such a significant position.

My sins were fast accumulating. Not only was I in love with a priest, but was now teaching Bible studies under false pretenses, while continually failing to mention my overt and regular acts of swearing, pot smoking, and increasingly immoral thoughts (hormonally-induced notwithstanding) about boys, when it came confession time.

"Bless me Father, for I have sinned." *And you have no idea.*

Yep, I was most assuredly going straight to hell, sacraments or no.

I didn't care. Finally, I was enjoying myself. Which was something, because most times, I was miserable. I was now sixteen and having recurring thoughts of either running away or downing a few extra Tylenols, or whatever was available, and wait for the devil to take me. I hated my all-girls school, hated my looks—and pretty much everything else about me—and of course, hated my mother. By now, she and I were hard enemies. Our daily communication was narrowed down to this:

"Why don't you just leave me *alone*!"

"You better listen up, young lady, the world doesn't revolve around *you*, you know!"

"You just don't understand!" Emphasized by the slamming of the bedroom door. (By this time, my brother had moved out, so I finally had a room to myself).

"You are in for a rude awakening, young lady," she'd scream through the closed door, "and soon as you get that through your head, the better off you'll be!"

It was a constant battle of wills, and I willingly gave her a run for her money. That is, had she any left after paying my private school tuition.

One day after a particularly nasty confrontation, I met with Father J in his office. I had called ahead and told him I needed to speak to him.

"I can't take it anymore, Father," I began, the minute I sat down in the leather chair in front of his desk.

"What's the problem?"

There was a difference in his tone of voice, but I was too swept up in my own agony to notice.

"It's my mother. I just can't live with her any more and I'm afraid if I don't get away from her, I'm going to go absolutely crazy. I mean it. She makes me *so* angry, all she wants me to do is clean the house and be her slave. She won't let me do *anything.* I'm so depressed, Father, and my school work is suffering . . . and I . . . "

I went on and on about how horrible and depressing my life was, giving him clear and concrete examples, including dramatic accounts of scenarios that had taken place between my mother and me in the past few weeks. It was awhile before I noticed that he was either not paying attention, or could it be? Not care?

I was expecting him to show true compassion as I ranted on: sadly shaking his wavy, hippie-haired head, sighing in sympathy, or reacting in some kind of favorable way (in my favor, to be exact). Instead, he simply got up from his chair and walked to the window. He stood there, gazing out impassively, at God knows what, saying nothing. I started feeling uncomfortable. And let down. Finally, I shut up. I was baffled, yet curious and anxious to hear what he had to say about all this. Surely he would agree with my idea that I should run off to California where my nineteen-year-old brother now lived.

"So you think you have it really bad, huh?"

Did I hear right? "Excuse me, Father?"

"The world has so many problems," he said, staring out the window. "You don't realize just how lucky you are . . . have no understanding what it's like on my end."

His eyes stayed fixed on the sturdy maple near the church parking lot as he continued. "Everyone thinks priests are granted some kind of amnesty from any *real* problems. Our job is to help *them*. So they unburden themselves to me." He paused, lost in his own misery. "There's a lot of pressure to always know the right thing to say, and do . . . how to guide people in their pain. Everyone wants me to help them with their problems, and *everybody* has problems. Or think they do."

I faintly heard something about how small and absurd my troubles were, compared to others, but was too shocked to be really listening. My face flushed, I couldn't look at him anymore. Here I was sniveling over a little tiff with my mother, he implied, when he had a flock of parishioners who relied on him for everything, including saving their souls.

Suddenly I was looking at Jesus on His last days. Angry with his apostles, questioning his own worth, and realizing that his days were numbered.

Wait a minute. Wasn't this supposed to be all about *me*?

My head bowed, I stared at the floor as he continued talking to the tree. My confusion struck me mute. He may be disappointed in me, I thought, but my disappointment was greater. I had looked up to him. I counted on him to make things better. In the last two years, he had made me want to be a better person, do good things—like attend church—because I wanted his approval. I wanted my priest friend to be proud of me.

And I had come to him for help. Like all the others, as he'd strongly pointed out. My shock turned to anger at his lack of concern over my problems, and his using me—a mere sinful apostle—as a sounding board. But I also couldn't help feeling embarrassed. And more ashamed than when my own dreadful mother chastised me.

Somewhere in this whirl of emotions and my own bemused thoughts, he had quit talking. The silence was oppressive. I was having a hard time breathing. We were both locked in our own world, yet shared a soundless room stifled with confusion, anger, and pain.

Something, perhaps the chirping of birds, brought him back to the present and he turned around to face me. When our eyes met, I saw the washed-out gaze of a bewildered and miserable man. And I got scared. If he, my adored priest, was flailing at his mission and questioning his own meaning in life . . . well then, we were all surely doomed.

"I'm sorry, Father," I finally murmured, rising from my

seat and heading, thankfully, to the door.

And I *was* sorry, for both of us.

"Guess I'll try and work it out." I opened the heavy, wooden door, and without looking back, shut it quietly behind me.

Not long after that, Father J left the church. His sudden departure fueled a flurry of rumors. "Father J left the priesthood because they wanted him to cut his hair." "Father J was kicked out after getting caught smoking weed. "Father J had a severe drinking problem."

I never found out what actually happened. A few months later, after saving enough babysitting money, I did run off to L.A. and spent my seventeenth summer with my brother. The break from my mother proved worthwhile for both of us, and I returned just before my senior year with a new appreciation of her, and her of me. But I stopped going to church, and like my grandfather before me, became a "non-practicing Catholic." It would be nearly two decades, and the blessed state of motherhood, before I rejoined the ranks of Catholicism.

I didn't think about Father J much after that. Probably on purpose. I'd once thought this holy man was flawless. Turns out, he was merely human, like the rest of us. Yet he had abandoned me in my time of need. And I hate it when people I admire don't live up to my expectations. Which isn't fair, of course. Live long enough and everyone is bound to disappoint you, one way or another.

Still, after Father's presence in my life, I began to behave myself. I figured out a few things. I realized that being a rebel only makes matters worse, and gradually, painstakingly, discovered that doing it God's way makes life a whole lot easier. And saves quite a bit of confessional time.

When I returned to the church some twenty years later, there was another priest whose youthful enthusiasm, compassion, and good liturgies reminded me of Father J. It was then that I recognized how I'd missed a unique opportunity so long ago. I should have went back that day and thanked Father J for all he had done for that little town parish. I should have told him how he made us think differently about issues that may not have touched us directly, but were important, nonetheless. And how his touch of humor in his sermons lightened the heavy truths. I should have told him how his compassion—a trait, I suspect, an ironic source of his burdens—taught us to understand others, which, in turn, helps us understand ourselves.

I should have told him that he had moved mountains in small ways. How, in one case, he had taken a rebellious, troubled teenage church truant and brought her, willingly, back into its fold, if only for a brief time. How he had gifted her with more understanding about human nature, and priests, than she could've have ever obtained at St. Isley's. That he had showed her, through example, that is never hurts to pray. But it can hurt not to.

I could have added, too, that, like the rest of us, he was allowed moments of doubt and despair . . .

I should have told him all of that. But at the time, I didn't know.

I can only hope that, somewhere along his journey through life, like the rest of us, he figured it out for himself.

3. Destination Freedom

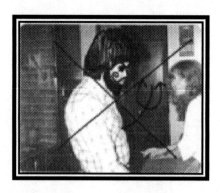

Boy Trouble

<u>Bad-Boy Syndrome</u>: An affliction in which a female is attracted to a male who's about as good for her—and irresistible—as a double-chocolate, double-cheesy cheesecake with cherry glaze, topped with French Vanilla whipped cream. This erroneous affliction can last anywhere from a few unnerving weeks, to an unfortunate lifetime. The only cure is when a woman learns to recognize the symptoms upon introduction, and runs—quickly—in the opposite direction. Which then allows her to be available for a kinder, gentler man who knows the true meaning of love, and respect, for women. And can make her smile.

*F*rankie made me laugh. Like the ones that came before him, his appeal to me was not so much his looks or apparent intellect, neither in which he excelled, but in his ability to bring laughter to my world.

I like that in a guy.

He was also—though he would never, ever, know this—the first boy I ever kissed. It was a whirlwind courtship brought about by the fact that I, at the time a school office "page," and he, serving time in detention, had some time to kill between classes.

Thus the beginning of the bad-boy syndrome I fell victim to for years.

"So whatcha doin'?" he asked nonchalantly, leaning against the wall, his light red hair luminous under florescent lights.

"Shhh, you're not supposed to be talkin' to me." I hissed.

He was standing in the corner of the hallway between the

principal's office and his secretary, Mrs. Myer's, desk. I sat at the small table across from him doing homework, like a good girl should, while waiting for Myers to hand me important notes to deliver to the teachers' classrooms. It was my first month on the job, having been chosen an office page the beginning of seventh grade because of my "exemplary" elementary school record. A record I would succeed in tarnishing within weeks, resulting in my first official firing.

"What do you call a girl with one leg?" Frankie whispered, all too loudly.

"Shhhhhh . . . ."

"I-*lene.* Get it?"

I tried to stifle the giggle. But failed.

He kind of reminded me of Howdy-Doody, the TV character with the freckled face and red hair that I hadn't seen since I was eight.

"I'm Frankie," the freckled face, red-haired boy said before spinning back around to face the wall as Myers approached.

"Deanna [oh, how I hated when they called me that], take this down to Mr. Klein's room please," Myers handed me a manila folder, and promptly returned to her desk down the hall.

"So your name's Dee . . . anna? I never heard that before."

I cringed. "I know, no one has. I go by my nickname, Dee Dee."

I would come to hate that moniker, too, years later, but at the time it was a far cry from the name my mother tagged me with. I was named me after Deanna Durbin, a 1940s singing star who, by the time I was born, had gotten fat, moved to France, and faded into oblivion before my generation ever heard of her. My mother wanted her daughter to be called something different besides the typical Debbie, Susan, or Kathy. I, on the other hand, would have loved typical.

Frankie was standing against the wall the next day, too. And the day after that. Our talks continued and I found myself intrigued with the eighth-grade class clown. That Friday, he walked me home from school. We stopped in front of my apartment building.

"Well, thanks for walking me home, Frankie, I gotta go now," I said nervously, turning to head toward the long driveway. I didn't quite know how one acts when it's time to bid goodbye to a suitor. He apparently did. As we stood on the busy main street with car after car whizzing by, he grabbed my shoulders, turned me to face him and pulled me against his tall, skinny body, planting a hard, lingering kiss on my lips. I was horrified. And thrilled.

Oh, my God, what if someone Mom knows saw us just now? was my first reaction. *Wow, that felt pretty good* was my second.

"Ok, see ya Monday!" he smiled, then darted across the street before I could respond.

What is it about bad boys that so fascinates the female gender? We all say we want a nice guy who treats us like a queen, is loving, giving, sensitive—all that fairy tale crap. Yet, when we actually meet a guy that fits that bill, they end up being "just a friend" because they're just not exciting enough for us. We instead go for the ones who don't call us when they say they will, who just "can't . . . seem . . . to find . . . the right job" (read: any job), or whose sole career goal consists of rising up the golden arches of succulent sex while 9 to 5-ing it by flipping burgers and dreaming of someday being the one who commands others to do the flippin'. The magic happens when we meet the guy who is the epitome of a parent's worst nightmare. Only to come to find out they are soon to be ours. It is then we aim to change them, to mother these poor misunderstood souls and help them overcome their bad-boy behavior caused undoubtedly by their disturbing childhood where they received no love.

My early crushes were too innocently juvenile to be really "bad," though I recognized their potential. Lesley Lawrence, the heartthrob of sixth grade, broke my heart after passing a note to Jackie, now my former friend, saying he liked her best. I got over him that summer when my fifth-grade crush, Donnie Allison, came back into my life the summer after seventh grade when, at our community carnival, he walked with me the entire time holding my hand. But after searching for him in vain that first week of school, I found out his family moved to Denver, or some such place, and I never saw him again. But by that time, I was playing spin-the-bottle at Carole's house (whose parents worked second shift) and discovered the art of kissing with Billy, who wasn't all that artful in his execution, but hey, it was a start.

Then came Blake, the true James Dean of Kennedy Junior High (even his name sounded Valentino-ish), who at fourteen, was already an experienced Casanova. After lending me his treasured 45 record of the Box Tops' hit, "Cry Like a Baby"—which I somehow took as a true love gesture— he was able to cross me off his ever-growing Make Out List after managing to kiss me several times, and cop a quick feel, before moving onto an older woman in the ninth grade.

I met Craig Duff, a gorgeous Brian Jones look-alike, at the Hullabaloo club that great summer of 1969 and fell crazy in love with him. But just as we were becoming more than friends, I was sent to the all-girls boarding school for my bad-girl behavior, and at fourteen, long distance relationships never seem to work out. That, and the fact that our subsequent nuptials would result in my going through life as Dee Dee Duff, a moniker that doesn't exactly scream "successful author," or any kind of grown woman you'd ever take seriously. So despite his great looks and pleasing personality, I was forced to face reality.

Reality came in a lightening-strike version of a sleek Italian rebel with a full head of dark wavy hair, bulging brown eyes, and an attitude that would make John Gotti swell with pride.

My mother hated Anthony straight up. Reason number one to call him mine.

He was bold, brash and drove a blazin' cherry-red 1967 hot rod Mustang convertible with a Road Runner sticker on the side window. He was *Perfect*. The romance began, once again, in the principal's office (where a girl is sure to meet the bad boy of her dreams). This time, we were both there for similar reasons. I had kick-started my delinquent period, he was perfecting his. In fact, Anthony had honed his so well that soon after giving me his class ring—which I proudly adorned with powder blue angora yarn—he was sent out of state, incarcerated at sixteen for stealing a car.

But I never forgot him, and measured all would-be beaus by him, with none quite living up to this ultimate bad boy. Three years later, when I was seventeen, I saw him again.

I'd just gotten back from California, where I'd spent my runaway summer, and had returned to finish high school to make my mother happy. In return, and probably to entice me to stay put, Mom bought me a car. A 1965 Ford Fairlane, complete with 8-track tape deck. To accentuate the "cool" factor, I wore sunglasses atop my head as I pulled into the gas station, window down with one arm sitting prettily across the car door.

"One dollar of regular please," I said in my coolest tone of feminine voice to the boy with the cute smile. *Why does he look so familiar*? I wondered. I watched him from my rearview mirror as he ran to the back of my car to give me gas (a sign of things to come), then swung around front to wipe my windshield with the squeegee thing. That's when it all came back to me.

I leaned my head out the window. "Is that you, Anthony?"

"Oh, hey, I thought that was you, too!"

Thus began a love affair I would soon live to regret.

By now, I had already learned a sad truth. The guys who were really nice and genuinely liked me, I promptly dumped. The bad ones, whom I really liked, usually dumped me (apparently I wasn't exciting enough). In addition, I was hooked on two soap operas in the early '70s: *The Best of Everything* and *All My Children*. Both of which featured exciting scenes with women who always loved the "wrong man" yet as a result, led exciting, intriguing lives. This left me with very poor judgment. [Not to mention, but I will—although it pains me to admit it—that I actually thought Anthony's nickname for me "*Dee Dee-Dumb Dumb*," was kind of cute. The self-respecting woman that this naïve, insecure, waif of a girl would grow up to become, would now have hog-tied him, sliced off his testicles, served them on a platter and make him eat his own balls for dinner before he'd ever insult a female like that again.]

Anthony passed all key prerequisites necessary for inclusion into my dull teenaged life. He was funny, charming (least I thought so at the time), with dark Italian looks. Unfortunately, he also had the celebrated Italian temperament that is often attributed to that nationality (though to be fair, there's also the Irish temper, the German temper, and so on and so forth). One year and many soap opera-ish episodes later, I no longer wished to have such an exciting life. Not that there hadn't been signs—even bright red flags!—early on. I simply chose to ignore them.

When wisdom finally forced its way into my still underdeveloped brain cells, I tried breaking up with him. But then, he'd begged for mercy while professing his undying love and devotion to me, and me alone. An unbelievably successful ploy. Lack of self-esteem causes teenage girls to believe that if a guy "loves" you, you better hold onto him as he may be the only one who will ever feel that way about you. And so, began my personal theatrical adventures of "*The Young and the Clueless.*"

Scene One - Going for a ride:

"Hey, why don't you get up on the hood and I'll take you for a spin in the parking lot," my prince charming says one spring day. We'd been sitting around my apartment while my mom was working, and had nothing else better to do.

"I don't know. What if I fall off?" my good sense screaming in my ear, before it took a leave of absence.

"No you won't, I'll go slow. It'll be fun," the boy in sheep's clothing tells Little Red Riding-on-the-Hood who, despite all evidence to the contrary, *trusts* him.

And so, I jump on the front of the Mustang. True to his word, he drives slowly and I begin to think, *Hey, this is fun.* Then his foot applies more pressure.

"Hey! Anthony, slow down! It's too fast."

He nears the end of the lot. My choice now is to jump off, or try to hang on as he gears up for the inevitable turn around.

I jump.

My hands hit first, then my face. Anthony stops the car, gets out.

"What the hell ya doin'?" Why'd ya jump off? How stupid can you be?" he says as I stumble to get up.

Nice guy that he is, he offers a hand. Blood is dripping from my nose, forehead, elbows and knees. As he helps clean me up, he reinforces the fact that I did a stupid thing jumping off, "You shoulda hung on. It's your own stupid fault."

And I believe him.

Scene Two – Prom Night:

"Everyone's going to Manners Big Boy afterward, let's go, too!" I say excitedly to Anthony as we're leaving my dreadfully boring all-girls-school senior dance.

"What? You know I don't have any money."

"How can you take me to my prom with no money?"

"I didn't know you wanted to go anywhere afterward. You know my job at the gas station doesn't pay a hell of a lot."

"I can't believe you!"

"Whad'dya want me to do, rob a bank?"

"Well, I'm sure you're perfectly capable of it!"

It wasn't the first time I'd alluded to his stint in prison

when I was angry at him. A few months later, I once again throw his past in his face. Which led to . . .

Scene Three – Highway to Hell

"You should go back to prison where you belong!" I said in fury one hot summer night when Anthony's no-basis jealousy and overall chauvinism sent me over the edge.

Oops.

I couldn't believe I'd said it out loud, and knew the minute it came out, that I'd pay for my big mouth. Plus, my timing couldn't have been worse. We were just getting onto the freeway ramp when those fateful words flew out of my mouth. He turned to look at me and I saw the crimson flares rise up in both dark eyes. He grabbed the four-on-the-floor gear shift and gave a new meaning to his favorite song, "Hot-Rod Lincoln." He floored the gas peddle and sent us flying down the highway like a scene out of *Cannonball Run*. The speedometer hit 120 in about six seconds, and I recall being exceedingly grateful there were so few cars on the road.

I was seeing my life pass before me, along with flashes of people's houses where they all sat contently, and safely, watching their favorite sitcoms as I feared for my life, deciding I had a lot of future plans that would necessitate my living way past a mere eighteen years. As the mile markers whooshed by, this scared shitless Catholic girl resurrected all the prayers she could muster and began pleading for a life extension.

*Our Father who art in heaven, I'm sorry for everything bad I ever did and if you just get me outta this, I PROMISE, I'll be the best Catholic girl you ever saw, save for the nuns, of course. After all, we both know I'm not real nun material. But I'll give it a shot from here on out. **REALLY. PROMISE.** Amen.*

It was the fastest set of prayers I'd ever prayed and I found it suddenly ironic that just a moment ago, I'd been worried that riding the freeway with the top down would muss my naturally frizzy and just-straightened hair. Oh, how our priorities shift in a crisis.

"Anthony! Slow down, *please*, come on, don't do this! *I'm sorry*, I didn't mean it, really. Anthony, PLEASE! I beg you. STOP! I'll never say that again. I PROMISE."

Unfortunately he couldn't hear my desperate pleads—what with the whipping wind and the radio blasting *"Mama told me not to come . . . that ain't the way to have fun . . . No."*

The night ended as one of those divine moments in life when you realize you are the lucky recipient of some amazing guardian angels who, in my case, would come through for me many more times down the road. Even when speed wasn't a factor.

As my boy wonder skidded sideways into the driveway of Home Sweet, THANK-YOU-SWEET-JESUS, Sweet Home, I waited anxiously until he came to a full and complete stop. Without a word, I wobbled out the car door, hoping he'd just go away. No such luck.

"Give me back my fuckin' ring," he screamed before I could make a clear getaway.

"Sure, no problem," I said, not faking my relief. With trembling hands, I wiggled and pulled and yanked until the antique ring let loose. The quarter-karat diamond silver engagement ring had once been Anthony's birth mother's. The woman who'd escaped his father, and in turn, abandoned him. She'd remarried years before, but he had since looked her up and renewed his relationship with her, which often included my going with him for visits. It was during one such trip that she gave her unruly first-born son her grandmother's engagement ring to give to me, whom she'd grown fond of. Perhaps seeing me as his redeemer. Fat chance.

Anthony grabbed the ring from my quivering hands, flung it across the parking lot, got back into the hotrod and peeled off, wheels screeching. The next day, he returned all calm and collected. I felt terrible about his mom's ring and convinced him to help me look for it. After more than an hour of surveying the concrete lot, we gave up. The ring was never recovered. So, too, could be said of our liaison. Had it been up to me, that is.

Anthony proved hard to get rid of. Any and all attempts at severing the relationship fell flat. So I decided if I couldn't break up with him, I'd get him to break up with me. The solution seemed easy. I was well aware of his disdain for girls who swore. So I became the most foul-mouthed teenage girl this side of Lake Erie.

"So what da'ya wanna do tonight?" he'd ask soon as I got in the car. And each time, I'd reply, "I don't give a rat's @&*#. Let's just *%## *goooo*, man. I only got two #%&* hours before I gotta be home. Make up your own *&*%$# mind!"

Anthony also hated girls who thought they were cool. So I became the coolest— lifting up my shorts-clad legs and hanging them out his just-washed Mustang window while snapping gum and puffing away on my smokes. Or when a hard summer rain forced us to roll up the windows, I'd prop my feet up on his freshly Windexed dashboard while cussing like a truck driver who had just realized he's gone fifty miles out of his way and ended up in Toledo. To my delight, Anthony would get so pissed off, he'd take me straight home.

"I don't know what's going on with you but you've changed and I don't like it," he'd say, squealing into my driveway. "Ever since you graduated from high school . . . "

Yeah, that was it.

I'd saunter into the apartment and my worried mom, who'd long since given up on my good senses, would ask, "How's things?"

"Things are going great!" I'd exclaim.

A day or two of independent bliss would pass before the Man-Who-Wouldn't-Go-Away would show up at my door saying he "forgave" me. And not to worry, he still loved me.

Clearly I had more work to do.

During one night of forgiveness, he asked me, again, to marry him. Thus, the catalyst that brought on my Academy Award-worthy performance.

"Wow, yes, that's a great *&%# idea! But I don't want some big fluffy, fancy hokey &%*#@ wedding . . .

I paused for affect.

"Hey! I got it! Let's get married at your gas station! How %&*# cool would that @#%& be!!"

"Are you #&*^# crazy?" I guess profanity can be contagious. He looked like his brains would burst out of his big Italian eyeballs, like in those cartoons. "What the hell ya talkin' about?"

"No, I'm *&^%# serious! It'll have to be small, of course [like we had friends] but your boss, Bob, can be the best man and I'll get my friend, Sue, as a bridesmaid. Hey, I bet we'll even get on TV!"

It took all the energy I had in my 110-pound body to stifle the volcanic Laughing Sal cackle combusting in my mouth.

"You're *&^%# crazy!" he said, again dropping me off at

my door of relief. "We ain't getting married at no gas station." He shook his head in utter disgust. "I'm not even sure I want to marry you anymore."

The words washed over me like a choir of angels showering me with warm, soft feathers of freedom from above.

"I did it! I did it!" I told my mother as I burst in the door. I finally came clean with her as to what I'd been doing all this time, and she laughed with what seemed like pride, or perhaps pure relief. "He'll *never* be back now!" I announced with confidence.

The next morning, I happily headed out to my car for work and saw a note stuck between my windshield wipers.

"Dear DeeDee:

I'm sorry I got so mad last night. I was just takin by surprise. But I thought about it and if ya really wanna get married at the gas station, that's what well do. I mean, if ya really want to. Love, Anthony

My mouth and heart joined in unison as they crashed to the ground.

After that, I simply told him to get out of my life. A request met with contempt and a series of ugly incidents. As many women with bad boys will tell you, these guys don't take no for an answer. After late night hang-up calls, stalking episodes (whereupon seeing me with another guy prompted him to throw a brick through my back car window) and another criminal act that involved his ripping out my car's distributor cap, thus disabling me from going anywhere I might meet someone sane. These series of events made me desperate enough to go to the police, who told me they couldn't do anything about it unless he *really* hurt me. I told them that if I was dead, I couldn't much put in a complaint then, now could I?

These *One Life to Live* episodes were fast-accumulating in my personal series of Life Lessons. The latest entitled: You Can't Fight Crazy.

And that's when I escaped to California, where I stayed until I figured my hot-tempered, jealous, ex-con first love was busy making another girl afflicted with Bad-Boy Syndrome perfectly miserable.

Perhaps part of the reason for my poor taste in men was that I didn't have much to go on. While I do believe that having no father around is better than having a bad one, it becomes inconvenient when daughters start looking for a male role model and hasn't any yardstick for comparison. Though I did have a grandfather, a good man who dearly loved his wife and treated her well, I always saw him in a grandfatherly way, not male role model way. After all, not many girls consciously look for a guy who reminds them of Grandpa. Though I'll admit there are those few . . .

Before my real knight-in-shining-armor finally arrived when I was twenty-six, I was more influenced by television male role models, such as Rodney Harrington from the 1960s TV night soap, *Peyton Place* (his fictional brother, Norman, was the "nice" one, therefore not nearly as appealing as bad-boy Rodney. Even Allison Mackenzie put sweet Norman in her "just a friend" category), the leather-jacketed "Fonzie" (who, though sweet, was a bit dangerous, thus far sexier than wimpy Richie Cunningham, who would forever be Opie to me), and Billy Jack, the hunky, rough-and-tumble, peace-loving karate expert who, in 1971, became a movie cult hero to hippies everywhere.

And despite the fact that movies and television continues to give impressionable young women horrible male role models to love by (always those way-too-good-to-be-true, six-packed hunks few real men can live up to), I am grateful that my daughters are blessed with a great one to look up to right in their own home.

But should they ever happen to veer off the level-headed road of decent males and find themselves breaking out with bad-boy syndrome, I will sit them down and relate my own crazy love stories. Complete with the life-threatening road-runner tale.

That—it is my motherly hope—should steer them, swiftly, back on the right track.

I Was a Teenage Hitchhiker

"*And* how are you lovely ladies doin' this fine afternoon?"

The bearded man with the weathered face and white turban atop his head was more jovial than Pam and I expected, which normally would've made us wary. But the opportunity was just too good to pass up. I'd never seen an authentic Rolls-Royce before. At least not up close. I knew it was the real deal, thanks to watching *Burke's Law*, the popular TV Show in the 1960s, starring Gene Barry—a.k.a. secret agent, Amos Burke.

But this Taj Mahal on wheels that pulled up to the berm of Pacific Coast Highway that sultry August afternoon in 1973, was more like the one John Lennon owned, which I'd once seen in *Teen Beat* magazine. Painted with bright psychedelic colors of swirling ocean waves, big puffy daisies, and multicolored peace signs, it even had a *Have a Nice Day* sticker—complete with sunshine-colored smiley face—on the hood, near the ornament of the gold naked lady.

Pam and I exchanged excited glances as we climbed in the back. How cool was this? Never in our wildest imagination had we'd dreamed we'd come near, let alone ride in, a car of such magnitude—both in size and hipness. "Wait'll our friends hear about this!" our eyes told each other. Our first vacation as working girls was off to a good start.

As Pam and I gazed in awe at our back seat surroundings, I caught a glimpse of our eccentric chauffeur in the rearview mirror. The old man resembled the Beatles guru, Maharishi Mahesh Yogi, a rumpled man well past his prime—sixty, if he was a day. With long, scruffy white mustache and beard, rimless granny sunglasses, that turban, and what looked to be pajamas, it was obvious this dude had long ago lost touch with reality. Then again, in Southern California, reality is subjective.

His younger companion in the passenger seat, a John Sebastian look-a-like, appeared more normal—Grateful Dead T-shirt, brown shoulder-length hair, faded jeans, and the standard granny glasses. A regular hippie who looked like he was just along for the ride. Maybe he'd gotten picked up, too, I don't know. It didn't come up.

"So where'ya all headed?" Mr. Maharishi asked, pulling back onto the busy highway.

"The beach, where else?" I said, figuring it was obvious by our bathing suit tops and frayed hip-hugger shorts.

While I sat busily gazing around the soft brown leather interior, Pam searched for an ashtray. Finding it near her armrest, she pulled out a Salem from her rumpled pack. She had a bad habit of sticking her smokes in her back pocket.

"Put that away!" the Grateful Dead guy barked, inducing a spark of fear. After all, these guys were way beyond anything in the realm of what our parents warned us about. I threw Pam an evil glance for lighting up without permission, but then, how could we've known not to smoke in here? It wasn't like we rode in a Rolls Royce every day.

"This is better for you," he then added, handing Pam the rolled joint. We passed it around and Mr. Maharishi cranked up the stereo. "Cisco Kid" by War was playing, and I half expected the car to magically turn into a low-rider, bouncing haphazardly to the lyrics, "*He drink whiskey . . . Poncho drink the wine . . .*"

We all joined in. "*Cisss-co Kid . . . waaas a frieeend of miiiiinnnne . . .*"

The song blasted through the open windows causing an appreciative nod at a traffic light from a tattooed biker, though the approval may have been in deference to the psychedelic car rather than the singing vocals. I was thinking how surprising it was that there was no air-conditioning in such a decked-out vehicle, but then decided it was more likely this guru didn't believe in using up the energy source. As the hot air blew across our cheeks, we told them where we were from, and the subject of music came up—always an animated topic amid stoned hippies. And certainly a welcome theme for Clevelanders, during a time we had little to brag about except for our well-tuned knowledge of contemporary music. We were always anxious to steer any possible conversation away from those tired jokes about "the mistake on the lake."

So of course, we brought up our city's real claim to fame.

"Oh, we'd see the James Gang all the time, at the Hullabaloo teen club," I pointed out nonchalantly. " 'Course that was before they hit it big."

"Wow, you saw Joe Walsh play at a teen club? That's far out. He's right up there with Hendrix, far as I'm concerned. Shit, that had ta h've been real cool, man," Maharishi was duly impressed. And when impressions counted—and riding in a Rolls Royce surely forced you to pull out the big guns—that one worked every time.

Ten minutes later, we were fast friends, and thanks to our hosts' generous peace offering, Pam and I were feeling no pain, laughing at everything said. We were sure this dude would be a real hit on the Carson show—save for the head towel.

Half a joint later, we were at our destination. The Rolls pulled up in front of a cottage-style house in Newport Beach as two young boys on bicycles stared in wonder. Apparently they'd never seen a Rolls up close, either—and way too young to have heard of Amos Burke.

"Now just head on down that alleyway there, and soon your cute little toes will be makin' love with the sand," Maharishi Man said, pointing straight ahead.

"Great, and thanks for the ride," Pam and I said in unison.

"It was all my pleasure ladies, all my pleasure. Have a good life."

With a wave of arms, the old man and his hippie sidekick sped off into the smoggy horizon, as our long straight hair blew across our faces in the Santa Ana winds.

Hitchhiking was no big deal in the '60s and '70s. It was what hippies did across the country, though some did end up on the late night news. But those morbid reports had little effect on most of us. The first time I stood on a street corner and stuck out my shaking thumb, I was sixteen and desperate for a ride. Most of my friends at the time lived some fifteen miles away. I had met Sue my first year at Andrews School for Girls, and after spending one weekend at her house, had met all her big-city hippie friends. They became the group I most wanted to hang out with. So whenever I couldn't get a ride, I hitched one. And though I admitted it to no one, I was scared to death most of the time.

And there were times I should have been.

I wasn't so naïve that I wasn't aware of the dangers of climbing into strangers' cars. And I wasn't one of those teenagers who thought nothing bad could ever happen to her. In fact, I was convinced that out of my entire high school, if only one girl were to get pregnant, overdose, or get into the wrong stranger's car, I was the one with the bulls-eye on my forehead. This belief—coupled with effective Catholic-raised guilt-ridden promises of eternal damnation—kept me from doing anything that would increase those odds. Except when I was desperate for a ride. So of course, there were times I had to make a break for it. Like when I spent my seventeenth summer with my brother in Orange County (the California area made famous by the TV show, *The O.C.*).

"The beach is quite a ways from here," Dennis had said upon my inquiry about a California tan. "But if you just go up the corner and turn on PCH, you can get a ride, no problem."

So I did. I stood alone on the busiest highway in Southern California in my psychedelic halter top and bell-bottom jeans (frayed on the ends), my Indian-style macramé purse holding all my beach goods on my left shoulder, and stuck out my right thumb, in front of a rush of zooming cars. I'd cringe when I'd lock eyes with the passing motorists—the old ladies giving me dirty looks, the old men winking (but thankfully moving on) as I'd wait for someone from my generation to pick me up. I was flush with embarrassment at stooping to this. Yet, I, a young, white Midwestern girl, forced myself to endure it all in my quest to become a glistening bronze West Coast girl the Beach Boys always sang about.

The cute boy who picked me up was probably no more than twenty, and had a nice warm smile. As he pulled back onto the street and asked where I was headed, I was already fantasizing how, as our eyes met, we would feel this alluring spark, like they do on the *Love Connection*, and he'd whisk me away to his hippie apartment in Haight-Ashbury and introduce me to all his cool hippie friends. He'd just happen to have an uncle who worked for *Rolling Stone* magazine, who upon our meeting, would be impressed with my poems he insisted upon reading, and—finding me amazingly talented—would hire me as its first woman reporter who got all the good gigs. Like interviewing The Mama and The

Papas (who I'd hang with one Saturday night because they found me so much fun), Long John Baldry (who I thought was terribly underrated, but as a result of my cover story on him would then be elevated to one of the top recording artists of the decade. Then Baldry would, of course, be so grateful that he'd thank me in the acknowledgments in his next album—which would shoot up on *Billboard* that first week to number two—with a bullet). And, of course, Mick Jagger, who, after my one-on-one exclusive would assure me a backstage pass next time the Stones played Cleveland.

In fact, Mick had just started asking me to sing "Honky Tonk Woman" with him on stage at that future concert when I noticed Cute Boy turning down a deserted street. In one swift move, he pulled over to the side of the dirt road, and stopped the car. Without a word, he leaned over to cop a feel, and my enjoyable rock 'n' roll fantasy switched to that of "Cleveland Girl Found in Abandoned Area in Costa Mesa, California—But Serves Her Right for Hitchhiking."

Luckily, my right hand was where it needed to be, allowing me to flip the door handle and tumble out of the car. As I rose to my feet, I saw his deep purple haze Chevy Nova peel away. I suppose he didn't pursue me because he figured I'd be more trouble than I was worth. Or maybe my boobs weren't big enough to make the ensuing struggle worthwhile.

As I ran up the hill toward the highway, my fantasies then switched to visions of my mother at home in Ohio sitting on the couch watching Channel 8. Just as she's going to make her way into the kitchen for a beer (this being her Wednesday night ritual) she hears popular news anchor Tim Gordon telling her to stay tuned to News at Eleven when he reports on the story of a former Catholic, not-too-bright Cleveland Girl—who incidentally, left a note to her mother that first day of summer vacation, then hopped on a plane to L.A. seeking more excitement, better drugs, and cuter guys—*Escapes Attack Just in Time*. Then he turns to his bleached blonde co-anchor and with a solemn yet sarcastic look, says, "Bet *her* hitchhiking days are over. Back to you, Nancy."

But ole' Tim Gordon would be wrong.

The next time I stuck my thumb out was due to circumstances beyond my control. I had gone down to the Akron Rubber Bowl with my brother and his wife for the 1972 Rolling Stones concert (which contrary to my former fantasy, I did not have a backstage pass to). We got back late, and I stayed overnight at their house. Everyone left early the next day for work, and I was left to fend for myself. I was anxious to get back home in time to see the next exciting episode of *All My Children*, so I walked to the nearest intersection and I, by now a seasoned professional, confidently stuck out my thumb.

It's amazing how you know when trouble is near. Mom always called it intuition, so I guess that's what was causing my heart to pulsate and prompt beads of sweat to form in my palm soon as I slammed the door shut.

"Where ya goin'?" he asked casually as I slid into his puke green Bonneville. He was a middle-aged man who looked like an insurance agent, with black-rimmed glasses, striped blue shirt and creased pants. Pretty regular guy. Harmless, if you'd asked me. So why did I feel this goose-bumping chill?

The vibe made me wary enough to lie and tell him I lived a half-mile closer than I did (I could walk the rest, I reasoned, and still make it in time to catch Erica Kane's latest deceitful adventure), but we weren't even that far when the conversation turned slimy.

"You're a pretty little thing," he said, looking over at me with a friendly but cock-eyed smirk. "Gotta boyfriend?"

Silence.

"Come on, I bet you have a boyfriend," His bulky hand glided toward my thigh as he continued to drive. "Or maybe I can be your boy . . . "

The traffic light flashed red just in time to make my move. I bolted out the passenger door and ran fast as I could, then snuck behind a big oak tree until he was clearly out of sight, and on his sleazy way.

Timing is everything.

And so are guardian angels who turn traffic lights. . . .

You'd think that would've cured me. And true, I didn't hitchhike for weeks after that. But soon as I got desperate again it was, as they say, like riding a bike.

But my level of anxiety had increased, and so I began saving up money for a car. I was twenty by then, and had just returned from L.A. for the second time, and got a job at a beauty shop. I arranged to ride with a coworker, Carol, until I could buy a decent set of wheels. One morning, Carol called.

"I'm not going to work today, can you get another ride?"

Of course I couldn't at this late notice. It was already 9 a.m. I had an appointment at 10. And so, once again desperate for a ride, I stood along a busy avenue in my professional hairdresser's white uniform and nurses' shoes, hair properly poofed and sprayed, and stuck out my thumb. A car pulled up rather quickly, but not quick enough. Seems I'd made an impression, I would soon learn.

I was thankful when I'd made it to the salon on time, and got right down to business. As I began shampooing my new client's hair, I notice her gazing at me curiously. She kept looking at me in an "I've seen you before" sort of way that was getting disconcerting. She waited till I sat her down and began discussing styling ideas when she interrupted my spiel.

"Hey, I knew you looked familiar!" she began, turning her chair around to face me for a better look. "Weren't you just hitchhiking this morning on Route 306?"

Busted.

As a new hiree at this particular job, I'd made a conscience effort to become a trusted stylist and accumulate a long list of clients in order to stop living on Frosted Flakes and Twinkies. I suddenly realized now, that in order to accomplish this, I had to begin acting like a civilized human being. It was time to take a hike when it came to hitching.

I told her of my dilemma, consciously over-dramatizing to win her sympathy. My story of a struggling teenager who was working hard to support herself—and eventually buy her own car—seemed to have done its job and after a heartfelt "Oh, I'm sorry, that's terrible," and even a "Well, I certainly admire you for not leaning on your family and being a burden to your divorced mother—good for you," she was kind enough to return the conversation back to her tresses and even give me a sizable tip.

The next day, I asked my mother to co-sign for me, and with my meager savings, I purchased a 1968 (only seven years old!) gold Camero with leopard interior. Of course, the sporty car was in no way close to a Rolls Royce—more of the low-rider variety. But it did sport a *Have a Nice Day* sticker on the passenger side window, which I took as a good sign.

And like the popular notion of going bra-less in the name of female liberation, this little hippie girl realized, finally, that whole hitching-a-ride thing was way overrated.

California Dreamin'

"Freedom's just another word for nothin' left to lose"

Janis Joplin

I want to die. To disappear off the face of this earth. Dead. Like my idol, Joplin.

I'm twenty years old and I'm lying on a battered old sofa in an otherwise sparse one-bedroom apartment in southern California. Alone. Scared. Pitiful. I'm afraid if I really do die here in my misery, I'll begin to rot before anyone starts to wonder about me. This being a Friday, my boss might start calling by day two of my no-show, but that means five days of decomposition on this dilapidated couch, or "davenport," as the adults in my family still call it.

Funny, about those odd terms they'd use, and the way they'd say things. The refrigerator was called an "icebox," a scarf was a "babushka," and a purse was a "pocket book." And words with o's were replaced with a's,, such as "get out the tomatas," or "grab that bag of potatas." My mother would always say she was going to *worsh* the clothes, which I found irritating as hell because it sounded like we were uneducated.

"Mom," I'd say in a high-and-mighty voice, "it's *wash*, not *worsh*" to which she'd get all huffy because a child should never correct a parent. Even if they were wrong. Now, it makes me sad at the thought of never hearing those incorrect words again.

116

I miss my family. This is surprising considering I'd spent years dreaming of leaving them. My entire adolescence was spent writing bad poetry full of anger, despair, and fantasies of flight—an independent woman making her own damn decisions. Yet, 3,000 miles away from home, I still can't make my own choices. Not the ones I want.

Last night, for example, if I'd had my way, I'd been chomping down on a nice, big, juicy steak. Instead, I had to settle for another damn bowl of cereal. Even the decision of how much milk I put on it was made for me because as I poured it into the bowl, the flow stopped short. I kept shaking out the carton with the pictures of lost children, willing more milk to magically spill out, but nothing came. *Well,* I thought, *least I don't have to worry about it getting all soggy.* I hate soggy cereal.

So tonight, I'm hungry again, but I just gave the landlord—a wrinkly old man with way too much nasal hair, who always looks at me the way I would a sizzling sirloin about now—my entire month's paycheck. Which means I'll be out of milk for awhile.

I've been lying here, all down and out, several miles from Beverly Hills, for what must be several hours by now. I can't stop thinking about how I ended up with such a nothing life. I had such plans, hopes, dreams. And here I am, living on my own in Southern California, just like I had planned. I have just now figured out the meaning of that old saying, *Be careful what you wish for.*

I had assumed by now, six months into my residence here, that I'd be living in a much nicer place, have an interesting job, and lots of cool hippie friends. (My brother and his friends that I knew have all moved back to Ohio by now, or wherever they originally came from.) Now, if someone were to give me a free ticket home right now, I'd be like the road runner.

Instead, I lie here thinking about those people I left six months ago. Those people, though not perfect (well, to me, Gee Gee comes close), who really love me, who actually care about me. And as I think deeper about it, I really didn't have such a bad childhood, as used to be my belief. True, I was "raised without a father," but that never really bothered me. My grandparents spoiled me, at least when Mom wasn't around. *Ok,* I think, *that's where it all went wrong.* Things went downhill when Mom got her own apartment, and took me and Dennis away from them. Oh, we saw them often, but it was never the same again. That's when I turned bad. And angry. And did stupid things.

As I lie here now, legs up over the back of the couch, feet pointing toward the ceiling, a light bulb appears over my head and I realize I was doing all those things to get someone to notice and stop me in my crooked tracks. But no one in authority tried to figure me out. I apparently wasn't worth their time or energy. They all considered me a loser, which made me act like one. I kept a mental list of all the chances they missed. The eighth-grade counselor who suspended me for getting beaten up when she should've shown some compassion for my "damned if I do, damned if I don't" predicament. That ninth-grade housemother, who hauled me downstairs one night and called me insubordinate. "Your attitude is the worst I've ever seen," she'd said. I remember gazing at her, thinking that—finally—I was the best at something. And the tenth-grade English teacher who gave me hope when she had us write in a journal. I could still see that "*A – Great Work!*" she'd written on the last page, and I remembered how good that felt. It was the only "A" I ever received in high school, and after that assignment ended, I received no more encouragement from her.

Then Grandpa died. Further fortifying my need to rebel. I was so pissed at the world.

Adolescence really sucks. You go through so much and no one seems to notice except when you misbehave. From seventh grade on, my life was a series of mishaps and anger. I wanted to be *happy*. I wanted to be free. To live an exciting life. To make my own way, my own decisions. Experience new things. Travel new roads. To meet a great guy who was cute and funny and who would think that I was beautiful.

Was all that too much to damn ask for?

Apparently so. And apparently, I haven't changed a bit. I'm still a dreamer. Still lost in my own fantasy world, as several people— most often my mother—have told me over the years. I thought California would be the answer to my dreams. I should be living in a hippie commune amid a group of other artists honing my creative craft and selling my brilliantly written prose to *Rolling Stone* magazine. And the *Los Angeles Times*. That'd be cool. This was my ultimate fantasy, to live the life of a . . . well, not really famous, but least a well-respected, sought-after writer. Yeah, that was it. In my world of thousands of dreams, this was my favorite. I suppose I could've gone to New York like many others, but big cities scare me, and besides I don't know a soul in the whole state.

"You better wake up to reality, young lady, or you're in for a rude awakening." My mother's words come back to haunt me. That was her absolute Number One saying. Number Two was: "The world doesn't revolve around you, you know. The sooner you realize that, the better off you'll be."

I guess I didn't realize it soon enough. Shifting positions, I move my head off the cushions so that it hangs upside down. When the blood rushes to my head, it doesn't make me feel any better, so I shift again, stretching out vertical on the couch. Damn. Turns out, my mother, who I pretty much thought was wrong 99% of the time, was right, after all. I really, really, hate to know she was telling me the truth.

So before I pop the fifty tabs of Sominex into my mouth, let's review. The only friend I have around here, Pam, moved out months ago with her boyfriend, and, hurt feelings still fresh, we don't talk much. I don't go out anywhere because I have no money, no car, and my job as an abused telephone solicitor barely affords me the monthly rent of $150, the utility bills, and the daily quarter for bus fare (though sometimes, it's not a quarter but a scraping of nickels and dimes, and sometimes even pennies). The first two weeks of every month are the worst, where I have barely enough funds left for food, mostly cereal, which is about the only thing I eat for days at a time. I've lost fifteen pounds the past three months, though I only needed to lose five. I'm living on *Heartland* cereal and faded dreams.

I'm a country/western song.

I can't go home because my family thinks—thanks to the lies I've become so astute at—that I am doing fine. Just fine. And I can't tell them. I still have my pride. And all this longed-for freedom. Yeah, great. I've learned the hard way that freedom isn't so free.

If my boss doesn't come look for me five days from now, I am going to be one ugly sight by the time Mr. Williams comes to collect the rent again.

If I'm going to do this, I have to get up. But I have no energy. Still, I have to force myself up because I'm in the living room and the pills are in the bathroom . . .

Suddenly Jagger jumps up on me, the beautiful furry silver-striped cat I picked up one day because it didn't have a collar and looked lonely. I knew how it felt. It was a cold November night when I found this little cat who wouldn't stop brushing up against me. Of course, I had to take her home. I named her after Mick, even though he's a she.

She now makes a full circle on my stomach, the tip of her long tail brushing my mouth, before she settles down in a ball on my chest. Her weight is like a heavy comforter. Her contented purring whispers softly, yet echoes loudly because it's the only noise in the room. At this, the lowest point in my life, I silently thank God for her presence. She gives me such comfort, companionship, and makes me laugh when she chases her tail round and round, as if she's doing it just to entertain me. Tears start running down my face, dripping onto her soft fur.

My West Coast adventure hadn't turned out at all as I'd anticipated. Not even the "never rains in California" part. Because it does. Especially in winter months. The year I spent there, it rained on Christmas day, all day. It was the most depressing Christmas I'd ever had. . . .

As I lied there in that dark room that April night in 1974, I reflected back on how it had all started out so promising. Nearly two years before, Pam and I had met at Higbee's Department Store in downtown Cleveland, where we had both gotten our first jobs at Higbee's Terminal Tower Beauty Salon. We hit it off immediately and went out a lot, going to clubs like the Mad Hatter (Wednesday night was "Stones Night" where the deejay played an hour's worth of Rolling Stones after midnight), the Agora Ballroom, and wherever there was music and cute guys.

"Hey, let's go on vacation together," I mentioned to her one night after a few Sloe Gin Fizzs. She'd known about my little excursion to Orange County two years earlier, so I suggested we go there for our first vacation as working girls.

"Oh, that'll be a blast!"

We set our sights for south of L.A.

The state of California held much appeal to us young Ohioans in the '60s and '70s. It wasn't just the lure of sand, surf, and sunshine, though that certainly helped when snow began covering our lawns in October and didn't melt till April. But the West Coast was where many of our favorite musicians lived:

Jefferson Airplane, the Grateful Dead, Jim Morrison, Janis Joplin, and Jimi Hendrix all hung out on Haight-Ashbury Street in San Francisco, and the Whisky A-Go-Go in L.A. and Bill Graham's Fillmore West. You couldn't get away from it. Everything that was considered cool was happening in "sunny California." It was Paradise, USA.

Thanks to my brother, who bolted back home after the 1971 earthquake, I knew the area. During our week vacation there in July 1973, Pam and I visited Groman's Chinese Theater, the Tonight Show (figures we'd get Joey Bishop, not Johnny Carson), Knotts Berry Farm, and Disneyland. In the interim, we made new friends, and spent the long plane ride home figuring out how we could live there.

October, 1973: It's a beautiful morning to leave on our first cross-country road trip. Pam picks me up right on time, 7 a.m.. We arrange all our stuff in her blue mid-sized Maverick. We set the AAA "Trip Tixs" on the visor. We put the jar of Goober's Peanut Butter & Jelly, and loaf of cheap white bread in the back, and head on down the highway.

"So whad'dya wanna hear first?" I ask, rifling through the box of 8-track tapes.

"How 'bout Grateful Dead," she says, lighting up a Salem. When "Truckin'" comes on, I crank it up and we sing to it as loud as our voices can carry. It becomes our theme song for the next four days as we venture down the road to Paradise, our hair blowing out the car window.

We have it all figured out. I sold Henry, my '67 Ford Fairlane, for getting-settled money, because Pam's car is in better shape. The Orange County bus transit system would suffice until I could afford another car. We planned to stay at our newly acquired friends' house (everyone, it seemed, lived communally, finances being what they were for independent-seeking kids barely out of high school), until we got jobs. We were going to be California girls, and feel those good vibrations.

The $500 from selling my car had seemed like an awful lot of money just weeks before. We envisioned making the L.A. scene every night and not looking for a job for at least a couple of months. By the end of our first week there, we were panicked. We couldn't afford a Jack-in-the-Box burger, let alone a night on the town. The 3,000 mile trip, even split between the two of us, had somehow burned a hole in our faded bell-bottomed blue jeans. Gas (even at thirty-eight cents a gallon), motel expenses (though a bargain ten bucks at Travel Lodge), the little amount of food (aside from the PB&J) we had sprung for dinner. Plus, we hadn't anticipated an unexpected $100 radiator problem we had to get fixed at a decrepit gas station in the middle of the New Mexico desert. All that put a sizable dent in our currency. The road trip, however, *had* been fun, with lots of laughs and one favorite photo of me "standing on the corner in Winslow, Arizona" in honor of the Eagles song, "Take It Easy."

So by the time we put down a deposit and paid the first month's rent on a small one-bedroom apartment, we were both ready to take whatever job we could get. Upon learning it would cost fifty bucks for a California cosmetology license, we desperately searched for alternatives.

"I don't know how to do anything else!" I tell Pam, flinging the want ads across the room. "I'm NOT going to work at McDonald's or Denny's. I want something that'll be rewarding and fun."

A week later, I apply at McDonald's and Denny's, where both managers say, "Don't call us, we'll call you," though probably not in those exact words.

And so I became a telephone solicitor. Pam fared better, getting a job in the wig department at a nearby May Company. Her good luck continued as, three months later, she found her true love and moved in with him. I quickly found myself alone. Except at work, where I had people in my ear all day, swearing and hanging up on me as I tried selling "Travel Packs to Tahoe." Still scavenging for bus fare after paying rent and utility bills, I occasionally treated myself to a 25-cent Hostess cherry pie, though I sometimes opted for apple.

I did, however, learn some things. I discovered that all the fattening junk foods are cheap compared to healthy vegetables and fruits. And no matter how much fat you consumed, if you only ate that, you could still lose weight. I also discovered something else. Guys in California expected things. I was still in search of that great guy who would help me "find myself." I hadn't meant in the back seat of a car. My first date was a bespectacled guy who thought if he took me out to dinner using his "buy one, get one free" coupon from his Diner's Discount Card, that he also got free dessert, in me.

"I'm looking for something to fulfill me. I want to find the meaning to my life," I was telling him in my best Dalai Lama voice when he asked why I moved to L.A. "Oh, I don't know how to explain it. I just want something more."

More didn't come after dinner, though he apparently thought more was due him, and I spent the rest of the night pawing my way out of his exuberant clutches. When he'd finally heard the o part of no, he dropped me off in the parking lot of my dreary apartment and I was left wondering if this Midwest girl didn't in fact belong in the Midwest. As a matter of fact, that was precisely what one date told me upon learning he wasn't getting any. "You should go back to farm country," he said in exasperation, hand finally pulling away from my crotch. I found the farm reference humorous because it said more about him than me. Apparently he thought the entire state of Ohio—including the large metropolitan vicinity of Cleveland—was rural. And so I also learned in that moment that a good manly six-pack doesn't always equate to good manly smarts.

All of my three or four dates were like that. Except for Jerry, who blessed me with continued comic relief. This disheveled hippie guy would show up out of nowhere and take me out for drinks in his beater. He actually called it "The Beater." While I can't recall what kind it was, I do recall that Jerry kept a butter knife in the ignition, as it was the only way the car would start (the key apparently long gone). We'd go out, share a few laughs over cheap beers, then come closing time, he'd take me home and pass out on my couch. A few times he even made it to my bed, where each opportunity for physical intimacy was subsequently squelched soon as he'd rub his long, sharp toe nails along my legs. Which gave him about a Rodney Dangerfield's chance at getting lucky. Which was fine with me. My attraction to Jerry began and ended with his ability to make me laugh, and the fact that he never pushed for anything else. Compared to my other California dating disasters, he was—elongated toe nails notwithstanding—close to perfect. But after a few months, he simply stopped showing up. I like to think that he went on to entertain and amuse some other lonely Midwestern girl.

As time wore on, I began to realize that maybe Dorothy was right. There *is* no place like home. With every weekly letter she wrote, my dear grandmother would offer to send me money so I could once again see my own backyard. And though it was exceedingly tempting, I, barely twenty, was old enough to understand that since I'd put myself in this situation, I should be the one to get myself out of it.

And that's how I ended up here, lying on a ratty old davenport Pam and I had bought at a flea market. With no one to save me, or miss me, as I mentally prepare to put myself out of my pathetic existence. That's when Jagger—this little cat who wants nothing more than to be loved—rises from my chest, nudges me with her head, and starts rubbing against my neck. Her incessant, lyrical purring begins again, and I realize how this soft, furry pet loves me with no conditions attached, and depends on me for her very life. I am suddenly not basking in self-pity anymore. I'm thinking about her. What will become of this helpless animal without me? Who will feed her when she's starving after five days with no food? Who will love her like I do? *She'll be fine*, I tell myself. Someone will take her in. With her supple paws wrapped around my neck, I hold her as I get up and carry her to her empty bowl and pour the whole box of Cat Chow into it, then refresh her water. *Least that'll hold her a few days*. She jumps down and starts eating. I stand there against the kitchen sink watching her munch away happily, obliviously. My heart hurts.

I take a deep breath and come to a conclusion. While it may work for some, California doesn't suit me. I am a Midwestern girl born and bred in the soul of the Heartland (even live on *Heartland* cereal for heaven's sakes). I need a change of seasons. I need to go home. . . .

And so I began making plans. I hoarded nickels and dimes until I had enough money for a one-way Greyhound bus ticket home - by way of Lake Havasu, Arizona and a six-hour bus stop in Albuquerque, but that's whole other story. In the interim, Jagger was apparently getting more sex than I had, and ended up pregnant. This gave me purpose. Having grown up with many litters, I knew how to take care of a mother cat. I quickly made her up a bed of ragged blankets and bed sheets in my closet, and there, she gave birth to six kittens, which I named after the seven dwarfs (minus Doc). Before I went back home, I met someone whose family had a farm (and they weren't even from Ohio!) and willingly took Jagger and her kin to their own Paradise, USA.

When I returned to Cleveland nine months later, people

would ask me, "Why would you leave the beautiful West Coast and come back to *Cleveland?*"

I'd tell them that it really does rain in Southern California, and there's nothing like the four seasons, and that even when the weather outside is frightful, the people here are so delightful.

I tell them that Cleveland is a best-kept secret, and there really is no place like home. (And that, in *Cleveland,* there is a city *and* a country.) And that you don't have to put out if you don't want to, because in Cleveland, there is no such thing as a Diner's Discount Card.

And I tell them that life is good.

And it sure beats the alternative.

Looking for Mr. Good Car

*T*hey say you never forget your first. Mine was a 1965 Ford Fairlane 500. Pea green. Like its new owner. I was seventeen, just returned from my self-imposed California vacation (the first one) and Mom had uncharacteristically decided to give her prodigal daughter a car upon her return. Mom paid $300 for the six-year-old car—a lot of money back then for a working single parent with no child support. I can still picture myself that blessed day I was let loose on the road.

"Mom!" I announced the minute I'd return from taking my driver's test. "I passed!"

"That's great, now get in here and mash the potatoes," she said, wiping her forehead with the back of her hand. It was a sweltering late August day but Mom insisted on making a dinner that required oven use, and after a hard day at the bank, was literally sweating over the hot stove. And bitchin'. A Lot. I was really mad, and disappointed, that she hadn't shared my enthusiasm.

All the more reason to make use of my new-found licensed freedom. I wanted to get the hell out of there.

"Why can't we just have BLT's?" which was my favorite and certainly more sensible than fried pork chops and mashed potatoes (this being pre-microwave days) in 90-degree weather. "Besides, I'm not even hungry. I'm going for a drive." This last statement in the disguised tone of one who'd been driving for decades.

"No, you are *not!* You're going to sit down and eat."

If *"whatever"* had been a term back then, I would've

responded likewise. Complete with the dramatic rolling of the eyes. Instead, I mumbled under my breath that I may eat, but I'm still going out driving. But in an attempt to soothe her looming wrath (and because she made me), I did the dishes. *Then* I grabbed the keys and fled.

No one forgets their first car, or the day they get their drivers' license because it's an affair to remember. Mine began that hot summer day in 1971. With my babysitting money (at fifty-cents an hour) I managed to put gas in the tank on a weekly basis. Though I could only afford a dollar at a time. Then again, thirty-five cents a gallon goes a long way.

Part of this love affair with our wheels-of-freedom involves music. A car is nothing without music. I cruised the neighborhood streets that day—my arm hanging ever-so-coolly out my window—to Don McLean's "American Pie" (*Drove my Chevy to the levee, but the levee was dry . . .)* as it blared out my car radio. Stereo? Not in 1971. Though it did have an FM converter—which was considered quite cool back then. But alas, the speakers didn't survive the first month. That, turns out, would be the least of my worries.

With a mother who never sat behind a steering wheel in her life, and no male guidance, I was clueless about car maintenance. For three blissful months, I obliviously drove my Fairlane around, never giving anti-freeze a thought. Actually, I didn't even know what it was. I learned about it the hard way, as with most things. One brisk October morn, my beloved car wouldn't start. A neighbor on his way to work stopped to take a look. His face grew dim.

"I'm afraid you cracked the block," he said, lighting a cigarette. "When's the last time you put anti-freeze in this thing?"

"What's a block? Anti-what?"

He shook his head and began explaining the necessity of this green fluid, what it means to crack the block, and that the bottom line was that it would cost more to fix than the car was worth. My mother, overhearing the conversation from the passenger seat, was none too happy. She'd not only just lost $300 in two months, but now had to go back to relying on coworkers again to get her back and forth to work (one of the reasons she had purchased the car, it wasn't solely to make her daughter happy).

"Now what're we gonna do?" she sighed. "You're gonna

just have to save up for another car, I can't buy any more."

Even I couldn't blame her on that. However, this new goal took awhile.

I'd been working on weeknights and Saturdays at a nearby beauty salon, sweeping and shampooing heads, but it wasn't enough for an automobile purchase. Plus, by then, I'd acquired a boyfriend who was happy to take me anywhere in his fiery Mustang, thus putting off any real need for me to get a car. When he turned out to be not exactly the man of my dreams, I gave up on men, and focused my attention to looking for Mr. Good Car instead. When I got a full time job out of high school at Higbee's downtown, I had to take public transportation, further increasing my desire for wheels of my own. Plus, when you're eighteen and still living with your mother, you just want to get the hell out of the house whenever, however, possible.

I eventually managed to afford (at the minimum wage of a dollar and ninety-five cents an hour) a boxy-looking Ford Falcon, the color of mud. It was a true beater, with no pad on the foot peddle and didn't exceed forty miles per hour, but a real bargain at fifty bucks. It got me where I was going and I didn't have to worry about speeding tickets. Not yet, anyway.

Within weeks, that car petered out and I quickly found a decidedly better-looking model. It was another Ford Fairlane, though I'd upgraded to a '67. I was so proud of it, I gave "him" a name. I found "Henry" much more reliable than my previous cars—or boyfriends, for that matter.

Mind you, back then, no nineteen year old I knew had a new car. That was something you worked up to. It's the natural progression of things, or should be. Nowadays, I'm amazed when I see kids driving through their high school parking lots with cars that match their graduation year. That's not the American way. It's against everything this country was built on—hard work and sacrifice. There should be a law forbidding new car ownership to anyone whose brains are still undeveloped and whose hormones are running in overdrive. . . .

But I digress.

Henry was maroon in color, ran like a top, and came complete with the requisite 8-track tape player. What more could a '70s girl ask for?

"Hey, I can make you a brass name plate for Henry," said Fred, a peculiar sort of fellow who made "art" out of items he retrieved from people's garbage. I'd met him in Oral Communications class at the community college where I was pursuing my love of journalism, and found him a lot more interesting than most guys of late, though not in the romantic sense. He was just odd enough to fascinate me and I enjoyed his eccentricness. Plus, Fred had been duly impressed with a poem I'd read in class about my new set of wheels:

"Henry is my real true love
Henry, I gotta take care of.
Henry runs on glue and tar
Henry is my Superstar. (This reference was inspired by the hit play at the time, *Jesus Christ Superstar)*

Henry likes the freeway best
But then he has to stop and rest.
Henry keeps me happy and sane
Henry is my Ford Fairlane."

Okay, I was no Walt Whitman, but who says only men have love affairs with their cars? It was this affectionate tribute to my automobile that prompted Fred to offer to make the name plate—complete with sticky tape on the back—which we promptly attached to my dashboard. It made me real proud.

Still, it did little by way of improving my driving skills. Seems finding a good car was only half the battle.

Looking back, it's a miracle I survived my younger years. The first time I got behind the wheel of a car—other than the Dodgem rides at Euclid Beach—I rammed it straight into a tree. I was sixteen, had no driver's license—not even a temp—therefore had no business whatsoever manning an automobile. But little things like that never stopped me from doing stupid things. And my buddy, Jay, who was one of my best friends and all too kind and trusting, had actually said OK when I asked him if I could get behind the wheel of his car that summer day at Strawberry Lane Park ("I'll just drive around a circle, I promise!"). I suppose we could blame it on what we'd been smoking for his taking leave of his normally good senses. I got in and hit the gas and upon that first slight curve, failed to turn the wheel fast enough, and smacked hard into the huge tree. I realized, right then and there, that I wasn't quite ready to drive. A year later, I had long-forgotten that lesson.

Driving meant freedom and I was more than ready for that.

I still swear I had nothing to do with my Driver's Ed teacher, Mr. H, searching out new career options after several nerve-racking excursions with me. All I know is he seemed mighty fond of his brake pedal over there on the passenger's side. You see, I had this problem with reverse. Soon after Mr. H defected and passed me on my driving skills (or lack thereof), I promptly backed into someone's mailbox.

It was the first week of my senior year. Mom and I had an agreement that I could drive to school (even pick up my friend, Vera), but I also had to take her to work and pick her up. There was just enough time between dropping Mom off at work, and getting to school on time to squeeze in our morning cigarettes. *If* we made a slight detour. Which meant having to turn around in someone's driveway. One day, I miscalculated and backed into their mailbox. Vera and I looked at each other after watching it crashed to the ground.

"OH, SHIT!" we screamed in unison. I threw it into Drive and sped out of there. My Catholic upbringing properly produced the right amount of guilt for leaving this scene of my little accident, but not guilty enough to own up to it. I simply found a new route to take to school.

But as any good Catholic knows, guilt can eat away at you. So the next time I backed into something else (it only took another year to repeat this offense. This time, in the parking lot of the college I was attending), I did in fact leave a note. Though to be perfectly honest, it wasn't my idea. Mentally adding up the money for a new front fender on that shiny Oldsmobile, I quickly surmised that I could actually live with the guilt. But then, I had a passenger with me. A good, *practicing* Catholic girl.

"You *are* going to leave a note, aren't you?" Sister Do-The-Right-Thing said, with matching glaring, nun-like eyes.

"Well, normally I w*ould*, but I could never afford to fix that," I confessed, hastily putting the car into Drive to move away from the awful crunching sound. "I don't have car insurance and I need books for my classes next term."

I could see her look of condemnation in the corner of my eye. That, coupled with the fact that I'd already reached my sins-for-the-month quota, forced me into submissiveness.

My friend was already digging in her purse for pen and paper.

To Whom It May Concern: I'm really, really sorry I accidentally hit your car. But although I'm a very poor, struggling student trying hard to make something of myself, I am willing to pay the consequences and make amends no matter how long it takes me. And it may take me a very long time because right now I can't even afford car insurance.

Thank you for your kind understanding and cooperation.

Sincerely, Dee Fedorko, sorrowful student and fairly new driver.

The owner was neither kind, understanding, nor cooperative. Turns out, he was the chief campus policemen of the college, and perhaps the title had stripped away his sense of humor.

Now hundreds of dollars in debt, I blindly moved on to my next driving adventure. Taking out my first loan, with Mom as co-signer, I purchased a sporty-looking 1968 gold Camaro, with furry, leopard interior. I was in love. It's true that the right car can make anyone look cool. I'd tool around town feeling all sophisticated, and as stylish as Farrah Fawcett.

I didn't feel too hip, however, the day I found myself and my "coupé du jour" hung up by one of those large, ugly orange barrels so prominent along Ohio's summer landscape. These pumpkin monstrosities also decorated downtown store parking lots. I've never been known to be terribly observant, so it's not surprising I didn't notice the overturned barrel lying behind my car as I went to leave the Terminal Tower one day. Oblivious as always, I headed straight for my leopard-on-wheels, got in and promptly put it in reverse. I hit the gas pedal and—whoa!

At first I thought I had a flat, since I could feel the lopsidedness of my automobile. I got out and couldn't quite comprehend what I was seeing. There was my beloved golden cruising machine looking like a cat in heat—front body crouched down, rear-end raised up. I had backed straight over the fallen barrel and rode right up on top of it, until it stopped in mid-roll.

Fortunately, a man, looking every bit as bewildered as I was, appeared out of nowhere with a jack, and kindly freed my car from the intrusive object that got in my way.

A few months later, another awkward event surpassed even that episode. By a long shot. It was a typical wintry Cleveland day. I was on my way home from work when I noticed my car was teetering on empty. I panicked and pulled into the first gas station I came to, and suddenly found myself riding on a sheet of ice, heading straight toward the gas pump at 20 miles an hour. With no time to slow down (and no way I was going to hit the brakes on ice), my car slammed directly into the ominous monster, which keeled over like one of Hulk Hogan's opponents. Lucky for me, the gas pumps had been turned off when the station closed earlier that day, due to . . . ice.

While a long line of cars waiting for the traffic light to change, I tried not thinking of my shocked, and highly amused, audience as I strained to quickly shift back and forth from Reverse to Drive, Drive to Reverse, until I finally cleared my way enough to slip-and-slide the thing out of there like a physically challenged ice skater, all the while checking in my rear view mirror for flashing lights. I made it to the street, and bolted down the road.

Word-of-mouth on an event such as this travels fast. Someone alerted the owner and police to the scene of yet another of my crimes as I hid out at my brother's house. I was pretty sure, however, that my identity would remain a mystery, since most witnesses were too busy laughing to jot down my license number. When I felt it was safe to go home, I walked into the apartment and was greeted by my excitable roommate who started telling me about some crazy driver who had knocked down a gas pump down the road.

"I past it just as the cop and owner stood there shaking their heads in amazement at this huge tank on the ground," she said. "You should see it!"

"I did," I said, feeling a shameful twinge of pride.

"Oh yeah?"

"Yeah. In fact, I had a front row seat," I assured her.

I was a fugitive at twenty-three.

It was at this point I began to wonder that maybe it wasn't my cars that weren't any good, but perhaps the driver had serious issues. I was never caught, however, and I'm fairly certain the statute of limitations have long expired by now.

And boy, had I been insured, I bet I would've seen an alarming increase in rates . . .

Unusual circumstances and speeding tickets aside (and there were plenty of those) my cars continued to "wreck" havoc on my finances, as well as my sense of security. I was still looking for that Good Car well into my twenties. Though, my early cheap affairs gave this writer a few good stories.

There was one car's ill-timing when its transmission decided to go kaput just as I headed up the highest, steepest hill in Kirtland, Ohio. I'll never forget the angry stares I endured from the drivers forced to go around me. Even at twenty-six, I was surprised how rude people can be, particularly when they're in a hurry. After ten minutes with no one coming to my rescue, I got out and walked the thankful few blocks to call for a tow.

During this same time period (my struggling college student days that lasted several years), another one of my short-lived cars caught on fire. While I was still in it. I'd been driving happily down the freeway, listening to Journey's *Wheel in the Sky keeps on turning . . . don't know where I'll be Tomoorrrooww*" when I suddenly felt my feet getting awfully hot. The song was on its last note when flames emerged from the floor. (I learned later, this was due to intense heat from the exhaust pipe, which was mounted too close to the floorboard, which caused the carpeting to ignite.)

I *knew* I smelled something . . .

I immediately pulled over, and a passing motorist kindly stopped and helped me put out the flames. After this latest fiasco, I considered leaving the car there and just propping up a For Sale sign on it. But then, I figured that probably wasn't the key to successful advertisement.

There was the car with the hole in the gas tank, which also happened to have a broken gas gage, making an accurate guess on the amount of fuel I could put in before it would leak out, nearly impossible. Each day for six months, I put in two dollars at a time. And prayed a lot. And still ran out of gas on occasion.

And good as Henry was, even he wasn't perfect. Those who recall old Fairlanes know that its front seats are like a bench, making it nice for dates to cuddle up close to the driver. However, the bolts holding down Henry's seat became so rusted, they gave way, as did the seat. So that if you leaned back, the seat automatically put you in a reclining position. While I wasn't crazy about this new feature, my dates found it a real plus at drive-ins.

Oh, the memories . . .

Maturity, a better job, and parenthood eventually turned me into a law-abiding, respectable citizen, with enough money to buy a relatively decent car, and my famed tales of my automobile adventures came to a gratifying halt.

Well, for awhile, anyway.

I have one more story.

I was older now. In my forties. But I have a habit of being in a hurry. This day was no exception. I left work in a rush, threw my car into reverse, not even noticing the big, beautiful boxwood bush decorating the side of my place of employment. (Which shall go unnamed, still not sure about current statute of limitations). I was unaware that my car had kidnapped an entire branch of this bush as I put it into Drive and headed down the road. It wasn't until I'd made it home, that I noticed something green sticking out the back of my white Lincoln. I got out and walked over to the rear and that's when I saw the large entangled twig hanging onto the bumper like the jaded claws of Christmas past. I gazed around for witnesses who may have tailed me home, and, finding the coast clear, promptly (but not easily, that sucker was really in there) ripped it free and dumped it into the garbage bin, thankful that it was the day before pickup.

I could've gotten away with it, too, had it not been for our friend, Bob O, who my husband and I saw at a party later that night.

"So, Dee, saw you drivin' down Munson Road today," he says casually, but his evil smile is a dead giveaway.

Oh. Oh.

I try the nonchalant approach.

"Oh, I must've been coming home from work." I respond. Casually. My evil eye matching his smile.

"Yeah, well, ya know, at first I thought it was December, you know *Christmas tree* season. But then I thought, well, *nooo,* it's only September . . . "

Ah, shit.

My husband of now many years looks over at me quizzically, then turns to the big snitch for clarity. The cat is out of the bag, and the rat runs with it.

"Sorry Dee, I just gotta tell this story," he says, chuckling, somewhat apologetically. "I was just two cars behind you." Then he turns to Jeff, still chuckling. "Ya know, I didn't know it was her at first . . . I just saw this humungous tree branch (*come on, it wasn't **that** big*, I want to say. But Bob doesn't give me a chance) on the back of this car's bumper. It was just bouncing along the road . . . bounce, bounce, bounce, all the way home." He was enjoying this way too much.

He then turns back to me, his hand wiping tattle-tail tears of laughter from his eyes. "It really was hysterical. Watching that branch clinging desperately to life with each bump. And there was Dee, just driving along, totally oblivious . . . ."

Well, okay, so there may have been a couple of minor episodes added to the list. But at least by then, I had both a good car *and* a good man.

And my children never once argued about buckling up for safety when their Mom took to the wheel.

This Bird Has Flown

"She packed up her bags and she took off down the road..."

That lyric from Bob Seger's song, "Sun Spot Baby," is easier sung than done. Sometimes you don't get a chance to pack up. And sometimes you don't walk, you run. You can plan the escape for months but when it comes right down to it, the execution of the act is not like heading for vacation.

"Now let me see, have I forgotten anything?" you say, looking around one last time before catching that flight to Disney World.

When you are leaving the person you at one time thought was your future, and further down that road decide on a different path, you most likely will be tossing shit in your car and stripping gears on your way out the drive.

My exit from my first marriage wasn't quite that dramatic. I didn't strip one gear, though I did throw in a half-empty suitcase and two startled cats before slamming the car door. The paralyzed look on my spouse's face was the last thing I saw as I pulled out the drive of our starter home. Because sometimes the person who's supposed to love you and know you the best hasn't a clue. It's not that you haven't tried explaining a hundred times. They are simply in denial. Or they don't believe you'll ever really do it.

Because neither do you.

Leaving is sometimes harder than staying. That's why some women, and men, who get abused physically, mentally, and/or psychologically remain in horrific relationships. It's the god awful, stinking, irrational truth.

I had several reasons for leaving, and thankfully they

didn't include violence. Tom wasn't a bad guy. He could be sweet and funny and kind. He had a childish manner that I, at the time, found cute. Also, at the time, I was attracted to men with dark, curly—and preferably shaggy—hair. And ones who weren't much taller than myself, which felt just right for hugs. Tom happened to fit the profile.

But he also believed women should be seen and not heard, and made a habit of confirming my worst fears about myself (like the frequent suggestion that I was sub-par in intelligence, and so needed his guidance), which only added to my own insecurities. But he said he loved me. That, in itself, can be seductive. So I settled, and married him for all the wrong reasons.

I did love him, yes, but I wasn't *in* love with him. We all know the difference. Tom and I had been friends since I was fourteen and he sixteen, so we were comfortable with one another. We were friends when he married his high school sweetheart, and when he joined the army, and while he lived in Germany. When he returned home, things changed between us. His marriage hadn't worked out, and I comforted him in his time of need, believing that it really *was* all her fault. Which was easy considering I never much liked her in the first place. And so we became a couple.

Mistake Number One. Don't marry a guy because you've been friends for years. There was no newness about us, no passion-driven, can't-keep-my-hands-off-you spark between us. We should've remained just friends. Yet the timing of our union was too convenient. He was on the rebound, and I was between boyfriends. I was also the last of my friends still single. That puts pressure on a twenty-three-year-old girl. Particularly one whose self-esteem is already low. It's like giving hard candy to a clueless two year old. They take it when it's offered, not knowing they could very well choke on it later.

I decided to marry Tom in large part because I loved his family. And they loved me. Even after we got our own place, we spent much time at his parents' house. His family filled a void in my life. And in that environment, Tom was charming and fun. He also had a quirkiness that I appreciated. Like this one: he liked smoking weed on top of his parent's roof.

"Come on, I've got you, I won't let go," he assured me the first time he talked me into joining him.

"You know I'm afraid of heights," I reminded him as I held tight to his hand and shakily proceeded up the slanted rooftop. Not looking down.

I was petrified, but also intrigued. It was 5 a.m., and there's no better place to enjoy a sunrise than in the country, on higher ground. And it had been worth it. We sat together, me still clasping tight to his one hand, while sharing a joint with the other. We sat still looking over the horizon of many colors, listening to the roosters crow and watching the bright summer sun slowly make its way to our view. It's one of those experiences when you absolutely must believe in God because nothing or no one but a Supreme Being could possibly make a sight like that. Tom and I were one with the universe. We talked and giggled (helped much by the pot), and for that small moment in time, there was no one else in the world but us.

That one perfect moment would later pacify me through all the times to come, when things got bad. Because I held out hope that we could, eventually, return to that lone place of bliss. I would finally realize, of course, that those kind of moments cannot be resurrected. No matter how hard you try.

Mistake Number Two. Don't marry him because you desperately want to be a member of his family. Because if and when the time comes to leave, you have to leave them as well.

At the start of our wedding ceremony, my new father-in-law recited a letter that he had written to me. It read in part:

"You are my daughter now. And I will love and protect you as one of my own. Welcome to our family, my new daughter."

How can you not feel absolutely loved by that? This was his special wedding gift to me. But it was much more than that. It was a declaration that I'd wanted my whole life. An assurance that I now had an active father in my life.

Tom's mother, too, welcomed me with a place at their dinner table, where there was always lively conversation, and occasionally, a good old-fashioned food fight. This family was right up my alley.

I had still not yet gotten to the point of confiding to my own mother about anything of importance, and so I turned to his. A mother of four, she had a talent when it came to motherly advice. So it felt natural for me to go to these two people for guidance whenever I was unhappy with their son. Something I later realized is not a fair thing to do to any parent. Still, they would listen, counsel, console. And made things better, if only temporarily.

To walk away from them in the end felt awkward and insulting, after all they'd done for me. When the time did come, I knew I'd miss them more than I'd miss their son. And that I would be leaving a part of myself behind.

Mistake Number Three is the most crucial of all. I mistakenly assumed we agreed that marriage was a partnership, and hadn't worried when we got to the "obey" part of our wedding vows (which I made sure to delete in my second marriage vow). Subservience was never my style. I was raised by hard-working, independent women who made all the decisions. So I was caught by surprise when this man who was once my supportive friend began treating me like I was more a servant than an equal. (There were red flags before this: After we'd begun seeing each other, he spent some time away in the Army Reserves. In one letter he wrote, "Won't it be wonderful when my divorce is final and we can truly own one another?" Those stark, blood-red flags waved wildly, stinging my eyes as they whipped across my face. But like many twenty-one-year-olds who only want to see what they want to see and not what's there—smack dab in front of them in black and white—I chose to ignore it.) When he began belittling my ambitious goals, things took a turn for the worse.

"You got your play school again today?"

This is what he called my attempts at higher education. He'd dismiss my serious need for personal growth. After all, I was his wife, my future rested in living out my life cooking his meals, listening to his problems, raising his kids. As such, it was ludicrous that I should waste time and money in pursuit of a silly, unrealistic, and useless writing career. Perhaps, had he known I was to write about him years later, he may have been a tad more supportive . . .

My chosen life partner often made me feel unsure, incompetent, and sometimes plain stupid. College gave me hope, encouragement, and satisfaction. And increased self-esteem.

Clearly, a choice had to be made. . . .

In every dramatic play, there is a final act. Each scene before it, leads up to that climax. And as the curtain opens for that last act, the scene can begin in the simplest of settings.

"So what's for dinner?" domineering husband asks three hours after submissive wife gives up on his arrival home and puts away the steak and potatoes.

"It's in the fridge, warm it up yourself," snaps wife with book in lap, studying for tomorrow's test.

Husband, not liking the answer, proceeds to grab wife's said book and hurls it into the garbage. The horrified wife is now sorry she hadn't done the same with his dinner.

"Forget that stupid shit and make my food," husband demands.

"Fuck you!" wife says, feeling the wings sprouting from her spine.

And that's how it got ugly and brought out the worst in two people who were basically not horrible people. He pushed—and finally—I pushed back.

Most stories have a moral. This is mine:

Sometimes you marry the wrong person for the wrong reasons. They might not be a bad person, just bad for you. When you stay, you slam all the potential doors to your future, and stifle your own personal growth. And in doing so, you keep that person from finding their true love, just as you keep yourself from finding yours. I think it really works that way.

I hated leaving. I hated leaving someone I'd known half my life. I hated leaving Dawn, our collie/shepherd who, whenever I sat crying on the couch would come up to me, put her paw on my lap and give me that puppy-dog look as if to say, "I feel your pain and I'm here for you." I hated leaving my mother-in-law, who was like a mother to me. I hated leaving his dad, who was the closest thing to a father I ever had.

I hated leaving this family with whom I'd shared so many meals, and so much laughter. I hated leaving the comforts of the place I called home. The walls I lovingly painted, the flower pots hanging in macramé holders, the kitchen where I learned to cook. I hated the fact that I would be alone, despite feeling so alone in my marriage. I hated the uncertainty, the sadness, the fear of starting over . . .

I hated it all.

But I hated staying more.

Postscript: A few months after I wrote this, Tom's mother died. Then six months later, his father followed suit. I attended both funerals.

It had been twenty-seven years since our divorce. Through those years, we'd run into each other now and then—a quick hello-how-are-you-doing-I-am-fine-nice-seeing-you-take-care," was the crux of our conversations. We knew the drill of polite avoidance.

The last time I'd seen him was in 1992. We were at a 40th birthday picnic of a mutual high school friend, and the conversation took a surprising turn.

"Can I talk to you a minute?" Tom came over and whispered to me soon as I arrived. Neither of our spouses had come, thus making it easy to step away without explanations. I had no clue what was on his mind, but he seemed nervous.

"I, ah, just wanted . . . to apologize . . . you know . . . for everything I put you through," he said, before looking at me with those dark eyes, brown as acorns. I couldn't think of a word in response, could not believe my own ears, but I believed his look of sincerity. He went on. "I realize it was all my fault, I wasn't a very good husband . . . and I'm really sorry."

This is every ex-wife's dream. How many times have we imagined the sense of gratification we'd bask in on that glorious day when the man who did us wrong *finally* owned up to his bad-boy behavior, *and* said he was sorry, *and* really meant it. I have to admit, I did gloat a bit inwardly. (I would learn later that he had joined AA, so, this was a required act—making amends to those you have hurt in your past. Knowing this at the time would've thoroughly dampened my enthusiasm of this joyful, triumphant moment.)

When I finally found my voice I heard myself saying, "No, it wasn't all your fault. I was young, too, and I wasn't ready for the responsibility of marriage."

What? Why was I saying this?

Because it was true. And something inside me—no matter how satisfying it felt to hear him sorrowfully admit his wrongdoings—couldn't let him take all the blame. Plus, it hardly seemed to matter anymore, so many years later.

"But thank you for saying that, it means a lot," I added. Then someone came over and broke the mood.

Still, it wasn't until his parents' death—two people I adored—that I came face-to-face with an epiphany that freed me from a hidden animosity I was not even aware of. I realized that, like my mother had done before me (that truth, thick with irony), that I had never rid myself of anger toward my ex-husband. I had simply gone about my life those past decades harboring a secret resentment and bitterness toward him, like a malignant tumor you carry around, blissfully unaware of its existence.

I guess if you experience enough funerals (and once you hit fifty, you get your share of them) you begin to realize a few things about life, and your relationships with others. Even when you don't think a relationship exists. But you see, time is often rewound at these sad occasions. Much talk of "remember when"—past events with family, friends, neighbors, and siblings, and the bond you all shared. Funerals, like those of Tom's parents, pushes aside the bad, and gives back the good memories. And a greater understanding of the nature of us humans.

For me, the funerals of my former in-laws reinforced the fact that the hardest decision I ever made was also the best one I ever made—for me as well as for him.

That decision came to me one September day in 1979. I had gone to church, my first visit in many years. It was a Monday morning, and not a soul was there. I kneeled before the statue of Mary, asking for her womanly guidance. We had a nice chat, her and I, got reacquainted. In the end, she left it up to me as to what to do. So I followed my heart.

What happened as a result (that is, a few years after our marriage's demise) was a miracle. We both ultimately found the right partner to spend our lives with. Tom and his wife have a son, now in his twenties. I met him at his grandmother's funeral. He's a good-looking fellow and, as I shook his hand upon introduction, I couldn't help think as I looked into his brown eyes, that he wouldn't be here had I stayed with his father all those years ago. And neither would my two wonderful daughters. Sure, had I stayed, Tom and I probably would have had our own children. But they would have grown up in a household full of unhappiness and contempt.

At Tom's father's wake, I realized that I really didn't mind seeing my ex again. That actually, it was good to see him. We'd come full circle, he and I. We're back where we started nearly forty years ago. We're friends. Maybe not as close as we were as teenagers, but we like each other again. And that feels good. With the anger dissolved, I'm able to see the traits I always liked about him. And that is freeing. It may be simple nostalgia, but I'm glad he was a part of my growing up, and my growing out.

And despite it all: the yelling matches, the lonely times, the mistakes numbers one, two and three, I have come to a conclusion.

That wings are for discovery. To seek higher ground. To see new worlds. And to land exactly where we belong.

And that regret and bitterness serve no purpose. For how can you regret a circumstance that ultimately puts you in a better place?

These are the kind of moments when God lets us see things clearly.

Even when we're not sitting high upon a roof top.

4. You Had Me At Vroom, Vroom . . .

Wild Boys of Summer

It is often said that girls are two to three years ahead of boys in maturity. This confirms my earlier statement that there is just one advantage for a teenage girl who has to put up with an older brother—the regular appearance of other boys. It works out particularly well when Mother Nature places you in a family with a brother two to three years older than you.

Perfect.

And so the opportunity was ripe when my teenaged brother started bringing home friends who became candidates for my romance-deprived heart—or at the very least—nice inspiration for my clandestine daydreams. The bonus came when these contenders were guaranteed to place dead last on Mom's "Boys-I'd-Like-My-Children-To-Associate-With" list.

Ah, yes. Life couldn't have been better that summer of '68.

It was the year of my introduction to Janis Joplin. And Jethro Tull. And Blood, Sweat & Tears (their debut LP, "Child is Father to the Man" remains my all-time favorite), among others who made life worthwhile. It was also the year that marked the end of the Andy Griffith Show, the Monkees (my brother did not see this as a bad thing), and my short-lived Greaser phase. It was a year that I, now a full-fledged teenager, was fortunate enough to have a seventeen-year-old biker brother. With dangerous-looking, and very cute, friends.

For some time now, Dennis had been associating with a swarm of long-haired, leather-clad, cigarettes-hanging-from-their-mouths, two-wheel riders with shit-eating grins on their faces. But that summer, he got up the nerve to bring them to our apartment.

This was a fourteen-year-old, not-so-good-Catholic girl's personal version of Hog Heaven.

To some, these guys may have looked a bit on the shady side, what with their motorcycle gang attire and all. In truth, they were just a bunch of boisterous, fun-loving, and actually really nice teenagers living life to the fullest. Though they were also, unknowingly at the time, gifting themselves with hordes of unseemly, corrupt—and ultimately humorous—memories they would later tell their grandchildren about.

Or not.

It was during this time my biker brother adopted the motto "*Born to Be Wild*" (after the Steppenwolf song, of course), and this new lifestyle certainly didn't warrant having a nosy, chatty, and thoroughly annoying, boy-crazy little sister. So whenever Dennis brought his friends around, he'd act like he had some kind of restraining order against me, forbidding me to come within fifty feet of his cool, badass friends. I was maddeningly forced to witness most of their actions from the sidelines (or when he was in his room with a girl, through a key hole).

That is, until Mark came to town. He was an "unruly" Texas boy whose parents had sent him packing to his grandma's house in the Midwest. She lived in Timberlake, a small village next to Lakeline—conveniently located within walking distance from our own grandmother's house.

We all have special moments from our youth that remain etched in our memory banks like a framed picture. Meeting Mark is one of my favorites. . . .

The slamming of the apartment door announces their arrival.

"Hey *Mouth*, Mom home yet?" Dennis shouts like he's alerting the neighborhood. His long, dark, curly hair—getting close to shoulder length (and decidedly closer to Mom following through on her threat that she'll cut it one night while he's sleeping)—is fanning out like a wayward Brillo pad because he'd just gotten off his Harley. I give him my baddest look because I hate his new nickname for me. He thinks it's funny, and when others laugh, too, it only encourages him.

I'm sitting at the kitchen table smoking a cigarette, which, had he been paying attention, would've answered his own stupid question.

"It's Friday, you know Mom doesn't get home till seven," I say, not looking up from *The Plain Dealer*. I'm reading Jane Scott's "What's Happening" column in the Entertainment section, checking what local rock bands are playing close by. Even though I'm too young (according to Mom) to go to the Hullabaloo teen clubs, I hold out hope that if I ever finagle a way—both in transportation and a foolproof lie—I'm there. Mark walks in behind Dennis saying something, and this boy's resonant Southern accent wills my head straight up, like a puppet on a string.

He's wearing a brown, buckskin jacket. And tight, flared, blue jeans. And the requisite shit-eating grin, complete with dimple (think Brad Pitt in *Thelma & Louise*). He throws his bike jacket on the chair beside me (the whiff of robust suede/leather permeates my sinuses), revealing a short-sleeved (despite it being October in Ohio) tight black T-shirt, and suede, fringed vest. His suede belt, too, has long fringes, that sway with each leg movement.

I think I'm in love.

Dennis's awful nickname for me is now put into question as *Mouth* is suddenly rendered speechless. Standing in front of me is a boy of the likes I've never seen before. He doesn't so much possess "Texas charm," as to ooze it. His smile comes easily, which makes you feel—even if you *are* his new best friend's unsophisticated little sister—like you matter. Like you, despite that horrible moniker your dumb brother has tagged you with, actually may have something interesting to say. And he, smiling at you, is ready to listen.

But nothing comes out.

Until curiosity gets the best of me. At a time when most kids our age have Beatles-inspired long hair, this guy is practically bald. Shaven, like some Army brat.

I want to sound cool about it, but I have to know.

"So what happened to your hair?" Yeah, real cool.

Mark flashes me this crooked grin and boastfully replies, "I just got outta DH."

I stubbornly ignore Dennis' dire threats of what'll happen to me if I don't "go away." Whatever punishment I may endure will absolutely be worth it. *Wow, Mom's gonna hate this guy!*

I learned his Detention Home stay was short-lived, and the charge was minor. No matter. Dennis had a cool, criminal friend, who was cuter than anything I'd seen in *16 Magazine*, or even that new mag, *Rolling Stone*. However, I would also quickly learn that Mark—though he's been in Ohio less than two months—has already acquired a harem of attentive hippie women at the ready. Each one of them older, prettier—and skinnier—than I am. So regretfully, I content myself with merely basking in the pleasure of his increasingly regular company, while enjoying my first James Dean crush from afar.

I even come to accept the fact that he'll never be mine, and begin to regard Mark as my "other brother," the one who's a lot nicer to me than the first one, and who makes life a whole lot more interesting. Starting with his willingness to let me hang out at his grandmother's house. (But only on Sundays, when decadent events are slightly more low-key. As if he and my real brother, now suddenly all protective, have this arrangement that I am not to witness all the rowdy, pot-smoking, law-breaking acts that take place there—though they'd soon let their guard down, finding it just too hard to feign good behavior, even in front of me.)

I'm sure Mark's Granny (we all call her that) didn't have a clue what changes were in store for her when her grandson first appeared at her doorstep. Within weeks, her tiny cottage-style bungalow became the mother ship for teenage aliens—a perpetually revolving door attracting every stray, wayward kid in a thirty-mile radius. And yet, Granny seems to take it all in stride. She keeps to herself—a quiet, religious woman who assumes the see-no-evil, hear-no-evil stance. Or perhaps the woman is simply a saint. A possibility given the large portrait of Jesus mounted on her dining room wall that must be a comforting reminder that someone is watching over her. But as Mark and his posse take over her home, she begins to spend an awful lot of time out of town visiting relatives, leaving these young sinners under the watchful eye of the Lord. Better Him than her.

Because I don't have much of a social life, I anticipate Sundays like a kid awaiting her day at the amusement park, where there is a guaranteed mixed bag of entertainment. I volunteer to clean the house to lengthen my stay among this growing group of misfit bikers. And one day I even cook spaghetti, with the help of Chef Boyardee. I know I can trust him because he's a Cleveland guy. But although I read, and reread, the instructions on how to cook the noodles, I'm befuddled when they stick together like Silly Putty as I try to dish it out.

"Hey, this is really good," Mark lies, as he lifts a fork full of thin-style spaghetti noodles clinging together like frightened children in a lake of watery red sauce.

No wonder I love this guy.

God knows what all goes on here during the weekends, but for me, Sundays are the best. The lively little house brings a thundering roar of motorcycles, a steady stream of teenage boys, and blasting, wall-vibrating rock and roll. This is where I get my first taste of Big Brother and the Holding Company, Grand Funk Railroad, and Jefferson Airplane. And where "In-A-Gadda-Da-Vida" becomes a life-altering theme song.

It is also where I learn about motorcycles. Parts, mostly.

In the winter of 1968, Granny's quaint living room becomes a motorcycle repair shop, with bike parts scattered throughout the lime green/gold shag carpeting, now covered with oil spots. Come spring of 1969, the rebuilt chopper is complete, and the gang goes hog wild with the celebratory revving of the motor, the choking of the throttle, and the ear-splitting, throaty roar, as Mark rides the bike out the front door to the sound of enthusiastic whoops, cheers, and praises all around (after all, it had been a communal project).

The neighbors in this quaint village of Timberlake, Ohio are not quite as impressed.

Dennis and Mark, and another boy, Bruce, became a '60s version of the Three Musketeers. They were best buddies, Harley enthusiasts, and though not trouble-seeking, often found it anyway. They were always together—"one for all, and all for one"—and when not on the streets, were often at our little apartment, now welcomed by my mother, who also succumbed to Mark's Texas charm. And Bruce, we'd known all our lives since his mother used to babysit us on occasion.

Having won over our mother became a fortunate circumstance for Mark when it came to several unfortunate "incidents." Like the night the police called Mom and told her to come pick up her born-to-be-wild son and his charming friend at the station. The situation proved problematic since my mother didn't drive, forcing her to call Grandpa, who came quickly—with melodramatic wife in tow—so that my entire family (save for me, who was told to "stay put") made a thespian appearance at my biker brother's first police station attendance.

The details of their being hauled into the station are fuzzy. Dennis and Mark hardly recall it, what with all the marijuana involved (smoking, not selling, I must make clear), and perhaps other influences. The only thing Dennis will own up to these days is the fact that, at seventeen, they'd been out past curfew and— while there is surely more to this story—once our Shakespearian mother and grandmother appeared, the police chief was probably all too happy to drop any and all charges, if that meant getting these people the hell out of his precinct.

As often happens with those "we'll look back on and laugh" moments, that's precisely what ultimately happened. The astonishing thing about the whole incident is that Mom eventually gained back her sense of humor and it later became one of her favorite "my son was a juvenile delinquent" stories. Though she never quite referred to it as that.

"Now Dennis, don't forget about that time I was called to go to the police station," she'd say (*and* with a little laugh) whenever those days were brought up. "You're just lucky I didn't make yas just sleep there."

After all, every story needs a hero . . . .

All those "remember when" tales seemed to be formed in the summertime, when life was ripe for anything remotely exciting or historic in our teen years.

And it is summertime that's as treasured as rare jewels in the Midwest. Three months out of twelve doesn't leave much time to pack in all your fun, and when you're young, the pressure is on. So, despite my big brother's best efforts to keep me from his friends, I managed to weave myself into their lives, and they, into mine. At fourteen, I coerce his buddy, Tim, to take me on my first motorcycle ride. At sixteen, I call Rich— often—whenever I need a ride somewhere, and—just as often—he complies (and never once asks for anything in exchange. Now there's a boy my mother likes). And Mark—still my favorite—hands me my first joint in the car on the way home from my first (finally!) night at the Hullabaloo.

And lucky for me, my big, protective brother was nowhere around.

It was one of those warm summer Midwestern nights you remember all your life—not too hot, not too muggy. While I had finally succeeded in making my way to the popular teen club, I had given no thought as to how I was getting back. Teenagers don't think that far in advance. All I'd been focused on was seeing my favorite hometown rock band, Cyrus Erie. This was one of the first groups of Eric Carmen's (who'd become an international celebrity, starting with the Raspberries, but at the time, was a mere child of seventeen). When the band quit playing and the club started to close, I, and my friend Sherry, began wondering how we were going to get home because ten miles was a long walk, especially after midnight. We were standing wearily in the parking lot watching everyone get into cars to leave, nervous about this latest quandary we found ourselves in, and searching out just who we should beg for a ride home. That's when I spotted the long fringes.

"Hey, there's Mark!" I shouted in relief at the sight of his buckskin jacket. There was no question that we were now saved. We piled into the back seat of his girlfriend's Volkswagen Beetle Bug, thanking him profusely for saving our ass. We were almost home when he lights up the joint and hands it to us without fanfare. He doesn't know we are virgins in this matter.

I had heard somewhere that the first time you smoke marijuana you don't get high. So I figured I had nothing to lose, even though Mom was always up when I got home. Turns out, that was not to be my experience. The light-headedness and giddiness I'd soon feel coincided perfectly with my turning the door knob to our apartment.

"Boy, I'm really tired," I told Mom before she could ask me anything that might demand an answer, which I now found myself incapable of.

I headed straight to my room and hit the bed without changing clothes, giving in to a sudden exhaustion. But I couldn't sleep. I was a little dizzy, but a nice dizzy, so lied there staring up at my Janis Joplin poster, trying to contact my idol telepathically. I was just about to drift off when a loud smash and the shattering of glass shook me out of my alpha state. The sound was so thunderous that it rattled our apartment building like an earthquake.

Now here's where I thought the marijuana might be messing with my young mind:

My upstairs bedroom window faced a small shopping strip. There was a Hough Bakery, a Laundromat, drug store, a Kroger grocery store, and a bar called Danny's Lounge. When I jumped up at the sound of all that racket and looked out my window, I saw the front part of an old Caddy sticking out of the now-smashed Kroger front window. I was now convinced that the pot I'd smoked had been laced with some kind of hallucinogen, which of course, was entirely possible.

"What was that?" Mom burst into my room to join me at the window. We both watched as the drunken couple stumbled their way out of the car—which wasn't easy considering its position on top of a stack of large peat moss bags. The woman in the driver's seat had mistakenly put the car, which was facing the street, in R instead of D, hit the gas, thus ejecting the car up and over the bags and into the big store window of Kroger's, finally coming to a stop halfway in. Once I saw that Mom, too, saw this same scene, I felt a bit relieved over my illegal indulgence. The next day in the store, I overheard the manager explain the night's events to a customer. "Yeah, and I bet it was real interesting when the lady was forced to call her husband to bail her outta jail."

This event may not have ended my pot-smoking, but it did teach me never to go drinking with a man who's not my husband, then offer to drive him home. . . .

Eventually Dennis's biker friends all went their separate ways. One went to Vietnam, and though he returned, no one recognized him as the once happy-go-lucky boy we had known. A few others were lured to California—or any place deemed better than Cleveland. And Bruce, the third of the Musketeers, decided one day to take a bunch of pills and end his life, leaving questions that were never answered, beginning with why. The rest of us simply succumbed, reluctantly, to adulthood: holding down jobs, raising families, living fairly normal lives. All becoming our own version of the dreaded "Establishment" we had protested against so vehemently all those summers ago.

In the meantime, Mark had disappeared. When he turned eighteen, he became a traveling man and was hard to keep track of. We saw him intermittently the next few years, but decades pass quickly. In 1992, I found a photograph of him and Dennis and suddenly realized we hadn't seen Mark since his last visit to

Cleveland for Granny's funeral in 1978. Fourteen years is a long time to ignore the kind of bond we once shared.

So one day I set out to find my other brother, my favorite wild boy of those adolescent summers. After a few false starts, I was amazed to find his name in a phone book—like a regular citizen. He, too, had settled down, ironically back in his hometown of Houston. I arranged for Mark to surprise Dennis with a phone call for his 41st birthday. It was one of those great moments that make you feel sixteen again. After that, we all vowed to stay in touch. And we have.

We're all in our fifties now—even me, the little sister, who began hosting an annual reunion for these boys from my brother's and my past. They come with their wives and girlfriends, or just a six-pack on their hips. Although several are now grandparents, some things haven't changed. A few still ride their Harleys, others still play in a rock band. In my backyard, over beer and brats, we talk about our jobs, our families, our friends. We laugh recalling how nasty Boone's Farm wine tasted. And play music. The kind that began with The Beatles. And we remark how the Fab Four changed everything. Thank God. We still damn disco, and now rap, for the demise of *real* rock 'n' roll.

And though we complain how it sucks to grow old, we're fairly happy with things. For we realize that no matter how the shades of grey have turned our hair, and time has wrinkled our skin and thickened our waists, and altered so many recollections, it cannot change an insurmountable truth:

We survived the '60s. And everything thereafter.

Some of those wild boys of summer weren't so fortunate. Yet they continue to take up residence in our mind's attic. And when the survivors get together, they are there, too, in nearly every "remember when" story.

Like a neighbor lady once told me so long ago: If you can count your true friends on one hand, you are truly blessed.

And so, when the chance comes to be reunited with those once on our "Whatever happened to?" list-the ones we once longed to share a beer with again—the blessed ones do precisely that.

Love in a Biker Bar – or
How I Found a Good Man

ℐ'm standing behind the bar wondering how I ended up here. There are long-dead stuffed animal heads hanging on the walls, perched above the bottles of Jack Daniels, Southern Comfort, and Mezcal (the tequila with the worm that floats at the bottom like a decayed turd). The furry deceased creatures include rabid-looking rabbits, squirrels, and a buck with that deer-in-the-headlights look. Most intriguing to visitors is the Jackalope (a obviously toyed-with bunny bearing antlers, humorously referred to as a "horny rabbit") above the cash register, mounted on a wooden plaque with long strings of sticky webs the spiders use as a tightrope. Sugar, the bar owner, whose tough demeanor reminds me of Barbara Stanwyck's "*Big Valley*" character, Victoria Barkley, is not known for her meticulous housekeeping.

Every one of these stiff creatures has bulging eyes that seem to be begging to hang elsewhere, such as a nice suburban den. Can't say I blame them. Looking up at the cluster of dust and muck that's formed on these ghastly varmints like dryer lint, I'm reminded that I, too, long to be somewhere else. But then, I really need the money. At this point, the alternative would be to take off my clothes in front of leering, drunken strangers but that career choice grates against my Catholic upbringing. Though I had, for a moment, considered it, the thought is just too icky.

And so begins my career at Sugar's Last Stand Saloon, where I am a "Sugar's Barmaid," meaning a breed of species infamously lumped into the category of "biker chick who can toss back a shot of Wild Turkey with nary a grimace" according to a recent newspaper article. This, despite the fact I don't live up to its esteemed moniker. Straight shots of anything make me grimace *and* convulse. I don't have a Harley. Nor a biker boyfriend. But like the other Sugar's girls, I can make conversation with just about anyone, and more than willing to work for food.

Who I really am is a struggling twenty-six-year-old divorcee who doesn't want anything more than to get her college degree and become a successful writer. Although, having a good man to encourage my art would surely be a plus.

But for now, I am a Honky-Tonk Woman.

This is a new career for me. I've gone from being a pretty good hairdresser, to a horribly inept telephone solicitor who couldn't sell a compulsive gambler a free ticket to Vegas, to a piss-poor, short-lived waitress who once dumped a basket of sizzling breaded mushrooms onto the lap of a nicely suited man— who looked like all he came in for was to unwind from his stressful job. Beer and hot fried mushrooms. The poor man mistakenly assumed the latter would go in his mouth, not on his pants.

I am still a pretty good hairdresser, but college is expensive and I'm determined to get through it. After my divorce last year, I'd found a small apartment, the upstairs of a house on Cleveland's east side, which I share with my brother, also recently divorced. Who doesn't have much money, either. We are quite the pair.

"Listen, why don't you come work at Sugar's?" my bartender friend, Laura, suggests when I tell her my financial woes. "She pays twenty-five dollars under the table. If you work just two nights a week, that's an extra fifty bucks!"

"Wow, that's pretty good," I said, thinking how four weeks of that added up to my monthly rent. But the notorious Sugars?

"Laura, uh, no offense, but I'd have to be *really* desperate to work in a biker bar."

Two weeks later, I'm desperately serving up fat, frosted mugs of Miller High Life with a Snake Bite chase.

As irony loves to have it, this was to be the start of a wonderful new life for me. God really does have quite the sense of humor . . .

My first surprise is that these big bad bikers who come in aren't really all that big and bad. Well some are rather beefy, with tattoos of skulls and naked women with long, flowing hair caressing their arms. But they show respect to the one who pours their drinks. I like that. I've been verbally abused as a telephone solicitor, frowned upon as a hairdresser, and stiffed more than once as a waitress, but as a bartender in a biker bar I am treated well. Go figure. Another strange but interesting thing is that most of these customers have nicknames. Even the women. So far I've met Bondo, Slick, Dago, Black Betty (*Bam-ba-lam*), Huckleberry, Peppermint Patty, Stutterin' Al, Deadhead, Donut, Panhead Mike, Weezer, Big Joe, Little Joe (who endears himself to me by saying I'd look good even in a paper sack—you gotta love a guy like that), Peanut, Tequila Willie, Funkadelic, Dirty Dave, Judy Blue Eyes, Brain-damaged Dave, Alcohol Al, JB Jeff, Bonnie Bell, and Bob O.

The writer in me finds the names, and characters, intriguing enough to jot them down for future writing prompts.

The biker women come in all shapes, styles and personalities, but none you want to mess with. This is proven each year, I hear, when "Sugar's Girls" participate in the Willoughby Bars' annual Tug of War contest, where they always take first place because they are the biggest, baddest, and bawdiest. And while some are actually quite friendly, there are those few who see me, the new barmaid in town, as a threat. After all, isn't this why I'm here? To steal away these guys with long, shaggy hair, knotted-up beards and ragged, ripped T-shirts that say "Free Mustache Rides" and "Harley-Davidson: Put something exciting between your legs?" Yes, they are a motley crew—which for odd reasons women find appealing. Me, I have a different agenda.

And yet, after awhile, they all begin to grow on me. I start feeling comfortable here and watch in amazement as these girls indeed toss back a series of alcoholic beverages, and hustle a pool game in the proud tradition of Minnesota Fats. But at the end of the night, they're just as sloppy and hard to pick up off the floor as their counterparts.

My coworkers and I often discuss noteworthy events here at Sugars, as we change shifts or finally get time on the other side of the bar. Sometimes I just sit and read the entertaining graffiti on the carved up wooden bartop (those boys see an opportunity to use those buck knives wherever possible). Nina and Lynette, who have become my new friends, tell me which girls to stay away from ("But how can you do that when you're serving them?" I ask. "Carefully," they reply. "Don't make conversation, don't smile at them - and above all, DO NOT talk to their boyfriends. Least not when they're around."). And so, with that wise advice, I manage to earn even the toughest girls' approval—after the initiation months of their watching and waiting for me to screw up, and me, not screwing up. I'm in.

My second surprise comes out of the blue, catches me unprepared, and distracts me. An issue none of them warned me about. I'm becoming attracted to one particular guy who is about as off limits as one can get. Of all the single guys that drift in and out of this god-forsaken place, I am drawn to a married one.

But I am not stupid. When JB Jeff—with kind eyes, charming smile, and good sense of humor—comes in and stays for long periods, I give him no more attention than the rest.

"Hey, Dee, how's it going?" Jeff says, coming in from his shift at General Electric. "I'll have my usual."

"Sure," is all I say and pour him his scotch and water.

"Thanks," he says, smiling that smile, then looks around. It's a Monday night, and the bar's mostly empty. "Sugar's not here, wanna play some pool?"

"Nah, I'm sure she'll be here soon," I say, then walk away to the other side of the bar and wash beer foam off the glasses.

Despite my cool exterior, we become friends. He sticks around sometimes until closing and keeps me company. He makes me laugh and we find all kinds of things to talk about. But as time goes by, the talk is mostly about how his marriage sucks. I, having been there, tell him he should try and work it out and suggest ways to do so. But they never pan out.

"She just won't compromise," he tells me each time. "It's her way or the highway."

I have no advice to that. It sounds pretty cut and dry to me. Still, I try my best to encourage him because, although I've had a few careers in my day, the last thing I want to be is a home wrecker, which to me, falls in the same category as exotic dancer, minus the exotic part. My life is challenging enough, thank you very much.

What surprises me most about this guy who lightly flirts with me, is that no matter how miserable he is when he comes in, he never really hits on me. This is an honorable trait. He stays, chats and leaves. He, raised Catholic too, doesn't try to kiss me or fondle me, or asks me out. Still, we both know something is going on between us. Our unspoken fear is that if the fire is lit, no telling how high the flames could go. It's absolutely terrifying. And yet, it feels right, even though it's wrong. Yeah, like that country song. I hate country songs.

"Why are you so worried?" Carol, another Sugar barmaid, and my good friend, asks me one night she's pouring and I'm drinking. I have finally decided to tell someone of my dilemma, and Carol is the kind of person a girl can confide in and know it won't go outside the door. She's smart, too, so I figure she'll steer me away from him with her wise words. "Look, his marriage is in the dumpster. We all know that. Just go with it. You both are disgustingly happy when he's in here. Besides," she adds, looking around. "You *could* do worse."

That makes me laugh, but her advice is not exactly what I want to hear. But I also know where she's coming from. Her one, true love was killed the year before on a construction site, and she knows that sometimes you only get one chance at something that good.

A few months down the road, my married biker is in the throes of a divorce and we start seeing each other, but only on the sly—"incognito" as we call it. We meet at bars outside the city limits. We tell no one, and it's kind of fun. But eventually, word gets out on the street. Some say they saw it coming. One girl asks Jeff, "Why do ya wanna go out with a Sugar's barmaid?" which hurts my feelings. A few others, too, join in disapproval because technically he's still married (seems even some bikers have morals). But those who know us well, welcome our couple-hood because it's clear to them that we have fallen passionately in love. And love is good. Even when it's complicated. Nine months later, between studying literature, taking tests, and pouring beers—just right with a fine line of foam on top—I quit my famed status as a Sugar's Barmaid. It had served its purpose. It gave me the means to continue school. But more than that, it gave me a good man, who would be the one who stayed.

It's been nearly three decades since our Sugar days. Jeff and I stop in occasionally at the bar where our lives both changed. That is, whenever Ma Barkley decides to open up, which is becoming rarer as time goes by. She's probably just plain tired.

Those wild times of the '70s and '80s have clearly taken a lot out of her. When we do visit, she's happy to see us and we catch her up on who's doing what, who still sees who. A lot has changed over the decades. But sitting in this ragged, time-worn bar, much remains the same. The mangy stuffed animals still hang in place, held up by the clogs of grit and cobwebs. The faucet in the girls' john still runs ice cold water through both taps. And as I sip my Rum and Coke, it appears she still buys the cheap stuff. Seems some things never change.

But the door no longer swings open with loud, high-strung bikers streaming in and out. No one really comes here anymore. And there are some faces we'll never see again. They're the ones who have ridden past us to that great Hog Heaven in the sky. Like my good friend Carol, who like me, never acquired a nickname. She did me a favor one Saturday night and took my shift so I could go on my first date with Jeff, and on the way home fell asleep at the wheel and crashed into a pole. A circumstance that haunts me to this day. Bonnie Bell, she died of brain cancer. Bob O decided to take a bike ride on a beautiful November day, didn't see a stop sign, smashed into a truck and died instantly. And Weezer. The guy just didn't take care of himself and his bad habits caught up to him. And Jeff's sister, Kathy, who also worked at Sugar's for a time and was everyone's favorite because she was sweet and laughed a lot. She fought hard against malignant melanoma—skin cancer—for two miserable years until her body had enough and she died at the ripe young age of 35.

And doesn't that beat all. Because there are others we all thought would surely have gotten there first (it's okay to say that, they thought so too). Like old George, who was old back then, and must be in his eighties by now. Sugar tells us he still comes around. And sometimes you can catch sight of Still-Dyin' Deke down the street at the bar that used to be the Peppermint Stick that for years was Sugar's competitor for biker customers. Deke, who never left his house without his brown cowboy hat and fiery attitude, hasn't worked for as long as we've known him, supposedly living off the royalties of some country song he wrote back in the '60s. No one ever remembers what song it was, but boy, that must be some royalty check. Anyway, he got his handle because whenever you see him and give a polite, "How ya doin' Deke?" he'll give you a rundown of his serious ailments and conclude with a dire, "Doctors say I don't have much time left."

According to our calculations, Deke's been dyin' now for more than twenty years.

Jeff and me, we're the lucky ones. We're one of the few couples of that motley crew still together. When people ask our secret to marital longevity, we credit common sense (don't yell when the other one's yelling 'cause they won't hear you anyway - that's one), and respect (we still say "Thanks, Honey," and let each other have a life of his or her own because you return with more to talk about). We're still each other's best friends. And we still make each other laugh. That's all the secrets we've got. What I don't mention because the time never seems fitting, is that through our years together, Jeff has managed to help me discover who I really am. It's been a slow, lingering process, but little by little, he's made me believe that I am pretty. And smart. And capable of doing anything I want to in life. And he allows me enough room to strive for it. He is my soft landing when life gets hard. This is what he brings to my table. It is his greatest gift to me.

When people ask us how we met, we recount our Sugar Days. The women are astounded that I not only found a good man in a bar, but a biker bar at that. "See," I say to them, "life is full of surprises."

Apparently, from Ohio, to California, and back, until I was twenty-six years old, I'd been looking for love in all the wrong places, like that Waylon Jennings song.

And here, the man of my dreams was nearby all along. Often just a few miles away. Passing time in a biker bar. Go figure.

I guess this is what they mean when people say no matter what our own plans are for the future, God can trump them.

My future came as an unexpected gift. Wrapped snug in a black leather jacket.

Rides of Passage

In 1993, I went on my coldest motorcycle ride ever. I sat on the back of my husband's Harley-Davidson to head out for a "memorial run," and was wondering if it was worth it. The temperature that early May morning was forty-some degrees—twenty degrees, if you count motorcycle chill factor. And despite my layered look—thermal underwear under T-shirt and sweatshirt and motorcycle jacket, jeans with leg-warmers, winter scarf over head and around neck, and leather gloves—I was freezing. And yet, as a group of us shivered down the highway at sixty miles an hour toward Cleveland, I felt my mood lift. There is just something exciting about the anticipation of riding with thousands of motorcycle enthusiasts.

And this day was special. It was the tenth anniversary of the Louie Run—the annual event that started in 1983, after Louie died. He was one of the only bar owners back then who actually welcomed the presence of bikers. And bikers are loyal. So those who frequented the Peppermint Stick Lounge, a longtime Willoughby, Ohio tavern (that, because of all the bikers, enjoyed a notorious reputation) rode on their motorcycles in his funeral procession. They then decided to ride together each anniversary and make it a memorial run, not only to honor lost loved ones, but to raise money for the living.

It has now grown from about thirty local riders to more than two thousand. Pretty impressive. Everyone was to meet downtown, so groups were coming from all areas of the North Coast. By the time we arrived at the designated Municipal parking lot, I was anxious for the chilly wind to stop whipping across what was still exposed of my face. But the glee I felt as I hopped off the bike was quickly replaced with a more intense concern.

I had to go to the bathroom.

And this vast parking lot was as vacant as an amusement park in winter. Looking around in vain hope, I began praying I could make it to the next stop where surely there'd be something resembling a restroom (sometimes we pray to God for the simplest of things). But no. Not even one of those ugly metal portable units made for such a purpose. Sometimes it sucks being a girl. Guys can go anywhere to relieve themselves (and often do), but girls need to be more discrete. Well, least I do. But it wasn't long after everyone arrived, that I, too, followed the girls to make nice with the trees. There are many rites of passage in this life.

Once all the bikes arrived, we lined up, two by two, to ride in a long procession for the next thirty miles to our final destination. As we made our way down the open road, we saw that our parade of motorcycles had attracted a sizable crowd the whole way out. As we waved to those on the hillside, those standing along bridges, and those on lawn chairs in their front yard, I whispered to Jeff that I felt like the queen. It's quite a sensation to be riding down a street and have hundreds of people cheering you, and waving at you, as you roar by. For those of us who have known isolation and rejection a time or two in life, riding motorcycles together generates a sense of comforting unity, and a feeling that you are a part of something bigger than yourself. It's a peace rally on wheels. And it feels really good.

But there are other times riding with a crowd feels awful. . . .

It's November 2001 and I'm sitting on the back of a Harley in line with some sixty bikers. In the twenty years I've been with my husband, I've participated in the Louie Run, Al's Fun Run, and various "toy runs," and "poker runs." All these events varied in number, anywhere from twenty riders to eight thousand.

But this time is different. Today, we longtime friends ride together to pay tribute to one of our own.

The roar of the motorcycles is just as thunderous and

stimulating as always. The long, steady stream of bikes of every make, color and year, is just as impressive. But no one is enjoying this ride. There are no smiles, no revelry. We are together to bury a friend. A healthy, hard working, loving husband, father, brother, son, and best friend to many. He left us in a "New York minute." That's all it took when, as he rode on one of fall's last Indian Summer days, Bob-O collided with a truck and was thrown from his bike. With one quick impact, his bountiful life ended.

After all these years, we still called him Bob-O. I don't even know how it came about, but it's how we referred to him back when we were all in our twenties. Back when everyone had a nickname. We weren't hoodlums, though I suppose some thought of us as such. What with the pack of leather, the loud and imposing motorcycles, the regular tavern visits. In reality, we were just a group of young people who shared a common bond—the bond of freedom, the bond of being different from the pack, the bond of exhilaration one can only feel when riding in the wind.

For those who don't know, this is the spirit of the biker:

For the most part, biker guys are just big boys. They revel in their boyness. They like to hop on their steel horses and have a good time.

Biker women, too, for the most part, are smart, kind, and strong enough to keep a heavy Harley standing—though their real strength lies within.

And most bikers work hard to make the money needed for their gleam machines. Most respect women. Children. People in general.

Most will take the leather off their backs to help out a friend. They love camaraderie. And they love to ride.

Back in our Sugar's Last Stand and Peppermint Stick days, we were the former high school misfits, the juvenile delinquents, the loners. Though a few were also the high school football stars, the cheerleaders, the Most Likely to Succeeds. Yet we were all one when we'd ride together. And in that sense, nothing has changed.

Except that we are all middle-aged now. All mature adults. We all have respectable jobs, have either raised our children, or are still "in the trenches." Many are grandparents. Many are watching over aging parents, while preparing for the future with 401ks.

And many of us still get together on a regular basis. Still love to ride our motorcycles. Still congregate in taverns. But nowadays, those gatherings are usually confined to the weekend, where many consume soft drinks instead of "snake-bites" and are home before the clock strikes twelve.

Bob-O was instrumental at continuing the male friendships created so long ago. In 1996, he founded an exclusive club called "Two-Wheel Tuesdays." It consisted of a select group of guys who met weekly in his garage. Its purpose was to provide a night out "with the boys," where they could drink beer, talk motorcycles, and swap stories. (Bob was a great and animated storyteller. We all know that had he not died in the crash, he would've used that horrific event as another opportunity to entertain his guests with an illuminating and dramatic tale of how he almost got killed that day.) These guys have been through many adventures together. They consider each other brothers. So it was no surprise that these big, strapping leather-clad men let the tears flow at Bob's funeral.

And because of this latest motorcycle death, people started asking me if my husband and I will continue to ride after this. I try to not sound defensive to those who clearly don't understand. But my only response is to answer the question with a question. Why do people smoke, overeat, drink alcohol, ride in an airplane, or participate in any number of sports where one can get hurt? Why do any of us do things we know are not particularly good for us, or that involve an element of risk?

I guess it's because we humans all need to find enjoyment in something. Something that gives us a moment or two of happiness. Something that brings us fulfillment. After all, there are many things we do in our daily lives that we don't necessarily enjoy, but that we must do if we are to provide a decent life for ourselves and our loved ones. So we need a release of some kind. We need to have fun. And since September 11, 2001, two months before Bob-O's death, that need is emphasized now more than ever.

And so we ride. We ride to liberate ourselves from confining offices. And cars. And even from the sometimes dull everyday-ness of our homes.

We ride to feel free. From responsibilities. From problems. And sometimes, even from lovers.

But we ride mostly because it feels really good.

And as we ride, we feel the wind brush our faces. We hear the busy din of traffic, or bask in the tranquility of an open country road. And we sense that freedom we so longed for in our youth.

Riding down the road, we look around and appreciate the planet's landscape, the world around us. We sniff the air. We get in touch with our thoughts. Our lives. And when we ride life's highway, we can think more clearly, which helps us deal with the responsibilities, the problems, the lovers.

And some of us, too, use that time to talk to God.

As Bob-O's six pall bearers stand next to their bikes, at the head of the funeral procession for this goodbye ride, his grieving father approaches them and says, "I'm not going to tell you all not to ride. You boys just continue on. And don't forget when you pass my house, make sure you give it an extra rev," he says, demonstrating with a turned wrist.

This is a man who understands.

And so do his son's friends who vow to continue those Two-Wheel Tuesdays. They know Bob wouldn't have it any other way.

We all know, too, that the next time we get together to ride, Bob will be there with us. He'll be there as the sun beats down on our gleaming Harleys. He'll be there in the landscape as we take to the open country roads, and as the wind brushes our faces.

He'll be there each time we ride in the wind, heading toward another adventure.

Just as sure as life itself.

5. Day Jobs

Dialing for Dollars

Orange County, California. November 1973. Way before "The O C."

*I'*m seated in a metal chair in a freshly painted, sparsely furnished, monochrome office. There are two housewifely women to my left, one Jezebel type chick to my right. We sit in front of black telephones, two feet apart from one another at a long metal table (like the cafeteria tables in junior high) that stretches from one wall to the next. Each of us is in various stages of twirling numbers as we read from the long sheets in front of us. We are dialing for dollars. And the incessant gyratory humming from the rotary phones is getting on my nerves.

"Hello there!" I say into my receiver, sounding like Goldie Hawn on speed. "My name is Sherry," I stop a minute to clear my shaky voice, "*and* if *you* can answer this one question, *you* can be on your way to a wonderful Lake Tahoe vacation! *And* even if you get it *wrong*, you're *still* a winner as we'll drop off a package of valuable coupons redeemable at area restaurants, hotels, and casinos right to your door! *Just* for answering the question—right *or* wrong! You can't lose!"

I want to throw up. I'm trying hard to sound cheery but the knot in my gut is unraveling up my esophagus like a tape worm, where it's lodged in my throat and I have to keep swallowing in-between pitches to force out what I have to say— with a smile.

I've never hated anything more in all my nineteen years. When Pam and I decided to move to sunny California, we envisioned lying on the beach on our days off from working at some beauty shop, then hang out at night with our new Orange County friends, whom we'd met three months earlier on vacation. In the six weeks we've been here, I've lost ten pounds (a good thing), have no money (bad thing), and the guys I've met all want just one thing—and it's not to take me shopping. I can't help feeling disillusioned. The Beach Boys always made it sound so cool.

The potential Tahoe winner is now screaming at me, her voice shrill and none too happy.

"How'd you get this number? This is _precisely_ why I have an unlisted number!" She then speaks as if I'm too slow to quite understand. "I . . . want . . . to . . . know . . . how . . . you got . . . my NUMBER?!"

My gut just tied a new knot.

"Well, ma'am," I say, my voice shakier than before. "I had no way of knowing that. You see, our list is comprised of all the numbers in the area code. We simply dial down the list."

"Well, you better scratch this number off your fucking list! Or I'll be reporting you to the phone company!"

The slamming of the receiver emphasized her point, right down to the blaring exclamations. I'm beginning to wonder if this nightmarish job will pay me back with permanent hearing loss. Sometimes I can anticipate the piercing slam of the receiver in time to pull it quickly from my ear before the predicted deafening thump. Other times, I'm in the middle of my rehearsed statement thinking I'm doing an admirable job and so the sudden bang takes me by surprise. Ouch.

I get hung up on a lot. Loudly and fervently. Sometimes, like today, the earsplitting slams come in succession. That's a lot of rejection considering that for five days a week—3 to 9 p.m.— I'm supposed to make close to two hundred calls a day. This is only day four, and I've yet to make a sale.

"Sherry, come in here," Mr. Atwell, the company president, calls out gruffly from his office door. He looks like Robert Conrad, from that '50s show, _Wild, Wild, West._ Though now, the muscular actor is best known for the Eveready commercial, in which he wears a tight white T-shirt and has a battery balancing on his broad left shoulder. He stares at you through the camera with a menacing tough-guy glare and says, "Go ahead, I dare ya" (to knock off the battery). The bit has become fodder for comedians, even Johnny Carson recently parodied it on the Tonight show. Mr. Atwell gets ribbed about it all the time. He acts like he doesn't like the comparison, but I think he secretly does. After all, Robert Conrad is quite good looking.

My new boss looks impatient as his slick Brylcreemed head pops out the open door. He's wearing a scowl, so I rustle up my papers into a neat pile feeling the other girls eyes shift to me, then back to each other. I feel their smirk as they keep dialing.

I enter the office, and he shuts the door behind me.

"Sit down," he says, motioning to the hardback wooden chair facing his mahogany desk. I sit. He walks over to his cushy leather chair on wheels. This is where I nervously sat for my interview a week ago answering the ad that lied, "High commission, easy sales! If you can talk on the phone, you can do this job! No Experience Necessary!" The "No Experience!" part had sold me, since after perusing a week's worth of want ads, I determined I sorely lacked much employable experience. Even after four years at a prestigious private all-girls' high school. Guess it would've helped if I'd paid attention.

My goal is to earn an extra fifty dollars to take my California Cosmetology test so I can at least do something I'm capable of. Until then, this seemed my only alternative. Pam and I had both interviewed for the "sales position," but her voice, Mr. Atwell said, was too soft for the job. Mine was "strong and clear."

"We never use our real names on the phones," he added, as if he actually participated in the phone work. He then welcomed me to Atwell & Associates, and added, "And because I think you'll do a bang-up job, I'll give you my personal favorite name. From now on, you'll be Sherry. I'm confident you'll do well here."

Turns out, upon further review, the man is a better businessman than a psychic.

"So what's going on with you, Sherry?" He's smiling kindly at me now and I had to wonder if he did that with all the girls he planned to fire.

"I don't know," I mumble, my voice quivering once again. "I'm doing everything you told me. People are so mean."

This wasn't the first time I was close to tears during this excruciating week. I try not taking it personally when people scream at me and slam the phone in my ear. But it sure was hard not to. And personally, I could hardly blame them. I almost made a sale a few times but the catch was, if they got the question right (or wrong, as a "consolation prize") they "can buy the coupon package for only $14.95." Once I relayed that bit of info, the screaming commenced.

"Are you fuckin' kiddin' me?" came first. Followed by "What the hell kinda prize is that if I have to pay for it?"

Then the inevitable phone slam. Though the polite ones murmured goodbye first. I rarely got to explain that the charge was "merely for tax and delivery."

"Let's play Tic-Tac-Toe," Mr. Atwell now says, pulling out a pad of paper and handing me a pencil. Soooo . . . we play a stupid child's game before he boots me out the door? My face must have revealed my confusion. He laughed.

"It'll help get your mind off it. Then you can go back and kick ass."

"Uh . . . well . . . okay, Mr. Atwell."

"Call me Ken."

It became our routine. At least once each day, Ken would call me into his office, using the same angry tone. "So the others don't know what's going on," he'd say winking. We'd then mark X's and O's for ten minutes or so, then he'd send me back to the table. His theory never made me a good telephone solicitor (or even an adept one) but I did manage a few times to beat him at his own game.

Despite my lack of sales production, I soon became the boss's favorite. He once told me it was because "I could trust you with a thousand dollars of my money," which was an incredible compliment considering the source. Tight-fisted Kenneth Atwell came to L.A. from Detroit with full intentions on becoming rich. He'd tried a dozen creative ways to achieve this, and a few actually came through. His most successful venture so far was an invention he'd come up with for smokers. A little filtering device you place on the end of the cigarette that supposedly catches the tar and nicotine before it invades the body and is "available only through mail order." I guess that made it seem like the package was coming from some huge warehouse, rather than a small rented office in Westminster, California. Whatever, it was working. He and his wife were now financially well off (even hints at millionaire status, though, as I come to know Mr. Atwell, er, Ken, this may be a slight exaggeration). They live in a large house in Riverside, and he drives a brand new 1974 black Eldorado.

Yet, although he isn't exactly always forthright in his business dealings, he seems to appreciate integrity in another person. And despite this Midwest Catholic girl's minimal employable skills, she does have integrity. Though she's quickly discovering—every day she has to scrape up bus fare—that this admirable trait doesn't pay the bills.

But being the boss's favorite does come in handy when, after several months of dire sales at this particular phone soliciting venture, Ken decides to change course, and gets rid of all his "sales girls." Except for me. Though perhaps loyalty has less to do with that, and more to do with the fact he's taking pity on me. Or even more so, like every male in California it seems, he aims to get lucky, since I'd be ever so grateful.

And the thing is, I am grateful he's kept me. I haven't been eating much, but I do need to eat. Ken gives me all kinds of odd jobs around the office just to keep me employed. His pay is pitiful, but I've applied at other places and no one seems to want me. Even my application at McDonalds apparently was tossed in the trash—further adding to my basement self-esteem.

So I stay. For the next six months, I endure the flirty comments that Atwell throws in from time to time that indeed borders on sexual harassment (that is, had I known about it in the 1970s). And yet, he and I do maintain a good—and platonic— friendship. We still play a quick game of Tic-Tac-Toe, and he enjoys telling me about this little business ventures, and how he golfs with Alice Cooper.

After seven months of barely surviving financially and otherwise, I tell him I'm going back home. He tries to talk me out of it, even quoting Thomas Wolfe with "you can't go home again."

But I can. And I do.
And I return a wiser girl.

There are a lot of mean jokes, and emails, these days about harassing, incessant telephone solicitors. Even detailed instructions on how to harass *them*. And in a way, I understand. While I was a shy and insecure nineteen-year-old at the time I had that horrible job, many who phone today are wholly irritating and relentlessly rude human beings who won't take no for an answer. But I always try and keep in mind that they, like I was, are only trying to make a living, and not even a decent one at that.

By the time I made my way back home in 1974, I had developed a new appreciation for the working-class woman. And especially, telephone solicitors. Who began calling me soon as I moved into my new apartment.

"Hello, ma'am," the young voice always greets. "My name is Cindy, and I have a great offer for you!"

I'd listen politely for a few minutes before interrupting. "Uh, Cindy, is it?"

Her banter in full sales mode, I'd be forced to crank up the volume.

"Hey, you . . . heeeelllloooo, can you stop the spiel for a moment?" I'd yell, raising my voice an octave or two. "Will ya listen up? Please don't make me slam the phone in your ear." That always stopped them short.

I could picture it all in my mind's eye. The befuddled young girl looking up from her prepared form, giving a quick glance around to make sure no one notice her veer off from her handout, or that her boss—probably a good-looking fellow— would poke his head out his office door . . .

"Excuse me?" she'd whisper in a confused voice. These girls weren't used to actually having a conversation with their phone customers.

"Look, I have some advice for you, Cindy. If that's truly your real name. I know where you're coming from. I've been there. And the job sucks. I know you're just trying to make a living. But how long can you go on with this nightmare job? People yelling at you. Swearing at you. Slamming the phone in your ear, day . . . after . . . day . . . after . . . day?"

I'd then pause to let it sink in. "Listen, I know. And let me tell you something. This will wear down your self-esteem, I tell you. You deserve better. People are so cruel, they don't see a person behind that receiver. Just a voice who always calls at the wrong time. Right? And God help you if you dial an unlisted number! Now that's a slam/dunk guarantee for abuse. I mean, even the old men in McDonald's would treat you better.

"So ask yourself, *Cindy*, if you only had one more year to live—and who's to say you don't—what do you really want out of your life? Is *this* it?"

I would then hear the mental wheels cranking through the phone lines.

"That's right, give yourself a chance. Go on out there and find your true purpose in life. Find a way out of there!"

Cindy wasn't the only frustrated solicitor who thanked me before asking me, just one more time, if I was *sure* I didn't want to take advantage of their great offer?

I like to think I made a difference in Cindy's future, and perhaps a few others along the way. If just one of those girls went on to complete her nursing degree, or graduated from business school, or finally got her beauty license, then I have done my job.

It wasn't even all that hard. And I never got hung up on. Not even once.

Suffering for My Art

She's slinking off the barstool in slow motion, helped by gravity and a steady round of Pabst Blue Ribbon Beer and Kami Kazi shots. A regular here at Sugar's Last Stand Saloon, she faintly resembles Ali MacGraw from her *Love Story* days, except this one's stringy brown hair frames hollow cheeks and is in a perpetual state of bed head. I'm sure she's in her mid-thirties, though tonight she looks like she's earned her AARP card. Her frail, worn body—clad in ripped, faded blue jeans and loose-fitting halter-top—is just about to where her knees hit the ground when her brawny boy-toy grabs her slender arms and hoists her back up, just in the nick of time.

"I think you better take her home," I tell him—nicely and with a pleading look— as I gently retrieve the half-empty beer can.

"I think you should mind your own fuckin' business!" the big guy growls.

So much for diplomacy. I'm just about to tell this *dude* that, in fact, it *was* my business when I am struck by a new sight before me.

I've heard the expression "eyes rolling back in the head," but never actually witnessed this amazing phenomenon. So I'm ill-prepared when I see it happening right there in front of me. Miz Kami Kazi is upright now and leaning back against the tattered barstool, long, limp arms hanging down like rag dolls. Her head is to the side, resting on her right shoulder. Her mouth is open (wide enough to surely catch one of those fruit flies swarming round her head after hovering over that shot glass), but her large green eyes (when I saw her sober once, they were her best feature) are looking up. Way up. The pupils rise to the top like a ping-pong ball in slow-motion. Now all I see, literally, are the whites of her eyes.

I am captivated. How does that happen, exactly? And will those eyeballs ever fall back into place so I can tell her that *It's Time To Go Home Now*? Obviously, young Fabio isn't budging, too engulfed in sucking down his Rolling Rock to catch his girlfriend's eyes rolling around like marbles.

I glance around the crowded bar for someone to verify this sight before me, in case *I'm* the one hallucinating. But two are shooting pool, and the others are alternately chatting, smoking, and drinking. Except for that one couple, there in the corner, who are too busy pushing their tongues down each other's throats.

What to do now? As one who serves the alcohol, I'm responsible for these idiots who swill down anything in front of them, then ask—no, demand—to "*gev mmeee another and make id goot.*" Ironically, it isn't the bikers who give me a hard time, it's the occasional outsider, the sloppy old drunk, or street-fighting man who, upon learning this is a "biker bar," heads straight here when feeling frisky, or looking for a rumble.

Or it's the alkies like the ones in front of me, out doing the pub crawl.

I sigh.

I'm not good at this. I'm not an in-charge kind of gal. I'm a wimp. I don't belong here. I only took this job because I thought it'd be *easy.* But there are some nights I feel as if I've earned a degree in behavioral science with the education I'm acquiring here just working for food.

Bartenders are supposed to refuse to serve inebriated customers ("It's the *law!*"). But no one tells you how to do it without getting into situations such as I now find myself. I can get away with mixing weak drinks once people clearly have had too much (they can never tell the difference), but you can't dilute shots and beers. And this is a shot-and-beer joint. Most times when I refuse to replenish them, they see reason, or at least their drinking buddies do. But there is always one or two who see me as their mother, or boss, who "can't tell me what to do." This forces me to pull out the big guns. And that would be the Matriarch of this Ponderosa, the Sugar of this Last Stand. She's not afraid to deny anyone, if it means the risk of getting cited. Me, I'm a chicken shit. Particularly when the customer's eyes, like Fabio here, are firing my direction, burning holes like lasers into my retinas.

Just as I'm about to summon Ma Barkely to help me kick this couple out, Fabio leans over the bar toward me. He smiles, nice like. Probably because he's finished his beer and his tab is overextended.

"Okay, I'm getting her outta here," he says, then pulls his date's limp arm over one shoulder, and they slink out the door.

He leaves no tip.

Of course.

Times were tough in 1980. America was in a recession, though no one in our political arena would admit it. When Ronald Reagan became president, he finally acknowledged what we already knew, and suggested we all "tighten our belts." Easy to say when your own belt is the size of California. Although this decade would later be remembered for its greed, it began with inflation, job losses, and record-breaking divorce rates. I was the poster girl for all three. I was divorced, flat broke, and had lost two jobs in a row that summer. But I'm getting ahead of myself . . .

Like many writers and artists, few hairdressers get rich through their creations. Although the '70s had brought new life to the hair business, thanks to Farrah Fawcett, Dorothy Hammel, and Bo Derek, whose stylish locks brought flocks of former hippie women back to the beauty shop. But then came conveyor-belt unisex shops offering haircuts for "just $4.99," forcing many good salons to actually lower their prices in order to compete. This was also before the media alerted the public that hairdressers deserve a decent tip. So most of us suffered in silence when the little old mink-clad ladies—after we strategically applied their blue rinse and meticulously set, combed, and lacquered up their hair so it stayed like cement a full two weeks—would slip us a quarter and say, "This is for you, honey," like they were handing us a twenty dollar bill.

Respect is hard to come by for a hairdresser. It's not like you need a college degree to "do hair." (Though many don't realize you must take chemistry, anatomy, electricity, and other not-so-easy fields of study in order to be licensed.) That popular logic proved its point the time I was wrapping blue and grey perm rods into a truck driver's hair (this was back when white guys wore "'Fros"—inspired by Link, the character in the TV hit, *Mod Squad*). He was checking out the other hairdressers when his eyes veered to the card with my picture on it, posted next to the mirror. He leaned in to read: *Ohio State Board of Cosmetology*.

"You need a license to do hair?" he asked, with bewildered expression. I wanted to answer, "Well, no, not really. That's just for looks, ya know. Actually, I woke up one day and experienced an epiphany. I sat up in bed and thought, "I got it! I think I'll go out there and cut people's hair for a living!"

What I actually said—with a smile—was, "Well, of course." This blunt response I figured should gain a little respect, or at least give the impression that his question was something a damned drop-out would ask.

I had given thought to changing careers before, but all I knew how to do fell under the umbrella of "the arts," which often translates to low income and near-poverty level living. I was still a "closet writer," taking courses here and there when funds allowed.

The best money-making opportunities came by way of business and retail—selling people just about anything. (As would be confirmed by the makers of "The Amazing Flowbee," that handy little haircutting gadget that, in conjunction with the recession, shaved off even more income from professional stylists. Though many cheaters returned when their illicit relationship with Flowbee turned ugly, and they'd come scurrying back to the experts for help.)

Suddenly, there were get-rich-quick opportunities everywhere for those who could convince people that anyone— their mother, sister, aunt, cousin, friend, neighbor or local hobo— can "do hair." After all, how hard is it to cut someone's, or even your own, hair? Or "dye" it? Or perm it into "lovely locks with no frizz!" The how-to instructions were right there on the box! The TV infomercials (the most popular being the "Fool-proof Frosting Kits for just $3.99") told you all about the "amazing ways you can get salon results right in your own home - *and* for *half* the price of expensive beauty shops!" Any idiot can do it. Or so was the premise.

The hair clients that did stick with us came less often,

tipped less money—if at all—and complained more ("$1 more for conditioner? Let's skip it then."). Financial reality soon forced me to realize I needed a second job. Although I had no prior experience, I became a waitress. A job that would give me yet another experience. One I wasn't anticipating.

Two months into the job, I got fired. It wasn't that I was a terrible waitress (which I was), or that I didn't follow directions (which I tried), but I was fired for not coming to work one Saturday night. Now let it be said, a month earlier, I had requested that night off to attend a wedding of a good friend. Yet the manager (one of those control freaks who see their title as a license to be a mean person) turned around and scheduled me anyway. I believe he did it because I *was* a terrible waitress, and he knew I couldn't come in. And so, I went in that Sunday for my regular shift and he told me my services were no longer needed . . .

No matter what the circumstances are in a firing situation, when you are dismissed from a job, any job, it attacks your psyche in a horrible way. Even if you were planning to leave in a few weeks, as I had, when someone says they don't want your services anymore—to get your things and get the hell out—you feel like a worthless piece of crap. In the eight years of being on my own, I had prided myself in being able to make my own living, no matter how meagerly. And now, I was back on the streets with my meager hairdressing job, couldn't meet my monthly rent, and was forced to move in with my grandmother for food, shelter, and sympathy.

It was June of 1980 and I'd been juggling college courses and fulltime work for months. With fall tuition coming up, I knew I needed to work in a busier salon. So I went where the money was. Or so I thought. I chose a nice salon in an upper-class neighborhood twenty miles away, where I could work as a hairdresser by day, and bartender by night. This particular salon required everyone to start work at 8 a.m., and 7 a.m. on Saturdays. Not favored hours for bartenders. Taverns stay open till 2:30 a.m., and by the time you kick out the drunks and restock the beer, you're lucky to be home by 3:30. Still, I managed to rise each day at dawn, and do what I had to do. By the end of summer, I was looking like something akin to what a tomcat would drag in.

While there were times I questioned my sanity for working at the bar (like those Kami Kazi nights), I felt less affection for this uppity hair salon. I didn't like most of my coworkers—"career stylists" who saw themselves as redeemers of the fashion world—who had no other outside interests. This gave me little to offer by way of backroom conversations. I never wanted to quit a job more, but I hated the thought of starting over at yet another salon. So every day I put on my big-girl panties, sucked it up, and walked in with a smile.

Meanwhile, word-of-mouth gossip about me had begun spreading through the whispered, smoky, backroom beauty shop channels. I hadn't told anyone about my second job, figuring it wasn't their business. As long as I did what was expected of me, that revelation was hardly necessary. Besides, telling them that I was moonlighting as a barmaid in a biker bar, might give the wrong impression.

But unknown to me, the husband of one of the hairdresser's drove past the bar each night on his way home from his second-shift job and would see my car in the parking lot nearly every night. Rumors began sparking like stray blue hair in a light socket. Although I never missed a day's work, and was always on time no matter what ungodly hour they wanted me there, my reputation as a nonstop party girl—confirmed by my hellish appearance in the mornings—convinced them all that I wasn't right for their sheer image.

"I'd like to talk to you, Deanna (my boss refused to call me Dee, while I refused to call him Richard)," Dick said, summoning me to his office with his nicotine-stained finger.

Of course, we all know what that means. Anytime someone—your mother, boss, or significant other—wants to "talk," you know it's not because they want to tell you how wonderful you are. He didn't have to go through the spiel: "It's not working out. Please don't take it personally (*!!*), I wish you *all the best*." But of course Dick did, in that very sequence.

Despite the fact I hated working there, I was flabbergasted. And hurt. And angry. If only he knew what I'd gone through, struggling to get to work on time. Every. Single. Blasted. Day. All summer long. I'd always done a good job, and never had a complaint about me. All that didn't seem to matter.

Why didn't they like me? I'd tried being friendly *and* nice. And now, just three months after that waitress job, I'd been "let go" again. I couldn't imagine what I'd done to deserve this tremendous streak of bad luck, and when I asked God why, He wasn't talking. I suppose He, too, had let me go. After all, I was a habitual no-show in church.

I wouldn't find out the true reason for my firing until weeks later, when a friend-of-a-friend-who-had-a-friend-who-worked-there revealed that they had thought I was a bar fly. *Are you kidding me?* Here, I'd worked my ass off for months so I could continue to go to school and become a writer (even knowing *that* wouldn't exactly make me rich), and this was my great reward.

But every disaster offers its own life lessons. This is what I learned from my latest: That there is always another side to every story. That sometimes a set of circumstances looks like one thing, when the truth is something else entirely different.

And that when someone says, "Don't take it personally," you are bound to take it personally. Because it is. You are personally deemed a loser. When they make it clear they don't want you anymore, you're right back on the school playground, the last one picked for the game. You are the unwanted morsel of candy—bit into, spat out, and left abandoned among the empty crumpled wrappers in the 16-oz. box of chocolates. You are the wad of repugnant chewed-up Juicy Fruit stuck underneath the school desk, or church pew. You are the unsolicited piece of junk mail that is so unwelcome people angrily rip you up microscopic pieces before tossing you in the garbage, then complete the act by dumping stale coffee grounds on top of you like a ceremonial burial.

You are, indeed, a worthless piece of crap.

No matter how much you ache to leave a job, or a marriage, you want to be the one who leaves. Not the one who is left.

"What am I going to do, school's starting up again, how am I gonna pay for it?" I asked my friend Laura, who always seemed to have an answer to many a life query. I was still working at Sugars, a blessing in disguise. This being a stifling Monday night in August, I wasn't surprised we were the only ones in the joint. Even the dead animal heads above me looked tired, hot, and bored. It was just past 8 p.m., and I was already drowning my sorrows with swigs from Laura's Bud Light (since I wasn't supposed to be drinking on the job).

"Don't you know you're now eligible for unemployment?

After all, you weren't fired—they let you go."

"Really?" My hopes suddenly rising. "Wow, that'd be great, then I could sign up for more classes, finish school earlier, and . . ."

My dreams were disrupted by the loud swinging of the squeaky front door. A rough-looking, cowboy-hatted disheveled man sauntered over to the bar like John Wayne's evil twin.

"Hey, you! Barmaid. Gimme a shot of Jack."

The drunk was by no means a regular. He was a lot older, and looked a lot meaner, as I glanced over at him from the other side of the bar. I hedged, thinking how to handle this one.

"Hey Bitch, didn't ch'ya hear me?"

"What do I do?" I whispered to Laura, fear gripping my stomach. "I don't wanna serve him, but I sure don't wanna piss him off."

"You better serve him," she said, a bit too blasé for my comfort. "Then go in the back and call Sugar."

Sugar lived next door, but that didn't guarantee she was home. I grabbed Jack Daniels, walked over to the ruffled cowboy, and poured the shot. The man stared at me with glazed eyes, which I tried avoiding.

"That'll be seventy-five cents," I murmured.

"Put it on my tab," he spat, daring me to dispute him.

"Uh, sure," I said, nervously walking away while motioning Laura as I headed to the kitchen door. She nodded slightly, ever the picture of cool and calm.

When I returned from leaving Sugar the "Help!" message, Cowboy was gone.

"Oh good, he left?" I asked Laura.

"No, he went to the bathroom."

When my buddy returned, he demanded another shot, slapped it back, then stumbled toward the exit. I didn't dare ask him to pay up before he checked out.

As he made his big way out the door, I ran behind to shut and lock it, but just as I gripped the knob, a knife whizzed past me, no less than two inches from my face. I then heard the squeal of tires that emphasized his departure, and I gasped knowing I had just escaped getting an unexpected face lift. Apparently Cowboy had managed to sneak behind the bar where Laura couldn't see him, and grabbed the butcher knife I kept behind the bar to cut sandwiches. Guess he decided to give it back before he sped off.

How nice of him.

You would think, after that little drama, I would've happily settled for an unemployment check and be done with serving people liquor. But no. I still needed the money. I stayed in time to add yet another dramatic installment to the continuing saga of *Cocktail Waitress for Hire*.

Tonight's episode is called, "Biker Saves Whimpering Barmaid Who's Working Nights to Better Herself, But Also Secretly Hopes to Meet the Man of Her Dreams Who Is Taking His Good Ole' Damn Time Makin' An Appearance." Brought to you by Captain Morgan and Budweiser, the King of Beers.

Our next exciting episode begins with said barmaid running speedily round and round the horseshoe bar pouring, smiling, and apologizing for not being fast enough.

"Heeeey, I need anutheerrr beer . . . hey, yooouuu . . . *BARMAID* . . . are you ffff-uuuuckin' deaf?"

I'd been on the job four months by then and was skilled at the smile-and-nod program, but this night I feel like an amateur. Gary, a regular here, is celebrating his 30th birthday, and everyone who's known him since grade school, it seems, is here to buy "whatever the birthday boy wants." The bar is knee-deep with bikers and strangers alike. And I'm the only one here to serve the drinks.

The jukebox is cranked up high as it'll go, upon request, and everyone's screaming my variety of handles over Hank Williams Jr.'s "Whiskey Bent and Hell Bound." Tonight I answer to "Hey You," "Heeeey, Barmaid," and "Yo, Sweetheart."

"Heeeey Barmaid," the old drunk yells as I whiz past him round the bar, "Giiimme a beer."

"Hold on a minute," I say (with a smile). But just then, I hear a crash. Apparently the old man didn't feel like holdin' on, and has smashed his bottle on the bartop. Glass shards and beer bubbles begin to spill into my stainless steel tub of dish soap. I halt in mid-run and hand him a bar rag, "Here ya go, I'll be right with you." But he grabs my arm before I can escape. "Heeey Biiiiitch, I'm not the cleaning woman, that's your job. Clean up this mess and giiimme a damn beer." The good, Catholic girl does as she's told and runs to the other side to retrieve Drunk 'n' Mean Man's beer. Hard as I try to suppress it, I start to cry.

That's when Bondo comes around the bar and puts his arm around me. "That guy givin' you trouble?" he asks with a hug. I can't speak because I'm sobbing. My tears are enough to give my biker friend the go-ahead. I stand there safely on the other side and watch Bondo walk over to the man, say something to him with a calm, straight face, and somehow performs magic. When I go back and set down his beer, Drunk 'n' Mean apologizes and tips me a five.

I now know that I've just become an honorary member at this Sugar's Last Stand Saloon. That this sweet band of biker gypsies will protect me as one of their own. My tears are replaced by a broad grin.

You know, some nights, suffering for your art really isn't all that bad.

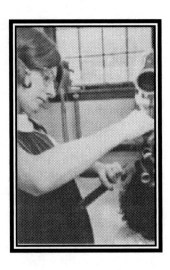

Memoirs of a Seasoned Hairdresser

ℐ'm sitting in the guidance counselor's office, my first time here as a total innocent. This is the meeting where we discuss my career options. Mrs. Bowman, with the ash brown, grey-streaked wavy hair and those horrid, round, black-framed glasses hanging from the bridge of her nose, is asking me what I want to do with my life. *How the hell should I know, I'm in eighth grade*, I think to myself. I do know I don't want to be a thief, a career I've discovered is not my forte. And my grades confirm I'm not meant to be a rocket scientist, either. Furthermore, I know I won't be following in my mother's footsteps. She's a bookkeeper at a bank. I'm presently flunking general math.

In fact, I haven't given much thought to my future at all. It seems so far away. I'm a fourteen-year-old juvenile delinquent (according to school authorities) who lives for today and whose main concern is if the boy I like—which changes on a weekly basis—really, really, likes me. Now this stern woman staring at me with eyes hovering over lined-trifocals, is asking me this huge question that seem to justify an equally huge answer. I realize I should say something profound like, "I'm going to join the Peace Corps," or "I'm planning on attending Harvard and eventually become the first woman President of the United States." Some shit like that.

Looking down at the floor for an appropriate answer, I spot an ant making away with a crumb twice its size and I'm reminded to eliminate "cleaning woman" as my career choice. Something, apparently, old lady Bowman and I have in common.

"Well?" she says, still gazing at me for an answer. I take my eyes off the getaway insect and focus on this Plain Jane's 1950's hairdo (it's now 1968). I envision how much better, and younger, she'd look if she'd only do something with that hunk of grey in front, and get a hold of a jar of Dippity Doo and plaster down that piece right there, stickin' up on the top of her head.

"I guess I'll be a beautician," I murmur.

Not exactly brimming with passion over my sudden decision, I'm nonetheless satisfied with it. At least styling hair is creative, and I like being creative. Plus, recalling the hours I spent when I was nine with my "Beauty Shop Betty" doll, equipped with pink curlers, matching pink hairnet, silver clips, and a "real working hooded hairdryer," I feel I've already had some hands-on experience.

Besides, I figure telling her about my frequent daydreams of being a writer would only cause her eyes to roll, given my current English grade. Truth be told, I know this woman doesn't give a rat's cowlick what my future plans are. She's already decided I'm not going to amount to anything, what with my past visits to her office. I can tell she has me tagged as one of those girls who'll surely get knocked up in high school and spend the rest of her life nursing babies at the kitchen table, puffin' on a Virginia Slim while her beer-bellied husband on welfare with the chili-stained undershirt belches in front of the TV set. I may not know how my life will turn out, but no way in hell I'm ending up like that.

My beautician response must have met this guidance counselor's expectations.

"Good," she says, happy to have something to write in her manila folder so she could get on to more promising students.

Back in the 1960s, being a beautician was a respectable enough career, but it did have a severe image problem. Mention "I'm a beautician" and the picture was set in the mind. A woman with a teased-up pompadour, bleached to a platinum shade of hussy, wearing a dye-stained smock, and smackin' pink Bubble Yum between queries of, "So what'll it be today (smack, smack) flip or pageboy?" or "How high do'ya want your Beehive?" or "Why don't we do a French Twist this time?" or "Ok, girls, who took my rattail comb?" Smack, Smack.

Still, it was the only thing I could think of at the time. I was immediately encouraged by all who now saw a glimmer of hope in my future. Bowman signed me right up for the 1970 high school's cosmetology department. And Mom seemed delighted with my choice.

"Now, that's a career you can always fall back on!" she'd say. As if, should I ever decide to try a more challenging field, I could at any time return to yanking strands of hair out of a plastic cap while inhaling vast amounts of vaporous chemicals for a living. That is, if I didn't end up in jail for failing to listen to my mother for the umpteenth time.

And so, I was a student "beautician" in the '60s, a "beautician/hairdresser" in the '70s, a "hair design stylist" in the '80s, a "beautician technician" (as Truvy in *Steel Magnolias* likes to call it) in the '90s, and finally, a "seasoned stylist" in the millennium. The titles changed nearly as often as the hairdos. And turns out, Mom was right. Thirty years and a zillion trendsetting styles later, it has indeed been something I've always fallen back on. And still enjoy, albeit part time. This career of enhancing women's beauty has also provided me with many writing prompts over the years. After all, there's no lack of available story material when one gets intimate with a person's lifeless locks.

What neither my mother nor I realized as I studied cosmetology, was that I'd get an equally worthy education about life, human nature, and how to write great dialogue.

Indeed, dressing people's hair and ego is a great platform for a writer. So long as you change the names, and hairstyles, to protect the craftily coiffed . . . .

My first job as a licensed beautician is at Higbee's department store on Public Square, because working in downtown Cleveland seems exciting, and sounds impressive. I arrive that first day with hair neatly combed in a high ponytail—the ends smoothly tucked under, cupped in a wide bun atop my head. I wear the required uniform—a rayon smock the color of Tang, white stretch polyester pants, and nurses shoes (to keep us "comfortable" after eight-to-ten hours standing in one place)—and a forced smile. I'm eighteen years old and scared to death that I'll do something horribly wrong and get fired on the spot. As I sit by the dryers, waiting for the manager to get me started at my station, two girls are standing in front of me. The tall blonde with Cleopatra eye liner is telling the heavy-set brunette with exaggerated flip, about the old lady in the waiting room.

"She's got a fuckin' *shoebox* full of blue hair that looks like cotton candy, telling Cantwell (the manager) that that's how much hair fell out after I gave her a perm last week! I *knew* that woman was trouble soon as she walked in! She probably had a psychiatric meltdown, and pulled it all out herself. The bitch."

I am dead meat, I think to myself.

This was the beginning of what would become my long hairdressing career. . . .

Your first job always stays with you. And working in a metropolitan city burrows itself into your soul. I can still recall the acrid scent of the busses' exhaust and hear their deep-throttled roar as they'd plow through the bustling city streets. I can still see them at the corner bus stops, picking up and dropping off downtown workers who'd throw coins into the slots. Clink. Clink. And I can still see the homeless men in their long, ragged, stained trench coats leaning against the fancily dressed store windows, or sitting cross-legged on the cement, watching with glazed eyes, as life passes them by, one stranger at a time. The writer in me still wonders what diverse circumstances separates those who live a privileged life with a paying job, home, family and friends, from those whose destitute existence is as crude and cemented as the lonely city sidewalks.

I remember standing at the Euclid Avenue street corner, squeezed between hordes of stressed-out downtown workers, waiting impatiently for the "walk" sign to make it in time for a seat at the luncheon counter. Every day, five days a week—be it frigid whip of winter or blazing scorch of summer—we all passed by these less-fortunates. One of them was particularly infamous. The scrappy old black man who persisted with the same ominous, reprimanding chant.

"God knows what you're doing! Repent now!" the rumpled vagrant yelled in outrage. His big, round black olive eyes would fix on you, and stare into your sinful face as his tootsie-roll index finger crookedly pointed your direction. No matter how many times this happened and you'd tell yourself, "he's just a crazy man," his look of absolute belief and firm accusations got you thinking twice about your actions. And wouldn't it be just like God to hide behind the guise of a demented homeless man to get His message across.

"God knows what you did last night!" was this man's specific mantra. Perhaps because he knew he'd be right on the money at least 50% of the time, his accusations often caused you to think that maybe he really *did* know what you did last night behind closed doors. Or in the back seat of a car. Whichever.

Those were my observations from the city streets. But the real training came from inside.

My cosmetology teacher, Miss Jordan, had taught us well. She emphasized the tipping benefits of being a professional, how to give a good head massage, and carve in the perfect finger wave. She also tried to prepare us for the real world. She'd emphasize the three topics you were never to discuss with clients: politics, money, or sex. She failed to mention, however (or perhaps I hadn't paid attention, a distinct possibility), how to handle it when the client herself brought them up. And they always do. In the real world, those are the things people most want to talk about. Therefore, Miss Jordan would've been wholly disappointed by my behavior my second day as a professional beautician.

I was concentrating on performing the perfect roller set on this middle-aged legal secretary when she geared the conversation toward the inevitable.

"You must be excited to be eighteen and now allowed to vote," the sly little woman said into the mirror, already marking me as easy prey. This was the first year eighteen year olds could vote, thus a perfect opportunity for her to defend her man.

"So which candidate are you going to vote for?" her inquiring mind wanted to know.

I quickly tried retrieving any kernel of advice Miss Jordan may have given on the politics issue, but was quickly sidetracked by the memory of my first introduction to Richard M. Nixon. It was November 1960. Our first-grade teacher had posted photos of the presidential candidates on the wall, and decided to conduct her own little poll by having us stand in either the Nixon line, or the Kennedy line, based on who our parents were voting for. I recalled hearing their names on TV and from my family, but now gazing at the men's pictures, I realized for the first time that they were not cartoon characters, as I'd previously thought. Then again, Nixon, with his long loopy face, shifty eyes, and hawk nose, wasn't all that far removed from that childlike concept. Next to the suave and kindly looking John F. Kennedy, this distrustful-looking Nixon didn't have a prayer. That image stayed with me.

So although something inside my brain shouted, "Don't say it!" my mouth was already open and the words streamed out the gate, heading straight for the huge red flag.

"Oh, I think McGovern will do a good job," I answered.

"WHAT?" the clearly Republican woman's half-jelled head jerked forward as if I'd just smacked her with my bristly Velcro roller. "You CAN'T be serious!"

She proceeded to tell me how naïve I was, enlightening me on Nixon's "vast experience and performance" and his "wonderful political record" (if it was so wonderful, why did he keep losing? was a question I didn't dare bring up).

From that moment on, I learned to concur with whatever a client said, and that peacemaking ability is one of the reasons why everyone loves their hairdresser. They not only listen, they vehemently agree with you. No matter what. For me, this was an early lesson well learned. And so, years later, when it came time for Mrs. Judy Jones (let's call her), to enter the salon in 1979, I was a wiser soul.

As everyone knows, hairdressers are like bartenders. People tell us stuff they'd never confide to their best friends or the person they're sleeping with. Most likely because those are the very people who are often the subject of their particular woes. Pillow talk has nothing over the sanctuary of the valued hairdresser. In addition, we offer a two-for-one kind of deal. We're a lot cheaper than psychiatrists, and the customer leaves the room with an improved coiffure.

People trust the person who dresses their hair and massages their head, despite the high-and-wide hairdos and variety of Miss Clairol hues we ourselves have adorned through the decades. They innately trust us with their dirty little secrets. Like we signed a contract or something. And yet, although nothing says we can't spread the word, most of us honor that sacred code of trust and ethics. We tell no one about Mrs. Hart's secret bank account that she's kept since marrying Mr. Hart. Or of recently divorced Meredith's healing scars behind her ears after her face has been stretched and snipped in her vain attempt to attract younger men. Nor disclose the name of little Sara's real father. Or speak to others about the aforementioned, mother-of-three, Mrs. Jones's infidelity.

We tell no one. Except other hairdressers, of course.

To be honest, though, I haven't had all that many shocking secrets revealed. Something I'm immensely grateful for. Knowing too much puts a lot of pressure on you. In my case, that pressure waltzed in the door upon Judy's—late—arrival, as she plopped down in my chair and requested pen and paper.

"I have to write my boyfriend and break up with him. I've had enough!" said the tall, bleached blonde with the sparkling, emerald cut, wedding ring. "If he thinks he's gonna see me only when it's convenient for *him,* well that man is *deeeaaaad* wrong!" Then, "Just trim up the sides a bit, honey, and blow it out smooth. You know, like how Susan Lucci's wearing hers now. You do watch *All My Children,* don't you?"

Her chilling emphasis on "deeeaaaad" was still echoing in my psyche, as I tried recalling the last full episode I'd watched of the soap opera. It was back in 1973 when the vindictive Erica Kane was still married to husband number one, Phil Brent, solely to keep him away from her rival, Tara Martin. Luckily, I had recently caught a snippet or two of the latest Erica adventure, and so, hoped for the best. With shaky hands, I reached for pen, paper and scissors. Once ink-deep into her Dear John letter, the hostile woman dashed off a three-pager, and by the time I reached for the blow dryer and round brush, she was signing "Love, Jude."

Between scribbling active verbs, descriptive adjectives, and several expletives, "Jude" revealed to me her torrid affair with her boss, who was also married, and the creep "had the nerve to always put *her* first!" This demure, silent hairdresser listened politely, and, as always, nodded in agreement at such audacity. After one good final spray, the now-happy hussy sauntered out the door in her Lucci-do and onto her melodramatic, clandestine life. After tipping me well.

Through the year I did Judy's hair, she'd complain about "the jerk" with each visit, write the occasional missive, then never seemed to actually break up with "the bastard." At one point she had me nearly convinced that the poor girl had no choice in the affair because her un-attentive husband (apparently there was a lot he wasn't paying attention to) was an even bigger bastard. That is, until I met the oblivious spouse. He arrived to pick his wife up at the salon—with their eight-year-old son in tow—while her car was being fixed. The man looked like a Ken doll, handsome, wearing jeans, neatly pressed button-downed shirt, and a clueless smile. I, having lots of clues, smiled back demurely upon introduction. As I shook his hand, I tried to mentally, willfully, intuitively, transfer my knowledge of his wife's extracurricular activity into his brain cells through my pumping palm, because I now felt sorry for him. And sorrier for their kids. It didn't work, of course, and because I left that shop soon after, I'll never know how it all transpired. Though I have a pretty good idea.

I moved on, year after year, hairdo after hairdo. I've survived The Beehive, The French Twist, The Flip, The Pageboy, The Bob, The Poodle Cut, The 'Fro, The Wedge, The Pixie (otherwise known as the Mia Farrow-gets-back-at-Frank Sinatra-by–cutting-off-all-her-hair Do), The Short Shag, The Long Shag, The Feathered Bang, The Lioness, and of course, the dearly beloved "Mullet." There were the styles named after the stars: The "Farrah Fawcett," "Dorothy Hammel," and The Great Gatsby Cut (otherwise known as the short, wavy, and sassy style of Daisy Buchanan (once again played by Mia Farrow) from *The Great Gatsby* film. I've spiked, and dyed, and carved initials into heads. I've molded strands of hair nearly every which way known to man. I've survived inhaling poisonous fumes brought on by formaldehyde tablets (now banned, because of its link to cancer), permanent wave and wig solutions, powdered bleach that dusts the air when poured into a bowl—cough cough—and ozone-killing aerosol hairsprays.

Through it all, I've worked with delightful girls and snotty girls and straight men and gay men and great bosses and not-so-great bosses. I've had good clients, nothing-to-say clients, and ones who've made me want to pull my own hair out. Yet now, in my third decade as a "seasoned stylist," I can honestly say that every experience, along with the good, the bad, and the what-was-I-thinking hairdos, has taught me many things about life and people, and, ultimately, reaffirmed my faith in human kind.

I've endured it all in the name of beauty. I am a survivor. Including that of the occasional difficult customer. Who Won't Go Anywhere Else. No matter how many times their hair "didn't hold" because you didn't use "small enough rollers." Or you didn't "tease it tight enough." Or that super-glue hairspray you used "just wasn't stiff enough." And yet no matter how wrong, or inept, you are at doing their hair, they stick with you. Despite your wanting, wishing, praying that they move on to another chair. Another hairdresser. Another life. But no. They want you. You begin to wonder if you have become their personal Pygmalion, and they only want to improve your life by showing you the way. She'll complain about something every damn time she walks in the salon, but insists that "No one can do my hair like you." Apparently.

So I've learned that, as a hairdresser, it's imperative you maintain a sense of humor, while humoring your clients. The day after the record-breaking 1986 Northeast Ohio earthquake, my favorite PA (a hairdresser term for Pain-in-the-Ass) client, "Sally," came in and proceeded to alert me to the biggest news item of the decade. As if the thunderous rumbling beneath my feet that day, coupled with the shaking walls that forced shelves of powdered bleach, Henna, and permanent wave solution to spit out their guts like a disgruntled Nixon-loving customer whose Final Net spray didn't turn out to be so final, had somehow escaped my notice.

"Yes, really. It's true," she proclaimed earnestly, in response to my simulated look of shock and awe. "*And*," she continued, "they say it was more than a 5 on the *rectal* scale!"

A hairdresser with less experience might've coughed up her Bubble Yum right then and there, whereupon the hocked-up pink goo would jettison from her mouth and into the dimwitted bleached blonde head, now held together with styling mouse, causing said customer to whip around and ask, "Don't you watch CNN?" Which may well have geared the conversation toward politics, money or sex. But no. By this time I, in fact, was a well-seasoned beautician/hairdresser/hair design stylist/beautician-technician/seasoned hairdresser.

I swallowed hard to force down the rapidly rising outburst, smiled stiffly and replied, "Really? Well, I certainly hope your hair stayed in for that one!"

She assured me that, yes, thanks to my expertise it had, in fact, stayed put very nicely. Then added, "But this time, could you make sure my roots are well covered 'til tint-time next week, and don't forget to conceal those healing scars behind my ears."

After all, only a hairdresser should know for sure.

Part Two

Love

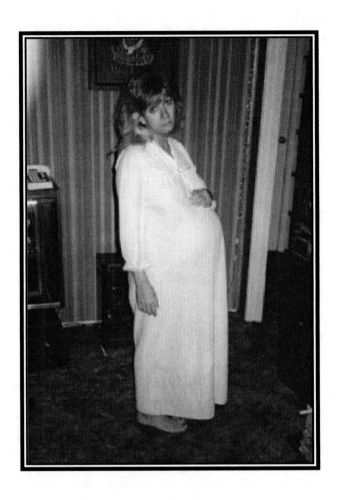

6. Adventures in Parenting

R is for Ruth – As in Babe

"*W*hat's her name?" my mother asks me on this beautiful Easter morning in 1987. An hour ago, I'd made her a grandmother for the first time, and relieved and giddy, I couldn't wait to call her with the news.

"Danielle, for Jeff's dad," I say. "And," pausing for effect, "Ruth is her middle name."

I don't hear what my mother says next, as I bask in the pride of this statement, knowing only she and I could totally understand its meaning.

"You need to get some rest now," the nurse tells me, coming into the recovery room with a pain pill. As planned, I'd received no medication, not even an epidural. I'd wanted to "go natural" although near the end I admit to screaming for "*something, anything you got*" to get me through those last few minutes of torture. But by then, it was too late. "No time for that now, honey," the older nurse had said firmly, "you're ten centimeters dilated. You're having this baby. *Now.*"

Danielle burst into the world, but in the process, I had pushed down so hard against the hard steel table, I cracked my tail bone. So I readily accept the small white pill sitting prettily in this nurse's furrowed palm.

"I gotta go, Mom," I say, "I'll see you at visiting hours."

I down the pill as Jeff and the nurse leave me alone with my thoughts, which basically consist of the knowledge that my life has just changed forever. From now on, every life occurrence prior to this joyous day would be referred to as "BC – "Before Children." And while there were times, particularly after my second miscarriage, that it seemed I'd never get to this place in my life, once in motion, it all happened fast. Even the labor, which culminated to a grand total of four hours. Other women, like my sister-in-law who labored for thirty-three hours, will really hate to hear that. But then, I felt I deserved this break after years of infertility, miscarriages, and heartbreak.

So now I was a real mother. But not of a son. Of a daughter. This was a surprise. While I was thrilled, and ever-so-grateful, to finally have this baby, I never envisioned myself with a daughter. In fact, it scared the hell out of me because I feared I'd repeat the same pattern that seemed to dominate in the women in my family. For generations, these mothers and daughters always had trouble understanding each other. Therefore, I didn't think I could ever connect with a daughter. Me raise a girl? I couldn't fathom it. Plus, my own mother always said boys were easier to raise (or perhaps she'd just been referring to me).

So, now, as I lie here holding this bundle of girl in my arms, I make a vow. "We're gonna break the cycle, honey," I tell her. I promise this child that I would be the mother *I* had always wanted: kind, affectionate, and understanding.

New parents are so naïve. . . .

By day three, when we're home alone and she's crying and I don't know what she wants, or how to make her *stop already!* I realize that promise is going to be harder in execution. If I can't even get her to stop fussing, how do I go about—day after day for the next eighteen years—ensuring that this innocent female child transforms into a self-assured grown woman with admirable qualities who actually likes her mother? How do I even begin to break the family cycle of problematic mother/daughter relationships?

God help me.

And the fact that I'd just given her a middle name I knew full well she was going to dislike every bit as much as I had, wasn't a good first step. After all, Ruth was such an old-fashioned name, and certainly not popular. Like Deanna. No one I knew had a name like that. Growing up, the name "Deanna Ruth" had only added to my insecurity and misery about being tagged uncool and different from everyone else. I gave little thought to the fact that

Ruth was my beloved grandmother's maiden name. One she still used even after she married. Gee Gee signed everything, Viola *Ruth* Jenkins. Being an independent-minded woman (one of the few common denominators among the females in this family), it was her way of holding onto to her identity at a time when married women were expected to relinquish their name immediately upon the nuptials.

But now, at thirty-three, I felt differently about the name. Gee Gee had been dead for five years, and I missed her terribly. I wanted to honor this woman who was more than just a grandmother to me, and who I knew would be absolutely crazy for this new child of mine. I also felt, somehow, if this baby I'd just given birth to carried her name, my little girl would also carry a part of my grandmother—and that lively free spirit—with her. Little did I know at the time, how true that would turn out to be.

And then, there was the case of legacy. Not just my grandmother's, but also our possible connection to a historic figure. I'd heard the Babe Ruth story all my life. Not the one everyone reads in history books. But our personal family ties to the great Bambino. As I got older, I came to appreciate, and be proud of, the significance of that famous Ruth name.

The story goes like this:

Cleveland Stadium, 1925. Gee Gee's brother, Cal, is sitting in the stands at the Indians vs. New York Yankees game waiting for the right moment to run down to the dugout and get the Home Run King's attention. By now, George Herman Ruth had been hitting balls out of every park for years and was an international celebrity. The Ruth family in Fostoria, Ohio, always wondered if the greatest slugger in baseball was related to them. Ruth wasn't a common last name, and published photographs indicated this man looked like "a Ruth," according to elder sources in Gee Gee's family. Right down to the round face and flat, wide nose. Newspaper reports confirmed that he acted like them, too. The spunk, the stubbornness, the restless rebellion. The hard part was finding out if it was so. Not much was known about this man, or his family background. Rumor had it that one day in 1902, Babe Ruth's father dropped off the "unruly" motherless seven-year-old at a Catholic boys' orphanage, where he remained through adolescence.

There was another trait of Babe's that was consistent with my grandmother's family (though in those days, hardly unusual).

Babe was a heavy drinker. Although the Matriarch of the Fostoria Ruth family was a teetotaler, her siblings and large brood of sixteen children, well made up for it. Alcohol flowed generously through the branches of this family tree. And so, in their view, this baseball wonder who shared their name must certainly be a sociable guy. And accessible. This is no doubt what drove Calvin Ruth to venture to the big city of Cleveland to meet the man he felt was a kindred spirit.

So Cal sat patiently on the green bench ready to seize his opportunity to prove The Babe was one of them. Finally, just after hitting a home run, George Ruth approached the dugout. Cal jumped up and raced down the steps before anyone could stop him. Separated by the wire fence, Cal, not much younger than thirty-year-old Babe, proceeded to call out to him.

"Hey, Babe!" he yelled. The other Ruth turned around to wave at just another exuberant fan, but before turning back around, the stranger said, "My name's Ruth, too, and I think we might be related."

Maybe it was mere curiosity, or perhaps the Babe noticed some vague family resemblance. Or perhaps it was nothing more than Cal's quick mention of getting "a few beers after the game" (wisely using the ball player's renowned weakness). Whatever the case, the great Sultan of Swat smiled, and told the spunky fellow the name of the hotel he was staying at, suggesting they meet up after the game. The two men who shared the same surname then stayed up all night sharing shots and beers while marking down the names, on hotel stationery, of family members each one could recall for any possible connection. Sometime around sunrise, it is told, they found a link.

The next day, Cal excitedly arrived home to tell his story, the proof in his pocket. The paper clearly showed that Babe's grandfather, and the grandfather of Cal and all his siblings, had been brothers. This was indeed a moment in history.

Cal never saw Babe after his storied encounter with him, but for years the man proudly kept that paper with him, showing it around to anyone who hinted at disbelief. "Got the proof right here in my pocket," he'd say, to those who doubted him. Cal's eagerness to prove the skeptics wrong ultimately became the family's downfall when the folded-up paper eventually became worn and somehow wound up lost in the maze of living.

But the story survived—alas with no concrete proof of its

validity—and was proudly passed down to each generation.

So it was indeed partly due to family obligation that I felt compelled to pass on this bit of legend in Gee Gee's lineage, with so few of her relatives left. But it wasn't the most important part. I'd given my daughter the name because I had learned a few things along my way to adulthood. That family names and tradition are an important part of who we are. And certain traditions are worth keeping. And honoring. I would inform this daughter of her legacy at an early age in hopes that she, unlike her mother, would appreciate the significance of the name and never complain about it. This, of course, did not exactly pan out. I'd later discover when this Ruth child was nine, that she'd been telling friends her middle name was Renee. I was then forced to pull out the big mother-guilt guns and refer her to the Bible, in which the name Ruth holds even more magnitude.

But that day in my hospital room on that bright holy morning, my mind was on my late grandmother. So I decided to hand down the very name I once considered so uncool, but now was so important. A name that also happens to carry with it a unique and interesting story about a baseball icon.

But it was *Viola Ruth*, not George Herman, who was the real hero in my eyes, and who I most wanted to honor. A woman who cooked and cleaned, sewed, shopped, and cared for her family. Who planted glorious flower gardens—even those Bleeding Hearts others say are stubbornly so hard to grow. And a woman who was as spirited as she was tender. As willful as she was loving.

When Danielle was twelve, my mother gave me a photograph of Gee Gee dated in the back, June 16, 1914. My grandmother, at age eleven, sits next to her school teacher, behind one of her many sisters, Vena Belle, and some classmates. Staring at the image of my young grandmother, I was shocked to see the image of my own daughter staring back at me. The little girl in the photo was the exact image of my first born child who bears the Ruth name. The resemblance was truly uncanny. And comforting.

But it wasn't until I began writing this piece eight years later, that I made another startling discovery. When I looked once again at that 1914 photo, my eyes focused on Vena Belle. Gee Gee's sister was sitting there in front, cross-legged, a big wide bow over her right eye, smirking at the camera. I was struck by what I saw, now for the first time. With photo in hand, I rushed to the library with all the anticipation of Cal Ruth, and pulled out some books on The Babe. And there it was. Confirmation. While there is no physical similarity between the Bambino and my grandmother, one look at Vena Belle with her pug, round face and wide, flat nose, no one could deny the family resemblance. Why hadn't I, nor my mother, notice that before? That photograph alone is all the proof we Ruth's need to verify that old family story.

In any case, it doesn't matter. While our connection to a historic icon is nice, it is the link I see between my daughter and a woman she's never met, that is the true legacy. For it turns out that I made the right decision that Easter morning two decades ago. Not merely by giving my daughter that family name, but by recognizing the need to break the cycle of complex mother/daughter relationships. Now don't get me wrong. My daughter and I most certainly have had our "moments." But we do understand each other. Even when it kills us.

My bundle of girl turned out to be just as expected for a Ruth. She is her great-grandmother's daughter. She shares Gee Gee's care-giving nature, and kindness of heart, as well as her name. And she is fiercely loyal to those she loves. But of course there's also that stubborn streak that has so often made me crazy. And still does.

Through the years of raising this Ruth, I recognize my grandmother in my daughter's expressions, appearing strongest when Danielle is at her most obstinate. She wears Gee Gee's face. Her determination. Her strength. Yet other times—when she smiles—she reveals her great-grandmother's warmth, and it seems, her wisdom.

It is those times—for a brief, cherished millisecond—I get to see my grandmother once again.

Fathers & Daughters

I'm standing on the sidelines watching this grown man frolic on the floor with our two little girls, who are giggling at his antics. I'm in awe that he can entertain them so easily.

"Daddy, Daddy, me next!" they scream in unison, fighting over him as he picks one up, then the other, and spins them around before dropping them, ever so carefully, back onto the floor.

It isn't fair, I think. On several levels. I'm the one with them all day. I feed them. I help them dress. I read to them. I take them to the park. The grocery store (where we have regular discussions on what's good for them). I take them to dance classes. The library. I make their breakfast. Their lunch. Let them watch *Sesame Street* and the *Ninja Turtles*.

But I also make them take naps. I make them have Time Out. Clean their rooms. I tell them why they need to share, and that they had better listen to me—if they know what's good for them. Danielle is five. Tiffany is two. They are beautiful little girls. They are sweet and loving at times. Other times, they are a handful—or to use one of my mother's favorite euphemisms—*rambunctious*.

And there is at least once a day when I find myself wondering if they had been switched at birth—both of them—because they can also turn into *those kind.* Those little out-of-control hellions I always point out to friends in restaurants, grocery stores and movie theaters and remark, "my kids will never act *like that.*"

Then they show up. Screeching. In my living room.

"I'M TELLING MOM! MOOOOOMMMMMYYY!! I HAD THAT FIRST, MAKE HER GIVE IT BACK!"

And:

"MOOOMMMYYYY, DANIELLE HIT ME!"

"BUT TIFFANY HIT ME FIRST!!"

And:

"MOOOMMMMMMYYYYY, TIFFANY PULLED OFF MY BARBIE'S HEAD AND THREW IT IN THE TOILET!!!"

As my Playtex-gloved hand carefully retrieves the blonde bombshell's head out of the water—that thankfully had been previously flushed—I feel the blood rushing to my own blonde head. I then send them both to their rooms so I can have my own Time Out. At which time, my mother's words come back to haunt me, ringing in my ears like a piercing whistle. "*I hope you have two just like ya!*" Another euphemism of grand proportions. And cast iron prophesy.

Those exact same children are now sitting demurely on the couch wearing halos, as Daddy retrieves a quarter from behind his ear.

"How'd you do that, Daddy?" they ask with wide eyes, between fits of giggles.

I'm wondering the same thing.

How *does* he magically transform these little hellions into such angels? And yet I have to remind myself, as envy washes over me, just how lucky they are—we are—that he is here. Physically and emotionally. This man, who goes to work each day and comes home to us, is the rock these girls will need in their future when forced to climb the mountains of adversaries they'll face in a male-dominated world. It wasn't something I thought about when he first brought up the subject of parenthood.

"Let's have a baby," Jeff said. On our honeymoon.

"But we're having so much fun!" I said, not equating dirty diapers, lack of freedom, and loss of glorious, glorious sleep, to a real good time. And while I did long to be a mother, I didn't feel quite ready yet to settle down to motherhood. When I began my new life with this man, I was twenty-six years old and just beginning to have fun. Finally, I had someone who enjoyed doing the same things I did, was interested in what I had to say, and introduced me to new things like van camping, fireworks on the beach, and crab legs dripping in hot butter.

I was also immersed in school and on my way to becoming a writer, which I'd wanted to be since I was nine and discovered the well-worn copy of *Peyton Place* on the bottom shelf of my grandparent's book case. Like those stolen literary moments, a new world had just opened up for me, and much as I wanted motherhood *eventually*, I wasn't at all sure I wanted it *now*. I didn't want to give up this new exciting life I was leading. Or the part of myself that I was just beginning to discover. I was also well aware that to do parenthood right, you had to be unselfish. And I selfishly wanted the fun to last.

Still, with Jeff's encouragement, I began thinking seriously about becoming a mother, something that had never before been an option. Until then, I had deliberately pushed maternal thoughts from my mind because I couldn't cope with wanting something I couldn't have. And until now, I couldn't have a baby. Not if I wanted to do parenthood right. And I did. I'd wanted children more than anything else in life, but I didn't want to bring another human being into the world where I couldn't fulfill its basic needs. Life is hard enough than to start it off on the wrong foot. I'd seen too many incidents where people weren't ready or *qualified* to raise a child. Having children was a monumental and serious undertaking. And I knew I could never—was too selfish to—give my baby to someone else. I also knew any baby I'd have would trump all my own personal needs. So I wanted to wait until I could provide it with food, shelter, love and my *time*.

In addition, looming large in my mind was the father issue. My number one consideration. The potential father of my beloved children had to be good daddy material. And now, here he was. A man I knew would be a good, loving and *present* father. And he wanted a baby with me. That romantic thought made me anxious to experience a family with this guy who had all the qualities I'd been looking for in a husband and father. And who shared my important values system. I also had to consider the very real fact that at twenty-nine, my ovaries were probably already beginning to wither a bit.

"Okay," I told Jeff, after a few more months of baby discussions. "I'm ready."

As I had predicted, when it finally happened (it took much longer than expected, four more years), life changed. And so did I. I discovered how wonderful it can be to be unselfish. And I learned that parenthood can be fun, too. Like right now.

Yet, as I observed this blissful scenario before me of this man bonding with his daughters, I couldn't help but feel a sudden pain, like a quick pinch in the heart, for what I had missed growing up. This special kind of relationship between fathers and daughters was inexplicably foreign to me. I had never really thought about that until this moment. Life with a father was something I knew nothing about. Though to be honest, I had never really felt the loss. After all, you don't miss what you don't know.

Until it's right there in front of you. And you suddenly wish—ache—that you were that five-year-old climbing up on this big guy's shoulders.

Watching this scene play out before me, I amazed myself at a new-found jealousy. What a wonderful thing this must be to have someone so big and strong to romp around with. To protect you from the big, bad world. For a moment, I let myself pretend I was one of these little girls, just to imagine how it must feel. To have this great protective presence to wrap my tiny arms around. How amazingly secure that must feel. Like a sturdy tree, or protective wall—an edifice of life energy that seals you from all harm. A safety net that catches you before anything could possibly hurt you. It must be like that.

As I silently mourned my own deprivation, my personal regret was soon replaced by an overwhelming joy that filled the hole in my soul. My babies had a father. A real one. The kind who was man enough to change their diapers and endure the occasional spit-up. A dad who watched cartoons with them and yes, roughhoused with them in the gentlest of ways.

I suddenly realized that I, too, had that now. While I may not be a little girl, and he may not be able to pick me up and swirl me around (though he has tried), this man gives me that steel armor protection I never knew I had longed for. I then recalled one of the few times I had given my long, lost alcoholic father any real thought.

I was fourteen, lying on the beach slathered in tanning oil, my little grey transistor radio at my ear. The deejay announced the next song, and though I had heard it before, when the Temptations sang, "Papa Was a Rolling Stone," they were suddenly singing about my own: "*Wherever he laid his hat was his home.*" I remember lying there wondering just where my father laid his hat at the end of a long day of drinking from a brown paper bag on the city streets . . .

I promised myself that day that my babies would have a papa who called *us* his home.

While I knew my daughters were too young to yet realize it, they were experiencing a bond, right there on that living room floor, that would carry them through their journey into womanhood—and invariably increase their chances for a good marriage. I'd read the statistics: A close and loving relationship with her father provides a young girl with self-esteem and a positive role model in which to guide her in choosing a compatible life mate.

Thinking about that, I felt a grand sense of pride and accomplishment that I was able to give my babies this gift (though in truth, I'd just gotten lucky). Something they would take with them when they'd leave this house as grown women. Because it was now engrained in their little bodies, this daddy saran wrap. And it would make them secure, confident, and strong.

On the flip side, raising girls seemed to also bring out the best in this man—who I knew had secretly hoped for a boy in the days we anticipated parenthood. A son with whom he could talk shop, work on motorcycles, and later share a beer with. All that male-bonding stuff.

But God had other plans.

Yet it took no time at all for Jeff to feel secure in his role as Daddy to these little women. He thought nothing of helping them with their homework (good thing, too, after Mom made a math error in our eight-year-old's school paper, which got me fired as the go–to homework person), braiding their hair or baking cookies with them. Though he also couldn't resist the urge to let them polish his Harley (while teaching them what parts go where and what does what), or have them stand by as he fixed whatever needed fixing. Like the chain on their bikes, or the wheels on their skateboards. I am comforted knowing these girls will be more knowledgeable when it comes to manly things.

I also know, unlike my generation of women who fought hard for viable rights, being female won't hinder these girls growing up in the millennium. Their only problem might be finding a man who can live up to a certain criteria. Their expectations will surely be high. As will their fathers'.

Mind you, the man is not a saint. There were indeed times he'd let out a distinctive lion-pitched roar when his cubs disobeyed or refrained from doing as they were told. But unlike mine, his outbursts are always more effective. I could yell in a pitch that could shatter glass, to no avail. But let Dad utter a single word in *that* tone of voice, and these same girls would stand at attention like little soldiers.

Yes, it's always made me mad, their civil obedience. And no, it never seemed fair. But I never complained. While he earned their respect with one howl, he gained their love with one hug. And the hugs always outweighed the roars—with no conditions attached.

It's been twenty years now since Jeff and I became parents. I once again stand on the sidelines watching this father, now in his fifties, fix our oldest daughter's car. She no longer lives with us, having found a man who has met certain criteria. But she still comes to Dad when something needs fixing. Growing up, she did indeed learn much about cars, and can identify most any apparatus in all those tool boxes in Dad's garage. But she still needs, no, *wants*, her father, when it comes to making things right.

She stands by now, too, because she knows he wants her to. After all, there is always something new to learn.

"Honey," he says to her. "Hand me that socket wrench over there," his voice echoing from underneath the hood. "You know, you're going to have to tell me sooner when this thing vibrates, or you hear a strange noise. Don't put it off," he warns.

No, I never had this, I think as I stand there observing idly. And yet, I realize at this very moment, that I, too, have reaped the benefits of having this father around—every bit as much as his girls have.

After all, I am one of them.

The Good Mother and the Bad Fairy Tale

"Mommy, guess what? This lady came to our class today and took me to the office and asked a bunch of questions about you and Dad and wants you to call her." My ten-year-old says this all in one breath as she climbs into the back seat. No "Hi, Mommy!" No kiss hello. Not even a "Can we go to the ice cream store?"

"She told me to give this to you right away." Danielle digs into her book bag for the card the woman had given her. So far, it'd been a good day. I'd had a successful interview with a hard-to-get source for the book I'd been working on, completed house chores, and still made it in time to pick up my girls from school at three o'clock. In good weather I walk, but this autumn day is chilly, so Danielle and her seven-year-old sister jump into the car. "I went to the office, too!" Tiffany boasts, not one to be left out.

"Don't get outta your car seat!" I say to Danielle. "Just give it to me when we get home."

Danielle's patience lasts until the minute I pull in the drive. She snaps open her seatbelt, leans over the front and shoves the business card in my face. She seems to know its importance, that alone raises a flag. I turn off the ignition and take a look. I have to read it three times before it sinks in. The stark black lettering shows a woman's name. Under it is her title: Director of Children's Services.

"Who was she, Mommy? Are you and Daddy in trouble?"

Why do children have to be so perceptive? I search my mind for a calm response and try to soften my expression to conceal what might surely look like gripping fear on my face.

"Oh, it's just someone who checks on things." I realize

what a feeble answer this is, but my tone suggests it's nothing for her to worry about. So she doesn't. The two girls hop out of the car, already arguing about who's going to be first to jump into the pile of leaves I'd just raked. I'm too numb to notice their flight. Nor the fact that I'm not breathing. Until forced to.

This must be some kind of mistake, I tell myself. The mere thought of anyone from the children's protection agency wanting to speak to me is preposterous. Me, who prides herself as a good mother. One who washes behind their ears, cooks them healthy meals, and reads to them in bed at night. Every night. And after prayers, I sing a lullaby I wrote just for them. And they actually let me do it without cupping their hands over their ears. They're still too young to realize Mom can't carry a tune to save her motherly soul.

If I'd ever been accused of anything related to my children it was of spoiling them (according to my mother), or being overprotective (according to my kids).

No, this kind of stuff happens to other people. People who truly deserve it. Monsters.

I walk into the kitchen, throw the card on the table, then open the refrigerator to start supper. But I can't remember what I was going to make. I'm imagining what those teachers must've thought when the principal came into the classroom and took my kids to the office. Did these teachers know why? Was it something they'd all gossiped about before the morning bell rang? I was a familiar face in Tiffany's second, and Danielle's fifth-grade classes. I'm one of the field trip moms. I attend every teacher conference. And least once a month, I come and join the kids for lunch. I'm a member of the PTA for heaven's sake!

I quickly snatch up the card to put it on my dresser before anyone comes over and sees it. In the secrecy of my bedroom, I look at it once again. That's when I notice the phone number. "She wants you to call," Danielle had said. *Oh, that's right! I'll call now and straighten out this crazy mistake.*

But I'm too late.

"I'm sorry, but I have left for the day," the business-like voice says. "Please leave a message and I'll return your call first thing Monday morning."

Monday! This was Friday. How could I wait through an entire weekend? What could we have possibly done to deserve this kind of torture?

When Jeff comes home, I show him the card and he looks as stunned as I am.

"What's this all about?" He's not asking me, he's asking the god of bad jokes.

Like any good mother, I somehow succeed in making life normal for the girls that night, despite my mental anguish. When they're finally asleep in their little beds, my torture escalates. Will this be one of the last nights I read to them, pray with them, sing to them? What's to become of our happy little family?

Sobbing into my pillow, I can't figure out who could have possibly made such a call. What kind of evil person would do such a thing to us? I begin mentally listing all the possible suspects. Was it the lady who gave me a dirty look when I reprimanded Tiffany in the grocery store the other day? At the time, I thought the disapproving gaze was meant for my active—and insistent—seven-year-old who'd wanted the box of overpriced cereal with all the processed sugar and added dyes "for color." Now I wonder if the woman thought I was being unreasonably cruel when I shouted, "NO! Not today," for the fifth time. Or maybe it was the neighbor guy my husband had yelled at about his dog depositing some unwanted material in our yard. Or was it some other disgruntled neighbor? A relative? Friend? Divorced parent with misplaced jealousy over our unbroken family?

I attempt to muffle my weeping so I don't awaken Jeff, but when his hand reaches out for mine, I realized he, too, can't sleep. He shares my pain. Anxiety. Fear.

For the next three nights, dark thoughts continue to drift in and out of my head like swirling demons. I recalled a news story awhile ago about a little girl who'd been beaten to death in her apartment by her own parents. Upon the gruesome discovery, neighbors and teachers had come forward with tales of suspicious bruises on the shy, quiet girl. Suddenly, it all made sense to them, they told reporters. They had often wondered . . .

Wondered?!

"I can't believe no one came forward to help that poor girl," I had said to Jeff as we watched the evening news. "They knew something was horribly wrong and did nothing? Not one person reported their suspicions?" The image of this defenseless girl murdered in a place she should've felt safe angered and haunted me for days. How could anyone do something like that? Clearly, those parents weren't parents at all. They were monsters.

Now we appear to be in that same category.

Could we really lose our children? This was no unreasonable thought. It happens all too often. There are always news stories of innocent people going to jail for a crime that, turns out years later, they hadn't committed. Which makes you wonder about the ones who are never vindicated. The ones who spend their entire innocent lives in a jail cell.

Would, could, that be us? What will happen to our beautiful little girls? Who would raise them into adulthood? Our parents are getting older. Our kids are very active. How could they keep up? Everyone else we know are either done raising kids or has their own to raise. Godparents? Yes, but that means these sisters would be separated. And despite daily skirmishes, they really are quite close.

Oh my God, this cannot be happening!

But it was.

The message said she'd be in her office at 9 a.m.. I call at 8:59. A frantic, near hysterical voice (after all, I'd had all weekend to think about it) was her Monday morning greeting. Her voice, in turn, was unnervingly placid. Just another day for her. They'd had a complaint, she said, and had to follow up on it. No, she could not disclose the person's name who called. When would my husband and I be home so she could pay a visit?

"Is now too soon?" I asked. I needed answers. I needed vindication. Jeff could leave work, if need be.

Sensing my anxiety, she agreed to "fit" us in the following day while the girls were in school.

That day, as we all sat around our family's kitchen table, Jeff and I learned about the protection of rights. The accuser's rights.

"We can't tell you who called but the complaints included loud noises coming from the house," she said, flipping through papers. "Loud yelling. Oh, and accusations that the girls were being force fed. Peas, to be exact."

"Are you kidding me?" I screamed, possibly reinforcing the allegations. "Of course I yell!" I yelled. "I'm a mom! Our own parents used to beat us when we misbehaved, and we know that's wrong, so we yell instead. I can never bring myself to beat them, so I yell. It's wrong and I'm sorry, but sometimes it's the only way I can get them to listen to me."

"You don't beat them?" Her question was directed to both of us but she was looking at my husband.

"I can count on one hand how many times I've spanked them in their lifetime," he told her. And it was true. He then repeated what he had often told me. "My dad used to get carried away when he'd beat me with the Marine strap. So I make sure I give 'em just one good whack on the butt with my hand, and that's it. Never more than one."

"Don't you have a paddle with the girl's name on it?" *Oh, my God*, I thought. Where was she getting her information? Suddenly our funny little joke was not the least bit amusing.

"Oh, that," Jeff replied. "I've never used it on them, but yes, I made a wooden paddle with Danielle's name on one side and Tiffany's on the other and kept it hanging over the stove to threaten them with when they get uncontrollable."

"Where is it now?" she asked.

We told her that we knew the sight of that paddle would be misconstrued, so Jeff put it away in the garage over the weekend. We then gave the woman some background information on our family. Our girls were happy children, and often very good children. But at times, they can be unmanageable. They're hyper. If we had believed in Ritalin, they'd be on it. Cute as these little girls were, there were times they could rattle a saint.

"The paddle was more of a joke than anything else," Jeff reiterated. "Something we'd kid about with friends who were going through the same thing."

We told her that yes, we did make the children eat their vegetables because if we didn't they'd probably have scurvy or some such disease. Especially Danielle. The picky one. The stubborn one. The one I was still feeding certain kinds of baby food, like spinach (which she in fact loved, go figure), and strained fruits at two-and-a-half because a kid can't survive merely on peanut butter & jelly and Mac & Cheese.

"What about the time you hit Tiffany with a hairbrush?" she prodded.

"What? I never . . . "

Then, I remembered. The day we were leaving for a vacation to Kelley's Island, I'd been brushing Tiffany's hair, and she wouldn't stand still. She wanted to go out and play. "If you don't settle down, Tiffany, I swear I'm going to hit you with this," I told her as I waved the brush in front of her face, for effect. The effect, apparently, worked. In her active imagination, it was as if I'd really struck her with it.

My heart sank. Everything this woman was mentioning was taken totally out of context. I then realized much of it was coming from Tiffany herself. She exaggerated everything. Every story she told was a wild conglomeration of fact and fiction. I'd often joke that, with her imagination, she was certain to be a writer. I'd always thought it was kind of cute. Except when her extremely active mind would cause her to have vivid dreams that often roused her, and me, several nights a week. Which wasn't so cute.

"I have to tell you," the woman explained, "we normally only interview the oldest child because the youngest ones often cannot distinguish reality from fantasy (that would be our Tiffany), but Danielle had so many good things to say about the two of you, and some real cute things that made me laugh. Like, after a hard day at work, her father goes into the garage and cranks up the stereo. 'That's how my Dad deals with his 'distress,' she told me, which I thought was hilarious."

She then returned to serious mode. "So we felt we better talk to the younger one to see if Danielle wasn't merely defending you, because frankly, some children want to protect a parent, even one who is abusing them."

This statement tightened the knot already in my stomach, recalling the murdered little girl from the recent news story. Would she have stuck by her parents if someone had tried to help her?

"Then I talked to Tiffany," the woman said, a confused look on her face. "Well, she kept changing her stories and events . . . I thought I'd better go ahead and look into it."

Tiffany. The one I always said was going to be a writer because of the whimsical world she often lived in. The trait I once thought so wonderful had turned on us.

As the probing continued, it occurred to Jeff and me that these accusations had to come from a parent of someone the girls played with because of the way the stories were misinterpreted. Children do say the darndest things. And sometimes it leads to this.

After touring our home, and checking the girls' rooms, our

explanations for everything must have rung true. "I personally don't see any basis to these charges," she finally said, walking to her car. "I'll make a report accordingly. We'll still need to conduct one unannounced visit and if everything looks good, you'll receive a letter in the mail stating the charges are unfounded. And the case will be closed."

A few weeks later, the letter came, but the closure didn't. From that day forward, I began questioning everything I said and did. My preconceived role as the good mother had been tarnished, and the scars remained.

The mystery as to who made the call, however, was solved days later when my head was finally clear enough for the obvious to appear. I knew who the caller was. It was a woman in our neighborhood whose child often played with ours. I decided to question another neighbor, Diane, who was friendly with this woman, about my suspicions. As I related my story, she must have felt my pain. Yes, she admitted, the woman had mentioned about calling authorities.

"But I didn't think she'd actually go through with it," Diane said, explaining that the woman often complained of hearing yelling and threatening of the children.

"I don't think she did it maliciously," Diane, always a kind soul, added in defense of the young single mother who lived with her father, and had problems of her own. I wasn't buying it. As fury rushed to my head, I'm sure my face was a dark crimson despite my efforts to remain calm. "I think she was just genuinely concerned because of things Brandon had told her, which she obviously misunderstood."

"*Obviously*," I scowled. "Do you have any idea what she put us through? You know me, Diane. I pride myself on motherhood. I try so hard to make sure these girls grow up decent and good.

"I'm a great mother!" I went on. "That woman doesn't know a thing about me! I never talk to her except for a few words or two. How could she so freely make such a call without asking me or saying something to us first? It's just so wrong."

I was devastated. My very integrity was being attacked— my entire identity as to who I was—questioned. All due to one phone call.

"I feel like going over and just smacking her," I screamed angrily. I was fully aware of this irony. That I was now threatening violence in response to violence, misjudged as it was. "She owes me a huge, and *sincere*, apology," I said, trying to hold back my frustrated tears.

But soon after, life resumed as normal. We never received that apology and I didn't confront the woman with all I'd wanted to say. Mad and hurt as I was, I've never been good at confrontations. And Jeff, somehow, managed to stay mum as well. We both feared our daughters might get wind of it, if we made a fuss, and they'd surely use it against us in their angry teen years. So, like the letter stating the case was closed, we realized that we, too, had to close the door on our anger and move on. But the resentment remained, burning inside me like a steady flame. Sundays were the hardest, particularly when the priest's homily was on forgiveness.

"Sorry, God," I'd whisper to the altar, "I just can't do that."

A few years later, the woman moved away. But the aftermath of my self-doubt continued to resurface whenever I punished the girls, wondering if I was being too mean, too tough, too unfit. As time passed, the memory of that dreadful experience lay dormant in my self-conscious. It helped, though, that I didn't have to see that woman anymore.

But then her father died. And she moved back in. With a new husband and his two small children. Interesting, I thought. It's been said that someone with just one child doesn't experience full parenthood because it's much easier to raise just one. But bring in another child and you have bickering, demands for attention, sibling rivalry, and multitasking at a serious rate. Now she'll know what it's really like, I couldn't help but gloat.

But by then, it hardly mattered. My girls were nearly grown. They were older teenagers, and good ones at that. I knew we'd done a good job. That fact alone was the ultimate vindication.

One day as I was returning from my walk in which I think deep thoughts, and do my best mental writing, I looked over and saw my old nemesis in her front yard, gardening. I gazed over at the one person who had hurt and angered me more than anyone ever had. What I saw was not the young single mother of yesteryear. This woman was older, a step-mom, with two small children running around in circles, carefree. I shivered. She reminded me of where I was not so long ago. The picture rekindled memories of days I so missed, the gaiety my children had brought to my world. That nonstop childlike energy I sometimes complained about, but usually enjoyed.

And for the first time, I realized I no longer felt bound by my long-held grievance toward this woman. I wasn't bitter anymore. No one was more surprised than I was by this revelation. I recalled the priest's words on forgiveness: It's easy to love someone who is lovable. It's easy to love and pray for your family and friends. That's no sweat on our part. The real mark of Christianity is when you learn to forgive, and pray for your enemies. That's the true test, and one that requires a tremendous amount of resolve.

You got that right.

Through the years, I'd made a few aborted attempts to forgive this woman who broke my heart. Who made me question my own worth in what I felt was my most important role in life. But hard as I tried, I still felt the resentment. I still heard the "*How could you have?*" ringing in my ears. So this struggle to raise my level of Godliness took a while. Until the day something clicked.

This woman may well have made that phone call all those years ago because she harbored some jealousy toward our family. Or maybe even *had* done it out of vindictiveness. But for the first time, I also considered the fact that perhaps she really believed that something wasn't right and wanted to "save" my children. She was wrong, of course, off base. But her willingness to get involved was commendable, nonetheless. I began thinking of all the children no one calls to save. And how many could be protected, and rescued, by one such phone call. So, despite the pain and heartache an innocent parent might go through as a result of such an act, people who honestly suspect child abuse should make that call. Even if there's a chance they are wrong. Because it just might save a child's life.

I realized something else, too. That if I expected to be forgiven for my past ignorance and bad behavior on so many occasions, than I'd be wise to do the same. I reminded myself that for the most part, we are all here just trying to do the best we can. Especially mothers. And I recalled a song that often plays in church.

"Let there be peace on earth, and let it begin with me."

As I headed toward my front door that day, I waited until the woman looked up. Then I waved.

"Hello," I said.

"Hi, how are you?" she said, smiling, a hint of surprise on her face.

Then the little boy and the little girl dancing around her smiled and waved, too.

"Hi, lady, how are you?"

"I'm good, kids, really good," I said, and felt a strange, but peaceful, lightness as I walked serenely into my happy home.

A Helicopter Mom Lets Go

&'m lying in my hospital room, arms wrapped tightly around my two-day-old daughter, all bundled in a blanket, crystal-blue eyes staring up at me. I'm grateful I have no roommate—it's just me and Tiffany getting to know each other. As the last among my friends to have children, I realize this serene moment will disappear in the time it takes to change a diaper. Danielle, who turns three next month, will demand more attention. As will my husband, who I know has been feeling neglected for months (my "with child" status made me feel fiercely protective, and oddly, virginal). There'll be a laundry basket that never empties. A perpetual rotation of feeding times. And sleep that won't come without constant interruption. So I resent it when a hefty, no-nonsense looking woman in nurse's clothing barges in.

"We have to take her back to the nursery now," she states, and grabs my baby before I can say, *Where are your credentials*? I've never seen this particular nurse, and wonder what happened to the last one, the one that looked like Mary Poppins. I'd just read a news report about a woman who, dressed in white, stole a newborn from a hospital. So when Cruella de Vil disappears out the door—with my child—I whip off the covers, slide into my baby-blue paper slippers and quickly, but quietly, tip-toe down the hall. I stand ridged against the wall and peep around the corner to watch the suspect as she enters the nursery. Although still all business-like, I see that she lays my daughter gently in the crib beside the other newborns. My heart decelerates and I head back to my room.

But I can't sleep. It's too quiet here without my baby's small but huge presence. I begin thinking of all that is now expected of me. I have yet another human being I'm responsible for. I'm on double duty. Every day. For the next two decades. And I know—confirmed by that whole follow-the-nurse act—that my lofty companion, that old Sense of Dread, has stepped on the gas.

Great. Just Great.

There is so much no one tells you, not even your own mother, about parenthood.

They don't mention that these small wonders will give you immeasurable joy, along with soul-crushing heartache. That, much as you love them, they'll be times you won't like them very much. That there'll be times your blessed children will make you so happy and proud you swear you'll burst from such intensity. Other times, they'll make you so infuriated you swear you'll burst a blood vessel.

And no one gets around to mentioning the overwhelming state of worry that will now be part of your psyche. As mothers, we're haunted with all sorts of imaginary fears that become our late night companions as we lie there contemplating if we're getting this parenting thing down right. Did we do the right thing today? Make the right decisions? Handle punishments the right way? Did we ask the doctor the right questions when we called at two in the morning when our baby wouldn't stop screaming. Or when our six-year-old had another ear infection. Or our teenager's fever hit 103. No matter what their age, we feel inadequate in this job of taking care of another human being. We're never quite sure if we've made the right choices, and when it's clear that we did not, we beat ourselves up. A lot.

When you first become a mother, everyone is too busy being excited to warn you about the dilemmas you'll be subjected to. The unanswerable questions. The continual on-the-job training. They don't alert you to the blood you're bound to see, if only from a playground scrape. They don't tell you of the sweat involved, be it physical, or mental. Or the tears you'll shed. Or that fear that lies just beneath the surface, then becomes reality when your child gets hurts and your motherly kiss can't make it better. This is fear's finest moment, when that Sense of Dread rises triumphantly to the surface.

No. No one tells you any of that.

And so, this Mother Hen—who was taken by surprise by all this—began monitoring her children like an air traffic controller. I was on duty 24/7. Our girls were extremely active, never walking when they could run. They wouldn't sit still, not even when watching the most captivating Disney flick. I quickly discovered I couldn't let them out of my sight. When Tiffany was two, for example, I put her down for her nap, and when I later checked to see if she was sleeping, she opened her mouth to speak and I saw the gleam of a penny on her tongue ready to make its way down her esophagus . . .

I had never known true panic until I bore these children. It's not something you can possibly prepare for. But I took this new job seriously. Even in my deepest sleep, my ears were on alert for the slightest cough, or smallest whimper. During waking hours, I took record-breaking bathroom breaks as they'd run around the house like little Indians—keeping the door open so I could make a fast exit in case of an emergency "MOMMY!"

After years of infertility, months of temperature taking, and two miscarriages, I was clueless to these realities of parenthood. Of course, I'd heard all the standard warnings. "Motherhood changes your life." "They grow up so fast." And, as one male nurse said the minute Tiffany was born, "Two girls? Start saving your money!"

No one warned me about the worry and the fear. Not even that pregnancy book, "*What to Expect When You're Expecting.*" I didn't expect the Sense of Dread that seeps in as soon as the placenta spurts out. Then sneaks into your diaper bag for a ride home.

SOD—we'll call it for brevity's sake—is an unwelcome, and often unwarranted, sense of doom that pumps through your veins like a blood transfusion, pumping you with gripping anxiety that strips every ounce of rational thought, making you a prisoner of paranoia. It's an overpowering feeling that something is sure to go wrong. And it has made me its special friend.

SOD makes itself known the day after I bring Danielle home from the hospital. I'm changing her—a soft, helpless thing no bigger than my cat—when I notice that her hands and feet are blue. Well, not blue-blue, but blue-ish. Enough to set off the panic button.

"Oh my God, what's wrong with my baby?!"

I set her in the bassinet and rush to the phone.

"My baby, she, her, I mean, her toes, hands, uh, they're like blue," I stammer. The pediatrician's nurse assures me that it merely takes some babies a few days for the circulation to reach those outer extremities.

"Don't worry," she says calmly, "It's nothing serious, she'll be fine in a day or two."

"Oh, good," I sigh with relief, regaining my sense of humor, "for a minute there I thought I'd given birth to a Smurf."

By now, SOD—recognizing easy prey—has propped its feet on the couch and made itself at home like an unwelcomed relative who drinks all your beer and smokes in bed. It's there during Danielle's bout with Croup, Tiffany's fall through a glass end table, and occasionally, for no good reason. Sneering. Usually in the middle of the night. So when my children are finally, peacefully, asleep, I feel a relentless need to get up, go to their room, and put my hand on their little backs to be absolutely certain they are breathing.

Sometimes, SOD even appears in doctors. Which takes a mother like me on a wild ride no astronaut can rival. Like when Tiffany was eight weeks old and developed a 102.6 fever . . .

I rush her to the clinic. The doctor checks her over, then takes me aside. He doesn't say, "We just want to make sure she doesn't have meningitis." He says—in a panicky tone. "At her age, it's very possible she has meningitis, and we have to deal with it *now*." He then holds my newborn down as he tries, over and over, to stick a needle in her doll-like arm to take her blood.

"It's often hard to find a vein in one so young," he explains in a frustrated tenor.

I barely hear this, nor do I hear my baby's cry, because I'm concentrating on her pained face—looking at me to save her—and trying to keep my heart from detonating and blowing us all into another galaxy. I want to grab my infant and run. To a place where children don't get fevers and mothers can vanquish all threats with a twitch of a nose. Instead, utter helplessness freeze-frames in my mind, and years later, whenever I recall this moment, that tiny hurting face looking at me so helplessly, still stings me with horror.

A few hours later, the blood test comes back negative. "Must be just a virus," Doctor Dread says now. "We'll give her Tylenol to reduce the fever and she should be fine in a few days."

He would be wrong. She is fine in a few hours.

But I wonder if I will ever be.

"Mommy, now that I'm in fifth grade, may I walk to school tomorrow by myself?" Danielle requests one evening at dinner. She seems to know that this appeal will hurt my feelings since I've taken her to school all her little life, so she's trying to soften the blow by asking ever-so-politely, and hoping that her sweet demeanor, and innocent little—practically batting—eyes, will have the desired effect.

"I can walk with Jason," she adds, gently, carefully, prodding. Seems she's already acquired an accomplice in this quest for independence. She thinks this will give her the upper hand because she knows I happen to like the sixth-grade neighbor. But SOD has jumped ahead of her, and suddenly I'm not sure I like him anymore. After all, he *is* a boy.

"We'll see," is all I can come up with.

As her luck would have it, I'm running late the next morning, so it sounds like a good idea. "Okay," I say, throwing sandwich and juice box into the brown bag, "But go *straight* to school, no stopping at Convenient or *anything*," I stress in my best really-mean-it mother voice.

"I *know* Mom," she says, and—as I hug her tightly, my kiss smacking her cheek—I can feel her eyes rolling. We rush off in different directions but when I wave to her and Jason as I drive off, my happy little girl doesn't see me. She's already chatting away as they walk up the street, as if her mother doesn't even exist. By the time I arrive at work, I can't concentrate. Although school is just a twelve-minute walk, I envision all sorts of horrific scenarios that could've happened along the way, even questioning the intentions of that eleven-year-old boy.

She's so young, maybe that wasn't the right decision. What if something happened along the way?

"Hello, Mrs. Johnson, this is Mrs. Adams, Danielle's mom? I was wondering . . . "

The school secretary puts me on hold for what seems like hours before coming back to assure me that yes, Danielle is safely in her classroom. I exhale deeply and go on merrily with my day.

When Tiffany reaches this same age, she, too, asks that I not walk her to school. Any. More.

"No one else's mom walks them to school," she says, as if this fact alone will change my mind. "I'm not a baby, you know."

"You're my baby," I reply, but she doesn't take it as a compliment. Perhaps because she really is the last baby I'll ever have, I feel even more protective over this one. So after hearing, "But you let Danielle walk that whole year!" for the hundredth time, I finally relent. On the last day of school.

I give her a long list of instructions for the half-mile jaunt, and remind her—repeatedly—of our family password because she has no one to walk with. My baby, walking alone. Still, I let her go because I *promised.* And thankfully, she never turns around. Because then she'd see her mother's shadow as she hides behind the big oak tree, watching every step that moves her child further from sight.

Rationale be damned. I am a *mother*.

When my children become teenagers, my symptoms go into overdrive. Summers are the worst. They want to go to the community pool. Their friends' house. The lake. The store. The skate park . . .

I get them cell phones. Have them check in every hour. Sometimes I don't wait for them to call. I call them. I find it increasingly hard to let them be on their own. Yet, I know I have to. I fully understand that they can't have their mommy hovering over them, lurking behind walls and trees.

All that logic, however, is lost on a mother with SOD syndrome. Who happens to also be a God-fearing Catholic.

It's a fight to the finish.

When Danielle gets her first job at fifteen, I take her there, I pick her up. When she gets her driver's license, I wait up for her. When she's not home five minutes after she's supposed to be, my heart begins to pound, palms sweat, stomach tightens. I discover to my dismay that even cell phones cannot expunge SOD, especially when you call and all you get is a voice message. I hold my breath and debate. Who should I call? Her boss? ("What time did she leave?") Her friend? ("Did she happen to stop at your house?") The police? ("My daughter was supposed to be home *five* minutes ago!"). As I begin dialing for defendants, my daughter saunters in, casually, and tells me the restaurant was really busy that night.

"Why didn't you answer your phone?" I ask.

"Mom," she says, rather impatiently. "I was driving and *you said*, not to use it when I'm driving."

Damn . . .

Still, I don't see myself as a "helicopter mom."

I'm just a person who doesn't quite know how to deal with this frightening, all-encompassing, overwhelming, tremendous love for another human being.

And yet, we deal. We wean our children from our bosoms, one baby step at a time. Not simply to prepare them for the outside world—a world we cannot protect them from—but also to prepare *us*. The mothers who, despite the late night hours, inevitable heartaches, and SOD affliction, have loved every minute of this job.

And so, with each birthday, I let up a bit. Give my daughters a smidge more freedom—with attached lectures on how it comes with responsibility. Year by year, after mother/daughter talks (in which only I do the talking), I leave published articles and books confirming our prior discussions on personal hygiene, boys, sex, and drugs (because, Lord knows, they won't believe me) on top of their dressers.

"Did you read that article?" I ask Danielle one day after school.

"*Yes*, Mom," she answers, knowing the test is coming.

"So what—exactly—was it about?"

"Stay a virgin until you marry."

She has made her own Cliff Notes, clearly having only skimmed the material.

"And why, specifically?" I urge.

She is saved by her younger sibling who barges into her room.

"Hey, Tiff!" She is suddenly thrilled to see her sister.

In dire emergencies, I've even risked full disclosure that their mother is not perfect (though by age ten, they'd pretty much figured that out) by relaying an anecdote or two about some lapse of judgment on my part that led to "important lessons learned."

Which always prompted First Daughter's favorite teenage complaint.

"Quit telling me what I should and shouldn't do!" she'd bark, muddy tears of liquid charcoal eyeliner streaming down her flamed cheeks. "You have to let me make my *own* mistakes!"

Second Daughter would go the sense-of-humor route.

"Now let's see, Mom, is that Life Lesson number 4, 266 or 4, 267?" she'd quip, sarcasm dripping from high-glossed lips. "Times have changed, Mom. You're so old fashioned!" Emphasis on old.

Yet with each episode that didn't end badly, the hovering mother blades would slow to a soft—though still consistent—whirl.

Until finally, the moment we think is so far away, comes . . . .

***

"After today, things will never be the same."

I'm thinking this as I fill water into the coffee pot and glance over at my oldest child, eighteen today, sleeping soundly on the couch. She looks peaceful, content, unmoved by the fact that this is the day she'll be leaving her home, her family. Forever. Not because she's off to college, but because she no longer wants to live by our rules.

She always said she'd do it. But things had gone fairly well this past year and she'd stopped talking about it, so I just figured . . .

Ever since our stubborn (like her father), rebel (her mother) daughter was thirteen, she's been counting the days till she would leave us.

"When I'm eighteen, I'm outta here!" she'd proclaim whenever we asked her to do something she didn't want to. Or told her she should find new friends. Or ground her when her grades were slipping.

"Oh, that's normal, they all say that," I'd hear from parents with twenty-five-year-olds still living at home. But I knew better. Although she looks and acts like her father, Danielle—my luck—inherited that fiercely independent gene so distinct in the Ruth side of my family. I cringe recalling the note I'd left my own mother at seventeen.

Mom, I know this will be hard for you to understand, but please try. I went to stay with Dennis for the summer. I'm not doing this to hurt you, I just have a lot of pressure and need to get away. I'll get a job, so don't worry that I'll just be running around. I promise I'll return for my senior year.

P.S. Here is a quotation I read in a book, The Prophet, called "Children":

You may give them your love but not your thoughts. For they have thoughts of their own. You may house their bodies but not their souls."

I then hopped on a plane to L.A. by myself and my mother would come home from work that day to find the note on the kitchen table.

As my age-spotted hand retrieves the coffee mug from the cupboard, I pause to think if I ever apologized to my mother for that little incident. No, I'm sure I didn't. I look over at the phone, suddenly wanting to call Mom right now and tell her I'm sorry for the selfish things I'd done back then. I was young and it was all about me. But I can't. She died a year ago, this month.

I suddenly feel abandoned. Twice. One through death, the other, sheer will.

My willful daughter now shifts in her contented slumber and I silently thank God she's never touched our liquor cabinet, sneaked out at night (least that I know of), or became a crack addict. I mean, there's a lot I have to be grateful for.

I pour the coffee into my cup, the one that reads in part: "*Love is patient and kind . . .*" and can't help but scoff. I don't feel like being patient or kind. How dare she do this to us? Eighteen years of weaning and teaching and worrying, and yes, reprimanding. Eighteen years of loving this child.

This child who thinks she's so ready to be on her own, yet at this very moment has dollops of zit cream dotted on her face, like Howdy Doody. This child, who wrote in her own leaving-home note to me yesterday (now I'm the one getting the surprise notes): "*I am an adult now, Mom, able to make my own choices. Please understand.*"

The pissy thing is I do understand. I left home twice before it became final, and with each exit, my mother's feelings never crossed my mind. I only thought "Freedom!" So the logical part of my brain tells me my child is not thinking of our hurt, our anger, our fear, at this time.

As I walk toward her, a memory comes to mind. Our first-born daughter is two and a half, and Jeff and I are laughing at how she always walks on her "tippy toes." Like the ballerina toy. The one where the dancer spins round and round, then takes flight . . .

"Danielle, it's time to get up and go to work. You fell asleep watching TV again." I gently rub her shoulders in a motherly way, my anger taking a momentary leave of absence. I tell myself she'll be okay because she'll always be willing to make a living. It's something her father and I have instilled in her; a good work ethic. I add this to my list of grateful thoughts. Though, after this day, it takes me many nights of her not coming home to think of any more. . . .

If you're lucky, there comes a point of salvation when your parenting skills are rewarded. When you begin to relax a bit (SOD be damned!), knowing your job is done, and the end result is admirable.

Sometimes that point, that moment of recognition—and relief—comes on your children's graduation day. Sometimes, it's the day they marry. Or when you see how they parent their own kids.

Mine came without fanfare. A moment in time on an ordinary day.

It'd been two years since Danielle had been on her own. One day, she found three abandoned kittens left in the back of her workplace, and brought them to her home. "I couldn't just leave them there, Mom, their eyes were still shut," she'd told me. She made them a homemade bassinet, researched kitten care online, and purchased special milk for them. She fed them round the clock, on breaks at work, in the middle of the night.

She brought them to our house one day. I sat on the floor with her, watching her lift each kitten—one at a time—cupping them in the palm of her hand, the other hand holding the tiniest of bottles. Feeding time. I watched my once rebel daughter coo to these babies, telling them how pretty, and handsome, how good they were. She then set them gently in the playpen she'd brought with her. So they could run free, safely.

"But this one," she pointed to the feisty striped one, "Now he's a little pistol. He climbed out of the pen the other day. I had to run and grab him quick before he escaped. I'd feel terrible if he got lost or hurt."

Welcome to my world, dear daughter.

7. Last Call . . .

Grandpa, the Baseball Fan

It's on those days when the air gets stifling and humid along the North Coast—and the Indians are winning—that I remember him best. Grandpa, sitting on the back porch with the Sports section spread out before him, a Lucky Strike in one hand and a palm-sized transistor radio in the other, pressed firmly against his right ear. That was his good ear. He was hard of hearing in his left, though we were never told why. My brother Dennis swears to this day that Grandpa wasn't hard of hearing at all. That it was just his "out" when Gee Gee was yelling at him to do something he didn't want to. He took equal advantage of this disability when he'd sit in the corner with a book, pretending not to hear the boisterous women in his life, his wife and daughter, snapping at each other, as they were prone to do, and often. The two women fought frequently for supremacy, making ours a lively and vocal household. While the adults held fast to the "children should be seen and not heard" rule, Dennis and I often wished this law applied to Mom and Gee Gee as well. So because no one ever told us much, we learned to live in a world of our own speculations, one being the cause of Grandpa's hearing loss.

Any tidbit of family details was revealed at the Saturday night poker games, which had just the right mix of relatives and alcohol to generate colorful stories, and give birth to my love for a good tale. Except for those enlightening evenings, we were mostly left in the dark—like household plants in the middle of the night, valued but merely existing—given no more thought until they needed watering the next day.

Whenever Grandpa took us for a drive, we'd pile into his car in anticipation, though it remained a mystery as to where we were headed. One time I asked, and Mom said, "You'll know when we get there." I accepted the answer because it made pretty good sense, and so entertained myself the whole way out by envisioning exotic destinations. Which of course set me up for disappointment every time.

On summer Sundays, however, it'd be just me and Grandpa in the car. We'd go to pick up his mother at her summer cottage at Euclid Beach Park where she, a Florida snow bird, stayed from May to October. We'd drive the straight shot down Lakeshore Blvd., which—at 25 to 35 miles an hour—took at least an hour, round trip. Longer if we hit the red lights. Sometimes Grandpa talked, other times he didn't say much, and I'd busy myself with the game of seeing how many traffic lights it took before a red one would stop us. If you timed it right, you could make nearly all of them, but if you didn't make one, chances were you got stopped at every one the whole way out. On these trips, least I knew where we were going—except for the time Grandpa threw me a curve ball and pulled into the gas station, but didn't get gas.

"How's it going, sir, gotta a minute?" Grandpa addressed the man in overalls and a Sunoco cap. Grandpa got out of the car, talked some more to the Sunoco man, then got back in, pulled the car into the garage, then got out again. As was my way, I paid no attention, already leaning over to switch the radio station—for just a minute—because the Indians' game hadn't started yet. That's when I felt the car rising. I whipped back up and looked out the window in time to see that I was trapped. The car was now closer to the ceiling than the cement floor.

"Grandpa!" I yelled. "What's happening?"

"Oh, don't worry, the man's just checkin' somethin' under the car."

Been nice if he'd told me, I thought to myself. But then I remembered that no one told me anything and that children— though I was practically eight—were not privy to any kind of useful information, even when they were scared. And I was. I'd always been afraid of heights (to this day, will not go on a Ferris Wheel, or anything that raises me above ground, and no, airplanes are definitely not in my comfort zone). Although, despite this fear, I *would* climb the wooden staircase with the six rickety steps that led to our attic where Dennis and I often played. I just never looked down.

"Why didn't you tell me?" I couldn't help but ask, calling out to Grandpa from the upholstered seat, while not looking down. He couldn't hear me over the loud drilling that was going on in that garage, so I sat perfectly still, breathing very softly so as not to rock the car, and was now sorrier than ever that I was a bit on the chubby side. My overactive imagination (that's what Mom called it, in a tone that suggested this was not a good thing) had me making one false move, forcing the car to teeter and wobble uncontrollably, finally toppling over whatever was holding it up, then slamming to the concrete where I'd experience whiplash or some equally horrible effect, maybe even die from my injuries.

After hours of horror that in reality was probably no more than three minutes, Grandpa's car began to descend, and like a fallen feather meeting a pillow, landed smoothly back into place.

"That outta do it," the Sunoco man said, and Grandpa slid back behind the wheel, waved the man off, and we resumed our normal Sunday drive to pick up my great-grandma for dinner.

Unlike my chatty, melodramatic women role models, who were subject to change in a soap-opera moment, Grandpa was cool and dependable, the family security blanket. Years later when *All in the Family* aired, I couldn't believe how much Carroll O'Connor looked like him—though in no way was Grandpa like O'Connor's TV character, Archie Bunker. My grandfather treated everyone with respect, no matter what the person's color.

He was also most effective in keeping my brother and me on the straight and narrow path of goodness. Whenever we'd misbehave, Mom and Gee Gee could yell in decibels that would rattle the earth's surface, but all it took was Grandpa's disapproving gaze to make you feel the red-hot blush of shame all the way through your soul and you never, ever, did whatever you did, again. He would've made a great priest.

The few times Grandpa got mad—actually raise his voice in anger—we knew it was serious. And Gee Gee was about the only person who could rile him to that point. When I was eight or nine, I recall hearing my frustrated grandma yelling, god-dammin' and sonofabitchin' him about some such thing (usually his slacking off at household duties, which Grandpa was not fond of, particularly if there was a ballgame on. I think this was less out of laziness and more because he just wasn't a "fixer"—evidenced by the outlet cover on the kitchen wall that for years read no/ffo because he'd screwed it in upside down).

No, he was not mechanically inclined, but then, he'd had no role model. His father died from TB when he was four, as did his two younger sisters about the same time. His mother later remarried, but not until he was on his own. Yet it seems growing up with no father or brothers, just his mother and frequent visits by aunts, produced my grandfather's greatest quality: a gentleness, appreciation, and respect toward women. A gentleman of the truest kind. But he wasn't a fixer. And for some time, he didn't need to be. He and Gee Gee rented the home where they raised my mother, so by the time they saved enough to buy their own, they were already in their late 40s. So he was sorely unprepared for homeowner repairs. . . .

When Grandpa surprisingly fired back at Gee Gee that day, I was scared that they might get divorced too, like my parents. Although he usually kept quiet, I knew these two drove each other crazy at times. And maybe, just maybe, his lack of motivation was his passive-resistance response to her yelling. She'd cuss him out for not mowing the grass, or taking out the garbage, or especially, listening to the ball game on the back porch when "other damn things need to be done." He'd pay no heed, despite the fact that surely the whole neighborhood heard, "Get that god-damn radio outta your ear and DO something around here."

There must've been an important game that day—maybe even a World Series where his team was dangerously close to losing—because, as he held that transistor radio tight to his good ear, leaning on the armrest of his corner couch, Grandpa shot back. I'd never seen him so angry, nor heard him yell at Gee Gee like that before, throwing in his own cuss words to rival hers. Lying on my bed listening to it all, I was convinced they were getting divorced. Now what would we all do? I relied on Grandpa to keep the peace in our family. To keep his wife and daughter from outright killing each other in their rivalry for family domination. I feared that Dennis and I would now turn out to be horrible human beings because Grandpa was the one who really kept us in line. Like I said, we respected Grandpa so much that if we were getting out of hand, all he had to do was call our name in that voice, and give us a look that was a cross between irritation and disappointment. Nothing made you feel more ashamed of yourself than if you disappointed Grandpa. He'd complete the look with the sensible motto, "Two wrongs don't make a right," which Dennis or I never knew how to respond to, and we'd straighten up pronto.

Grandpa's sudden outburst must have shocked Gee Gee, too, because she finally grew quiet as she put the roast in the oven, and by the time our Sunday dinner was on the table, I noticed she had also made Grandpa's favorite dessert—mincemeat pie. After that, things went back to normal and my grandparents never uttered a word about divorce.

I loved watching TV with Grandpa no matter what was on, or how boring. We watched a lot of game shows together, like *Concentration, Password,* or the *Match Game.* Grandpa worked second, sometimes third, shift. On third, he'd still be home when I got off the school bus. I'd go straight to the kitchen cupboard, grab the box of graham crackers, pour a glass of milk in which to dip them, and plop on the couch across from Grandpa's chair. Summertime was the best, when baseball brought Grandpa mounds of happiness—except of course when his favorites were slipping. I loved seeing his face when he watched those games. And he'd watch them all, not just the Indians. He never got animated, jumping up and down and screaming like some guys. That wasn't his style. He was nonverbally intense. When "his team" was winning, he'd smile a contented grin and utter an occasional "now we're talkin'." When they were losing, he'd sit quiet, as if mentally willing the player to hit it out of the park, or catch a fly ball. Although he never talked about it, Mom told me years later that he used to coach kids' baseball leagues, and I remember thinking he'd obviously missed his calling. He worked for more than twenty-five years at Willard Battery, then somewhere else which I can't recall, loading up heavy boxes onto trucks. I don't think he liked doing any one of those jobs, not one day. But Ralph Jenkins did what he had to do as the dominant breadwinner of our three-generation family.

His rewards were listening to the ballgame on the back porch on a hot summer day, or watching it on TV. So I learned to love the game, too. I also learned a few other things. One day, right after we watched the St. Louis Cardinals win a game that propelled them to the 1965 World Series, Grandpa switched the station to the *Match Game*. I don't recall the other celebrities on the show, but one stood out above the rest. Jayne Mansfield was introduced and came out from behind the curtain with her little Chihuahua resting comfortably on her huge breasts like its own personal pillow. Hips swaying to some unheard beat, she sashayed over to her seat with the other panel guests. I'd just gotten Grandpa a beer, which was our routine.

"Honey, wanna get your old Grandpa another beer?" he asked, too comfortable to get out of his plush red easy chair with the fringes on the bottom. As was our custom, I ran to the fridge, snatched the brown longneck P.O.C., grabbed the silver opener with the wooden handle, popped off the cap, took a big swig, then ran back to the living room and handed it to him. I didn't like the taste of beer at all, but I liked seeing Grandpa smile. And he always did when I'd return with his beer and he'd see the telltale bubbles rising to the top.

"Sure you didn't take a sip?" he asked with a big grin. We both knew the answer to that one. I jumped on the couch across from him and replied, "Nope," giving back the same knowing grin. This was our special game and the one and only time I could lie and get away with it. As I plopped back down, I heard Gene Rayburn refer to Jayne as "sexy."

"What's sexy mean, Grandpa?" I was ten at the time and knew a lot of words because reading was my favorite activity, but this one was a new one to me. While I waited for an answer, I noticed Grandpa grinning even wider than when I handed him his foaming beer, but he didn't respond right away. I could tell he was giving this some serious thought and it occurred to me that maybe I shouldn't have asked, that perhaps it was one of those things children shouldn't hear. But I knew he'd eventually tell me because this was Grandpa I was talking to, a man who, unlike other adults, was always straight up with me.

His silence increased my curiosity, so I anticipated the answer all the more.

Finally. "It means attractive to the opposite sex," he said, trying his best to hold in a laugh, I could tell.

Well, then. This was interesting. I was aware that the opposite sex meant boys, and as I glanced back at Jayne, with her big ruby lips—curvy as her hourglass figure—and her curly mass of puffy, platinum hair and humongous boobs hanging out over her fluffy, powder blue low-cut sweater, I knew exactly what he meant.

When we learned that Grandpa had lung cancer in the fall of 1969, I wasn't all that surprised. He smoked a lot. He once told me he had started when he was twelve. So that added up to fifty years of smoke-filled lungs. What did surprise me was how fast he declined when given the lung cancer diagnosis, and how seemingly accepting he was of his fate. He took the illness as he took life, compliant. After all, it was what it was. I never heard Grandpa complain before and he didn't now. I was fifteen and entrenched in my rebel period, but this news about Grandpa deflated my insolence. I tried hard not to cry when I called him one day and, after waiting a bit for his coughing fit to subside, asked how he was doing.

"Well, I don't feel so good today," he said dryly, as if I'd asked him the weather report and he was simply stating that there were dark clouds ahead. His submissive matter-of-factness gave me the same crumbling feeling I'd experienced when he used to give me that dire look of disappointment. I wanted to tell him I loved him, but our family never said that out loud, so I didn't know how. When I hung up the phone with him that day, a week before he entered the hospital for his final inning, a series of events played out in my head.

Those rides to pick up Grandma at Euclid Beach. The Saturdays I'd go with him and Gee Gee to the neighborhood bar where he taught me to shoot pool. And that day I got suspended from my private all-girls' school for protesting against the Vietnam War on the front lawn of the campus. (This didn't sit well with school administrators since their reputation was everything and the front lawn of the campus was right on a main street where car continually passed by. Which was our point.) He was disappointed, I could tell, when he picked me up, but never said a cross word to me about it. I think maybe, just maybe, he admired the fact that I had stood up for what I believed in. But telling me that would have naturally made me feel right, although the act was wrong, and getting suspended was wrong, and two wrongs don't make a right.

Then I recalled that night long ago at the poker game when he said offhandedly that if he died tomorrow, he was okay with it. I wondered now if that was still true. I'd bet money it wasn't.

We sure weren't okay with it, not my mother, brother, me

or Gee Gee, as we surrounded his hospital bed. It was Christmas, and there he was with tubes up his nostrils and looking totally miserable. Yet, we were all acting like we were spending the day at some Holiday Inn, giving him wrapped presents and talking cheerily, like it was any other grand celebration. I don't remember any of the gifts we gave him, except for one. I don't recall whose gift it was, just remember his face when he opened the brightly colored paper to reveal a pair of thick winter gloves. No one else seem to notice (or if they did, ignored it) his frown that said, "Don't you people get it, who're we kiddin' here? I won't ever be using these."

And he was right.

The next day, my grandmother—who'd been with him all day—had to get to the bank before it closed. She kissed him goodbye, told him she'd be right back. She didn't want to leave this man, not for a minute. This man she'd spent forty-three years with. Whom she'd loved, and fought with, equally hard. Who always had his arm around her whenever they'd go out. And who she'd sit right next to, in the middle of the car seat, when he drove—leg-to-leg—like lovers at a drive-in movie, prompting those who witnessed it to remark, "Oh, isn't that cute?"

She didn't want to go to the bank.

But this, of course, was his opportunity. He'd been struggling to stay alive for our sake. It was just like him to wait until Christmas passed, and because he'd never want Gee Gee's last memory of him to be his gasping for that last breath, he waited patiently for her to go. That's when he made his exit. Although Gee Gee made record time running to the bank and back, Grandpa was faster, and when she returned there were nurses surrounding him and the doctor quickly whisked her away from the scene and broke the news to her. Grandpa probably hadn't considered that in leaving her so slyly, she'd feel guilty the rest of her life for not being there.

When my brother called me with the news, I was alone in our apartment listening to the new Crosby, Stills & Nash album. Dennis said Mom had left work and rushed to the hospital (not a driver, she had to get her boss to take her) because Grandpa died.

As I hung up the phone, the first thing I noticed was our Christmas tree, and cursed it for all its false promises, mentally shaking it so hard the ornaments and silver tinsel strings went flying in protest.

Soon after they all returned that night, the electricity went out in our apartment for what seemed like no good reason, and we were left to mourn our loss in the blackness of the living room, only deepening our anguish. Mom and Gee Gee sucked down beers in the dark while discussing which relatives to call, what arrangements to make. Dennis and I sat quiet in our miserable thoughts. The few candles my mother managed to find did not brighten the dark shadows of the night, and eventually Dennis went to a friend's house, leaving me with these two grieving women who were fooling no one that they were keeping it together so well. At fifteen, I couldn't grasp, nor did I want to, the thought that I would never again have this man in my life, ride with him in the car, or see him sitting in the corner with that transistor in his good ear.

The following day, I overheard Mr. Pearson, my grandparent's neighbor, echo similar thoughts as he gazed at my grandfather in the casket. "Hard to believe I won't be seeing him anymore, sitting out there on the porch listening to the ball game on his radio." I had to fight off my instinct to smack him right then and there. Because his saying it out loud somehow finalized the truth.

Today, when I close my eyes and think of my grandfather, I prefer to remember this:

I'm feigning sleep as I hear Grandpa come into his bedroom. He and Gee Gee always let me sleep in their big bed on poker nights because, unlike my room, it has a door, so I don't have to listen to all the jabbering through the wee hours. I like to pretend I'm sleeping so I can bask in this special moment. He slides both arms underneath me and gently scoops me up from their bed, to carry me back to my own.

I make sure I'm all limp-like as he holds me, while managing to tilt my head towards his chest so I can feel his protective presence, his strong, beating heart. If he knows I'm awake, it will take away the magic. This sacred moment of tenderness between a grandfather and his granddaughter. I think he secretly values this, too, as much as I do.

In fact, I am sure we both treasure this brief moment in time because it is the only way—seeing how our family isn't demonstrative—that the two of us are allowed this quiet sense of love, like a soft hum from his transistor radio.

G as in Gregarious

She is holding me just like a mother would. And not letting go. Even though my tears and dripping nose are sopping her cotton housedress. I don't even know why I'm crying. I fell off my bike, but I'm not hurt. The blood between my thighs doesn't hurt. Still, it's scary. And I feel stupid. In the film I saw about it—just two months ago when our fifth-grade teacher took us girls to the other room to watch it that last day of school—the woman kept saying how "normal" it is. And Gee Gee is repeating the message.

"It's okay," she tells me as I sob into her chest that smells like roast beef and carrots. "You're fine. It just means you're a young woman now."

I'm only eleven. I don't feel much like a woman. Don't want to be a woman. I want things to stay the same. To be held like a child by my grandmother. To go outside and play till suppertime. To ride my bike without feeling something wet on my seat.

Gee Gee makes me lie down on my bed and brings me a TV tray with two orange chalky baby aspirins (which sparks memories of when I was five and crawled up on top of the stove, poured out a handful, and proceeded to chew a bunch of them before everyone woke up, because I loved the taste. Which still amazes me that I didn't barf them all up) and a steaming cup of Lipton tea on a saucer.

"Here, Honey," Gee Gee says, placing the tray down on a chair next to my bed. "This'll make you feel better."

Fat chance, I think. But I sit up to slurp the hot liquid anyway because when Gee Gee offers you anything to eat or drink, you don't want to hurt her feelings. It's why I'm chubbier than most of my friends. At Gee Gee's table, if you don't take seconds, she thinks her cooking isn't any good.

She goes back to the kitchen, leaving me to wonder how my life will change now that I'm "a woman." Will I still be able to play Barbies and Chutes & Ladders with Jackie next door, who's only ten and hasn't a clue what yucky "womanly" stuff is ahead of her? Next thing you know, I'll be wearing an ugly bra because the mirror keeps showing these bumps on my chest that are growing bigger. Will all the boys now look at me the way the Cartright men gawk at women in *Bonanza* (they don't see ladies often on that prairie, but when they do it's like a Setter's tail pointing straight up at attention). I'm not sure I'm ready for that kind of lurking from boys.

And will I have to stop "acting silly" and be all serious and unhappy like my teacher, the lady at the corner store with the perpetual frown or . . . my mother? I think of that part in the Bible where it says something like, "There comes a time when you must abandon childish ways" and I want to know why we have to when we don't feel like it.

When my mother comes home from work, Gee Gee calls her over and there's whispering in the kitchen. Mom opens the hall closet, and I hear rustling as she digs down deep for something that must be buried pretty good. Finally finding whatever it is, she approaches my bed.

"Gee Gee tells me you're a young woman now." Oh brother, not her too. "Here, I've got these books I want you to read."

Geeze, let me guess. I look at the two pamphlets. One's titled: "You're a Young Woman Now!"

Mom leaves and I flip through drawings of the "menstrual cycle" and learn all about this new womanly life I'm going to lead—apparently for the rest of my life—that involves Kotex sanitary napkins (the included sample looks like a mattress big enough to accommodate Barbie, Ken, *and* their future brood), a bizarre-looking stretch "belt" with snaps (which I have not a clue what *that's* for), a calendar for marking those "special days," and accounts of all the joys of being—yep—*A Woman*. If an overdose of baby aspirin didn't produce barfing, this should certainly do the trick.

But Gee Gee somehow makes it all better. After supper, she brings out my favorite dessert, strawberry shortcake (which I know she was saving for our more formal Sunday dinner), and tells me I don't even have to help with the dishes afterward. "You just lie down and rest," she tells me with knowing eyes.

Maybe this won't be so bad after all.

When I wrote something in fourth grade about my grandmother, the teacher read it out loud in class and I shot my hand up immediately to correct her.

"It's not GeeGee," I announced, "it's *Gee Gee*. Like ga, or guess, or (using a new word I learned in the library) *gregarious*."

Mrs. B looked surprised. I thought it was because of my sudden outburst.

"My, that's quite a word," she said, a little lilt in her voice. "Do you know what gregarious means?"

"Social," I replied, feeling very smart.

My teacher smiled. "And do you know what *that* word means?"

She had me there and we both knew it. "Not really," I replied, feeling not so smart.

All I knew was that gregarious sounded fanciful and fun— like my grandmother. And that the "ga" sound was the right way to say her name. Gee Gee. It wasn't her given name, which was Viola, but it *was* given to her. By my brother. When he was a toddler, he couldn't say "Grandma." It always came out, Gee Gee. So when I came along, as with everything else Dennis did, I followed suit. The nickname seemed perfectly suited for her— even Mom referred to her as Gee Gee when talking to us.

As a social, gregarious person, Gee Gee was always chatting with the neighbors, who she often exchange recipes and just-baked dishes with. When she and Grandpa went to Wally's Bar nearly every afternoon after grocery shopping, or errand running, they socialized with all the patrons, new and old. On weekends, they might even go into town to The Corner Bar, on E. 185th Street on the border of Euclid and Cleveland, to see their big city friends and, after a few beers and shots of whiskey, would dance to the jukebox that played songs by Glenn Miller, Lawrence Welk, and Guy Lombardo. Ralph and Vi were big hits wherever they went.

When I was little, Gee Gee and I had our own social hour. Dennis would be in school, and Mom and Grandpa would be at work, leaving my grandma and me to hit the streets. She'd put me in Dennis's Radio Flyer wagon and off we'd go to Culp's Bend, the bar named after both the owner, and its position at the well-known curve on Lakeshore Blvd. When I got old enough for soda pop, she'd tell the bartender, "And Dee Dee here'll have a Shirley Temple." This was a real treat because I personally liked all the Shirley Temple movies, and drinking the dark, sweet cola stuffed to the top with cherries (Bob the bartender was a generous man) allowed me to pretend that I was the cute and peppy Shirley for the duration of our stay. Gee Gee, in turn, would order up a ginger ale, with a shot of Kessler's on the side. An hour or so later, we'd make the half-mile trip back home, both giddy from a good day in our happy world.

Gee Gee and I took many trips together, always on foot because, like my mother, she didn't drive. Depending on the day, the season, and pressing household chores, we'd first exercise to Paige Palmer on TV, then go out to shop, and socialize. Our excursions to Shoregate Shopping Center were my favorite, even more than Culp's Bend. This walk included a variety of joys, starting with the game of seeing how long I could kick the same stone on the way there.

"That one's too close to the street now, pick another one," Gee Gee would often say, forcing me to start all over. Sometimes I didn't feel like kicking, so would count all the birds we saw, or imagine that I lived in one of the many houses we passed. My favorite was an A-Frame set back from the boulevard. There was not another house like it, and I'd imagine my bedroom was at the top level, with a bear-skinned rug on the floor, and a bed with a dressy pink canopy, and ruffly quilt covered with fancy dolls.

The long shopping strip was nearly a mile away, and the new McDonald's with the big golden arches was conveniently located halfway. So we often stopped for a break, ordering fifteen-cent hamburgers, a paper sack the size of a pocket stuffed with salty fries, and a milkshake (vanilla for me because I was allergic to chocolate, a devastating hardship), then sit outside on the golden bench. We'd then make our way to Shoregate and its many stores. Federal's Department Store had two floors of nearly everything you needed: clothes, household goods, even appliances. There was also a drug store, jewelry store, record store, candy store, bowling alley (where I'd get kicked out of, at thirteen, for shooting pool underage), Kroger supermarket, and Uncle Bills, another department store, but with more stuff.

But our favorite place was Woolworth's Five and Dime. Gee Gee got all her makeup there, which included a round flowery box of Coty face powder and compact with little mirror attached, Maybelline eyebrow pencils and mascara, and Revlon lipstick called "Certainly Red." Being gregarious, she took pride in her looks. We'd then go to the nylon aisle to get her "stockings," which she always rolled up with round elastic stretch bands to just above the knee.

"Let's see what they have over here," she'd then say, the cue to venture over to the children's area where I'd get a new Cupie Doll, or glittery pack of little girl stuff, including dazzling play bracelets and rings wrapped in stiff clear plastic. And maybe a new hairbrush for my dolls.

After making our purchases—and if we hadn't eaten at McDonalds—we'd sit at the lunch counter and order our usual fare. It was always busy so we'd have to wait for an empty stool, which left more time to browse, and buy.

"Okay, now, let's sit before someone else takes it," Gee Gee would say, soon as two stools side by side were empty. "Ready for a hotdog and Coke?"

Need she ask?

The smell of those hotdogs sizzling on the grill made you hungry even if you weren't. And the very sight of those wide, thick buns captured your taste buds. The hair-netted ladies manning the counter would open the buns flat, butter both sides, then slap them on the grill besides the searing dogs. It was worth passing by McDonald's for this.

The casual walks, the hopping up on bar and diner stools, the eating of hot dogs, the chatting with neighbors, the lying on the floor in front of the TV set doing the Rocking Cradle (where we'd lie on our bellies, hold onto our ankles, and rock back and forth) with Paige Palmer to "flatten that tummy area" . . . all reminds me of life with Gee Gee. Yet there was so much more.

Gee Gee was at her best in the kitchen. Cooking grand meals, or a simple grilled cheese sandwich and tomato soup, was her way of showing her love because hugging and kissing were reserved for tragedies, like death, or getting your first period (which, to me, felt like the same thing). Her Sunday dinners, especially, were testaments to your ranking with her that week. If I came home with an A paper, for example, dinner would be my particular favorite: ham, baked beans and potato salad with

Pineapple Upside Down cake for dessert. If Grandpa did something to win her good graces, she'd make a special mince meat or blueberry pie just for him, carving a big R (for Ralph) into the top crust. (Though as previously disclosed, she also made it for him after they'd have a fight). And she always made the standard holiday fare—turkey for Thanksgiving and Christmas, pork and sauerkraut for New Years, corned beef and cabbage for St. Patrick's Day. But none of those meals matched the specialness of the ones she made just for you.

Then sometime between my childhood and adolescence, my mother, brother and I learned that Gee Gee had a secret past. Which shocked us all because Gee Gee was not one to hold back much. Not her feelings, or her opinions—nor did she do it daintily. My grandmother was vocal. And a true master at the art of cursing. She could cuss out anyone at any time, sharply and in running monologues. Though most times, it wasn't directed at a person, but at a thing. If the pie crust broke on its way around the pan, she'd spit *"Jesus H. Christ!"* (After all, she took her baking very seriously.) If the thread refused to be harnessed through the sewing needle, she'd spit *"god-damn, son-of-a-bitch . . ."* It was never just one word, but a string of obscenities that blew out like gusts of funnel clouds whipping sideways, and best you just let her rip till she ran out of momentum.

Although Gee Gee was kind, loving, and giving to her family, she was capable of dishing out venom if she deemed it necessary. Or, worse, she would merely expunge your very existence from planet earth. Such was the case with Harry. Her first husband must have pissed her off so badly she simply erased him from her history, like one does with an Etch-a-Sketch.

My own mother didn't even know about Harry Day until she was in her thirties, and a relative from Gee Gee's hometown of Fostoria let it slip one night. As most things do when alcohol is involved. My mother couldn't have been more shocked as the two women sat chatting in the kitchen sucking down beers after the bar had closed. But when Mom pressed for more details, cousin Bea stopped short.

"Don't you ever mention him to her or she'll have my head for telling you," Bea warned, adding only that the man had been a friend of Cal's, one of Gee Gee's nine older brothers, and considerably older than she was. How old, or how long the relationship lasted, was never disclosed. Bea had sealed her lips.

All Mom ever figured was that it must have been short-lived since Gee Gee was twenty-three when she met Grandpa.

After my mother died, I found old letters from 1919-1921, written in pencil—yet still legible—all signed "Love, Harry." These affectionate notes remarked on how much he enjoyed a spunky girl like her, and how he just couldn't wait for WWI to end so they could finally settle down on the farm of his dreams. That right there must've sealed his fate. As a gregarious, social girl, Gee Gee would've gone stark raving mad with no one but cows and chickens to converse with. Of course, there must have been more to the story for Gee Gee never to acknowledge his existence. And yet, one has to wonder why she'd keep his letters in a pretty floral box for more than sixty years, right up until her death. My guess is that she simply forgot the box was there, tucked far down in the bottom of the large wardrobe cabinet, just as she'd "forgotten" him.

Viola Ruth was born in the small railroad town of Fostoria, Ohio, the fifteenth child born to a couple who finally stopped at sixteen. She apparently couldn't wait to get out of that stifling little town, and her opportunity presented itself when she was sixteen and her older brother's wife took ill and needed help taking care of their young son. She hopped on the next train bound for the exciting big city of Cleveland.

She worked for a few different companies, but was at Willard Battery for the longest, retiring there in 1960 when the company closed. She then used her bountiful energy on us; cooking, baking, sewing, and creating a beautiful yard filled with colorful flower beds of brilliant tulips, hyacinths, and daffodils, along with an enviable bush of hard-to-grow Bleeding Hearts. The flourishing red rose bush extended up one side of the house where you could enjoy its beauty as you washed the kitchen dishes.

And when it came to Dennis and me, our grandmother was our greatest ally. The two adult women in our household fought almost constantly over us. Mom trying to enforce "her" rules in how she wanted us raised, and Gee Gee—as Matriarch—thwarting her at every turn by giving in to us, and sticking up for us whenever we got disciplined.

"Don't yell at her, *I* gave her the chocolate cupcake!" Gee Gee would scream. "It's just one for Chrissakes. Not worth griping about." Then the next day I'd break out in a rash because of my allergy, granting Mom more ammunition. "See! That's precisely why she can't have chocolate!" Mom would say, showing Gee Gee my arms. Still, this was Gee Gee's house, which gave her ultimate power. So after they'd go round and round like this for one reason or another, Mom would eventually give up (albeit, not demurely), slam the bathroom door shut, where she'd remain for a lengthy period, or until Gee Gee settled in to watch the evening television shows, and life returned to a series of the Marlboro Man, Ovaltine, and Alka-Seltzer commercials.

"*Plop, Plop, Fizz, Fizz, oh, what a relief it is.*"

And it was.

Gee Gee was the one person Dennis or I knew we would call, were we to ever land in jail. And she made sure to speak up if she thought we were doing something that would get us there sooner. Or that might even make *her* an accessory. When Dennis and his new bride stayed a few months at Gee Gee's before getting their first house, our wise and protective grandma made sure to say something the day they moved out.

"Now make sure you don't forget about that plastic bag you got up there in the attic. It's in the corner, by your box of dishes," she whispered to Dennis, referring to the ounce bag of marijuana she came across when looking for something else. Her knowing tone of voice told him that there was no use trying to pass it off as oregano.

And when my first boyfriend, who was clueless as to my culinary dysfunction, asked me to make potato salad for his family picnic, Gee Gee came to my rescue and whipped up a huge bowl full, complete with paprika sprinkled on top. "Oh, it was nothing," I casually told the boyfriend who seemed so impressed. No lie there.

For Gee Gee's seventy-eighth (and ultimately, last) birthday, I took her to lunch at the Top of the Town, a skyscraper restaurant in downtown Cleveland. Although I was still afraid of heights, I faced my fears because making this day special for my aging grandmother was more important. Later, the family surprised her with a big party at her favorite bar. Vine Lanes was a bowling alley with a huge bar inside that had provided many fond memories for me as a kid and adolescent. The best were the Sunday afternoons our family spent there after Gee Gee's famous afternoon dinners, after Grandpa died. That August evening was a perfect celebration, and I believe her last real good time.

A few months later, I stopped to check in on her because she hadn't been feeling well. I opened her front door to see Gee Gee trying to walk the few steps from the small living room to the kitchen, tightly gripping the walker she'd had since hurting her leg years before. I don't recall our conversation, how long I stayed, what I did for her. I just recall her expression. How she looked at me when I appeared in her doorway. It was the first time I'd ever seen true fear in my grandmother's eyes.

Hopelessness is a son-of-a-bitchin' feeling, to borrow from one of Gee Gee's common phrases. When someone you love is leaving you, and you both know it, it sucks out all the energy each of you once had. Except in Gee Gee case. She replaced this feeling of helplessness with another kind of energy. Anger. When those people took Gee Gee to the nursing home, she was mad as hell. To her, going to a nursing home meant they were giving you up for dead. So when I came to visit her on her second day there, holding stacks of her favorite reads: *The Cleveland Press*, *National Enquirer, True Detective* and *Star Magazine*, she demanded I leave. "Just go, please," she said as kindly as she could. But her eyes told me she meant it. While I understood her anger at fate, her dismissal of me broke my heart. But as always, I did what she told me.

"She's giving up," the desk nurse said when I asked why she was lying there in a darkened room with all the shades drawn. "We can't get her to eat, or cooperate in any way." Then she added, "She's very stubborn." Oh, yes, tell me about it. The infamous Ruth family trait had taken over. I left, holding in the hysterical sobbing until I got to my car. The pain in my chest had nothing to do with a physical ailment.

Doctors said my grandmother's kind and generous heart was enlarged. The term struck me as ironic. Her big heart was killing her. And breaking mine. The next day she went into a coma. I swear she did it on purpose.

Three months later, Gee Gee miraculously emerged from unconsciousness (and with her mental facilities amazingly intact). We excitedly rushed to her side. She was smiling, as we all were. Hope had returned.

"You look too skinny, haven't you been eating?" was the best greeting I could have wished for. It meant that nothing, really, had changed. She'd been asking me that question since the day Mom moved me out of her house when I was twelve. As if without her doing the cooking, setting it in front of us, then, before that last bite was swallowed, holding out another spoonful to dump on our plates, we would surely perish from malnutrition.

"Yes, Gee Gee," I laughed. "Actually I've been eating a lot."

She threw me that "don't bullshit me" look, and I wanted to tell her that to be honest, I was starving. Starving for her Sunday dinners. For her special birthday cakes, and the left-over batter she always let me eat. For those children's books she'd read to me. And for the way she'd held me when I became a "young woman."

But I couldn't mention any of this, because we all knew those times were gone. We also knew, assured by her doctors, that this renewed perkiness was only temporary.

If it wasn't for hopelessness, we could have said and done quite a few more things that last month of her life.

"Hey Gee Gee," I'd say. "How about you and me taking just one more long walk to Shoregate? We can stop at McDonald's along the way. And still have room for one of those Woolworth's hotdogs with all the works?

Then my gregarious grandma would smile and say, "Well, okay, but after that, we have to stop for last call at Culp's Bend."

And that's just what we would do.

Father of Christmas Past

𝒯he last time I saw my father I gave him twenty dollars. Dennis and I were in Dad's one-room dwelling on Cleveland's west side, which consisted of a dilapidated couch, a TV with aluminum foiled "rabbit ears," and the unsteady wooden table we were all sitting at. Dad was telling us he was between welfare checks and asking if he could borrow some money. Dennis said he didn't have much on him. I searched in my purse and found the Andrew Jackson in the pocket of my checkbook. I was going to deposit it in the bank later that day to pay my gas bill. But I wanted my father to eat.

I was twenty-five years old, freshly divorced, and hardly ever had more than five dollars on me. Still, I handed it to him, despite the fact it was a few days before Christmas and I really needed the money.

"Honey, you know I'll pay you back," he said. "I know, Dad." I knew that he meant it when he said it, even if it would never come to pass. I'd only been in touch with my father the last seven years, and then intermittently, but I knew him to be a sweet, kind, sensitive man. I also knew him to be a man who needed alcohol more than he needed us. As I drove back home that day, I recalled the first time I realized this.

"I would've rather lost Joe to another woman than to his drinking," I overhear Mom tell Grandpa at the kitchen table. I'm seven years old and often force myself to stay awake so I can eavesdrop on these late night conversations between my mother and her dad. It's the only way I get any information at all, since adults never tell kids anything. It's also the only time my mom's voice sounds soft, and not mad at the world.

So I lie here, eyes closed, and listen. It's easy enough. My bedroom has no door. It's in the extended corner of the living room, where the never-used fireplace is. My grandparents' small house has only two bedrooms. One is theirs. The other, my brother's. My mother sleeps on the couch on the opposite side from my "room." On Tuesday nights (Wednesday's her day off from her job at the Cleveland Trust Bank), she waits up for Grandpa to return from his second shift job on the loading dock so they can sit in the kitchen and have a few beers. Oftentimes, Gee Gee goes to bed, leaving the two of them to have lively discussions that I don't always understand. Like when they disagree about something called unions, or talk about relatives who always have some sort of problem. But I secretly enjoy hearing about it all, nonetheless.

Grandpa must not have believed what Mom was saying.

"No, really," she insists. "I could've understood that better. It would've been easier to handle."

I don't think I believe her on that one. Even at seven, I find it hard to believe my mother would've "understood" or "handled" another woman luring her husband away. After all, I've seen *Divorce Court* and *Perry Mason* on TV. I know what betrayal means. Though I also know that some adults look for happiness in the liquid that flows from tall brown bottles. . . .

My mother and father met at the Engel-Fetzers Furriers on Huron Road in downtown Cleveland where they both were working in 1947. She never talked about their two-year courtship but I'd heard over the years that my grandmother (and possibly my less-outspoken grandfather) didn't want her marrying him because of his drinking. Which seemed ironic to me, even a bit hypocritical, because she herself came from a long line of drinkers. Then again, that's probably why.

So the marriage was short-lived. My parents were already separated when I was born, with Mom and Dennis, then three, living at her parents' house. Over the next few years, Daddy would magically appear at Christmastime, like Santa Claus, bringing a gift for everyone, and then disappear until the next year.

In these scenes, Daddy was always kind, jolly, and happy to be there.

But there were other times my father brought havoc to our household. . . .

As Mom tells Grandpa how sorry she is about her circumstances, I lie awake in bed reviewing my daddy moments. I think about the gifts he would bring me when he'd arrive, and how excited I'd been that one Christmas when he brought me my very own electric train set, like the one Dennis had. I can still smell its burning engine when it had stopped working an hour after dinner, and can hear my grandparents and Mom argue about whose fault it was. Was it because I left it plugged in too long? Was it because Daddy had probably gotten it at the Salvation Army? Yes, that was probably it, they decided. I think hard and try to recall what he looked like. His wavy brown hair, always combed neatly, with perfect part on the side and secured with that slick "little dab'll do ya" stuff. And I remember his eyes, though that makes me jealous. They're the color of Lake Erie on a clear day and I always wish I'd gotten them instead of the "hazel" color I got stuck with—a shade not even good enough for Crayola.

As Mom and Grandpa change the subject, I think of that time Daddy came over and it wasn't even Christmas. And how upset I got because he was there to take my brother fishing, and I wasn't invited along.

"I wanna go, too!"

Grandpa looked like he was just about to call me "Little Me too" again, but Gee Gee interrupted.

"Fishing is a boy's activity," she said, trying to make me understand about "fathers and sons." But to me, it sounded terribly unfair. Why can't girls fish? Although had I been perfectly honest, with the yucky worms and all, it didn't sound like my kind of thing.

"Besides," Gee Gee said, "The *Wizard of Oz* is on tonight!"

She knew this was my favorite movie of all time. It played on TV just once a year—the only good thing about March—and I never missed it. Still, I felt left out.

Those few times Daddy came, he and Mommy always talked to one another real politely, like strangers. Like people sharing a bus ride and forced to sit together. But sometimes, I'd catch Mom giving him those mad looks that I never saw her give anyone else. Not even when Dennis and I were at our worst behavior. . . .

When Mom and Grandpa get on the subject of jobs and unions, I get bored. I hug the covers up close to my neck, scrunch the pillow against my ears and try to go to sleep. But then I remember what happened last fall.

"Hi, Honey, how's my little girl?" my father says through the phone receiver. He sounds especially pleased that I answered. "Oh, Daddy, Daddy! Hi! When ya gonna come see me, Daddy?" Suddenly my grandmother appears out of nowhere.

"Gimme that phone!" she says in a mean voice she's never used at me before. Gee Gee rarely yells at me for anything. I'm her grandbaby, whom she spoils incessantly, to the disapproval of my ever-disapproving mother.

She grabs the phone out of my hand and starts swearing before her mouth meets the receiver.

"What the hell are you calling here for? You son-of-a-bitch!"

I run to the big, soft living room chair that's my favorite, and try hard to block out the bad words by putting my hands over my ears. But it doesn't stifle the screaming. I slink down further into the cushion of the overstuffed chair in hopes it will swallow me up. I can't make out Gee Gee's words anymore, so I release one hand to try and learn what's making her so mad.

"If you ever call here again you bastard son-of-a-bitch, I'm calling the police!"

That's all I hear before the slamming of the phone. Then Gee Gee comes over to me. She kneels in front of me and puts her hands on the chair arms. She's still so angry her face is all red, and then says something I'm sure she doesn't mean.

"Your father isn't a good man. He isn't caring for you. He doesn't love you, Honey."

I didn't know, then, about my father's failure to pay child support. Or about his brief stint in the US Marines that led to his AWOL status. Or how alcohol can bring down a good man.

All I knew was that Daddy probably wasn't coming over for any more Christmases.

"He does too love me!" I argued. "He was real happy to hear my voice on the phone, he wants to see me." I'm crying so hard, the words come out in constricted gulps. "And I wanna see him!" I add when I can catch my breath.

"Now, don't cry, Honey," Gee Gee says softly. She tries to hug me, which had always worked in the past. This time, I push her away.

But she doesn't move. "You have us," she says. "We love you, he doesn't. He doesn't help your mother. That's why he can't come here anymore."

My father did not appear the next Christmas, the year I learned that Santa didn't exist. I figured the same could be said of my father, so it became easier to tell people I didn't have a father, than to say the one I had didn't love me. It took many adult years before I understood that he loved me as much as he was able to.

It always comes as a surprise to people when I say I didn't give my father much thought after that. It may have been an unconscious decision to wipe him from my mind, or perhaps because he had rarely appeared in my life as it was. Nonetheless, I went on to lead a normal, fairly happy childhood, and never really missed his presence. When I was eighteen, my brother informed me that he had "looked Dad up."

"Guess who's coming to dinner?" Dennis announced one day to Mom and Gee Gee, though maybe not in those exact words. Thirteen years had passed since any of us had seen or heard from my father. My brother's wife, who was close to her parents, had convinced him to get reacquainted with his father. The search didn't take long. Dennis found him at Stella Maris, a Cleveland alcohol rehabilitation facility, where we learned Dad spent a lot of time, to try the sober route, or in winter, to keep from freezing to death on the bitter city streets. It appeared time does heal, somewhat, as Mom and Gee Gee were surprisingly accepting of this news. I suspect because they felt the importance of our getting to know him. (Or perhaps for us to realize they'd been right about him all along.)

A few weeks later, Dennis and his wife Laura pulled into Gee Gee's drive with my father in tow. Dad had evidently spent some time at the Salvation Army's clothing store and arrived looking like a bible salesman in a pale blue suit, matching tie and shined up brown leather shoes. His dark wavy hair was still parted to the side, and I noticed his shirt matched his Lake Erie summer blue eyes.

And he was sober. For a moment, I'd forgotten that he was a nonfunctioning alcoholic.

"Hi, Honey," he said, hugging me tight. I saw mist in his eyes, and remember thinking I'd never saw a man happier, or more nervous, than he was at this moment.

But I felt nothing. I could only respond with a meek smile. This man, so caught up with emotion, was a stranger to me. A nice, sweet stranger.

"Dinner's ready," Gee Gee announced.

The table was set. Mom and Gee Gee sat on one side, Dennis and his wife across from them. Dad sat on one end, claiming my deceased grandpa's chair, and I sat on the other, across from him—like bookends holding in a stack of mysteries. As we ate roast beef and potatoes, I would sneak glimpses at my father, searching for traits that I may have acquired from him. That's when I noticed his prominent nose. *Figures,* I thought, *that I would get that nose, rather than his Lake Erie eyes.*

Conversation was stiff, but ongoing.

"They say it's going to be miserably hot this summer," said Gee Gee. "I don't know how I'll stand it."

Then Mom. "Joe, you remember Aunt Grace, don't you? She died, you know . . . it was terrible . . . such a shock . . . And Helen, well, I haven't seen her in years . . . I don't suppose you see your sister Mary, do you? I wonder how her kids are doin'?" she rambled on.

The words spilled out, one after another, as if any dead air might suck us up like a vacuum hose and fill our baggage of guilt and regret like leftover soot. After we all devoured dessert, Gee Gee cleared the table, moved the doilies, and shook out the tablecloth to make way for poker, a game that always brought relief and lively banter to our family. As spades, hearts, clubs, and diamonds flashed around the tabletop, the stifling air began to clear with each scoop of winning pennies. It appeared that Mom and Gee Gee had somehow managed to bury the past and live in the present. After that, Dad became a fairly regular Sunday dinner guest.

A few years later, in 1977, I asked my father to walk me down the aisle at my first wedding. The night of the rehearsal dinner, Dad became Santa again. This time it wasn't a used train set, or doll with missing hair. The man came up to me and gave me an envelope. "Go ahead," he urged, with shiny baby blues.

"Open it." I did as told, and pulled out three one hundred dollar bills.

"Oh, that's too much!" I exclaimed wondering at once where the hell my father—who far as I knew never held a fulltime job since marrying my mother—could have managed to acquire such funds. But I didn't ask. I didn't want to know.

"Take it," he said, firmly pressing my hand. He seemed so proud to be able to do this, I couldn't deny him.

"Thanks, Dad," I said, managing a smile.

With all the dinners consumed and cards that had passed in those reunion years, I assumed that Mom had forgotten certain issues about my father, just as I had. So I thought nothing of asking my estranged parents—one minute before the music began—to participate in the Bridal Dance, along with my new husband's parents.

The photo of my dancing parents at my wedding is not in any keepsake album. The reminder is too painful. The snapshot shows my properly suited father, markedly drunk, holding my mother in his arms (left hand clutching her right, right arm snuggling her waist), smiling blissfully with glazed eyes. My mother, in sparkly silver mother-of-the-bride gown, is trying, unsuccessfully, to keep her distance as they sway to "Let Me Call You, Sweetheart." She is not smiling. The scowl on her face is one I'd seen before, that same stern look I noticed years before when no one else did. I came across the photo not long after my father died, and recalled the moment when the song was over and the bridal party returned to their seats.

"That's the hardest thing I've ever done," she whispered to me in exasperation the minute my father released her.

"*The Hardest Thing I've Ever Done.*" Her words echoed in my ears. It was quite a statement, considering her many past struggles. At that moment, I suddenly realized that I, the excitable bride, had failed to take my mother's feelings into consideration. I had forced her to dance with a man she had once loved and hated, at their daughter's wedding. Where emotions run high. Where a two-minute dance can replay a lifetime of regret. And disdain.

My mother quickly walked away then, leaving me standing on the empty dance floor, alone with her pain. . . .

When my father called me on Christmas morning in

1979—two days after I'd given him the twenty dollar bill—he was drunk.

"I wanna seeee you guys. Wanna seeee you on Chrissstmusss," he tried talking clearly, but the slur was evident.

My father could never afford a car, and was never capable of driving one. It had been snowing all night and was still snowing when he called, so I'd been debating whether to make the trip to pick him up for Gee Gee's annual Christmas dinner. Normally, he wouldn't be drunk till somewhere between poker and dessert.

"I can't waaaait to seeee you, Honey. Your daddy loooves you."

That's when I knew I wasn't going to pick him up. I knew the money I'd given him had been spent on booze. That really pissed me off.

"I'm sorry, Dad, but the weather's just too bad outside. And they're calling for more snow."

With that statement he began sobbing over the phone, begging me to come and get him so he could spend Christmas with his kids. I cringed. Guilt pumped through my veins, but so did disgust. Damn him! He had spent money that I couldn't afford to give him, and instead of using it for food, my father spent it on liquor. I had to wonder why this revelation surprised me so. It's what alcoholics do.

I repeated my rejection several times, as one does to a drunk who doesn't understand the first ten times you tell them something.

"Don't worry, Dad, we'll come get you next week for dinner. I promise." He was still crying when I hung up. I felt like crying, too. But didn't.

Five days later, I got the call no one wants.

"Your mother's on the phone," the salon receptionist said just as I walked to the desk for my next waiting appointment.

Mom wasn't quite sure how to say it. This was news they say you shouldn't give over the telephone. But then, she had little choice. She didn't drive, and to tell me to come to her place right away would make the situation worse, more dramatic.

"I'm sorry to tell you this at work but I just got a phone call," she paused. "Your father is dead. They found him in his apartment. They think it was a heart attack."

I stood there holding the phone a minute or so before

saying calmly, "Ok, Mom, I'll be right over."

I remember hanging up the phone. I remember going into the bathroom. I remember locking the door behind me. I remember the whole surreal scene, like an Edward Albee play. My knees buckled with the clicking of the lock and I slid slowly down the wall next to the toilet until I reached the floor, my sodden face buried into my lap. My emotions tightfisted in my stomach.

And I remember how baffled I was at this reaction. After all, I'd barely known this man who was my father, nor had he really known me. In the end, we'd had never held an in-depth or serious conversation about anything that really mattered—life, relationships, or if he ever regretted not seeing his children grow up.

I'd spent years not giving him a moment's thought. Only if something sparked it. Like those who only eat turkey when it's Thanksgiving. It's not that they don't like turkey. It's just that they don't think of eating it the rest of the year.

But he *was* my father, if in name only. After burying my feelings toward him for years, I now had to bury any chance at a better relationship with him. And so I sat on the bathroom floor of the beauty salon and mourned the father I barely knew. As I did, I recalled my last daddy moment. How he'd begged me to come and get him for Christmas dinner, and how I refused him. His last words to me kept ringing through my head, and I wondered if he may have known he didn't have long, given how adamant he'd been. And I, the mean-spirited, selfish, bitch of a daughter, stripped him—and us—of one last time together.

Guilt has an evil way of shredding your insides.

"Is anyone in there?" the customer's knocking disrupted my self-hatred.

"Just a minute," I called out, and forced myself up off the floor. Grabbing wads of toilet paper, I blew my nose, and looked up to meet my horrid reflection in the mirror. I bent over the sink to splash my reddened face, then willed the image in the mirror to suck it up and be a big girl now.

I opened the door.

"My father died," I announced to my gaping coworkers. "I have to go."

Then I walked out to arrange my father's funeral.

There's a saying that goes something like, "If you lend

someone twenty dollars and never see that person again, it's still probably worth it."

In time I came to grasp its meaning. I had come through when my father needed me. In giving him all the money I had, I had shown him generosity, forgiveness, and acceptance. And though he didn't spend the money in the manner I'd expected, he used it as he saw fit. He spent my gift on something he needed, even more than wanted. And I'm sure it gave him some comfort, in a way only addicts understand.

I never really knew my father. I can't comprehend how he lived. What he thought about. Why he did what he did. Why he didn't do what he should have. Perhaps if I'd asked him, he couldn't tell me, either. His life was like Lake Erie—mysterious, often murky, certainly lonely. Blue eyes looking into the cloudy shell of an empty bottle.

It was agreed that my sailor brother would spread our father's ashes into the lake that we all knew better than we knew him. I was not present for that event. Did not need to be.

When I think now of my father, I am content. I'm at peace with the notion that perhaps the greatest gift this man had given his children was in not having us grow up knowing, or seeing, too much.

It's what some might call, a blessing in disguise.

Letters to Kathy

Too few stop to pass the time
Guess that's how it goes
So sure that there's much more than this
When really no one knows . . .
- from Rosewood Bitters, by Michael Stanley

January 1991

Ðear Kathy:

I still hover safely by your bedroom door. During the past year, your tumors have been growing outside your skin, and they are—I hate to say it and I'm sorry—they are grotesque. There is just no other word to describe it. They look like moon craters—purplish black blobs the size of grapefruits—sticking out on your neck, your arms, your chest, and from what I hear, your legs, too (you are always under a blanket now, as you lie in bed anticipating death). A lot of people have stopped coming to see you. It's too painful for them (ironic, since it's nothing to the pain you suffer). You don't even see much of Melissa now. It would be too upsetting for a twelve-year-old to see her mother like this. It's upsetting for us adults. Your boyfriend, after living together for two years, has abandoned you. All you have now is your family.

You have a loyal, loving family. But it is your mother who suffers the most. She is now your nursemaid. Every day she gives you sponge baths, cleans and dresses those bed sores, and does it all, somehow, without letting you see her heartache. I don't know how she does that.

Who would've thought all those fun times at the beach, the regular campouts, the customary slathering of baby oil on your skin would be your death sentence? People still think you can't die from skin cancer. Most have never heard its proper term, malignant melanoma. And I wonder if, even you, thought that a simple scrapping away of the odd-looking moles was all that was needed to send you on your merry way. I don't know. We never talked about that.

I know you appreciate that your brother Jeff and I stop by, though not nearly as often as we should. And as you know, I never go near your bed. I just can't seem to get close to those tumors. That one time you were in the hospital, I remember how shocked I was when I called you and you said they'd taken out *twelve* tumors, and that there were still some left (I guess they felt a dozen was enough for one day). I didn't visit you then. I was "too busy." To be fair, I *was* busy, since Tiffany was a newborn and I was trying to adjust to having two small children. I thought it was enough that I keep in touch by phone and offer my support—long distance.

But to be honest, that was only half the reason. The other truth . . . I'm ashamed to tell anyone. You see, somewhere in my psyche I'm afraid I'll catch it somehow. I know, I know, that's so *crazy*. How can I think that? It makes no sense. But they still can't convince people that AIDS isn't contagious. As if just being in the same room with an inflicted person can expose you and trap you into its snarly web. Like a dream catcher. Only this would be a nightmare catcher.

I can't help thinking "what if" the so-called experts are wrong about the AIDS thing. Or we discover that they (whoever "they" are) are outright lying when they say you can't catch it except through blood or saliva because they don't want to create a panic.

But this isn't AIDS. It's cancer. The disease, besides heart, that experts say we're most likely to die from. But that's supposed to be when we're old, not in our thirties. Yet this is something you don't hear much about—it's still "rare." And the logical part of my germ-phobe brain knows this cancer is not contagious, so I feel like a real idiot. But I'm a mother of two now, and paranoia is my new companion.

So there I stay. Safely by the door. Just in case . . . .

Winter 1989

Dear Kathy:

I've decided to write down my thoughts to you and I don't know if I'll ever even give you these letters, but I need to do this. Because lately all these memories keep creeping into my head, and I want to document them. So that if, *when*, you get better, we'll have other things to talk about than "the time you had cancer."

I'm thinking about that Michael Stanley Band concert on New Year's Eve, 1981, at the Richfield Coliseum. What a great time that was, huh? Jeff and I had been together about a year then, and you and I became fast friends. I still have that picture I took right before we left for the concert. I was ready to take it and you were chatting with Jeff, and I had to tell you to "Hurry up, get in the picture," and you ran to join your sister just in time. And there you were, as always, smiling.

Remember all of us piling into that black van of Jeff's? We were all talking at once, smoking cigarettes, passing joints, drinking Hawaiian Shooters from a pitcher. The radio was blasting MSB songs on WMMS. Their "Heartland" album had just come out, and "Lover" was every woman's favorite song (and "*Thank God for the man who put the white lines on the highway*" everyone's favorite lyric). At the concert, we didn't sit down once through the entire show. Dancing and singing to every song . . .

We sure laughed a lot back then. On the way home we were all quiet, though, burned out from the revelry, but looking forward to another year of partying. We never thought much beyond the present. We lived for today, like that Grassroots song.

And now this. Everyone says you are the last person who should have to go through this. And it's true. You are sweet and kind and funny, and oh so full of life—it seems like you're always laughing. Well, least until that first tumor appeared. And you have a daughter to raise. So it really isn't fair. Melissa's just ten, and the two of you have already had your share of difficulties, heartache, challenges. After you're gone—that is, if you don't beat this, and if there's anyone who could defy the doctors grim diagnoses, it'd be you—people who have known and loved you will say they miss your distinctive voice, your hearty laugh. But your daughter has no idea what you sound like. She can't hear that great laugh of yours, or know the sound of chirping birds. And when you'd use those flash cards that show simple words, she can't speak them. I've always marveled at how you took all that in stride. I recall how you'd sit patiently on the floor, signing to your daughter. You'd shake your head firmly when she'd get a sign wrong, and make her do it again. You wanted her to be able to communicate to the world. To you.

I never heard you complain about all those times you woke in the middle of the night to give her that medicine for her juvenile arthritis. And all the times you had to take that child to the doctor. All the time, and energy, you spent teaching her how to live in a world of silence. You were determined that she be strong (like you are now) and self-reliant (like you can't be now), despite her many health issues. You took signing classes so you could share thoughts and knowledge with her. When you and Terry divorced, she was just three. You then made it your personal mission to be everything your daughter required. It was almost like it was you and she against the world. I think that's how you viewed it. Even when you did get a chance to go out with friends, you talked about her the most. "Melissa did this . . . Melissa did that." Strangers overhearing you would never guess the problems you both faced. Because that never defined either of you.

And cancer doesn't define you now. It makes me mad that doctors seem to already be writing you off. Ironic that this is one of the cancers with a caustic stipulation: the easiest to cure, *but* only if it's "caught in time," in which case you are doomed. Yours crept up in a sly and devious manner. And now, here we all are. Your parents, your five brothers and sisters, and all your friends, refusing to accept, or acknowledge, this death sentence. We stubbornly cling to hope, and discuss only what's next on the agenda to get you well. Because the only way we all can deal with it is to have some semblance of optimism in the face of those ominous statistics. Because you, my dear sister-in-law, deserve better than to have anyone give up on you so easily.

You know, though, as I look back to last year, I think you did suspect that something was wrong early on. And I, too, recall a nagging little thing in the back of my mind (intuition?) telling me that something wasn't right. But I consciously chose to dismiss it.

It was when you were babysitting Danielle last year. She was just over a year old, and you were about the only one we trusted to watch her. When we came home, you were lying on the couch reading a medical book.

"Kathy, of all the books I have," I joked, "you're reading that?" I thought you'd say that you just found it fascinating reading. But instead you said, "I was looking something up, I've got this thing." Or something to that effect.

Sometime soon after, you went to the doctor and they told you about the tumor in your abdomen. From then on, your life has been as series of tests, and blood work, and operations to remove those tumors that are multiplying faster than fungus in a petrie dish. "They" say—if doctors don't catch this type of cancer early—patients die within eight months.

But here you are—more than a year later—*surviving*. The disease is ruthless, tormenting, and heartbreaking. But we all say, you're tough. A fighter.

A fighter who is slowly, painfully, losing the battle.

You are only thirty-four years old.

It really, really isn't fair . . .

I just thought of more of my favorite memories with you. Remember when we went to the movies and saw *Mask*, with Cher and my movie star crush Sam Elliot? (God, that deep voice of his . . .). I can't believe that was five years ago already. Remember how hard we tried not to cry at the end, when Rocky Dennis died?

And I will *never* forget that time we took Melissa to the carnival at Shoregate Shopping Center. You had that old beater with the hole in the floor board, and Melinda, then just three, took her shoes off in the backseat and we discovered too late that one shoe must've fallen out the car by way of that hole. Me, I would've been so upset, even mad, because now you'd have to go and buy another pair, and none of us were making much money. But you thought it was hilarious. You started laughing at the absurdity of it all. Which made me laugh, too. We drove the rest of the way home cracking up, with Melissa, quiet little Melissa in the back seat of her own silent world. You always saw the humor in most everything. A trait that would ultimately serve you well down another road.

Now if you'd ask my mom for memories about you, she'd

jump right in with the stories of those times we took her to the E. 185th Street Festival. Jeff would babysit, and you, me, and my mom would do the "Pub Crawl." With so many bars on that street, it was a good thing we could walk to Mom's apartment! We'd talk, and laugh, and giggle all the way home. You were—are—one of my mom's favorite people. "I really like that girl," she'd often say after seeing you. Those times were fun, but the memories are clouded now by that last time we went. It was last August, and as we sat in the bar, the final crawl of the night, you started telling me about the latest tumor doctors had found, and how they were going to try and take that one out, too. You mentioned the blood work, saying something about some new experiment they were going to try on you. Something about filtering out white and/or red blood cells. I don't know, alcohol soaked up the details. Details I really, still, don't want to know.

But I do know this.

Like my mom, you are one of my favorite people, too. I never thought much about how great a person you really are, until my wedding to your brother. I was all aflutter that day, all excited to marry this man so perfect for me. So, of course, I wanted everything to be just right. Ever the helpful one, you were already there when I arrived at the apartment where we'd be getting ready, and you saw the look of disappointment on my face.

"I can't believe it," I said as I walked in the door. I'd just returned from picking up my "bouquet." "All I wanted was just one red rose with baby's breath and a little ribbon, and look at this rose! It's half-dead already, it'll never last the day in this heat. It's supposed to be 93 degrees today!"

"Here," you said, taking it from my hand. "Maybe all it needs is some water." You set it in a vase to try and liven it up, then told me you had to go somewhere real quick and promised to be back before we were ready to leave.

I busied myself with other details and was standing in the living room wearing my wedding dress when I heard the door open. I swung around to see you there, holding in your hand the most beautiful blooming red rose I have ever seen.

"Here you go," you said—as if it was no big deal. You then proceeded to take the lackluster bouquet apart and totally redid it with the fresh budding rose.

I get choked up every time I think about that simple little thing you did for me, which wasn't a simple thing at all.

266

Then again, such a thoughtful, unselfish gesture was so like you.

Which makes me feel even more awful about how I'm dealing with your illness.

Just like those people who no longer come and visit you, I am just as bad as they are, as I stand by your bedroom door instead of sitting by your bedside holding your hand. And isn't it just like you to somehow understand and not hold it against any of us. Those who don't come, and those who do come—but don't get too close—are forgiven. I find this amazing. I can't even forgive myself for being like this. For my absurd paranoia.

But get this. I'm really angry toward your former boyfriend for not sticking by you. When I mention this one day as you lie on your death bed, you say simply, "He couldn't handle it." And I want to scream at him, "Oh you poor fuckin' thing. Can't handle it? *None* of us can handle it, dumb shit!"

This all makes no sense. You of all people. The kind one. The one with the little daughter who can't hear and needs you so much. You, the one who laughs so easily. And yet, you're handling it better than anyone.

This all really sucks.

April 1991

Dear Kathy:

Did I ever tell you how much Danielle loves that little plastic record player you gave her when she was two? With those colored records that play those nursery rhymes? Even at four, she still plays it. And even when she—and Tiffany, who I'm sure will be playing with it soon—outgrows it, I will save it. After all, they won't have much to remember you by. I'll put it away in the attic and years from now, when they have their own kids, they can show it to them, and tell them how they used to play it for hours. By then, it'll be an antique, like the first telephone. Still. I hope they remember . . .

We all know it's only a matter of time now. Last week you told me about your conversation with Kelly, Melissa's step-mother.

"We've been talking everyday—for hours—about how to raise Melissa," you tell me. "We even laugh at the funny things she does."

It fucking breaks my heart.

Then it shatters, as you add. "I told her yesterday, 'She's your daughter now.' "

You don't cry when you say this, you simply state it matter-of-factly.

"I'm going to get some water downstairs, want anything?" I said, and of course we both knew I needed a moment to gain my composure.

My own daughters are four and one, and I cannot fathom being strong enough to say those words to another woman. Even if I liked, and trusted, her. I'd stubbornly hang on to the fantasy that I would always be their one and only mother. Because I'm so much more selfish than you are. You, my friend, my sister, are a saint.

You also realize that we have to face reality. That there is no more hope. No more operations. No more experiments. You have just days left.

The other day I heard that Louis Armstrong song, "What a Wonderful World," and I recalled the time I was visiting you and that song (now in an ice cream commercial) came on TV, and you said, out of the blue, "Oh, that's one of my favorite songs." I stood there thinking, how can that be? A wonderful world? Are you fuckin' kidding' me? I would be so angry at this world right now, if I were you. I'd probably be even angry at God. I just don't get how, even a trouper like you, can think that way at this point.

May 21, 1991

Dear Kathy:

The cancer has invaded your brain. So at least—hopefully, you don't actually realize what's happening. I wish you could've heard your brother, my husband, call the radio station the other night, and dedicate Zeppelin's *Stairway to Heaven* to you. It was his way of saying goodbye because he can't quite summon up the nerve to see you like this.

We are left to bide our time and wait. Wait for that phone call.

And finally, it comes.

Jeff isn't home, and I decide not to call him. I'll just wait.

I am lying here with Danielle in her little bed. Baby Tiffany is sleeping soundly in her crib. And Danielle, now four, has just drifted off. I lie here looking up at the plastic glow-in-the-dark stars on the ceiling and wonder where you are going right now. Does that stairway to heaven get you there fast? Or are there different pathways you must take. Are you watching your life flash before you right now? If so, I hope you're reliving that MSB concert. And that *Mask* movie we so loved (hey, maybe you'll meet the real Rocky Dennis) . . . .

June 1991

Dear Kathy:

I've just had a weird dream about you this morning. The kids were sleeping in, so I decided to go back to bed. And that's when you came. You were floating above me, up in the sky, kind of glowing, in a light powder-blue nightgown. I could see you so vividly. I started crying, and apologizing all over the place. "I'm sorry, Kathy, that I wouldn't come near you when you were so sick, I am so . . ." and you stopped me with your hand and shook your head. "Do not be sorry. I am *so* good right now. Do not be sorry for me. Do not feel guilt. It's all good. Really . . . ." You didn't actually speak the words, it was like you put it into my brain telepathically.

Then you shot up the sky like a bright, dazzling meteor.

I awoke with a start. And as I sat up in bed replaying it over in my mind, I don't believe it was a dream . . . .

Fall 2007

Dear Kathy:

I made you a promise at your funeral. I whispered to you that I wouldn't let people forget you. Especially my children. I told you that I'd write something about you, for you. A few months later, the words came to me easily, in poetry form:

October 23, 1991

It's your birthday today.
Where are you? Are you happy? Relieved? At peace?

Are you aware of us, the ones you left behind?
We, who think of you, love you, miss you?

It's a beautiful day today, this autumn lull.
Is your world more radiant than the bright sun now shining through this clear, blue sky?
More vibrant than the earthly glow of amber and crimson leaves now scattering across the land, from the gentle sway of the wind?
My children are at play, happily oblivious to so many things in life.
Of people who will come and go in their lives.
Yet, that's what it's all about.
People.
By simply living our lives, people enter it.
Some we forget, some we reject, others we embrace.
I embrace knowing you.
Your easy-going manner. Your casual helpfulness.
Your dilemmas, your strength
Your laughter – OH! Most certainly your laughter!
Of course, I do miss you. Though I missed you long before you actually left.
You've touched many a life here.
You continue to do so.
What a Legacy!

Happy Birthday, Kathy.
See you again. Someday.

Love,
A sister.

Now. Just a few more things before I go.
I want you to know I've been paying attention. Besides that "weird" dream, I have fully recognized the other "weird" happenings since you've been gone. Like that very day you came to me in that dream and later that afternoon, I took the girls for a walk to the beach and out of absolutely nowhere Danielle starts singing "Somewhere Over the Rainbow." Man, you kind of freaked me out on that one. The girls hadn't watched *The Wizard of Oz* for months and I'd just been thinking of you, and there's Danielle–who doesn't make a habit of just belting out a song unprompted—singing the

song that reminds your family of you. Wow.

A few months later, I had another dream. We were all sitting around your mother's table having dinner and you are there, but you weren't talking. Not a word (which really isn't you). It was rather unsettling. But not as unsettling as learning some days later that your brother, David, had had the same exact dream. How is that possible? How could any two people have such a similar dream? Yet, it felt just like something you would do. So we mentally filed it away under "gift" and never spoke of it again.

And that time I took Melissa to the circus with my girls. I thought I had brought enough money (*Boy these things are expensive*, I remember thinking), until we were standing in line and I was reading the prices on the board. I was getting nervous, hoping the kids wouldn't want too much candy and stuff, or those fancy balloons, because I barely had enough to get us all in. I was nearing the ticket window, practically breaking into a sweat in fear these kids wouldn't be able to get anything, then get bored, and what I meant to be a happy time would end up being something the girls would later tell people, "Our Mom wouldn't let us get *nothin'. Everybody* was all eating cotton candy, and carrying animal balloons, and there we were, just sittin.' With nothin' . . . "

Just then, a man approached me.

"Excuse me, ma'am, but I have an extra ticket. Can you use it?"

I was stunned into silence, so just nodded my head. The man smiled, handed me the ticket. I mumbled a grateful thank you before he disappeared. I never saw him again.

I knew right then that was your handy work. So, thanks, Kathy. Melissa and the girls had a great time.

And each one took home a balloon . . .

But then came the time, a few years after they'd spread your ashes on your cousin's farm (you wanted to be somewhere beautiful and it sure is), and we were visiting. I went up on that hill alone, to talk to you. Afterward, I returned to the house—everyone else was outside somewhere—and as I opened the door, the radio was playing "What a Wonderful World." I stood there, chills running through me and I, again, started to cry. But it was a reassuring cry.

And finally, finally, I got it. About that song. When you had remarked about how you liked it, you were saying that you appreciated everything there is that makes the world wonderful—nature, family, laughter. The world truly is full of wonder, and while you hated to leave it, you were grateful to have been a part of it.

Yes, I get it now.

We didn't know back then, Kathy, but we do now, about the dangers of the sun and causes of skin cancer. How it can kill. Yet you wouldn't believe how many still lie in the sun incessantly. And those tanning beds that had just come out when you were first diagnosed? Remember they said how safe those were? Well, not so much now. But people still bake in them. But then, people still smoke, too. And yeah, it's true we could get hit by a truck tomorrow . . .

Although cancer takes away so much, it can't take away our memories. And thanks to your kind, bubbly, and helpful nature, we've got some great ones of you.

Your name still comes up often, you know. And when it does, I sometimes say (forgetting your other siblings are present), that you were my favorite in the family. But it's okay, because whenever I mention this to anyone who knew you, it never comes as a surprise.

After all, you were everyone's favorite.

And Tigger, Too

He was six weeks old, sitting comfortably atop an empty dog cage, paws tucked under his tiger kitten frame, calmly observing the bustling scene around him. I was twenty-three, and late for work. But I'd promised my brother I'd take his dog to get boarded while he and his wife went on vacation. I had no plans on falling in love when I barged into the animal shelter. I was too busy holding back Dennis's German Sheppard, who had his eye on a sweet cocker spaniel, and feeling the pain in my hands from gripping the leash so tight. Amid all the commotion—the barking, yipping, and meowing—I so wanted to be out of there, like yesterday.

"Hi, I'm here to drop off Bandit," I shouted to the stout white-haired lady at the counter.

"Yes, we're expecting him," she shouted back. "Here, just sign this form and we'll take him back."

"Wow, that's great." I like expedient personnel.

But then my eyes shifted to the right, and I saw that tabby face.

"Ah, what a cool kitten," I said, pointing to the corner. "He doesn't seem a bit ruffled by all the noise and barking dogs."

"Yeah, he's a tough little guy, nothing gets him rattled," she said, handing Bandit over to her helper. "Someone dumped him out of car few weeks back, and he came right up to the door and meowed like he'd just come for a visit. But he was a mess. Fleas, worms . . . and the poor thing was starving. We brought him up to snuff, though. We dipped him, gave him his shots, pumped him up with Kitten Chow and he's doing great." Then as an afterthought, "He's up for adoption, ya know."

My new first husband and I did not need, nor desire, another pet. We had a frisky Collie/Sheppard mix named Dawn (his), and a half-Siamese cat named Yahtzee (mine).

"Ahh, I wish I could take him, he's really cute. And I like his attitude," I said, as the kitten stretched his back, shifted positions, before settling back down again. All with an easy-going stance. "But I already have a dog and cat at home. And my husband's not even crazy about cats."

"Sure I understand. I just really hope to find the little guy a good home. He's a real sweetie, very affectionate. We named him Surprise because of his sudden appearance at our door."

As I drove to work, my mind was less on what I was going to say to my boss about my tardiness, and more on that tiger kitten. *Surprise*? That's no name for that cat. It didn't suit him at all. If he were mine, I reasoned, I'd name him Tigger. Yep, that was a perfect name for this little cat.

When love grabs a hold of you, it permeates your entire being and you can't think of nothing else but the object of your affection. By lunch time, the thought of someone else having that cat was inconceivable to me. On the way home, I ignored the turn that led to my house and headed straight for the animal boarding shelter, praying I wasn't too late.

"I changed my mind," I told the woman soon as I threw open the door. "I'll take him. I just have to have that cat."

"What about your husband?" She said, placing him in my arms like a newborn baby.

"I'll talk him into it," I said with more confidence than I felt.

So began a love affair that lasted the next eighteen years.

Some people are dog-lovers. They like the way their dogs get all hyper soon as they walk in the door. They welcome the dog's neediness and willingness to do anything to make them happy. Some even think that because Dog is God spelled backwards, they are holy spirits wrapped in fur. While I can appreciate all that (though not sure about the Dog/God thing), I grew up with a menagerie of felines. So I understand cats' independent nature (which some, usually dog-lovers, mistake for arrogance). I appreciate their suave, free-spirited, yet affectionate (albeit choosy) personality. Unlike dogs, who hover, and pant, and jump, and drool (and that's fine if you like that sort of thing), cats cuddle up with you on the couch (well, okay, only when they feel like it, but still), they rub their soft little bodies along your legs (well, okay, only when they're hungry . . . *still*), and they purr. Now, that's the thing. No other animal purrs. And there's hardly anything more soothing and life-assuring than pressing your ear against its furry form as you lie in bed at night. It's the ultimate de-stresser.

And just as there are people who, upon introduction, you feel an instant connection to, there are certain animals that draw you in the same way. Like they're your own personal pet angel. You can have twenty animals in the span of your lifetime, but chances are, like lovers, one of them is going to be extra special— "the one." And as with humans, that bond can last forever.

For me, that was Tigger. And he has quite a story. Several, actually. He was the epitome of that saying, "cats have nine lives." This handsome tabby began life abandoned, a kitten discarded along a busy highway. Later, he would change residents on a regular basis, due to his twenty-something owner's topsy-turvy life. He would find himself accidentally boarded up in a pantry (that curiosity thing got the best of him). He would be kidnapped by a jealous ex-wife who, until forced to fess up, claimed he'd gotten lost in a snow blizzard. After miraculously being rescued from said kidnapper, Tigger would then get side-swiped by a car, where he'd limp home with a broken jaw and other head injuries that left him blinded in one eye.

All before the age of four.

Guess I should've named him Lucky.

But I'm getting ahead of myself. Let's go back to the beginning . . .

At the time I fell in love with Tigger, I was married to a Gemini, the sign of the twins. I often kidded that I never knew which twin I'd come home to because Tom had two distinct personalities. One was gruff with no sense of humor, the other was sweet and humorous. When I married him, I naively thought I could eliminate the bad twin and bring out the good one for all time to come. That's how you think when you're twenty-something.

Fortunately for me and Tigger, I came home that day to the Good Twin.

"Can we keep him?" I asked, using all my wily, womanly, and new wifely ways.

As were Tigger's ways, soon as Tom mumbled a resigned okay, he adjusted beautifully to his surroundings. He made friends with Dawn and Yahtzee (though that took a few days), and wisely endeared himself to the house master. This smart little tabby seemed to instinctively know that this was his ticket to kitty paradise.

The paradise part was short-lived, however, and two years later, we abruptly high-tailed it out of there. Him, me, Yahtzee, and a box of books. After a few more moves, we settled for a time at Gee Gee's house. It was here that the water heater guy finished up his day's work, and so, replaced the section of the wall that covered the pipes in the back kitchen pantry. Apparently he didn't notice that my inquisitive cat had crawled in, and proceeded to board Tigger up, too. That night I looked for Tigger everywhere, especially when I began hearing a faint, far-off meow. I followed the desperate cry, finally settling near the kitchen corner, and, realizing what happened, summoned my brother immediately for help. At two in the morning. Dennis rushed right over, not for my benefit, but because Tigger had also wisely endeared himself to my brother as well.

When I met the man who'd become my second husband, he had three cats—leftovers from his own first marriage—despite his claim that he, too, was in no way a cat person. I gave Yahtzee to a friend, but insisted on keeping Tigger. "It's a package deal," I told him. Jeff wasn't crazy about the idea but figured, how long can a cat live, anyway?

Tigger was an indoor/outdoor cat despite vets telling you it's safer to keep your cat indoors. But he had a wild streak, and insistent meow, that demanded he be let out for new adventures, which often involved his returning home with a dead mouse or fish in his ever-proud puss. He'd look wounded, and surprised, when I'd shriek at his capturing talents. But then would repeat the activity, as if determined to impress me with his hunting and fishing triumphs. His adventuresome nature did have a positive side. I never once needed a cat box. Tigger would meow at the door when nature called, and return in his own good time. No matter where we set up house (and as I mentioned, there were several), I could let Tigger outside, and he always came back.

The day he didn't, I knew something was wrong.

"Tigger, Tiiigggger, where are you?" I called repeatedly that Friday morning as swirling snow whipped around me like slaps of frozen confetti. He didn't respond that Saturday, nor that Sunday. By now I was as frantic as any mother whose child is missing. Finally, that Monday evening, Jeff was forced to relay the bad news.

"She took him."

"What do you mean she *took* him?" I asked, feeling intense heat rising inside my head. Jeff's ex, let's call her Winifred, had been coming around our house lately for one reason or another. The last time, we weren't home, and she took it upon herself to take back her two cats, scooping up mine for good measure. Divorce can be ugly.

"She told me Saturday what she did," Jeff confessed. "I told her in no uncertain terms that she'd better bring him back by today. That's why I waited to tell you. I didn't want you upset."

"Upset, *UPSET*??" I growled. "The bitch stole my cat!"

"But she promised me she'd bring him back, so I waited. I'm sorry. I should've told you."

I hate crying in front of anyone, particularly a fairly new lover. Yet this time I didn't care. I wanted him to visibly see my pain.

"You sat back watching me tear my hair out, crying myself to sleep every night . . . and you *knew*?"

It was our first fight. He stood there letting me rant, and in my blinded fury, swing at him (which surprised even me, since I'm a peace-loving Aquarian, and, let us not forget, a harmony-driven Catholic). Turns out, this would be the only fight we'd have for years to come. I believe the man learned a lesson.

But the kidnapping incident was a long process. When the vengeful thief finally called, I begged and pleaded for my cat's return. "I don't know where he is," Winifred stated nonchalantly. "I didn't think you wanted the cat because it was outside with the others, so I took it to my grandmother's and it took off."

IT? She had called my beloved pet an "it." Had she'd been standing in front of me, I'd have hauled off and smacked her so hard she'd still feel the sting today. Not even my ex-husband had summoned this kind of rage in me, and I purposely kept God out of it because I knew just what He'd say. And I didn't want to hear it.

Winifred's grandmother lived on a country farm some thirty miles away. I slammed the receiver down, and gazed out the window at the heaping mounds of snow. How could any animal survive in this below-zero weather? I felt physically sick. And didn't know how to deal with feeling fear, misery, and intense hatred in one searing lump of emotion. My little three-year-old cat, who had gone through so much with me and my crazy, erratic life, was out there somewhere in the middle of the worst snow storm of the season. I was devastated.

I placed an ad in the paper, and cried into my pillow every night while imagining my poor innocent cat—a pawn in a hostile divorce—freezing to death in a forest of wild animals. Then, a month later, someone gave me an idea.

"Do you know it's against the law for her to come onto your property and take something that belongs to you?" said my friend Laura, who missed her calling as a lawyer.

"Oh, really?"

At her suggestion, I called the county prosecutor, and poured out my heart to him, hoping he would take me seriously. The man must have been a cat owner because he immediately understood my anguish and asked me for Winifred's phone number. Which I didn't have.

But I did have her mother's work number. Two days later, my cat miraculously appeared at my doorstep as the captor sped away.

Tigger was home.

After that, our lives, both Tigger's and mine, became more stable. Jeff and I married, bought a house, had children. Tigger was the most tolerant of his species. He endured these two little children, who wrapped him up in baby buggies, and hung him upside down by his hind paws ("Put Tigger down!! That's not how you hold a cat!"), and chased him around the backyard to see how fast he could run. In retrospect, I'm amazed he stuck around. But he seemed to understand that they were merely having fun at his expense, and never seemed to hold a grunge. He still came when they called him, still gave them his best purrs. Like I said, he had a great attitude.

My girls began throwing birthday parties for him, complete with hat and cupcake made of Fancy Feast (the expensive stuff, served only for this special occasion—with Tender Vittles sprinkles, of course) and the appropriately numbered candles. By the time we celebrated his eighteenth birthday on July 5, 1995, we all knew that my Tigger-Tom, as I liked to call him, was dying. I'd been taking him weekly to the vet for glucose shots so he would eat, because he was rapidly losing weight. Once a robust, stocky tabby weighing in at about fourteen pounds, was now barely four. My feline soul mate, the one who, whenever I'd pick him up, would relax his entire body flat against my chest, wrap both paws around my neck, and literally hug me. My cat, who never uttered a complaint when my children tormented him, who loved me every bit as I loved him, was not going to be around for another Fancy Feast.

I began praying that I would find him lying peacefully in the yard one day so I wouldn't have to make the call to end his rapidly declining life. I wanted it to be God's decision. Not mine.

"You know, we can't keep doing this. Eventually his kidneys and other vital organs will fail," Dr. Dole told me on the last visit. This vet knew our history. Dr. Dole was the one who had saved Tigger's life when I brought him in that day, fifteen years before, when he'd been hit by a car. No one had expected him to survive such injuries. But Tigger was tough. He pulled through.

But we all knew he wasn't going to this time.

Dr. Dole then added, "You don't want him to suffer."

No I didn't. But at the time, I was suffering more. I couldn't face being the one to make the decision to end his life. But as with most things in times of tragedy, the decision was made for me. Two weeks after Tigger's birthday, I went outside to feed him—he still loved the outdoors, though he no longer ventured further than our yard—and our eyes, like that first meeting, gazed understandably at each other. He walked slowly, pathetically, toward me with a weak meow, and I saw, and felt, his pain. I could hear his silent pleading to let him go. To not let him suffer any more. I knew, damn it, that it was time.

Before we put him in the car, I talked to Jeff about burying him in our backyard. But we had hard clay soil, and coupled with our limited tools and no advance warning, I had to admit this wasn't a good plan. I'd heard horror stories of animals digging up remains and feared our daughters might discover Tigger's while happily playing outside. However remote the chance, I didn't feel like gambling. I prepared the girls with the news that Tigger might not be coming back from the vets, then wrapped my now two-pound elderly cat in his favorite blanket. As Jeff drove, I talked to my little friend and ran my hands continuously over his lithe body. I was amazed that his fur was still as soft as the kitten he once was, so long ago. I held him against my heart the whole ride there.

"Would you like to stay with him during the process?" asked the lady at the desk. I looked at Jeff, then at Tigger, and knew there was no way I could. Feeling him fall helplessly limp in my arms would be too much to bear. The smart cat who knew me as well as anyone, knew this, too. With glazed eyes, Tigger looked into my own watery ones and seemed to communicate with me in some telepathic way that he understood.

The lady then appeared at the door that would led to my cat's demise, and gently took his weak body from my arms. As I looked at him one last time, and kissed his furry head, I flashed on all our adventures. We'd been together longer than many married couples. He'd been with me through so many life trials, from when I was a twenty-three-year-old girl, to a forty-one-year-old woman. That's a lot of love. And after all of that, all I could do was wave goodbye.

Walking out without him was the hardest part. It was the end of an era. There would be no other cat like him for me. Yet I felt grateful I'd been so fortunate to have had such a cool, loving cat who gave me such pleasure, and comfort, through most of my adult life.

We all have people in our lives who, by simply taking part in our existence, somehow make us whole human beings. And when they leave us, they take a piece of us with them. And we are never quite the same again.

If we're lucky, we get to have a pet that gives us untold moments of joy, companionship, and laughter. And when we lose them, we feel a void, we miss their presence. But we also realize how much they've given us. And how much we've learned from them. Like how to be patient for our food (and other things, too). And how to accept a person for who they are, without judgment. And how to love, with no conditions attached.

When our beloved pet leaves us, we are truly never the same again.

We are better.

Pennies From Heaven

*Gee*Gee was always finding pennies.

My mother often said this, and I can confirm the fact. Gee Gee and I would be walking at a good clip on our weekly stroll to Shoregate Shopping Center when she'd suddenly stop, bend down and say, "Oh, look, a penny!" She'd say that every time, as if it was a new occurrence. Or we'd be in a grocery store. Or bank. Or while she was in the yard planting her bed of flowers. "Must be my lucky day," she'd remark smiling, placing the copper coin in her apron or pocketbook.

And so, years after her death, I couldn't dismiss the rash of pennies that began appearing in seemingly intentional spots, as if purposely placed there solely for my benefit. Now I'm aware that pennies fall, and people find them. That this is not out of the ordinary. I'm also aware that some people would pass off my own personal penny experiences as mere "coincidences," despite the story I am to tell. And that's not to say there haven't been times this Catholic girl (now a pretty good Catholic girl) held doubt that these events were no more than flukes. But too many times, I've run out of reasonable excuses.

My mother, and her famous quirky thinking, is what started the chain of events that led to these all-too-frequent "coincidences."

"Next time you come over, bring me a copy of your book's cover," she told me over the phone one day in 2002, right after I published my first book. We were planning a trip to the cemetery to honor Gee Gee's birthday.

"Why?" was my sensible question.

"You'll see," was her nonsensical answer.

I humored her and arrived at her house with a color copy of the cover of my new book. In the car, she explained her odd request.

"I read somewhere that if you want them [dead loved ones] to know what's happening in your life, you should bring something concrete to leave on their graves when you visit them."

It was just the sort of thing my mother would take and run with. Although she didn't always go to church, she had total faith in God, the afterlife, and the occult. Her favorite sayings were "Everything is meant to be," and "Events come in threes" (like deaths, and weddings). She would also talk about, and to, her dead relatives, as if their spirits were hanging out with her at all times. And she loved psychics. She read Edgar Cayce and Jeane Dixon, and watched The Amazing Kreskin on TV. And more recently, was a huge fan of Sylvia Brown. Mom also had a Magic 8 Ball (that Mattel toy used for fortune-telling) on the end table in her living room.

And then there was the Ouiji Board. When I was a teenager, she'd often prompt me to play it with her. I'd agree when I was bored out of my mind. Or grounded, with nothing better to do. But then I couldn't ask the questions I really wanted answers to, because then she'd know what I was up to. And the freaky thing was, there were times that I didn't ask, and ole' Ouiji Board told anyway, which really sucked. Like one Saturday night when I was fifteen.

It was one of those times I was bored *and* grounded, so was a prisoner in my own home when Mom suggested we play the rat-me-out game. I suppose she brought it out to cheer me up, and perhaps even felt bad about my incarceration over something as dumb as not doing the dishes.

"Okay, I'll go first," she says, all excited-like.

We sit face to face, the mystical board on our laps. The tips of our fingers are lightly touching the three-legged pointer thingy (I know now is called a planchette) that has an uncanny ability to move on its own accord. The board has letters of the alphabet inscribed on it, along with a "Yes" on one end, and a "No" on the other (apparently when it only feels like giving yes and no answers). Those who play this odd game believe there are supernatural forces at work. That those in the spirit world will come forth and spell out answers to your questions when you set your fingers on the pointer. Skeptics, on the other hand, believe it moves due to unconscious thoughts by the player. Either way, it's weird.

"Will I have a good time next Friday," Mom begins because she plans to go to the bar that night where her favorite band is playing.

The pointer whips around the board and lands on "Yes." Good, I think. That'll make her pleasant for the next week.

Then it's my turn. I ask a generic question like, "Will I pass math?" (which I'm presently flunking). It spells out W-O-R-K O-N I-T. Which isn't what I want to hear.

We go back and forth for awhile. Then my turn comes around again. I can't come up with another generic question and am sidetracked because I'm busy thinking about Kevin, a bad boy I met recently at the Hullabaloo. He rides a Harley and told me he'd meet me this Sunday at Squire's Castle (a local hangout in the Cleveland Metropolitan Park) and I'm wondering if he'll have a joint or two for me. Suddenly, and without warning, the Ouiji Board begins to whip around like it's indeed possessed.

"What? I didn't even ask it anything," I say as it whirls around. Finally, it begins to spell something out.

"N-O . . . M-A-R-I-J-U-A . . .

Oh, shit. I know where this is going and try to force it in another direction. But it's a stubborn little planchette. N . . . A.

Unfortunately, my mother knows, too, what it's saying. And gives me an accusing look.

But I play my hand well.

"Boy, where'd that come from? Sometimes this thing makes no sense at all."

And she buys it. Or appears to.

In hindsight, the Ouiji board game gave us time together that wasn't spent arguing, and except for that little tattle-tale incident, and though I'd never admit it to my mother, I had just as much fun with it as she did.

So when Mom made this odd cemetery request, I simply went along with it. After placing the bouquet of flowers on Gee Gee's stone, my occult-believing mother stuck a handmade cardboard stick with the book cover between my grandparents' headstones. "Look what your granddaughter did!" she exclaimed proudly. I cringed, but said nothing. As we drove away from the site, the sign stood high on the hill, like a banner for all to see. To visitors, I was embarrassingly sure it appeared to be some sort of ludicrous, quirky, and certainly tacky, marketing gimmick—*"Hey, Dead People's Relatives! Look over here, I have a book out. Available outside your vicinity"*—it seemed to screech.

But Mom was getting older, and after years of being disagreeable, I was now the dutiful daughter. Even for this. My only hope was for a huge storm the likes of Kansas to whip up suddenly and send the sign flying. But then, who knew where it would end up?

Then, lo and behold, right after that visit, the pennies began showing up. It was as if Mom's idea took hold, triggering something in the cosmos. If you believe in that sort of thing.

The first one showed up in church, appropriately enough. The Sunday after our cemetery trip, I stood up to go to Communion, looked down and spotted a penny between me and my daughter's foot. A few hours later, my husband and I went for a motorcycle ride and stopped for a drink at a local tavern. I hopped off the barstool to leave, and saw a penny, again, right by my foot.

"That's odd," I said to Jeff, "That's the second one today. It reminds me of Gee Gee, she was always finding pennies."

That's when it hit me.

"What are you doing?" Jeff asked, watching me as I began surveying the entire floor of the bar. Not another penny anywhere.

Two days later, I was teaching a class on rock and roll history in Cleveland, the subject of my book (which a copy of its cover now graced a nearby cemetery). I went over to the window to close the blinds in the room, and there was a lone penny lying on the sill, right where I stood. The cycle was in full force. The copper coins began appearing, on a weekly, sometimes daily, basis in distinct places. I found them at work. In parking lots, right beside my car door. On the seat I was about to sit in at a restaurant. And, of course, in my house. One morning I walked into the kitchen to make the coffee, and there lay a penny, clear and bright on the floor. Wouldn't I have seen it when I turned off the light the night before?

After awhile I'd start looking for them, expecting them, but then they'd never appear. I realized I wasn't going to find a penny when I looked for one. God isn't that obvious. Mom, of course, got a huge kick out of hearing of these findings. I couldn't help begin to believe that my grandmother was confirming Mom's silly belief, and so knew of my recent accomplishments, and was giving me a thumbs-up. Or in this case, heads.

Then suddenly, the rain of pennies stopped. As quickly as they'd begun. The drought lasted nearly two years.

In April of 2004, I got a frantic call from my brother.

"Mom just got rushed to the hospital," he said.

The next few days would've been a blur except for a couple of notable events.

The third night of Mom's comatose state, we were standing over her bedside—me, Jeff, Dennis, and our friend, Lynne—as she lay there unconscious. I hated seeing the tube in her nose, as it reminded me of the last time I saw Grandpa. Doctors said Mom's heart was extremely weak, and "it doesn't look good." All we could do was stand there gazing at her, and listen to the incessant beep-beep-beep of the machines. Lucky for us, Lynne was a nurse, and could explain in laymen's terms what was happening.

"See this number here," she said pointing to the heart machine, "That means her heart is only working 25 percent. And this . . ." pointing to another contraption ready to explain more. But I didn't hear the rest. It all added up to one thing. My mother was dying.

"I gotta get outta here," I said, and the others followed.

As we walked down the hall, the tears welled up, making everything look blurry. Yet, in the midst of my hazy vision, I managed to see the penny. Right in front of me, so close I was about to step on it. I stopped in my tracks.

"Oh my God," I said, looking at Lynne, who knew about what we now referred to as The Penny Story. I picked it up, but in my sadness I felt confused.

"I don't know if this is a good sign or a bad one," I told her. "Either Gee Gee's telling me not to worry, that it'll be okay, or that my Mom's on the way to see her and my grandfather."

I didn't think at the time, the penny might have meant both.

"I need a drink," I said to Lynne, who, in fact, would have her own penny stories after Mom died. After all, Mom had taken a liking to her.

So we went to Cebars, the place we always took Mom on Sundays for the Blues Jam Night. Upon entering the doorway, I headed straight to the restroom to wipe my red eyes. I did not see a penny when I placed my purse on the shelf. But when I went over to pick up my purse to leave, there was a penny under it. A chill washed over me.

It was Lynne's turn to say, "Oh my God."

"What does this *mean*?!" I asked her, as if she knew.

"It means she's here," Lynne answered, and I realized I had to be content with that thought.

The pennies were back. I'd find another one just two days later, again in Cebar's bathroom, after our hospital vigil. These two findings so close together and in the same area, had significance because it was there, in the ladies restroom, where Mom and I (now friends) would brush our hair, fix our makeup, and chat about whatever came up. Silly as it seemed, it was kind of "our place."

Another week of worry and uncertainty went by before Mom began to breathe on her own, and she was finally released from her life-saving constraints.

"Mom, you're not going to believe this," was practically the first thing I said to her after she had "come to." I was excited to be able to talk to her again, even though she wasn't able to talk back. The breathing tube had done some damage, and it hurt too much for conversation. We all hoped there was time for that. "I found three pennies since you've been here!"

I told her about the penny in the hospital hallway, and the two at our favorite bar. She smiled, and her eyes seemed to glisten. I knew she got a huge kick out of that. So I was surprised that I didn't find a penny when she died a few days later.

The morning of her funeral, our cousin Doug brought in a roll of newly-minted pennies. I passed them out to those who either knew the story, or would appreciate it. Then, one by one, they placed a penny in her coffin as they said their goodbyes.

Then a strange—Ouiji board-worthy—thing happened.

Mom and I often had ongoing discussions on which psychic was authentic—Sylvia Brown (Mom's choice), or John Edward (my choice). She always tried to convince me of Sylvia's great abilities and would call me every time the renowned psychic was on The Montel Williams show.

"Just watch her, she's amazing," Mom would say over the

phone, where she couldn't see my eyes roll.

The Wednesday after her funeral, I was home keeping busy, as one does when in grief. My teenage daughter had been watching TV, but then left the room, the TV still on.

"Danielle," I yelled, "You didn't turn off the TV again!"

I grabbed the remote controller and when I looked up, there was Sylvia Brown. Of course, I remembered, it was time for the Montel Show. I smiled thinking that Mom would be watching now, if only . . .

Just as my index finger was about to press the off button, a man in the TV audience stood up. "I have a question for Sylvia," he began. "Is there any real significance to suddenly finding pennies everywhere, because ever since my mother died, I'm coming across them everywhere I go."

I froze, the chill moving up my spine to my open mouth. Sylvia told the man that yes, coins are a way the dead communicate with loved ones. I couldn't believe it, seems Mom was *still* trying to convince me about her favorite psychic.

But that isn't the end of the story of my Pennies from Heaven. After that, I waited anxiously to find more pennies, and as before, I didn't find them when looking. But they still appear when I need them to. The last day I was in Mom's apartment, the men came by to get the last of her furniture (I had donated most of it). After weeks of calmly dividing up her things, the finality of her death hit me in the emptiness of her condo. The sobs came in spurts. When it came time for them to remove my mother's dining room table, there in the center was one lone penny.

"Thanks, Mom" was all I could utter.

There was the time I picked up a phone book one day at work and a penny fell out of it (who has ever found a penny inside a telephone book?). The day my daughter told me she was moving out, I stood looking down at the floor thinking, "What am I going to do with this child?" My answer came back as I spotted two pennies at her feet. One for her, one for me, I presumed. *You gotta let her go,* their presence seemed to say, *Don't worry, we're here. She'll be fine.*

Each penny discovery brought its own brand of chills. Like this one:

It appeared in the grand tradition in the Wizard of Oz, I call it my "Good Deed Day."

I'd just cleared out the back seat of my car from all the

newspapers that often accumulate there, and then drove to a local store. The day before, I'd purchased some items, one being the latest Rolling Stones CD. When I returned home, I discovered I hadn't been charged for it. If you've read Chapter Two, you know what circumstances brought me to becoming an honest human being. Of course my first thought was, *Oh, cool, I saved a few bucks.* But then, my upbringing and the fact that I now consider myself a good Christian, invaded my conscious like an unwanted Jehovah's Witness at my door telling me to repent. I knew that if I didn't make it right, the CD was good as stolen. Plus, I had to admit that if I had been short-changed instead, or if the woman hadn't given me an advertised sale price, I'd righteously march back to the store to make clear the mistake and demand my money.

So I had to go back.

"I'm sure you don't get this too often," I began. The woman in the blue smock looked puzzled. "I bought this CD the other day, but somehow I didn't get charged for it. I'd like to pay for it now." I did enjoy her confused look.

"It wasn't rung up?" she replied after a few silent moments. "Well, that's really nice of you, most people wouldn't do it."

While her comment was reward itself for my good deed, I also realized that honesty is apparently so rare these days, that when carried out, it rather baffles people. As I walked toward my car, and opened the driver's side door, I went to set something in the back seat, which I'd just cleaned out no more than twenty minutes before. And there, lying by itself on the seat was a brand new shiny 2005 penny. I placed it in the palm of my hand and drew in a breath. Then I exhaled, smiling. *I should be used to this by now*, I thought. *Hi, Mom. Hi, Gee Gee, Grandpa.*

Hi, God.

This was my reward for being honest. And what a reward it was.

I sat down behind the wheel and stared at the penny. *In God, we trust.* I flipped it over. *E Pluribus Unum.* "From many, one."

Precisely.

The copper coins don't always seem to come from my family members. The day I wrote about my writing mentor and good friend, Lea Oldham, I took a walk, thinking about what I'd written about her, and stepped on something. A penny. I bent down to pick it up. It was dated 2001. The year Lea had died.

And they don't always come for my benefit, it seems. The day I found out Vera, one of my oldest friends, had breast cancer, I found a bright shiny 2008 penny directly at my feet. It seemed that my mom, who knew her, was telling me that she would be fine. And she is.

They have appeared in meaningful ways to my cousin Doug, who Mom considered a second son, my husband Jeff, and to my friend, Lynne, who was with us in the last days of my mother's life. Her latest penny appearance, particularly spine-chilling.

"You're not going to believe this," Lynne calls to tell me. "I found a penny in the paint department today, where I was picking out a color for my bathroom," she says excitedly. "Then after I chose it, the saleslady mixing it, looked up the name and said, 'Oh, that's called 'Fostoria Glass.' And get this," Lynne added, "the color is light green, your mom's favorite."

Things come in threes, my mother often said. A Penny. Her favorite town and place her relatives worked. And her favorite color. All within a few minutes time. *Hi, Mom.*

I come from a long line of good, strong women who loved family and friends, and while they didn't always go to church, had a real sense of the wonders and miracles of life, death, and God. And through example, faith, and many stories, they passed these values on to me. And now my daughters (who, of course, know the penny stories) know that I feel the best gift I can give them is continuing this tradition of love and faith in God, and a belief that there's more to this life than we understand.

Coincidences?

I think it takes more effort and energy to try to dispel these occurrences, than to simply accept them. And I take comfort in the fact that I'm not alone in what I believe. In fact, I'm in good company. In the book, *"This I Believe: The Personal Philosophies of Remarkable Men and Women,"* there is an essay by Albert Einstein, written in the 1950s. It reads in part: "The most beautiful thing we can experience is the mysterious—the knowledge of the existence of something unfathomable to us, the manifestation of the most profound reason coupled with the most brilliant beauty."

Pennies from heaven?

This I believe.

8. Wine, Women & Wisdom

Girls' Nights Out

*T*he guy's slick, greased-up naked hips are gyrating to the pounding, throbbing primal drum beats of "It's Raining Men." *Hallelujah.* The song rises in chorus as Adonis struts over to us. He then springs up on top of our table like a bobcat, nearly spilling my Harvey Wallbanger, still gyrating—always gyrating. He's offering himself to us, eagerly awaiting the promise of our hard-earned money stuffed into his gold glitter pouch that barely covers his family jewels. We can feel the thumping bass in our throats and chests. *"Tall, blonde, dark and mean. Rough and tough and strong and lean. It's raining men!"*

The colored strobes surround us like search lights to the disco beat, through a fog of smoke aimed at making the men more mysterious. This guy's sweaty booty is so close to me, I can smell the Musk he splashed on himself before coming out. He now combs through his Elvis-black jelled locks with his brawny fingers of his right hand while cupping his muscular derriere with his left—for more thrusting and grinding. Round and round, back and forth goes his hips as his glazed eyes meet mine because I'm the only one looking at his face.

"Ya want some of this, I know you want it," his cocky expression tells me.

What I really want is to find the nearest exit, or at least a cocktail waitress and change my drink order. I suddenly don't want to partake in a beverage that now gives me visuals of being banged against a wall by Harvey.

Or whatever name he's using tonight.

"Whoo, Hoo, oh YEAH!!" Carrie, next to me, screeches in my ear. *She's* the one who wants "some of this." This was her idea.

"Hey, let's go to Cowboy Joes Friday, it's Male Revue Night!" she'd suggested that Wednesday I was feeling kind of down. "The guys are real hunks. There's one that looks like John Travolta but with blonde-streaked hair. Another one is more subdued, acting all innocent and shy, like John-Boy (this being 1979 and *The Walton's* is still on the air). But I bet if ya get him in bed . . . whoa! OH, and *Br . . . ii . . . an.* Oh. My. God. Would you believe he slipped me his card last time (*yes, actually, I would*) and I lost it! (*Believe that one, too*) so I gotta get him to ask me out. You just gotta see his muscles (*Do I have to?*). *OH,* man! They actually *RIPPLE.*"

It appears Carrie is a regular.

I was unaware of this. While I've known Carrie and her family for a few years, she and I have never hung out. But she now feels I should get myself "back out there." Because I've just left my husband. So apparently I'm supposed to go right out and find a new one.

Please.

I'm not looking for a rebound. I'm not looking for anything. Because I don't know what I want. But I do know what I don't want. And I don't want some GQ kind of guy who preys on the horny aspirations of jiggly, giggly women. I am so clearly not one of them. "I'm not looking," I had told her.

"Hey, look at that one!" Carrie points across the floor to another half-naked stud waiting in the wings. *Mr. Do-Ya-Think-I'm-Sexy* has already jumped ship and moved on to a new soirée of possibilities—after claiming his green paper tokens, of course, from all the girls at this table. All but me. I have exactly four dollars and some loose change in my purse and he ain't gettin' it.

"Bad Girls," that incessant disco tune by Donna Summer, is blasting through the speakers now, and it seems everyone here wants to be one.

"How 'bout a Screwdriver?" the waitress suggests when I tell her I want something different but don't know what. I wince.

At this point in my life, any slight reference to a horizontal activity with a man repulses me.

So what the hell am I doing *here*, I have to ask myself.

"I'll just have water," I tell her. She is not happy.

Just as she walks away, here comes *Briii . . . aaan.*

"Oh my God, *there* he is," Carrie screams. "Yoo Hoo, BRIAN! Over here!"

As Brian thrusts our direction, I feel a desperate fear that this is all I've been missing the past few years. And for a milli-second, I want to dash back to that house in the 'burbs with that stifling man and unfulfilled dreams and just vegetate and forget about being happy. Maybe happiness really is just an illusion, like that Temptations song. *This is what becomes of the brokenhearted. Filled with sadness and confusion . . .*

I am going to end up all alone. I will never have children. I will be a spinster. Or perhaps, a nun. If they'll have me.

"Got any more dollar bills?" Carrie's friend, Jane, yells into my left ear, the smoke from her cigarette burning my eyes.

"No," I yell back. Jane, who's on her third Long Island Ice-tea, grabs a left-over buck on the table, presumably meant for the waitress, then jumps up on her chair. She waves both arms like she's in desperate need for a taxi, until the next guy—who first came out in white tails and top hat to the tune of *New York, New York* but is now wearing just a white, glittery (*of course*) loin cloth—finally spots her and heads our way . . .

I don't belong here. A nice Catholic girl. In a place like this.

God could not be pleased.

Then again, it wouldn't be the first time.

Looking around this barn full of women with their cat calls and wanton, or rather, *want him*, behavior, I suddenly recall the time I was in eighth grade and called the Roxy Theater looking for a job. My girlfriends and I were off school that day and the four of us were at Debbie's house because her parents were at work. Everyone was bored, so I decided to liven things up.

"Hey, how 'bout I call the Roxy and pretend to be a stripper?"

They all screamed in the affirmative.

Me, being the only one who reads the newspaper regularly, had seen tons of ads for sexy girls at the Roxy. *No experience necessary.* I wondered if I could pull it off.

"*Heellllooo*, yes, I'd like to speak to the manager," I say in my best fourteen-trying-to-be-twenty—and sexy—high-pitched, come-hither voice.

He gets on the phone.

"Yeah?" he answers, rather surly. You can see through the phone lines he looks like Ralph Kramden, but is wearing a loose-striped shirt—buttoned-down to show his black, chest hair that curls in tight loops like ring worm—and his thin, tight lips clamped down hard on his wet chewed-up Cuban cigar.

"*Heellllooo*, my name is *Caaandi* . . . with an *I* (I add for authenticity). I've just moved into town and was wondering if you need another girl . . . "

"You 21?" he barks.

"Oh Yes Sir!"

"Then stop in, between two and four, and we'll talk."

"Oh, thank you Sir! You won't regret it."

I hang up as my support group rolls over on the floor, holding their stomachs, and howling.

I'll do anything for a laugh.

Truth be told, I was just trying to be cool in front of my girlfriends. Now, I realize that, at twenty-five, I'll still do anything to fit in. I flick my cigarette lighter and check my watch. 12:30 a.m.. The night's still young. *Damn.*

I lean over to Carrie, whose eyes are tearing with excitement (helped along by several shots of Tequila) and say loudly in her ear, "I'm outta here." She looks at me, surprised, shrugs, then whips her head back to see what's coming next. So to speak.

I walk out into the October chill, light up my last Salem, and congratulate myself for driving. After my first few nights out with the girls, I learned that there is always one who wants to leave earlier, or stay longer, than the driver wants to. This always becomes a problem and I decided early on that I would drive myself and meet my friends at our destination. This way, I can leave when I want to. Like now.

By the time I get into my Plymouth Arrow (the only material thing I managed to keep after my marriage died—though that, too, would ultimately come to a screeching halt), I'm crying. The feeling of utter failure and loneliness overwhelms me. I just don't know where I fit in life.

I'm not into this "Male Revue" stripper thing. Or this raunchy place that sweats liquid sex, and reeks of Musk for Men. I may be newly single but my dream of Mr. Right doesn't come with a rhinestone g-string, slicked-back hair, and ego the size of a Town Car. Those kind of guys leave me cold. They're not my type. My fantasy man has more substance, is a bit more complex. A bad-boy, but not too bad. One who has a good heart. Say, a romantic guy like John Denver, but with a touch of no-holds-barred Mick Jagger.

And I surely am not going to find *him here*.

And apparently, I'm not going to find a girlfriend who understands where I'm coming from. While I have a few friends—now all divorced, too—I feel detached from them. Like I'm thirteen again, and still cannot connect. Still feel like the odd one. . . .

I lie there that night in my lonely bed as visions of my history of relationships—with guys and girls—swirl in my head like ghosts of failures past. Guys who wanted more of me than I could, or would, give them. Girls I thought were friends until I'd learn otherwise. And sometimes, the two merged. Like my high school friend, Jenny, who always seemed to need a ride home from school, and my then-boyfriend, who was always happy to oblige. I was clueless to their mutual attraction until the day when I, sitting in the middle of the front seat, moved the mirror to check my makeup and saw Jenny in the back, perfectly in line for said boyfriend's view, her skirt hiked up strategically to show what she had to offer. And here, I'd thought he'd been checking the mirror so often for safety . . .

And that's when, lying in my bed at four in the morning, I had an awakening of sorts. While I did consider never trusting anyone ever again, male or female, I quickly decided that attitude would cause me to be bitter and alone for the rest of my life. Then again, though I didn't want to be alone the rest of my life, I also realized that there were many nights when being alone was a wonderful pleasure. That I could sit contently on the couch with a comforter and a nice glass of wine and watch a sad, or happy, movie and be thoroughly content. I didn't need to always be out on a Saturday night.

That's when I promised myself to never go anywhere—with the girls, or on a date—just to go out somewhere because I didn't want to be home alone. Because, truthfully, I actually enjoy my own company.

That's the first step to being on your way to liking yourself. To trusting yourself. To knowing exactly who you are. But it's only a baby step. You see, this knowledge takes a while.

It's not until most women are in their forties, or even fifties, that Girls Nights Out become exactly what they should be. A get-together among friends who really like one another, and more importantly, like themselves. Who are out solely to converse with other women, not on the prowl for other men.

Somewhere between junior high cat fights, and bad-boy syndrome, and trying to be someone we're not, we women discover ourselves, and find camaraderie. We begin to bond. We become allies instead of competitors. Friends, instead of backstabbers.

Somewhere on our long way to womanhood, we realize we've all been through the same ordeals. Even the girls we used to envy. We learn we've all had our family "issues." We've all been screwed over. We've all had our hearts stomped on by some good-looking, sweet-talkin' jerk. We've all had those moments we've felt horribly insecure and unsure of ourselves. We've all had our times under the covers, when we'd just want to lie in bed and stay there the rest of our lives.

We've all had our ugly-duckling moments.

Moments we've felt like complete losers.

Moments we acted in a way we'd later regret.

Moments we'd just as soon forget about.

Yes, even the cheerleaders. The "Most Likely to Succeeds." The ones who stole our boyfriends, or husbands. They, too, have their stories.

And while there will always be women we'll never meet up with at Starbucks, or whose numbers we'll never have on our speed dials, or include in our prayer list (though, those are exactly the ones who should be, if we are truly a Good Catholic Girl), we realize, even with our enemies, that we share common ground.

So after years of fighting with each other, with our mothers, ourselves, we wake up one day and discover that, despite so many complex issues and personalities, we are more alike than different. And we begin to share our lives with one another. We become confidantes. And through this sharing of our time, our stories, our lives, we discover how very much we need each other in this world.

And if we're lucky, that includes our mothers, too.

It's one of those blessings we hadn't realized has been there all along because we'd been too busy combating against it. When the fighting stops, we find peace within our sisterhood.

And find that we *really* like doing stuff together outside the parameters of the *Y* chromosome.

So we no longer need half-naked men thrusting their wares in front of us (though we now can see the humor in that) to be entertained.

And Girls Nights Out, or Girls Days Out, become this:

We do lunch. And split the three-decker fudge cheese cake.

We go to movies together. We see "*Love Story*," and "*Forrest Gump*," and "*The Notebook*." And one of us always remembers to bring tissues (with lanolin).

We see plays.

We meet at the park with our kids and complain about our lack of sleep, and sex, and brain power, while our children climb the monkey bars.

We get together at each other's houses for pizza and wine (or whine). And watch *Sex and the City*.

We go to the beach. And to spas. And say nothing about the weight the other has gained. But are first to notice, and comment on, when the weight's been lost.

We meet for Happy Hour chocolate martinis, where we giggle and gossip and gorge.

Our girlfriends are there when we take our wedding vows. When we bring home our babies. Or when we just feel like talking.

They are there when our mothers leave us, forever. When our boyfriends, or husbands, leave us.

And when our children leave us.

They are there, ready to celebrate, when we get that long-for job, or hoped-for promotion. Or when we *finally* get that college degree. Or meet a great guy and just have to tell someone.

They are there to remind us of all our good qualities. They help us like ourselves again. Or, for the first time.

They are there when one of us is told we have cancer. And they are there, too, when told we have beaten it . . .

Our girlfriends are there with open minds, open hearts, open arms. And an open bottle of Chardonnay for the good times. Mezcal for the bad.

Because they understand what it's like to be female.

My Best Friend's Weddings

The boat sank.

A sure sign of things to come.

Of course, I could've told her that. Well, maybe not about the boat, I mean, who could've predicted that? But tying the knot with bachelor number three? That was right up there, or rather, down there, with the Titanic.

And I sort of did tell Alice—we'll call her—that. More than once, actually.

"I'm not sure you can trust him," I said, the time he wasn't where he'd told her he was.

"I don't think you can depend on him," I said, when he lost a job and, months later, was "still looking."

"Why don't you go out with that nice guy, Ben?" I whispered, when I noticed Ben's hopeful gaze towards her at the Tiki Bar.

How do you tell your best friend—your love-ya-like-a-sister best friend—that she is following that stupid and half-crazy rabbit right down the hole to what seems like an enticing little place (what with the funny characters and all) that leads to exciting little adventures (including a fun-looking Tea Party) but in reality, is a surreal wonderland that doesn't really exist, and they'll be no tea for her. That one day, she'll discover that it was just a hole, where she was growing smaller. And festering. Like a mushroom. In a dank, lonely forest. Then, upon this awakening, she'll rub her eyes and find that it's all been just a silly dream, and hop on along, to a merry life.

But, as they say, that only happens in the movies.

"We talked it all out—talked for *hours* and he really seems sincere," Alice tells me on the phone in an almost giddy voice. She and Bill had moved to Florida two years earlier. Where, six weeks after moving into their newly purchased home—he announced that he wasn't quite ready for a commitment, and well, could she move out? And now, twenty-some months and several liaisons later (not all with Alice), the man gets this sudden change of heart.

"He says he can't live without me and is actually *treating* me like it. He's begging me to take him back, and get this—he even wants to marry me. Says he's really ready now. What do you think?"

She always does this to me. She asks for my opinion.

Through the past two decades of our best-friendship, we've been through all kinds of life changes. Our history is jam-packed with *As the World Turns* moments. This one is a mere continuation of her on-and-off-again relationship that began splintering soon after that move to the Sunshine state. So let's start there.

"I think I'm going to stay here," Alice is telling me. It's the closest thing to a decision I'd heard her utter in weeks. It's the fall of 2002. She is a thousand miles away, and has been freshly abandoned by The Mad Hatter. I miss her, and want her to come home. She wants to remain where the sun seems to always shine.

"Asshole," I say after each play-by-play she gives, leading up to the missed goal. She'd been describing the events of her past month. The night she saw him "just talking" to a girl in a bar. The night he didn't feel like making love. The night he never came home. Then finally, the night he told her he thought it "might be best" that she find a place of her own.

"I can't believe this is happening," she says. Repeatedly.

"He's just an asshole," I say. Repeatedly.

My stomach is in knots. I can hear—can feel—her pain as she sobs into the phone while cleaning out the backyard pool, *their* pool. Soon to be *his* pool. I want to fly down there and grab his lying, cheating neck with both hands and swing him round and round like Wonder Woman, until he disappears, like Jimmy Hoffa.

"What do I do?" her quivering voice asked me at the start of this conversation. Does she stay down south? Move back to Ohio? Either way, she must start her life over—again—and, as she continually emphasizes, at the ripe old age of forty-five. She doesn't see that this unhappy circumstance could possibly lead to better things. That it may not be as hard as she thinks. My best friend is a strong person, stronger than she gives herself credit for. But sometimes one person, by way of deceiving words and actions, can make you too weak to save yourself. That's where friends come in. But right now, my life jacket is too far away.

Why—I wonder those nights I stay up worrying about her—do bad things really do happen to good people? The trouble with Alice is, she has too good a heart. She's the kind of person who can hear in your voice message when something's amiss, stop what she's doing, call you and say, "Okay, what's wrong?" And you end up spilling your guts to her. Because she's there for you, will listen, and acknowledge your angst. And you know what you tell her won't go any further. The girl is a steadfast, loyal friend. And that's the thing. She's the most loyal person I know. She strives to do the honorable thing. Like when she became pregnant twenty years ago, a bit unexpectedly, and decided she should marry the father. Despite certain qualms that kept nagging at her. Which she kept to herself. Until we were on the way to her wedding.

"You know, Dee, I'm not sure I'm doing the right thing," she tells me in the car, exactly one mile from the church.

"What? What are you talking about?" I whip my head toward her, forgetting for a moment I'm driving.

"Hey, watch the road!" she says and starts to laugh, which is always a chain reaction with us. So I start laughing too, and for a brief moment we're just two young women on the way to every girl's dream come true. But then the moment passes. I veer back to my side of the road, feeling baffled. And worried.

"I don't know," she says, looking out the side window. "It just seems like I should be happier right now. I don't think I'd be doing this if I wasn't pregnant."

Now she tells me. Two whirlwind months of planning and shopping and setting our sights on "making her an honest woman," with a guy more than willing to own up to his end of responsibility (although we're not at all sure, since his children are grown, that he wants this, either).

And actually, husband number two is a nice guy. And they both have a lot in common. But for the next fourteen years, they won't be able to make each other happy. And that's all Alice really wants. It's all anyone really wants.

So eventually Alice conjures up the nerve to leave him. To search for true love. A few years later, she's convinced she's found it in Bill. Despite a clash of personalities. Despite his obvious flaws. Despite his tendency to make her miserable. But she is determined. Because she is loyal.

This is what happens, all too often, when a father tells his wife and nine-year-old daughter that he's going to the store, then never comes back. Ever. It is the legacy Alice's father left her with. A legacy that taught her to settle for less than she deserves. And to fight, even when what you're fighting for is no longer valid.

The irony of it all is that Alice can have her pick of men. She laughs hysterically whenever I tell her this (which I do rather often because she needs to hear it, though she still thinks I'm full of it). With her bountiful, coffee-colored hair (that would change to blonde in Florida), and matching dark eyes, she can get by on looks alone. Yet, she also has been gifted with other appealing traits in the gene pool of life. Aside from physical beauty, she's one of those people they say "lights up a room" merely by walking into it. And she's fun, so she makes friends easily. Men fall for her easily.

Even through the difficulties of divorcing husband number two, she remained strong, and survived many traumas afterward. I knew she'd come through this one, too. I just needed to convince her of that.

"You should stay," I agreed, ignoring my secret wish to have her back where we shared so many girl moments. All I'd heard for years was how she wanted to live amid palm trees, sandy beaches, and warm sunny skies. And it's what she needed now. More than she needed me. "You know you want to stay, and damn it if you should let some self-centered jerk who doesn't deserve you, ruin it. Get a job, find a place to live, make new friends . . ." I sighed. "Stay."

And she did.

After years of experience, you get good at giving advice. I wasn't there for husband number one, but after learning the details, I'd have told her to ditch him, too. We didn't meet until a year later, in 1980, when we were newly minted divorcees seeking shelter in the most unlikely of places, Sugars' Last Stand Saloon, serving up whiskey and beers. Our friendship blossomed under the leaky roof of this biker bar, fueled by common interests and shots of Hawaiian Shooters. Through the next two decades, we talked about growing up without a father. And how we loved the Beatles (even though she was a John girl, I gave her credit for rebuffing the pervasive Paul trend). About being "hippies" in the '70s. And how our favorite album was Blood, Sweat & Tears, "Child is Father to the Man," back when Al Kooper was in the band. Another common element: We'd both married in '77. Both divorced in '79.

We've been each other's friend, co-conspirator, and life cheerleader. When talking about each other to people, we don't say, "my friend," we always, *always* say *"my best friend."* We are Lucy & Ethel (I'm crazy Lucy to her practical Ethel), Thelma & Louise (well, except for the driving-off-the-cliff part), and The Bangor Sisters (except for the ex-groupie part). So when she caught the bouquet at my wedding in 1983, fate seemed to be making plans.

"You're next!" I laughed in her ear, still hugging her as she held my flowers, now wilting in the 93-degree heat—a result of having an outdoor wedding.

"Get outta here!" she screamed, throwing her head back in laughter.

Nine months later, she married the man who gave her a daughter. Naturally, I stood up for her. An honor I would employ, in many situations, from that day forward.

When Alice gave birth to Callie, who would be her only child, Alice called me (at 5 a.m.) with the news, and we stayed on the phone until it was time for me to get out of bed and go to work. She knew, despite my genuine happiness for her, how hard it was for me to hear about the joys of motherhood—seeing how I was struggling with infertility. But, like everything else, we got through it by staying close. By talking. And laughing. When I finally became pregnant, then miscarried, became pregnant again, and miscarried again, Alice kept insisting I was meant to be a mother. That in time it would surely happen. And she was right.

Motherhood, as with wifehood, brings unique challenges. The kind only other women understand. We were each others' sounding board and therapist. Thursdays were our Nights Out. On Fridays, it was pizza and wine nights. Our children would play together and eat pizza while we'd commiserate our various struggles over wine.

Every summer party we attended, the two of us would sneak away for a stroll down the street, drinks in hand, divulging secrets or to just talk about our husbands, mothers, children—life. We never ran out of things to discuss, and we possessed an uncanny ability to make each other burst into fits of laughter. The kind that causes sides to ache, and uncontrollable hiccups, which would crack us up all the more.

We are sisters in spirit. Before she moved to Florida, we talked nearly every day, shared many evenings, and kids' birthdays, at each other's houses. Even swapped clothing. Well, actually only that one outfit. The sleeveless, red-and-silver striped pantsuit.

"This is so cute!" I remarked to Alice one day at the mall.

"Oh, yeah, it is. How much is it?" she asked, turning into Practical Ethel.

I flipped over the tag. "Oh, well, it's $24.99," I mumbled, reading her mind. We both worked part-time so we could be home with our babies, so spending that kind of money, frivolously, was not an option. We stood there staring at it, imaging ourselves wearing it.

"Hey, I got an idea!" I said in my best Lucy voice. "Let's split it."

"What?"

"We'll split the cost, and take turns borrowing the outfit. It's not something we'd wear all the time, anyway. We both wear the same size."

Her expression was a cross between "you're nuts," and "this has possibilities." Finally. Miss Practical gave in.

"Well, let's just hope we don't wanna to wear it on the same day," she said, heading to the checkout . I agreed. Because although we rarely got into a spat, it had better not be over something as trivial as a cotton garment.

The pantsuit lived a good life, taking turns in our closets, going out to special, and separate, occasions until we both tired of it. One of us finally gave it to Goodwill, though neither of us can remember which one.

But Alice and I shared a lot more through the years. We've had our share of joy. Our share of tears. Our share of not always being pleased with one another. But, like sisters, we always understood that our relationship is unconditional, and unbreakable. Unlike romantic ones.

I'm thinking of this shared history now, and how maybe she should've returned home before Bill had a chance to worm his way back into her good graces. So now, in 2004, she's telling me that, after spending a year-and-a-half reclaiming her life, Bill is back in it. Professing his love, devotion and promises of marriage. And I'm debating, as she carries on, how I should tell her, exactly, what I think. And then it's quiet. She has stopped talking. She is waiting. Waiting for me to give her my blessings. Waiting for me to voice what she wants to hear.

There's a lot I could bring up. A lot I could remind her about. But I've been here before. I know more now. I've learned the cold, hard truth. That no matter what you tell someone, no matter how much they ask for your opinion or advice, they are going to go right ahead and do what they want to, anyway.

And Alice is going to follow that damned friggin', son-of-a-bitchin' rabbit right into the hole. And there's nothing I can do about it. No matter what I say, the girl loves him. And she is fiercely loyal.

"You have to follow your heart."

I say this instead of, "I don't trust his actions. I don't think you can depend on him. Why don't you fall in love with someone else?"

Because saying it will only hurt her, and ultimately, our friendship. If I tell her to run—fast—away from him, she'll end up pining for him, perhaps the rest of her life, and secretly blame me. She wants to give this one last chance, and I have to let her. Part of the responsibility of being a trusted friend means you have to step back and just be supportive. Before. And after.

She calls the next day to confirm the wedding date.

"You *will* come down and be my maid of honor, *again* [she laughs], right?"

It isn't a question, for either of us.

"That's what best friends are for," I say.

They're also for standing by helplessly watching that best friend choose another guy who you just know is going to break her heart. This guy who Alice—as is her style—loves unconditionally, will become lucky husband number three.

But who knows? By now, she's convinced me that maybe,

just maybe, this will work after all. Hope can be a contagious drug.

So maybe I'm wrong, I think as I stand there on the ship's bow listening to Bill promise to love and cherish my best friend. Maybe I'm wrong, I think. I'm praying for wrong.

The wedding took place on the steer of a nice Hatteras boat—borrowed for the occasion— overlooking a beautiful harbor, the glaring Florida sun beaming down.

A few months later, the boat—interestingly named *Last Resort*—sinks to the bottom of the ocean in the middle of a fierce tropical storm. There were no casualties. Though, you could count one. The marriage it once hosted, soon sinks as well.

Key West, May 2007: My best friend and I are jumping on a bed, laughing hysterically. (We try to see each other once a year. I go to Florida, or she comes to Ohio.) As always, and through everything, nothing has changed between us. We're still being silly together, and rediscovering our inner child.

"You're crazy!" she says, as she bounces up, and I down.

This is true. It *was* my idea. Once again, I was Lucy, and she was Ethel, who had to be talked into another of my crazy antics. Our men (hers is new) sit outside on the balcony patio with beers in hand, shaking their heads. Here we are, two old broads (I can just hear Alice say, "Hey, speak for yourself!") jumping on a hotel bed. Like monkeys. Like sisters who the babysitter can't control—because no one can tell us what to do. Not anymore. It's the kind of freedom you only get once you've earned it. And we, now motherless with grown children, and grown wisdom, have earned it.

The laughter that echoes in the room sings triumphantly, and lasts long after we both get out of breath (which happens all too quickly) and flop onto the bedspread.

"Oh my God," Alice says between chuckles. "That was so fun!"

"Yeah, let's do it again!" I say, and we have one last giggle before returning to our middle-aged senses.

I am thrilled to hear that laugh again. My best friend has the greatest laugh.

April 2008: I'm driving down the highway talking to Alice on my cell phone, which—yes, I know—is a bad habit. But then, at this stage, I don't have many left.

"Hey, I'm getting married!" she says, while I'm driving in the fast lane. A sure way to get me killed.

"WHAT??" I yell, trying to pull over because I'm having a hard time controlling the car.

Now here's where some might think my best friend is really crazy and a glutton for punishment. That, by the time your children are grown, there is no good, sensible reason to get married again. Particularly if prior experiences in this matter, have been, let's say, unsuccessful.

"Now I know this sounds surprising," she says, as I get off the nearest exit and turn off the ignition, for my own safety. "But hey, life is short. And after two years, we still get along great. He's the only one who's ever treated me this good."

She's right about that. Jeff and I have gotten to know this guy. We've seen them together. We see that he always puts her first, before himself. That he gives her what she needs, with no conditions attached. And he really, truly, wants to spend the rest of his life making her happy. Now, that's a good man.

There's a saying that goes, you are meant to go through what you do, to get to where you are today. Today, Alice is honestly, deservingly, happy. Sometimes it just takes a long time, a lifetime, to find the right person. And as my best friend, my love-ya-like-a-sister best friend, says, "Hey, I'm no quitter," then laughs that great laugh.

Alice has moved on to a merry life.

Take that, Mad Hatter.

How My Mother Got Her Groove Back

*T*his is a story about triumph.

A few months before she died, Mom and I were at a bar, as we often found ourselves, listening to a polka band. This night, between the oom-pah-pahs, my mother began reflecting on how life was in "her day." The music, as music tends to do, sparked all kinds of recollections. She talked about childhood memories and odd relatives. Of dates she went on before "I met your father" (her face scowling a bit), and all the letters she'd received from "the boys in the war" (which I'd find in shoe boxes after her death). Her eyes then moved from the dance floor to her Gin & Squirt, and she said to the drink, "I've had a pretty good life."

Whaat?

I forced myself to contain my bafflement. Throughout my childhood and adolescence, my mother had been an unhappy, distant, moody, and oftentimes, bitter woman. According to most everything I knew about her life, Mom—who would turn seventy-five in a week—had been miserable most of the time. It had been only in the last fifteen years that she seemed happy, and content.

Had time and age, somehow, magically erased those awful years? It appeared so.

I looked at her stunned as she met my gaze. Just then, a spunky white-haired man wearing a Hawaiian shirt, tan dress pants and brown oxfords, offered his hand and whisked my mother away. I sat there stirring my Rum & Coke, watching this woman who I rarely understood, bouncing up and down, twirling round and round to "In Heaven, There Is No Beer" in her silver sequined tennis shoes. This smiling woman, who right now seemed to not have a care in the world, was not the woman who had raised me. This one, who replaced her, was cheery. Self-assured. Sure-footed.

This one knew how to have a good time.

I have photographic evidence that my mother had had some experience in that regard prior to having children, but then she stopped. She simply wasn't in the mood. And who could blame her? After just a few years of living her own life, she'd been forced to move back in with her parents with two small children in tow. And get a fulltime job while other moms stayed at home donning aprons, baking cookies, and hosting coffee klatches. (It took me my whole life to see it this way.)

And so, with each birthday my brother and I passed, Mom would declare, "The older you two get, the younger I get!" I didn't get it. She'd recite the phrase often as time made us grownups and it baffled me for years. That is, until I became a mother and began seeing the benefits of your children growing up.

If you do it right, there's a lot of sacrifice that goes with parenthood. Your priorities change. Or at least they should. Then before you know it, as the saying goes, they're making their own way in the world, leaving you behind as they venture onto other relationships and another life.

And there you are. Free to do what you've been holding off for decades without worrying about babysitters, or where your kids are, or what the neighbors will think.

What to do now?

My mother chose to dance.

Whenever she could, that is. Having never learned to drive, she often found that getting where the music was, created a challenge. But Mom usually found a way. She had friends, she had neighbors, she had cabs, and she had me. When she couldn't get a ride, or afford cab fare, she'd settle for dancing in her living room. I never actually witnessed this, but she'd get a kick out of telling me about her two-stepping with her cat to her favorite country music or big-band station.

And she became proficient at it. Or maybe it's something that naturally comes back to you. I remember how surprised I was by her sense of rhythm when I started going out with her. After I got older, and she, younger. Our dates became more frequent after Gee Gee passed away, and Jeff, my then husband-to-be, was working second shift. I'd pick Mom up at her apartment, we'd go to dinner, then hit the bars. This is how I witnessed the great transformation from Mom One to Mom Two. Mom Two was fun. And social. And interesting. Over drinks and music, we could discuss any topic without the parent/child gene getting in the way. And we could tear up the dance floor, like real friends. Without either of us realizing it, our former relationship as strict mother vs. rebel daughter slowly dispersed. As we bopped to the music, we began to like one another.

It was a change I'm sure my mother found especially gratifying. Throughout my childhood and adolescence, I had steered clear of her most of the time, choosing instead, the gentle and nurturing arms of her mother. Which created hormonal chaos in the female-charged shadowbox in which we lived. Things only worsened when Mom moved us out from under Gee Gee's reign. My mother's joy of finally having her kids to herself—and being the ruler of her own roost—was quickly overshadowed by the realization that she and her daughter were strangers.

It took years, but we finally came together. And music became our common denominator. That, and parenthood. When my children were little and I needed, myself, to get away, I knew Mom was always available. So one Friday night each month, Mom and I went out. Sometimes we'd go to a new bar, if they had a "good band" (according to Mom), but always ended up at Earl's Lounge, an old neighborhood shot-and-beer place where my family knew most everyone. There we'd share anecdotes, swap parenting adventures, and dance. Me in my biker boots, she in her glittery, rhinestone tennis shoes she got on sale at K-Mart for $7.99. When I was young, I could never have imagined my mother in such happy shoes.

Mom Two knew all the latest dance crazes, including— I'm afraid—the Macarena and the Chicken Dance. Which is fairly embarrassing—no, scratch that— *wholly* embarrassing when you think of watching your now elderly mother, who constantly drummed in your head throughout your childhood about being "ladylike," dancing around with a roomful of people, squawkin' and flappin' her arms up and down, hen-style.

"Aw, come on," she'd urge me at the first note, waving her arms toward the dance floor.

"Sorry, Mom, that's one dance I'll pass on," I often said.

She got me up a couple of times, though, when I'd had enough cocktails to make it seem like a good idea. Strange that, some years later, I'd wished I'd said yes a few times more.

When there wasn't a live band playing, Mom hit the jukebox. My mother was a jukebox junkie. And not just for the "old standards." There was no rhyme or reason for her varied taste in music. Mom's gauge for any song was the music itself, not the lyrics. So although she loved anything recorded by Elvis, her favorites ranged from Eric Burden's "House of the Rising Sun" (I often wondered if she knew it was about a Louisiana whorehouse, though by the time she became fun it wouldn't matter), David Lee Roth's "Just a Gigolo," and Joe Diffie's "Prop Me Up Beside the Jukebox (If I Die)." Mom especially loved that one.

"Make sure you play that song at my funeral," she'd say, every time that song came on. For years, Mom had been preparing for her own funeral, as if the event was right around the corner. If someone she knew was dying in the hospital, it was a perfect time to reiterate, "Now, don't you dare keep me on life support." Returning from a funeral, she'd remind me, "And I don't want you giving some long eulogy about my life, and no big display of pictures, either. Just play my favorite songs." (After she died in 2004, I'd find a dusty 8-track tape in a box, labeled with song titles she wanted played at her "goodbye party." Considering 8-track tapes were rarely used by the mid-'80s, it appeared my mother had been expecting to go for a long time.) I would respond to her request with this: "Mom, you keep talking about a party you won't even be there to enjoy!"

"Oh, you bet I will! You can count on that!" she'd say, raising her right arm straight up, as if already dancing. Although she was no longer a "practicing Catholic," my mother had a firm belief in the afterlife of the human spirit.

Although Mom hated her picture taken, the few photographs she did like were the ones of her dancing. Her greatest joy as a child and preteen was her tap-dancing lessons and subsequent recitals. Her mother had been a seamstress, who made all the outfits for the dancers' big events. Every photograph of my young mother in her elaborate dancing outfits shows her elation. Her smile is wide, her eyes gleaming. Her face, brilliant. Mom's favorite memories of those times were of her dancing on a big snare drum, looking like Shirley Temple, with black patent-leather shoes and ribbon bow ties on her happy feet.

My mother's biggest regret in life was that she didn't

become a *real* dancer.

When Mom was thirteen, the doctor had told my grandmother that her daughter should quit dancing lessons because it was preventing her from getting her menstruation (likened to today's female athletes who don't get their periods for months on end). My mother was devastated. She fought, she reasoned, she tearfully begged her mother to let her keep dancing. But like any God-fearing mother, Gee Gee followed the doctor's orders.

And Mom soon got her period. In exchange for her bliss.

I knew the story well as she repeated it often. "I could've been a great dancer, I had rhythm," she'd point out whenever a particular song made her twelve again. And she was right. She did have rhythm, and proved it during those mother/daughter outings to the local taverns.

Whenever she'd get on the dance floor—even in her seventies—my mother came down with rockin' pneumonia, and the boogie-woogie flu.

I was still thinking about Mom's offhanded remark that evening, when she returned to her seat after the polka dance. That's when I saw that her face was beaming. Suddenly I understood what she'd meant by the "pretty good life" comment:

This was a woman who had endured many years in the shadow of her mother, whom she'd loved and fought against, with equal fervor. A woman who struggled to raise two children without the support, financially and otherwise, of a man. Who, for twelve years, didn't have her own bed, or room, but slept on an old couch in her parent's living room. Who worked most of her life as a bank teller, and then an office worker, a job that, in its last ten years, she'd grown to hate. Who lived life on her own terms—even when it would've been easier to be more agreeable. Who loved music, dancing, family, and friends, and discovered along the way those were the things that held the key to her happiness.

My mother was a woman who, after years of labor, heartache, and regret, ultimately showed them all, including that misguided doctor, that she could not be beaten. That she would dance again. And did.

In the end, my mother had triumphed.

The last time I danced with my mother was the night of my fiftieth birthday. By now, we were very much in step with one another, and when she'd ask me to dance, I did. Even the chicken one (well, okay, not every time. After all, I have my pride). On Sunday nights, Jeff and I would pick her up at the little condo she so proudly had, somehow, managed to pay off. And we'd make our way to Cebars, another shot-and-beer place that held a weekly blues jam night. We would spend the evening partying with friends, who all thought my mother was cool.

"I love your mom's shoes," people would say to me. By now, she owned several pairs of happy shoes, all with the requisite glitter and rhinestones. They became her trademark.

I remember thinking on this birthday night that my mom had come a long way. At seventy-five, she'd turned out okay. As we danced, I thought of all those years we didn't get along, and I knew it had to be some kind of miracle that time had made us friends. In fact, she'd become one of my best friends. And my biggest fan.

"I need more copies," she'd tell me every time one of my articles came out. When my first book was published, she told everyone she saw—the neighbors, the ladies in the bathroom at my book launching ("My daughter's the author, you know"), the postman, and the people at the discount store she went to every Wednesday. And she was always remembering just one more friend, or relative, she wanted to send a book to. When I was a guest on a local radio station that didn't come through all that clearly in her area, she fiddled for an hour trying to get it in, so she could hear every word. My mother's enthusiasm and pride in me became one of the things I'd miss the most after she stopped dancing.

It happened that my mother's wake, in April 2004, fell on a Friday night. I walked into the funeral parlor with CDs and boom-box in hand and told the director to turn off that dismal "funeral" music. My mother would have none of that! We played country music. We played rock 'n' roll. We played the blues.

We played what Mom wanted to hear. And I saved Diffie's tune for last. I didn't care if a few elders thought it was in poor taste.

"I want you to have a big party, play those songs I told you to, and dance."

And this time, I did as I was told.

And so, the night before her funeral, in a room filled with

flowers and photos of Mom (a rebel till the end, I had my say-so when it came to pictures), we played her favorite songs, and in the end, a few of us danced. And as I clapped and swayed back and forth with Mom's best friend, Bev, I heard my mother's voice.

"Now that's what I was talking about!" she said.

Then we all went to the bar.

A week later, I found three pairs of glittery tennis shoes in Mom's closet. For a split second, I thought perhaps I'd use them sometime, because we wore the same size. But they weren't me.

I placed them in the Goodwill box, figuring if they worked for my mother, they just might be a perfect fit for some other struggling woman. A woman in dire need of getting her groove back.

Part Three

Legacies

9. What I Know So Far

Perseverance is a Virtue

My mother lies there quiet. Eyes closed. Breathing through the tube taped to her mouth. Like driving past a bad accident, I cringe at the sight, but cannot stop staring. Or thinking. I stand by her hospital bed and I can hear, *hear*, her voice. The slight lilt it had. The wisdom that came from it, along with the nonsensical. I stand there numb, recalling all those times she'd be yappin' away and I'd be thinking about groceries I had to buy, or my daughter's upcoming school recital, or what I was writing about—anxious to get back to it. So many times I wasn't listening. Just nodding my head at the appropriate times.

She did, after all, have a tendency toward run-on sentences . . .

"Mom?" I say, touching her swollen arm. "I'm going to step out now. I'll be back in a minute."

This time, it is she, not listening.

I go directly to the nurse's station. There is only one lady at the desk, seemingly engaged in paperwork. I interrupt anyway. She raises her head and gives me a *Now what?* look.

I ask my questions quickly to get them all in, make my anxiety known. She rises from her chair and stands before me, bored, as if she's been asked to recite a Walt Whitman poem to a class of imbeciles.

"Your mother is very sick."

Her voice is not kind, it's scolding. Like a mother who's told me ten times to pick up my room and ready to smack me into action.

But I want to go first. I mentally slap her tight insensitive face and send her flying out those automatic doors where she lands on the fucking leaves of grass.

After a week of this, I have no patience for anyone. I've been sitting here day after day, hour after hour, with my comatose mother in this room of tubes and wires and indifference.

I look at Nurse Pursed Lips, a face with clearly other things on its mind, and stare. How stupid did she think I was? It's Day Six of my mother's stay in this god-forsaken unit and I do know what CCU means. That's not the point. I want details. Like what those bleepin', beepin' machines attached to her do, exactly. What those ever-changing numbers *mean*? And why is my mother's right arm so grotesquely swollen, bruised? And that tube snaking down her throat—that *has* to be painful, despite that nice male nurse reassuring me last night that she feels nothing.

And this: If my mother is in such a drug-induced coma, why does it seem like she's aware of what is happening? Why, when I began talking to her in this coma on Day Four, did I see a single tear trickle down her right cheek?

"The doctor will be in later, you'll need to direct your questions to him," the woman says in a rushed tone. "You'll have to excuse me now."

No, I don't believe I will. I can't excuse a care-giver who really doesn't give a shit.

But before I say it out loud, she steps away, taking with her all that she knows.

Ok, I get it. You people are terribly busy. Have lots of patients. Can't explain things to family members lest you say the wrong thing and they sue your ass. I've got all that. What I don't get is that I thought part of your job was to be compassionate. To be kind. To wear a smile as clean as your uniform in your world of frowns.

I go back to my mother's room like a good girl and sit in the hard wooden chair by the window. Boy, would Mom be pissed, I think. How many times had she told us not to let "them" keep her alive through a machine? That lone tear told me of her pain, but was it also expressing her disgust?

"But this is different, Mom," I whisper. "It's only temporary. Trust me. Ya gotta keep the faith."

After all, it had always sustained us before.

This all happened so fast, with no forewarning. She'd been her old self since they removed that lump last year. We'd practically forgotten about it. Her breast cancer. My mother, the trouper, was feeling great. She had refused doctors' suggestions of precautionary chemo and radiation treatment. "I'm seventy-four, and want to enjoy the time I have left," she'd say, knowing the devastation those treatments can provoke. Who could blame her? She *was . . . finally*, enjoying her life. Why put her through that hell now? And so she went on with life as if cancer had never interrupted it. Mom was once again healthy, energetic, fine.

But unbeknown to us, my mother had congestive heart failure. And sometimes, the disease doesn't show itself until, one day, all hell breaks loose. Mom had gone out to dinner with Bev, her friend and neighbor, and was home by seven. Didn't even go out dancing. But she seemed fine, according to Bev. Mom ate and chatted about her family, like any other day. Then, two hours later, she couldn't breathe. *Really* couldn't breathe. She ran across the driveway to Bev's house, who called an ambulance. Mom had fluid in her lungs, medics said, a common symptom of CHF.

"I'm afraid things don't look good," the emergency room doctor said that first night.

"How long has she been smoking?"

We counted.

"I guess about 60 years," Dennis said. The doctor shook his head at my brother like it was the wrong answer. He then walked out of the room, leaving the stifling air of hopelessness swirl around us like left-over smoke from Mom's last cigarette.

"If she makes it through," Doc had said, "She can never smoke again."

I can't imagine my mother not smoking. It was part of who she was. It gave her pleasure in a life that had allowed so few.

On Day Seven, I sit in the chair gazing at my unresponsive mother and suddenly recall the time when this particular scene played out in reverse. . . .

Mom is sitting next to my hospital bed. I've just had my tonsils out and open my eyes to see her in an uncomfortable looking chair—where, I'd hear later, she'd been all day—waiting for me to "come through" the ether I'd been given that morning. I start to gag and spit up blood, and she grabs a blue round plastic bowl for me to spew into.

"Now don't forget you can have all the ice cream you

want!" she says with a smile, a weak attempt to make it all better for this miserable eight year old.

I shudder at the memory. A memory I hadn't realized was still there.

"How's Mom doing today?" one of the nice nurses says, entering, disrupting.

"You tell me."

But all I get is a comforting smile as she checks those blinking numbers and writes them in her chart.

She leaves to continue her rounds. I stay to continue my wait. I wait for a sign, any sign. As that damn machine Mom's hooked up to, slowly, effectively, extracts my faith. Beep by Beep . . .

Throughout our relationship I was never real clear on what my mother expected from me. But as I sat there watching her, waiting, I knew two things to be true. We both had far exceeded each other's expectations of one another. I liked to joke that my mother, after those rough patches, had "turned out pretty good." She, in turn, would boast about her daughter, the "successful writer," to anyone half listening.

And although she wasn't always a church-going Catholic, she harbored more confirmed faith in life—and whatever comes after—than I did at this moment.

Faith was something I had always relied on. It had been my most reliable companion. Standing quietly on the sidelines until I'd seek it. And there it'd be. But now I felt abandoned, locked inside a dark basement warding off the swarms of rats that kept me up at night.

I wanted my mother back. I hadn't realized how much she defined me, how she was always on my side. We'd be sitting at her favorite bar, drinking Gin & Squirts and I'd be complaining about some coworker, or some event that happened that sucked, and she'd always agree with my assessments. "Well, that's ridiculous," she'd say in support. And, "Well, they're just plain idiots." Then, "Let's have one more before we go." Somehow her agreement with my take on things always gave me the sweet sense of vindication, if only imaginary.

And to my enjoyment, she never tired of my endless stories of every little thing my children did. In fact, she embraced them. That meant everything.

It had taken years, decades in fact, for us to become friends. A slow process, but somehow God had ultimately made us true mother and daughter. It was a gift I felt certain came by some great miracle. Now I sit here helpless, wondering why God doesn't wake her up. And my faith and reliance in Him is disappearing into that sterile bed.

A week ago, I'd been on the phone with Mom, setting the date for our annual road trip to Fostoria, her "party town." She was near giddy with excitement. I often thought it ironic that she would so love the small town that her own mother couldn't wait to flee. *She was so different from her mother,* I thought. *Then again, so am I.*

I get up from the hardback chair, and go back to her bedside. "Oh, my God," I gasp. Lying against those pallid sheets, I suddenly realize just how much my mother looks like my grandmother right now. I never saw a resemblance before, between the two. They were never alike in any way. I suddenly notice now that I'd been coloring mom's hair the same shade as Gee Gee's—something I doubt either of us realized. And now this seventy-five-year-old woman lying here with closed eyes and auburn-enhanced hair looked exactly like her own mother. I looked away, then back. It was true. Eerie as this was, though, it seemed right. As if Gee Gee was lying here, too, with her. As if the two most influential women in my life had merged into one.

And the one lying here was the one I often dismissed in my life. I left my mother out of many important events. I robbed her of personal moments she rightfully deserved to take part in. Like being involved in my weddings. I never once asked her, either time, to come with me to shop for my wedding dress. Or pick out the cake, or flowers. And I never had her be present when I had my children. I had waited until the historic event was all over, then called her with the news. I was a terrible, self-centered, rotten daughter . . .

But then, somehow, someway, I hear my mother's voice and she intuitively shakes me out of my self-imposed guilt. I am reminded that, had I actually taken Mom shopping with me for a wedding dress, we would've never agreed on one anyway. She would've *had* to give her opinions, which would've influence mine (refer to Chapter Two), and this would change a nice mother/daughter outing into something not so nice. And I had to also remember, that there was no way Mom would've wanted to be anywhere near that hospital room while I was giving birth. She was, what is now referred as, old school.

So while I feel a bit better about myself, my relief doesn't last. My mother is still lying in that bed, motionless. Quiet. Dying.

I put my hand on Mom's, the one that's not all puffed out (I learn later, that was caused by an inept nurse who screwed up her IV, probably Pursed Lips) and stare at that ominous machine that's, somehow, sustaining her life. I was never a numbers girl. Good with words, incredibly bad with numbers. They were never important to me before. Yet now, I desperately want to understand those digits that light up like a score from a pinball game. I want to make sense of them. So I can put two and two together and make life. This all seems too much like death.

And then, hope.

On Day Ten, my mother comes out of her coma. Her lungs, previously filled with fluid, have cleared up enough to allow her to breathe on her own. Gone is that bleepin' machine, the unsightly tube, the waning faith. My mother is back. We had weathered the storm. We have persevered.

Her voice is raspy as she struggles to talk because having a tube down your throat for more than a week must feel like sandpaper in your esophagus. But she is effective in her gestures. Especially the one I know so well. She is flashing me her disapproving look. I first take it to mean she just wants the hell out of here. But then her eyes shift from me to the TV, the TV to me. Then I get it. The nursing staff, in an attempt to keep her calm after a couple of thrashing bouts (and wouldn't you, if you couldn't *breathe*), put on some kind of yoga channel with waves crashing against a shore along with musical sounds of seagulls hawking. Continuously hawking.

My mother hates water, birds, and music that doesn't make you dance.

"Oh, Mom, how could they?' I say smiling, reaching for the controller. "They don't know you very well, now do they?" Mom smiles back, weakly, and I click on *Wheel of Fortune*. She nods. Much better.

Day Twelve, I arrive early to a surprise. Mom is out of that bed, sitting up in a chair getting ready to graduate from Camp CCU to her own room. "She's moving up in the world," a smiling nurse says.

"I'd like some ice cream," Mom says in a hoarse voice. This, right after being told she can now take in small amounts of liquids.

"Oh, not just yet," the nurse says. "Let's try some water first. And tea."

Mom makes a face. "Ice cream is better." Then she grins. Her sense of humor is back, too. I want to tell her she can have all the ice cream she wants. But it'll have to wait.

"I know," Smiling Nurse replies. "But we have to take baby steps. If things go well, maybe you can have that ice cream tonight." Then turning her head towards me, she whispers, "Such a good sign she wants to eat. You know, everyone here is talking about her progress. We really didn't expect such improvement."

Expectations . . .

We have already told my fun-loving mother that her life has to change. No more cigarettes. No more gin. No more dancing. Yet, she seems okay with it. She seems just happy to be alive.

Faith . . .

She's fought demons before, so she's ready to take on this one, too. No big deal.

Perseverance . . .

I lean over my mother's chair. "Looks like you're in good hands, Mom," I say, smiling. We're all smiling. We are kids anticipating a trip to Disney World. Or Fostoria.

"I have to go now, Mom," I add. "I have to go to work."

I can't explain to her all the work I've missed. She doesn't know how long she's been here. She doesn't know how much hope we'd lost. But now, I can walk out of this room feeling relieved. I choose to ignore the fact that my once-vibrant mother now looks like a frail, old woman in that chair. It's too heartbreaking to acknowledge. So I concentrate on the fact that she is getting better. And that machine is nowhere in sight.

"I have to work both jobs, tomorrow, so I'll see you Wednesday. For sure," I promise, leaning over to place a kiss on her forehead. It will be the first day I miss since the ambulance brought her here a lifetime ago. She nods to me. My independent, hard-working mother understands about making a living. "I'll call you tomorrow morning, okay?"

"Oh, that's fine—I'll be here!" she sings.

As I walk down the corridor and out the door, I have no clue I'll never see my mother again.

Mom had several sayings I grew up hearing. One of them was, "When it's your time to go, it's your time, and there's nothing you can do about it." It's one of the first things that came to mind when a nurse called the next day to tell me, "Your mother's taken a turn for the worse. You'd better get down here."

I immediately called my husband, who came and got me at work. I knew that's what hospital people say when there is little hope, and that in all likelihood, my mother was probably already gone.

And there was nothing I could do about it.

Still, we rushed. My brother beat us there.

"The doctors did everything they could to save her," the nurse recited to us in the hallway. "But it happened very fast. She didn't suffer."

It was a blood clot. Of all things that would take my mother down.

Yet it was almost as if Mom had devised the most efficient way to make her exit. She didn't want life support. She didn't want to end up in a nursing home. She didn't want "to be a burden to you kids."

"I have to tell you," the nurse added, "She did get her ice cream last night."

That made me smile, envisioning Mom enjoying every bite.

My mother, my strong and tenacious mother, had her way in the end.

For weeks after my mother died, I began wondering where—exactly—had she gone. I wanted to know. For sure. And without a doubt.

But doubt began to plague me. Me, a woman who always believed in a higher power. Me, who prayed every day since I'd learned how (even as a rebellious teen). Me, who taught my children that God is real, and will always be there for them.

Me. Now of little faith.

Mom would be so disappointed.

Still. The "what ifs?" persisted. What if there is nothing beyond this one trip in life? What if we die, and it's like when you're under anesthesia and there is only darkness, forever. What if I never really, *really* see my mother again?

These thoughts . . . despite a sign to the contrary that, for a time, I'd forgotten about.

One day, years ago, I was driving, taking Gee Gee to the grocery store, as I did every Wednesday. We were stopped at a light and both of us noticed the brilliant sky before us. Bright rays of glowing sunlight streaming through the billowy clouds, like Star War beams. Gee Gee pointed to it and said, "Oh, look, someone's going to heaven." I remember thinking what a great thought that was. It was one of the most beautiful things I'd ever heard my grandmother say.

On that last trip to the hospital with my husband driving, I was sitting in the passenger seat gazing out at nothing, afraid to even think. Halfway there, I looked up in time to see the clouds begin to part, and saw the streams of sunlight beaming through. It was beautiful, and confirming. I knew then that someone was going to heaven. And I knew who.

Still, I questioned other signs as well. After all, they could all be just coincidences, I told myself. I wanted confirmation. To have my mother suddenly appear walking through a locked door, like Jesus, where I could touch her and believe. I wanted absolute proof that she was, somehow, still around.

I began to question how all the unexplained events, people, places and things in the world happened. This of course only produced more questions. If in fact, there was no rhyme or reason for all the wondrous ways nature, and human beings, work, then how is it so many things fall into place at just the right time? How do flowers know that it's spring and time to bloom? Or squirrels know winter's coming and bury their food? Or new mother birds know how to care for their young? *And how the hell do blades of grass spring up through cracks of hard cement?* That one always boggled my mind.

And how do people know that it's their time to go?

The questions were endless, but the answers were clear.

Somebody or something had to be in charge.

There simply was no other explanation. I'd been right all along. There was a higher power orchestrating it all. It makes perfect sense.

Realizing this had nothing to do with my Catholic upbringing. Had nothing to do with wanting to believe. It had everything to do with living life and observing and seeing how everything has its place. Even though we don't always understand how, or why.

***

It's a month after my mother died, and I'm sitting alone in an airplane. It's the first time I've flown by myself since I was seventeen and took off to California in a desperate attempt to get away from my mother's hold on me. But this time, I'm headed south. I need to be with my best friend, the other woman who will listen to me rant about an event that sucked, then vindicate me with her comments.

"Are you okay?" the woman seated next to me says, offering a Kleenex. I hadn't realized I was crying.

"I hate to fly," I say, dismissively wiping the tears with my hand.

"Oh, me, too. But I've learned to just grin and bear it. Have a drink."

I order a Gin & Squirt.

Soon after I return back home, I dream one night that Mom and I are in my car, going shopping, and she is yappin' away. Her voice is loud, clear, real.

And I am listening. . . .

I read somewhere that we are not human beings having a spiritual experience. Rather, we are spiritual beings having a human experience.

I would come to believe this to be true. When I saw that stream of sunshine upon learning of my mother's death. When I found that penny lodged underneath her dining set. When I grabbed the phone the other day to call her about something my kids did . . . forgetting When I remember her favorite poem, "Don't Quit," that so reminds me of her. Or when I'd hear her tell me in a dream that she is fine. Happy. Then starts to sing . . .

So many moments, I feel her presence. One spirit communicating with a mere human. On those occasions, I am reminded my mother and I are not so different, after all.

We both persevere.

Fifty Is Not for Sissies

My face is falling. I look at this middle-aged person in the mirror with the droopy eyelids and sagging skin, and realize, horrifyingly, that this is probably the best I'll ever look.

I gaze at my cheeks and recall how my youngest daughter, at six, used to pinch them in church and say, "You have such spongy cheeks, Mommy!"

Ever press your finger into a sponge? It makes an indent that stays put that way for a minute before returning to its initial shape. My whole body seems to be in sponge mode. They should call me Bob. Except I don't wear square pants.

I'm doing the press test at my reflection when I suddenly notice some wrinkles—not those cute, little etchy crows-feet adorned by still-attractive "older" actresses that somehow make them appear more sophisticated—rather, mine are in the puffy areas below my eyes, like my mother has. Had. Why hadn't I noticed *that* before. Shit. I grab the hairbrush from the cabinet and brush back my bangs to examine my forehead – no wrinkles there, thank God. But then I see my eyebrows, which I haven't plucked in twenty-some years. That's because I hardly have any. When I was an insecure, self-hating, peer-pleasing teenager, I became obsessed with my unibrow. Every time I looked in the bathroom mirror (and how often do teenage girls do *that*?) I'd pluck and pluck and pluck like a mad scientist attacking each faintly emerging threadlike outgrowth in a vain attempt for Twiggy brows. Even after every, single stray hair had been ripped out, I'd keep doing it, like a bulimic's need to purge. Finally, the origins buried in the underlining papilla gland acquiesced, and declared a truce. Those menacing little hairs got the message, and never grew back again.

And that's precisely when thick, full eyebrows came into vogue.

Shit.

And now, after years on my feet dressing hair, the veins on the back of my legs look like railroad tracks. Purple railroad tracks.

And oh, how I mourn my waist. Used to have one, you know, but it's hiding under this saggy mountain of fleshy flesh. It only reveals itself if I lift up my flabby, saggy breasts. OH, there it is!

My once "hour-glass" figure has shattered, the shards distributed haphazardly around my swollen body that is now referred to as "apple-shaped." My mid-section has blown up—or rather, out—like a balloon, so that it droops over the waistline (now a cruel ironic term) of my jeans like twin blobs of silly puddy, and stubbornly refuses to budge no matter how many tasteless, cardboard rice patties I slowly, agonizingly, devour. How much easier it would be if I were to grow just a few inches taller to stretch it all out.

And then there's this: When I do happen to have a good hair day, and my face is covered nicely with "age-defying" makeup and my best (slimming black) outfit, my hands—with their own set of wrinkles, puffed out veins, and telltale "age spots"—don't just give my age away, they suggest I'm even older than I am.

It all seems absurd considering that in my mind, I am still twenty-nine, thirty at most.

And yet, despite the fact that I loathe these horrific changes in my body, I am happy with this older woman who looks back at me in that unforgiving mirror. Like my forties, my fifties—which I'm now well into—has provided me with exciting opportunities, new experiences and knowledge, new friends and colleagues, and a forever-changing perspective on things. And I really do appreciate it all. When people ask my age, I'm weirdly proud to announce it. Like I'd just won a prize or something. I suppose given the way we boomers grew up: smoking, drinking, drugging, and other foolhardy behavior, I have reason to be proud I've made it this far. Or more like, relieved.

Especially considering the weekend I've just had. . . .

Nobody likes hospitals. Except maybe people who work in one—and then probably just a handful of those. It's not just the clinical, antiseptic feel of these structures, it's the foreboding thoughts, and inner ramblings, of doom that swirl around the brain of those who find themselves praying—probably more than usual—amid those white, Spartan walls, that you'll make it out those doors in relatively good shape.

So I wasn't thrilled when the doctor called me to give me what should've been good news.

"Your thyroid tests came back negative," she said. With the symptoms I'd been having, this news was disappointing. Because it would've been an easy answer. I like easy answers. "I want you to go to the emergency room."

There was true concern in her voice, enough to keep me from saying, "Sorry, this really isn't a good time for me. I have a window open next Wednesday, however."

"We need to find out what's going on. This could be serious." (She declined to say, "at your age." But I heard it anyway).

Like I said, nobody likes hospitals, and most have a particular disdain for emergency rooms. If for no other reason than they make you wait *forever*. Though there are of course, scarier, more horrifying reasons. Nonetheless, whoever came up with the phrase, "the waiting is the hardest part" (*Tom Petty?*) had to have been in the ER at the time.

So I'm waiting. I sit and sit and sit. I try to lose myself in the book I've brought in a useless attempt to not think of what they may discover about my racing heart, my palpitations, my endless fatigue, my occasional lightheadedness, and the weird pressure I feel in my head. But I can't concentrate in lieu of the stifling, crazy, paranoid thoughts that insist on creeping in. It's something you can't control. It's what the brain—particularly a brain of a person, say, over forty—does in times of uncertainty that leads you to the Emergency Room.

What if something is really wrong? I've experienced heart palpitations lots of times through my adulthood, but these last few have been worse, more intense. What if I have a bad valve? What if I need heart surgery? What if at fifty-two—and a half—my days are numbered.

The lady calls me in.

"Do you have a history of heart problems?"

"No, but there's a lot in my family," I say, remembering. "My father died of a heart attack at fifty-three (*Oh My God! I'm Six Months Away!*). And both my mom and grandmother died from complications of congestive heart failure . . .

"But they were older, in their seventies," I add, quickly.

Still, it all doesn't sound good to me. Neither does the next question.

"Are you an organ donor?"

"Well, yes." *If it comes to that.*

"Do you smoke?"

"No. Not for the past twenty-one years," I state proudly.

"Drink alcohol?"

"Not a lot. About four, five times a week."

Having just said that, I realize that it does, in fact, sound like a lot. So I quickly add, "But rarely more than two drinks a night. Ok, three on weekends."

"Recreational drugs . . . ?"

"Nope," I say honestly, but wonder, does she mean in a lifetime? The answer would have been different twenty-five years ago. Before kids and common sense kicked in.

She sends me to another room and another lady, who needs to know how I'm paying for all this. After that one gets all the insurance info, I'm sent back to the hallway chair with an assurance that "Someone'll be with you in a moment."

Yeah, sure.

I sit back down, and my cell phone goes off. It's my brother. I turn it off. I don't want to talk to him right now. It reminds me of when our mother was in the hospital. Could that have been over two years already? I don't want him freaking out. We're the only ones left in our family. This thought leads to another. And another. I begin contemplating my mortality. My daughters. *They're still young, teenagers yes, but too young to be motherless. And grandchildren. Oh, how I look forward to that! Children are so cool. So precious and cute. My girls will be great mothers. I already know this. I want to see it. I want to laugh when they're going crazy with these kids and I can say, "And you thought it was easy, huh?"*

My eyes begin welling up. *And what about my book? This one. It's not finished yet. I want to be home writing it. There's still a lot I need to write about, a lot more to do to make it right. To make it complete. To make it publishable.* I pull out a Kleenex. *Damn. What the hell am I thinking? This can't be happening. I'm too young. There's still so much I want to learn about, to experience, to continue to grow into the person I'm just beginning to become. To like.*

I've got plans. And lots of them.

Okay, God, I'm well aware of that saying, "Just tell God you've got plans . . ." but don't laugh. These are really good plans, and there is so much more time I want with Jeff and the girls, and all these great friends I've acquired over my time here. And words of wisdom—got those too. I want to share what I've learned so far . . . and . . . and those yet-to-be-born grandkids . . . I've got stories to tell them. Hugs to give.

Please God, make this okay. I promise I'll do good things.

The automatic doors swing open, and a woman about my age leads her frail-looking grey-haired mother into the waiting room. The woman is smiling as she helps Mom sign in. Smiling, like she's just entered a party. I find this odd. I observe her a bit longer and determine that she's one of those people who wears a permanent smiley face, her way of making everything bearable. She reminds me of that Katherine Mansfield short story, "Bliss," in which the wife knows her husband is having an affair, but goes blithely about her merry way, choosing not to deal with any upsetting issues. I'd like to put on my smiley face at this point, but my spongy cheeks won't move.

"Deanna Adams." A voice calls out.

They give me a gown, and take me into a back room where they have me wait some more on a bed behind a curtain, like I'm a prize in *Let's Make a Deal*.

What's behind the curtain? An anxious fifty-something broad who wants the hell *outta* here!

They take my blood-pressure ("My, it's awfully high," says the nurse. *And wouldn't yours be?* I mentally say back.). They x-ray my chest. They take my blood, all the while monitoring my heart. Hours pass, when finally, a slow-moving heavy-set female nurse—who looks like a candidate for this very spot—tells me they have found nothing.

"Oh, okay, whew, I can go home now, it'll pass . . . right?"

"Not necessarily," she says grimly. "You say you don't feel right, your blood pressure is sky high and your complaints of palpitations are a sign of something. We just haven't figured it out yet. We want to admit you into the hospital for observation and more tests."

"But I can't," I tell her adamantly. "I have an important presentation in Akron tomorrow . . . I have to be there."

"Well," she sighs, like a mother to an unreasonable child. "We're telling you that you need to go in, and if you refuse (her next words come out like a bite), you are going *Against Medical Advice* and you must sign a form saying so. Did you drive yourself here?"

"Yes."

"We recommend that you don't drive until we find out what's wrong. It's too dangerous."

I. Want. To. Go. Home.

"Well, if everything so far looks okay," I prod, "then it can wait till, say, Sunday, right?" (That's my next "window.")

Heavy Sigh. "That's not what we recommend."

I sign the form. Then, just as I'm about to leave, the overweight woman—who probably smokes too—says, "Just know that if it's arrhythmia, something can happen so fast you won't have time to call 911. You'll be dead. Like that." (She snaps her fingers).

I bristle at her harsh words. But my need to be home overshadows the fear.

And so I go.

But after I'm home for an hour I get nauseous (one of the "warning signs" to go back to ER *immediately*), and the nurse's ominous words continually pound inside my head like a drum roll. I get scared. I leave messages for the coordinator of the conference I'm supposed to speak at the next day, and Jeff drives me to the hospital where they admit me, put me in a bed, and hook me to a machine. More waiting. More questions. More blood-pressure rising fear.

Finally, they have a room for me, "Third floor, Step Down Unit" the nurse announces to the orderly. *Step down. Well, that doesn't sound too bad,* I think.

The clip-clapping sound of the wheels beneath me as my moving bed rolls down the corridor, to the elevator, to another corridor, is disconcerting. Arriving at my destination, they have me stand up, and guide me to a scale (five pounds less than yesterday. *Now* I lose weight!). They lead me to my new bed by the window in room 5B, next to the sleeping woman, who looks about ninety if she's a day. It's 1:30 a.m., and I am pissed. I am tired and I want my own bed. My own home. My own family. My own peace of mind.

They've got me terrified now. And, as usual in these cases, I call on God again. And Mary, too. *Don't you remember, God? We've got this thing goin'. I'm down here learning, you're up there teaching. You'd have to agree I'm not done learning. I'm your work in progress. You can't be running short on instructions now, and I'm more than willing to learn more . . .*

And Mary, you're a woman, you understand. I've got all these womanly issues, tasks to complete, love to give. You know, all that good stuff we women are meant to do.

A nice male nurse, with an Indian accent I can barely understand, enters the room and lo and behold, asks more questions. He senses my irritation. "I'm su surry, ma'am," he says, in that accent we usually hear over the telephone, when we really need someone who can talk plain English. "I know you vant sleep. I jest must ask you bery few questions and I be gone. I prumise."

For the next thirteen hours, I'm left to ponder my fate as I'm jabbed, pumped, poked, and prodded, while hooked up to a "twenty-four hour" monitor, and questioned some more. And get to know my new roomie, who looks just like Granny from the *Beverly Hillbillies.*

"What's wrong, dear?" she says, pulling back the curtain soon as day breaks. "You look too young to be here."

I couldn't agree more.

For politeness sake, I tell her what's going on.

"Do you have a pace-maker?" she asks. Seriously.

"No, I don't," I say, feeling this is all too surreal. It might make an interesting movie, possibly a humorous one, if not for my leading role in it.

Granny is nice, sweet. And talkative. I don't want to be rude, just want to read and pretend I'm somewhere else. When she finally gets quiets, now absorbed in her *Animal Planet* program about the life of rabbits and other road kill (volume on HIGH), I gratefully return to my book. (Later, I overhear Granny tell her husband that a rabbit's life expectancy is only three years. "Really!" she tells him, as if it's the most interesting thing she's heard in years, "It's 'cause they get killed by other animals." So at least I've learned something during my stay.)

I'm reading *House* by a Cleveland author, Michael Ruhlman, whom I've met and talked with on occasion. The Cleveland writing community is, thankfully, a small world. We all support one another and often work together at conferences and other get-togethers. Despite where I am as I read it, I'm enjoying his book, not just because it's a memoir of someone I like and admire, but also I share his appreciation for our hometown. But as I read the chapter called "Return Pain"—what he describes as a form of longing, nostalgia, sentimentality—I become a part of his words. When he describes his family's first meal in their century-old house ("Roasted chicken, baked potatoes, green beans with lemon and butter") I get this overwhelming desire to rush home and make my family this meal. I want to clean the house as I've never cleaned it before (starting with those messy cabinets I normally just throw pots and pans into, hurriedly). I want to light scented candles all around my wonderful house. I want to be, truly, a domestic goddess whose housewifely skills are perfection.

Because I realize I haven't been the best in that category. While I can say I keep a fairly clean house, it's no museum. It is lived in, as they say, mostly because of all the magazines, newspapers, and books all about. And unlike those real domestic goddesses, I don't put any real passion into the scrubbing, dusting, polishing, and everything-in-its-place job of it all. There is a reason why they call it "household chores." It is precisely that. Never-ending chores. A mind-numbing routine that, frankly, bores the hell out of me. I've always found it useless to be fixated on being meticulous. Because in the grand scheme of things, how important is a perfect house, anyway?

Oddly, it now seems absolutely important. Just as important and priceless as my husband and daughters. My family. Who are really what matters in my world. Even more than writing, which I also have a passion, a need, for. And families rely on the mother to surround them with a homey atmosphere that is clean and neat—with no clutter. Clutter. I cringe. *Oh, have I failed.*

I'm crying when Indian man returns to take my blood pressure—again—and I silently beg God for the umpteenth time to get me out of here so I can become the most perfect, fixatedly meticulous, wife and mother.

My family needs me, I want to cry out. And I need them. I'm on this floor with all these old people who most, I'm sure, have had time with their grandkids, had their career peaks, had their chances for sparkling houses and home-cooked meals. Not to mention sewing. And gardening. All those things I really don't do. But now I think I should start.

I realize I'm not being fair to these elderly people whose lives are equally as important as mine. That I'm being selfish. Still, I can't help at this moment feeling robbed.

I've just finished my lunch of tuna salad and fruit cup when a priest walks in.

"Oh, hello, Father John," Granny says. I am relieved to learn he's here to pray with her, not to give anyone in this room last rites. After they repeat the Our Father and a couple other prayers, he moves on to me. He doesn't ask me why I, a person who looks too young to be here, is here. He doesn't ask me if I'm a Catholic, or even believe in God. He simply asks if I'd like to say a few prayers with him. Having just had a running monologue with God these past few hours, I think perhaps it can—with such an impromptu appearance of a holy man—be what I need to increase the effectiveness of my requests.

And miraculously, a few hours later, a nurse comes in and tells me I can go home. Once again, they have found nothing wrong. I have "passed" every test. They set me up with an "event monitor," which I am to wear for a month. The following week, I run my ass off on a hospital treadmill while hooked up to an octopus of wires, like a car engine that needs a good start, until the doctor says, "You are just fine. There's nothing wrong with your heart."

I want to kiss the ground. I want to kiss the nurse, the doctor, that priest who offered his prayers. The prayers that have been wonderously answered. Because within weeks, I am feeling perfectly healthy. No palpations. No tiredness. No complaints. As if it was all just a bad dream.

Thanks, God. I owe ya.

And so I go back to my life that was so rudely interrupted. I go back to doing everything exactly as before. I don't become a domestic goddess, though I do, two months later, get around to making that chicken and green bean dinner. And I must face the reality that, like Popeye, I yam what I yam. And I yam no domestic goddess. When I tell Jeff of my fear of not being the best wife and mother, he begs to differ.

"You are a terrific wife and mother and there's not one thing I'd change about you. To me, you *are* perfect." And I'm reminded why I married him.

And so I go back to critiquing the mirror. I go out and purchase an "advanced" facial peel that promises to "reveal younger-looking skin and diminish wrinkles." One application and my face puffs up like a chipmunk's. If that isn't bad enough, I awake the next morning to see that I can play connect-the-dots for all the zits that have emerged overnight. *This was not what I had in mind when anticipating "younger-looking" skin,* I think to myself. I promptly dump the jar of lying cream into the wastebasket and decide to just stick to tinting my roots, which I'm proud to say, still shows no signs of grey.

Life is gloriously back to normal. With one small change. I inhale thanksgiving with every breath. I love my people more intensely than before. And I thank my buddy, God, every morning I wake up. And Mary, too.

Because I realize that I am one lucky spongy-faced, middle-aged, flabby-waisted, eyebrow-less, purple-veined legged broad. Who is really, truly grateful for it all.

Music Saves

It came to me in a dream.

A really weird dream.

The thunderous, earth-shattering, God-like voice trembled through the skies, demanding, "Let it be *Music* to occupy your Muse," as if it were the most important commandment in life. We of little faith were caught off-guard by the sudden show-stopping rumblings, and furious parental tone.

Whoever was talking was clearly pissed.

The entire planet seemed to be tipping on its axis. I could hear echoes of swooshing, threatening water all around me, like I was caught in the middle of a tsunami. And yet, there was a disturbing lack of fearful screaming that would certainly be understandable under such circumstances.

I happen to be in the bathroom at the time. Not a place to be when the universe is tilting upside down. I kept envisioning toilet water spurting up like an oil well, and me in this claustrophobic cubicle with no way out. The door seemed to be locked, and I started to panic. I frantically jiggled and jiggled the knob for what seemed like hours, as water splashed about. Then, miraculously, the door opened. I escaped just in time to hear the all-encompassing Voice reiterate, with fuming words, about the impact of music.

Oh great, I thought. *And me, with not one iota of musical talent.*

The heady Voice shook me awake and I lied there—as anyone would—trying to decipher what the hell that was all about. Was it just a fluid dream or something more significant? After all, it was a dicey time in America. A few years after 911, things were not looking up. More and more of our troupes were fighting in the Middle East, and at the time of the dream, the country was on Orange Alert due to a revelation about a new terrorist plot in Britain. So maybe there was something to this, I couldn't help but think. After all, if any one thing could bring peace in this world, it would be music. Everyone loves music. Music brings people together. It creates a mood. It can make people happy just hearing it. And even when it makes you sad, it's a kind of a healing, cleansing sad, like the conclusion of a good cry. And it certainly drives the great Muse spirit. I mean, look at the music of Beethoven. Rogers and Hammerstein. Bob Dylan. Bruce Springsteen. Enough said.

In fact, I had never thought of it until that dream, but the very word *Music* is a derivative of *Muse*.

Hmmm . . . .

And there's nothing like a song that can evoke a once-forgotten memory. Even for those suffering from Alzheimer's. I know this because when I go to the assisted living place once a month to cut the elderly people's hair, many can't recall what they did five minutes ago, but when the old records play in the afternoon, everyone comes alive and sings and not one misses any of the words from some fifty years past. They then proceed to tell me how old they were at the time, about their former "beaus," and what they were doing when that song was a hit. And that's the magic. Music not only drives a Muse, it allows us to live our lives over by recapturing moments in our lives, if only for a lyrical moment.

And Lord knows, I've tried to go on some musical path, encouraged by my mother, who indeed loved music. My brother Dennis and I were always getting musical toys at Christmas and birthdays. One year it was a xylophone, which I don't believe influenced me one way or another. I was only four, so I was more attracted to the bright colors of the keys, than to the levels of plunking sounds you can make by hitting them with that stick with the ball on the end. It wasn't long after that we got bored with it, and it made its way to the bottom of the toy chest. The following year, Mom went way over budget and purchased little accordions for us, inspired by weekly doses of that local TV show, *Polka Varieties*. She thought this was so adorable that she immediately took our picture playing the matching wind instruments, and wrote on the back of it, "Beginning of a polka band?" That answer came a few weeks later when they, too, joined the ranks of the forgotten land of children's toys. As did the flute. The plastic saxophone. And the harmonicas.

One Christmas, "Santa" brought us matching tambourines. Now this I could get into. As one prone to showmanship (or showwomanship), I loved the fact you could dance and wiggle and make a silly fool of yourself while shaking that thing. I especially liked playing it when *American Bandstand* was on. But that's how I discovered my deaf ear. No matter how I tried coordinating shaking that thing along to the records Dick Clark was playing, I was never quite in synch. Seems I was better at the theatrical part of playing it than the musical part. I believe my mother discovered this truth as well, because the next year, I didn't get a musical instrument. But my brother did. It was a ukulele, which I guess in ten-year-old Dennis's mind was not very cool, so I quickly confiscated it. But one night when the relatives were all over for poker, our cat, Tippy, decided to do a little concert. She jumped on the couch where I'd left the little guitar, and began plucking at the strings with her claws, which brought howls of laughter from the audience. And while I agreed it was kind of cute, I had to admit that even Tippy could play the thing better than I could.

I was quite disillusioned.

But then came the Beatles, and a trip to Petromelli's Music Store in Euclid, Ohio. My brother wanted a guitar. And Mom—believing there was still hope for a music star in the family, and knowing by now, it wouldn't be me—signed him up for guitar lessons. Soon after, the teacher saw enough ability in Dennis to persuade Mom to make that purchase.

"If Dennis is getting a guitar, I should get something, too," I told Mom, gazing into the store window at all the shiny instruments. That's when I spotted the drum set. It was blue, my favorite color, and was all sparkly, like a sky full of diamonds.

"That's what I want!"

"Girls don't play drums," Mom said in a tone that marked "end of discussion."

Here we go again, I thought. I knew if I continued to prod, I'd hear the other repetitive excuse. *"And besides, he's older."* Some things never change.

I knew that no matter how I fought, I wasn't getting that drum set.

So after that, I resigned myself to just appreciating the

music that others, with God-given talent, create. While enjoying the memories that music provides . . . .

I'm five years old and sitting on the floor of my brother's bedroom playing Conway Twitty's "It's Only Make Believe," over and over on the little record player because it's the most beautiful song I've ever heard. I sing it loud because no one's in the room but me and I can pretend I'm Dinah Shore. (She's the pretty lady who sings, *See the USA in a Chevrolet* . . . .)

I'm six years old and playing at my neighbor Jackie's house. We're swinging on the swings in her backyard, and as we ascend to the top, we yell, "It waaaas aaann . . . Itsy-Bitsy, Teeny-Weeny," and as we descend, we scream, "Yellow Polka Dot Bikiniiii." On and on, as we go up, down, up, down, singing the story of the girl in the scant bathing suit who's afraid to come out of the water because she's afraid people will see. (My thought is, then why'd she wear it in the first place? But the songwriter doesn't say).

When I hear "I Wanna Hold Your Hand," I'm ten years old, standing in my bedroom singing into my hair brush, and wondering when, and how, I'm going to be the girl that Paul, then John, then George (Ringo would always be "just a friend") finally chooses to take my hand.

I don't hear "Singing in the Rain," much anymore but when I do, I'm a teenager, staying at my grandmother's house. I'm lounging in Grandpa's chair (he's working third shift) watching old movies with Gee Gee (who I run to whenever Mom and I have a fight, which is usually every weekend). We watch Gene Kelly skipping over puddles, and though he's way older than me, I have a crush on him because he's just so nice, and cute, and has great rhythm. (Soon I would see him in "*Marjorie Morningstar*," which increases my great love for him.)

And right now, this very minute, MacArthur's Park is melting in the dark and all the sweet green (or is it cream?) icing is flowing down, and I can't tell you what in God's name that one's about (I mean, come on, who leaves a cake out in the rain? Well, unless it's fruit cake). This song transports me back to age thirteen, when my life began to really change, and when songs didn't have to make sense. I like this one for its dramatic overtones. Plus, it reminds me of the Herb Alpert and the Tijuana Brass with that album cover of the Spanish woman covered in whipped cream. Because, at this age, I babysit every weekend (just to get out of the house) and the couple have the LP, and it sure beats the hell out of their Engelbert Humperdinck and Tom Jones collection.

Then, in 1981, something happened to the music.

It was called MTV (Music Television).

It was quite a concept. Songs made into videos. With "veejays" (video deejays) to talk to you in between. There were only five MTV veejays at first, and my favorite was Nina Blackwood—even before I learned that she's a native Cleveland girl. I liked how she could get away with that crazy hairstyle that somehow worked for her. We boomers all watched the videos every chance we got. I fell in love with John "Cougar," (who later added his real name, Mellencamp) was fascinated by Madonna (though she'd soon disappoint me with her publicity-driven sexual antics which, in my Catholic girl psyche, desecrates the blessed name of the Mother that is her namesake), and felt akin with Cyndi Lauper because, after all, we girls really do just wanna have fun. And when our own hometown heroes, the Michael Stanley Band turned up on MTV, all Cleveland rockers—who never get any respect—felt vindicated.

The peak in this new attraction came with Michael Jackson's mini-movie "Thriller." Now if that doesn't make you want to sing and dance. . . .

We were all having quite a marvelous time of it, enjoying this new-found form of musical entertainment, when I, for one, realized something horrible.

I was driving down the road one day in 1986. MTV had been on the air for five years by then. My car radio was playing all the hits from the early '80s era, and somewhere between Joan Jett's "I Love Rock 'n' Roll," and Prince's "Little Red Corvette," I noticed, as I was singing along, that I was thinking about their videos. By the time "Leather & Lace" came on, it hit me.

MTV was robbing me of my own personal musical moments. I wasn't thinking about where I was, or doing, when the songs first played, I was recalling the videos. And this time, it was intercepting my wedding memories.

That Stevie Nicks song was the first on the tape Jeff and I had made to play at our wedding ceremony. As our guests stood outside facing the beautiful lake where we'd both grown up, we all listened to the lyrics that so epitomized Jeff's and my relationship.

Whenever I hear this song, for the rest of my life, I want it to be about my wedding. I want it to be about our love. Not about a damned video.

I noticed this, again, after I saw the video for Billy Idol's "White Wedding." That too had played at our wedding—before I'd seen the video. I merely knew the words and felt it was a good song to play right after the ceremony. Because it *was* a "nice day for a white wedding" and it *was* our great chance to "start again." But a few days after we returned from our honeymoon—still in romance mode—I saw Idol's video of that song on MTV. It was nothing like I'd pictured in my mind as a great wedding song for two divorcees starting life anew on a fine sunny day. On the contrary, it was filled with dark images. I was horrified. And heart sick. Especially when I told a friend about it and she'd remarked, "Yeah, I was wondering why you chose *"that song."* Silly me, I'd been concentrating on the lyrics, and had missed the televised visuals. Now, Billy Idol and music television had stripped away one of my most precious memories. I never watched MTV again.

I went back to listening to music instead of watching it, now with more intent on remembering what's happening in my life as each song plays. It's a small gift I give myself.

There are, of course, a few memories brought on by songs that we'd prefer to forget. Like when I woke up to the radio that day in December 1981, and heard that John Lennon was murdered. I thought I must be having a really bad dream. But then my radio station kept playing his songs, and referring to the crazy man who shot him. I felt the same devastation upon hearing about Harry Chapin, whose concert Jeff and I attended on our first date. And John Denver. The other day, I heard "Thank God, I'm a Country Boy," and though it's a happy song, it now makes me think how sad it was, what happened to him. The plane crash and all. Which then makes me think of Buddy Holly. And Jim Croce. And Lynryd Skynyrd. I can't for the life of me figure out why God takes those who bring us such beautiful music, then strips them—and their Muse—away. And while none of us know the answer to that, we are at least left with those great songs to enjoy. And that's something.

So when God's forceful, demanding voice thundered in my dream that night, I woke up trying to figure out what it all meant. Then I realized He had said, let music *"occupy"* your muse. As in absorb. Utilize. Inhabit. Take possession of.

Sounds good to me.

I guess that's why, when I feel I want to relive my adolescent memories, I occupy myself with rock 'n' roll.

When I'm feeling a bit melancholy, I occupy the blues.

When I feel the need to write about life and longing and love gone wrong, I turn on a country song. And occupy.

And when I feel like dancing, it's Big Band music. Or the Rolling Stones.

I really do believe that music can save us. Like that great, inspiring song, "We Are The World," written in 1985 to bring peace, love, and aid throughout the world.

A world that's so very fortunate to have music to occupy its muse.

What a concept. And what a blessing.

What We Keep, What We Leave

This is not how I should be spending the first hot, sunny day of summer, I'm thinking. My kids should be here—like all those summers before—happily playing, giggling and splashing in that pool outside my mother's front window. But time has changed everything. My little girls are nearly grown. Their activities these days consist more of shopping (for clothes, as well as boys), texting friends, and figuring out how to outwit their parents.

As I stand looking out my mother's window at that pool, I hear laughter from my children of yesteryear. But now it sounds like mockery. *Ha, Ha, those days are gone*, it chides me. *And you will never get them back. Ever.*

I simply cannot grasp the idea that my children will never swim in that pool again. That I'll never hear Mom chat away, as she and I watch them splash about. And laugh. *Ha. Ha.*

Oh, for heavens' sakes, I say, in my own mother's tone, get a grip. There's too much to do today to get all sentimental . . .

I haven't moved from this spot since I walked in the door. I'm standing in the middle of my mother's living room, just staring at all the stuff that surrounds me. "Where do I begin?" I say this aloud, despite the fact there is no one here. My mother left this place abruptly, rushed to a hospital she would never return from. And now I'm left to clear out the condo she loved so much and I can't seem to move. What do I keep? Throw away? What would she want me to do? It all seems too overwhelming when I haven't even accepted the fact that I, at fifty (disturbing in itself), am now an orphan.

For days, weeks and months, I sort through my mother's life. I can't believe the things she saved. Everything is kept, or rather, preserved, in plastic bags, or wrapped in newspapers, and placed in boxes or dresser drawers. For larger items, there are stacks of huge green (her favorite color) plastic containers she bought at the discount store. Getting rid of her furniture and clothes is the easy part. She wouldn't care what I do with those things. And her cat? My daughter reminds me, and her father, of when Grandma said she wanted Smokey to be hers. What could Dad say to that? And so, we take her home with us, despite the fact our spoiled feline is less accepting to the family addition.

But what about the rest of Mom's things? The old pictures in old frames of old relatives I couldn't identify in a lineup? Letters and cards from people I've never met? How can I simply toss it out knowing they meant something to Mom?

And so I don't. They find a place, somehow, in my house. More months go by before I feel strong enough to go through more items. Still, I save more than I discard. Because through these items, my mother speaks to me. Literally.

She has left me notes. Opening an old jewelry box, I find old women's watches, clasp earrings, and a ring with a piece of paper attached. "This was your grandmother's," it reads. I smile as I hold yet another cherished piece from a woman I still miss after twenty years. More items, more notes. "Great Grandma Carter's locket from Great Grandpa." "Gee Gee's thimble she got from Block Company (at least 62 years old!)." And "My necklace given to me by Uncle Ruth when I was six months old." My mother is telling me this as I hold a keepsake with her faded baby picture in it. There are antique brooches and bracelets and even old letters— from service men, as well as love letters my grandmother kept (from *both* husbands). There are stacks of saved greeting cards and other letters from family and friends that span decades.

And copies of every single published article I ever wrote.

There are also copies of poems my mother wrote. The ones she penned for my brother and me marking important events in our growing lives. When I open another drawer, I spot a couple of "Cash Explosion" tickets (she watched the TV show every Saturday night). She must've been saving them for one of our birthdays because this, too, has a poem attached:

If wishes could come true
This would be my wish for you.

To see you on the show
Winning lots and lots of dough.

Such silly little ditties, from the heart.

And of course, dozens of black-and-white snapshots. One, in particular, disarms me. It shows a woman casually sitting on a motorcycle like she owns it. And there's no doubt this woman is my mother. My mother—who always warned me about the dangers of motorcycles—sitting on a two-wheeler before she became a mom. I'm amazed. I wonder whose bike it was. And if my mother did more than just sit on it. Did she ride? Even just around the block? I want to know this. But I never will. Like so many of the pictures I find, this one has no date on the back. And there is no note, or poem, accompanying it. Like it's there to simply make me wonder. I hear my mother chuckle. *There's more to me than you thought,* she seems to say in a faraway laugh.

The wastebasket half empty, I put all these things in a special place. And realize now why we, known as packrats, save stuff. So much of my mother still lives through these items that, like the women before me, I will keep them, too. They are part of our legacy. They are part of all of our histories.

My mother taught me to love music.

She didn't teach me how to get rid of stuff.

A year later, I decide to pay my mother a visit. I drive down the long, winding road that leads to the place where my first family rests. I stop right in front of Mom's grave, shut off the engine, and sit in my car. "See," Mom often told me, "I'll be right on the road so you can wave at me as you drive by." I do better than that. I pull out a CD and put it into the player. Then I crank up the volume, loud enough to shake the earth. I play the song in an odd hope that she'll hear it. "Steal Her Love," is a cover song our favorite local band, The Alan Greene Band, played often on those Sunday Jam Nights. It was the song we always, always danced to.

A few cars pass by, and I'm sure they're wondering why this lady is sitting in the car blasting music in a quiet cemetery. I don't care. I sit and cry and sing as the song plays out, and mentally dance with my mother. When the music ends, I say—

loudly—"That was for you, Mom." Then I start up the car, and drive off. I retrieve the CD, and switch to the radio, which I'd left on a country station. The song that's playing is almost over, so I only hear the last verse, "Just you remember me . . . ."

When I was fifteen, and incarcerated at an all-girls school, when I wrote this poem about mothers:
> Mothers have a tendency to do all the right things
> But they seem to forget of that word, understanding.
> They never forget how to yell and recite
> But when it comes to understanding, they never do it right.
> When you have a problem too hard to work out
> You can't seem to tell her of what it's about.
> Well no one is perfect - not North, South, East or West
> So give your mother credit on what she does best."

Turns out, my mother was best at several things. At setting examples. At showing me courage in the face of hardships. At loving me.

Even when she didn't know how.

Homecoming

*T*hey say the only constant in life is change. Anyone who returns to the place where they once dug for China, swung on the swing set while singing at the top of their lungs, or laid in the grass envisioning snowmen in the clouds, knows how true that adage is.

Hometowns change, grow, and build condominiums. Most do anyway. Not mine. That little town of Lakeline, Ohio, is pretty much the same as it was fifty years ago. The massive trees that line Lakeshore Boulevard still hover over the village like a protective canopy. Young families still raise children here. Older residents still grow their own tomatoes. And though I'm not certain, I imagine they still share a few with their neighbors.

The houses here are pretty much the same, too. Well, some have been updated. Others have modern additions. Not so with the little bungalow I grew up in. It did not receive an addition, but rather, an amputation. The utility room, where I had watched the births of many litters of kittens, and where my family kept cases of Black Label, POC and Pabst Blue Ribbon Beer alongside bottles of Kesslers and Seagrams, is gone. Along with the adjoining porch, where Grandpa listened to the ballgames on his transistor radio.

I know it was necessary, based on the last time I walked its grounds. But still. . . .

When my grandmother died in 1982, I swore I'd never return to that house. When the last truck came to haul away all the stuff we couldn't use, or that simply wasn't usable, I stood there in the backyard, reviewing twenty-eight years of life moments, and said my goodbyes. But two decades later, I unexpectedly found myself back in that yard. Blame it on the all-too-impatient driver behind me honking his horn, forcing me to either pull into the drive or move on already.

For years, I had moved on. But this time, my daughter forced my hand.

"Let's get out, Mom, and look around," my inquisitive thirteen-year-old said. For years, she'd heard stories of her mother growing up in "Gee Gee's house." And she was at that age when she was actually interested in my life, which I knew wasn't going to last much longer. I pulled in.

"Well, aren't we getting out?" Tiffany prodded as I sat there numbly, the motor still running. How could I tell her I was afraid?

And ashamed. This did not look like the house I grew up in.

After Gee Gee died, the mayor of Lakeline bought it—for a country western song—fixed it up, then rented it out. His renters stayed sixteen years, but it had now been vacant for nearly two. Or rather, abandoned, like an orphan. Overgrown grass and tall weeds now shadowed its view. The once white picket fence is now faded grey, with dark spots where paint had chipped away, like the years. Boarded-up windows concealed its many life stories. And everywhere Gee Gee's vibrant blossoms once filled the yard, there is not a bud in sight.

I passed this house often because I lived just ten miles away from it. But each time I'd get close to the address, I'd divert my thoughts by turning up the car radio, or talking to my kids, in order to drive on, as if it was just another house on the way to somewhere else.

Now my youngest daughter and I were sitting in the car gazing at the rundown building that used to be my childhood home.

"This is where you lived?"

I cringed. It was not the house I'd described to her.

"It didn't look this bad back then," I said apologetically. Tiffany glanced at the mailbox. It sat atop a wooden post now. Ours was always stuck between the oak's thick, broad trunks (my grandfather's answer to a pole).

My daughter read off the numbers: "33602."

"Lakeshore Boulevard." I added. It was an address forever etched in my mind. I could've recited the old phone number, too, but Tiffany was already out of the car.

By now, curiosity had gotten to me, too. "Well, no one's gonna kick us out." I turned off the ignition.

After Gee Gee's death, my mother had suggested that Jeff, my soon-to-be husband, and I buy the small dwelling.

"No way," I said in a voice that shouted final.

"But why?" Jeff asked, clearly dumbfounded. "Don't you want to live in the house you grew up in? You always said it has great memories for you."

We were driving to our rental home after another day of clearing out my dead grandmother's house. We were both in our own thoughts when he stopped at the light. He turned toward me.

"Look, it's a great opportunity. You always said renting was a waste of money."

I said nothing. The light turned green. As a last ditch effort, he added, "I realize it doesn't look like much now, but we can fix it up. Make it ours."

He didn't get it. It wasn't that I didn't have a happy childhood there, and cherished memories. But this little house across the street from Lake Erie held currents of sad ones, too. The people, the cats, and neighbors that had made this house a home, no longer existed. I couldn't imagine myself living there again. I was no longer the child that once occupied it. Besides, it could never feel like my home. This was Gee Gee's house. It could never be mine.

Yet now, as I walked slowly toward the house, I felt a sense of ownership. Like I had every right to traipse through this yard, despite the twenty years that had passed.

As we headed down the driveway, I began telling Tiffany about the flowerbeds that once lined it. The various colors of tulips, hyacinths, and big full roses that had graced the front yard and surrounding that tree that once held up the mailbox.

"It must've been really pretty," she said. I could tell she was trying to make me feel better, as was her way.

"Yeah, it sure was," I barely answered. "Your great-grandmother took a lot of pride in her gardening." The images were coming fast and strong and I had to catch my breath a few times as life suddenly went backward like the rewinding of a movie projector . . .

I'm twenty-one and raking the fall leaves covering this yard. I'm doing this to help out my seventy-one-year-old grandmother, whose declining health has been keeping her from doing things she never had problems doing before. I'm thinking how the yard looks so much smaller than I remembered from my youth. Like my ever-weakening grandmother.

I am ten. I'm sitting down on the picnic bench in the backyard with my grandfather, who's listening to the ball game on his transistor radio. I know that baseball is his favorite sport, so I've become a fan, too. Even though I find it hard to pay attention when you have to listen to it on the radio. It's so much easier to keep track of when you watch it on TV. But Grandpa seems to prefer it this way, like the mental images of the homeruns and the strike-outs are far more entertaining in his head. I sit quietly because I know I can't talk to him until I hear the broadcaster announce a commercial. But I don't mind. I just like sitting here with him and watching his changing facial expressions, depending on the hit, the miss, or the score . . .

I am nine, and I don't understand why my mother gets mad so much and slams the bathroom door and stays there for long periods of time. I know nothing of her struggles. Of being the only woman she knows who is divorced. Of having to live, at thirty-three years old, under her parents roof, and rules. Of having to sleep on the couch each and every night of her life. And how frustrating it must be to not even to have a room of her own where she can go and have a good cry. All I know is that my mother is not like the others I know, or see on TV . . .

I am eight. I'm dressed in a fancy white dress and white patent leather shoes and feel like one of my dolls, the bride one with the veil. I've just made my First Communion and everyone's here at the house. My grandparents (who love a good party), my mother, brother, the neighbors, and some of my favorite relatives. Even my first-grade teacher (one of Mom's few lady friends because her husband, who also works at Cleveland Trust, drives Mom to work and back). I'm enjoying being the center of attention, for a change. And although I'm still pretty confused by all the rules and commandments and prayers this Catholic church now demands of me, I think I can handle it. Though I do tell God in private that doing everything my mother says, is kind of pushing it, in all fairness. Doesn't He realize how difficult she can be? But I promise Him I'll try. But warn not to expect too much. . . .

Now as my daughter, who's a much better child than I ever was, walks with me to the white picket fence, I pointed out the magnolia tree. "We always knew it was May when that tree would be in full bloom," I told her. The tree wasn't in bloom—this being September—but from the looks of it, I suspected it hadn't bloomed in many a May. We got to the front door and this is when I drew in some more breaths. The brick walkway that welcomed all those relatives on poker night was broken up in big clumpy pieces, like someone had beaten it with a hammer. We pressed our faces to the window that had no board covering it. I knew we couldn't go in, nor did I want to. There was something sacred about my memories of its insides that I wanted to honor. I wanted to remember it as it looked in my head. And on so many occasions, in my dreams. I still had dreams, oftentimes, where current events played out in this old house. I always thought that was weird.

As we continued our walk toward the back of the house, I told my daughter how all those cats would roam the yard and climb (and get stuck in) the big trees. I recounted stories of Uncle Denny's tree house (and how he never let me up), and showed her the exact place I dug for China (and ignored the odd look she gave me). She asked a few questions and I answered, but it soon became clear that that was then and this is now, and I didn't belong here anymore. We left and went back to 2003.

Amazing how you can love a house. And how it can break your heart when you see it abandoned, and in such disrepair that you hardly recognize it as it stands in front of you, its yard full of leafy debris.

It's also strange how a house can remain a part of you, how it becomes a part of who you are. How a small and simple house can be the stage in which your dreams play out.

In those dreams, my childhood home remains as I best it remember. The grayish blue shingles. The blooming rosebush that creeped up along its outside walls. The open yard in which this child ran, played, pretended. In those surreal moments of twilight, events take place in rooms of a house that' s filled with life, with the family, neighbors, and cats that helped mold this adult.

I told my mother about us stopping at Gee Gee's house. But I didn't mention its condition. I didn't tell her that I believed it was going to be torn down, because I knew it would upset her.

Mom was seventy-four by then, and didn't need that kind of heartbreak. The following year, just as the house was being refurbished with new vinyl siding, new windows, and basic sprucing up, my mother died. So I never got to tell her that the house was going to live on.

One summer day, a few years ago, Jeff and I were out for a motorcycle ride. As we headed toward Gee Gee's house, I suddenly asked him to pull in. The drive was filled with cars and trucks. New owners were working on it. That old curiosity thing had taken hold of me, again.

"Hello, I grew up in this house," I told the lady on the other side of the screen door. "I was wondering, could I come in and see it?"

"Oh, sure, just watch where you walk," she said, stepping aside.

That should've been my cue. Some things are better left alone.

I walked inside my childhood home for the first time in twenty-four years. And I was immediately sorry I did. The place was in shambles. They had stripped that beautiful knotty pine wood paneling that always seemed to protect its inhabitants. Gone were the fancy French doors I once slammed on my brother's face. Gone was the '50s furniture I remembered. Gone were all the people who had wandered in and out. This was so not Gee Gee's house.

I didn't blame this nice couple who were restoring it—was even grateful it would survive demolition. But in their doing so, it had stripped a huge chunk of my life.

"That was too weird," I said to Jeff as we hopped on the bike.

"Yeah, now you'll probably dream of that house tonight."

"I always dream of that house," I answered him.

But it's a house of a different kind. A house of another time. Another era. The house I knew only exists in the attic of my mind. And as we rode on down the highway, I realized that's where it will remain, cobwebs and all.

What I Want to Tell My Children

Dear Girls:

      I was watching Oprah's *After Show* the other day and she was saying how at twenty-five, she felt disappointed because she hadn't done much with her life. And I thought, *That's another thing we have in common!* (Okay, I know what you're thinking, kids, "Get real, Mom, you and Oprah don't have anything in common. Let's see: She's black. You're white. She's like a gonzillionaire. You have like $1.60 in your purse. *And* she's personal friends with Jay-Z and all those famous people *you* only *read* about.")

      But that's not what I mean. You see, me and Oprah, we think alike. We both agree on human issues. And we've experienced many of the same things. We both grew up loving the Beatles and the Supremes. We both watched the *Partridge Family*, and *Mary Tyler Moore*—faithfully. We both have god-awful school pictures we can't escape from. And get this: We were born just three weeks apart from each other. So we're practically twins! (She's the older, wiser one.)

      That should all account for something—despite the fact that she's actually doing something to change the world. Although, having raised you two to be decent human beings, I feel I've done my part for world peace. . . .

Now as I was saying, I know exactly what Oprah meant. When you hit that big milestone of a quarter of a century, you think you should be all set in life by then. That you should already be there, or at least on your way there—wherever *there* is. After all, you have certain expectations (or at least your parents do) as you head toward adulthood. Women feel they should have met their prince charming by then, or started their family, or be halfway up that proverbial ladder of success—like to a talk show or something.

Or at the very, very least, figured out exactly she wants to be when she grows up.

But it doesn't work that way, my children. So I'll begin my list of what I want you to know with this:

It Takes Decades To Be Who You Really Are.

Sounds weird, huh? At eighteen, or twenty-five, or even thirty or more, you're still a work in progress. Hey, stop that rolling of the eyes! It's true. Through your various life stages, you think you know who you are. But as those infomercials say when selling those Ginsu knives: "*But wait! There's more!*"

Oh, so much more. You've heard how snakes shed their skin, layer after layer, year after year? This is a sign of growth. The young snakes shed more often than the older ones because growth is more rapid in babies. Once they become old snakes, they don't need to shed as much because the design that's been hidden underneath that whole time has finally been revealed. They've reached that stage in their little reptile lives where they are at their most beautiful in color and content.

Of course, you know where I'm going with this analogy. Humans are like snakes (I'm sure you already know a few people who take this similarity all too literally). And as we get older, we get wiser, less restless, and more colorful, as each layer is shed. The exception—in snakes and in people—is when their environment isn't right, or the frequency and amount of nutrition is limited, or where there's been injury.

But if all goes well, by the time you're middle-aged like me, you'll be looking mighty fine, inside and out. To yourself, if no one else. And you'll be great with that. Trust me.

When I turned twenty-five, I was so depressed. You'd have thought it was my 80th birthday and all I had to look forward to was a walking cane and a male nurse named Arthur Ritis.

Everyone, it seemed, knew where their lives were going. They had direction. Me, I was stagnant. In limbo. I guess like Oprah. But unlike Oprah, I was married by then. That's supposed to be one of the main life goals for women. So I thought this would make me happy. Make me feel like a real adult. Turned out, marriage wasn't at all like I thought it would be. Instead of feeling all grown up, with my own house, my own car, my own dollar and sixty cents, I felt imprisoned. Like when a fly gets stuck between the window and the screen and buzzes around frantically looking for a way out. It felt like that.

That's how you know you're not where you belong.

My husband (you remember, I told you about the "other" one) had thrown a party for me to celebrate this milestone birthday. All five of my six friends showed up. Which was even more depressing, to realize I didn't have that many friends. My big night was spent sitting around drinking cheap wine, smoking a few joints, and watching TV. I was bored to the core of my being. I should've been out dancing and laughing and flirting with the bouncer at the local bar. But I'd have never been "allowed" to do that. Because even though I was at the prime of my life, I was *married* and so, considered practically dead.

In addition, along with an unfulfilling marriage and few friends, I hadn't published one thing I'd ever written. Now, here's the crazy part. I'd only sent out one manuscript in all those years I'd been writing. *And* I'd received a hand-written, personal rejection letter, which I now know, in my writerly wisdom, is actually a really good thing. It means you got close enough to warrant a personal note, and all it takes is a little more tweaking. But no, based on that one-time negative response, I considered myself a total failure.

Oh, that's sooo twenty five. . . .

Remember that one morning, Tiffany, when you were crabbin' about having to get up so early and go to school? You said, "You just don't understand, Mom! All *you* have to do is pour your cup of coffee, go into your little office and type all day. *In your pajamas!*"

Oh, sure, it may look like that . . .

I sighed, and in my ancient wisdom, I placed my hands on your young shoulders and replied, "Honey, it took me nearly fifty years to get to this place in my life. So get your butt to school and learn something. You've got about thirty more years to go."

But this, my dear growing daughter who thinks her mother has always had it easy, is what you have to look forward to. Not the part about working in your pajamas (though that *is* nice), but the grand discovery of knowing what you're meant to do in this life. That, through trials and many errors, you find a way to do it, *and* get paid for it. (Be it monetarily or spiritually. Though the latter pays bigger dividends.)

For most people, this all takes awhile. But you'll know it when you realize how much you love doing what you do. Every day. And can't wait until tomorrow, so you get to do it again. Because you've earned the right. You've struggled and worked hard. (Most likely, let's say, in at least one shitty job that seemed only worth it when you got to write about the horrific experience in a book. Or you run into that old boss who, years before, fired you—at your own book signing, or perhaps the taping of your hugely successful talk show—and he now sees that you're really not a worthless piece of crap, after all.) And you can smile recalling how you suffered.

It's called sweet justice.

And that's when you know, my dear daughters, that you have become the person you really are. When you can wake up each morning and thank God for all your blessings, including the person you are that very day. That person with all the little quirks, and the clumpy cellulite, and the venial sins. And you thank Him for giving you all that experience: the good, the bad, and the divine wisdom that He's still not done with you yet. That you still have some growing to do. Still have a few more layers to shed . . .

What fun.

Now here's the other stuff I want to tell you:

- **It's Not Enough to Simply Get by Day to Day**. Make your life count for something. *Live*, don't simply exist. If God wanted you to be a slug, he'd have made you one. So you have an obligation to Him (or Her, we really don't know), and to yourself, to be your best person, and do good things. Because as far as we know, we get one good sprint around this block. As my good friend, Lynne, says, "This is not a dress rehearsal, folks." So think about what you'd like to be doing in a year, or two or five. Then take steps toward that goal, whatever it is. Start with today. And sure, there'll be days when you won't feel like doing a damn thing toward any goal. Call that your Mental Health Day. But only give yourself one like every three months or so. (And please don't take them on work days. Weekends are great for Mental Health Days and you'll keep your job). And please, please, don't sit around watching TV and smoking dope (a popular pastime in my day, which I never quite understood, it's so incredibly *boring*). That won't make you happy (that buzz won't last nearly as long as the exhilarated feeling of a worthwhile accomplishment). Get out and be active in the world. Be a *part* of the world.

- **Find a Good Life Partner.** Don't be in a hurry to get married. Even if you think you've found the right person, take your time. Get to know who *you* are, before having to discover who someone else is. And please, please Pay Attention—to everything about that person you are dating, or have fallen in love with. Notice how he treats his mother, children, animals, the elderly, the waitress. And don't for one delusional minute think that you'll be able to change that person into what you really want. He is what he is. If he has a lot of flaws you don't think you can live with, you're better off going solo. Trust me on that. Make sure that person meets your needs, and supports—even encourages—your own personal growth. And make sure he makes you laugh. It'll never be all the time, but it should be a lot of the time. If you're not having fun with that someone, or feel special with that someone, consider him a waste of your precious time, and move on.

- **Learn Something New Every Day**. Your brain needs nourishment just like the rest of your body. Feed it knowledge. It will enrich your mind, as well as your soul. Even if you get to where you want to be in your career, or become a gazillionaire, there is always more to learn, new things to experience. Read. Read. Read. A good book, or just the newspaper, so you can be informed on current events. This will allow you to talk to anyone about anything—a worthwhile asset in business, and in life. And keep learning. Go back to school to get your degree (*never* use age as an excuse not to, that's just stupid), or take a class, or workshop in something that interest you. Always wanted to paint? Learn how to do it, and paint, damn it.

- **Make Time For Your People.** The people you love, who love you back. Including yourself. There's this trend going around American society where everyone is busy, busy, busy. And while I believe that's a good thing (so long as you're doing good busy stuff, like spending time doing what you love, which should include your job), sometimes you get caught up in the whirlwind, you forget to make "Play Dates." This is different from a Mental Health Day, which is a lazy day. A Play Date is exactly that. A day to do whatever makes you happy—with someone, or by yourself (because you are your people, too). Spend a day lolly-gagging around your town. Go for a hike. Or bike ride. Or a nice walk in the park. Swing on a swing set. Go to a show. Have lunch with a friend. Spend time with children and animals (they will surely reacquaint you with your inner child). Whatever you feel like doing for a day. And make a *personal* phone call (not emails, not texting) to someone you haven't talked to for awhile. Call your significant other every day, just to say, "I love you." And above all else, call your mother. And your father, too.

- **Remember: Success is Defined by How You Treat Others.** I've known a few successful people in my day, and I've known some real shit-heads. The truly successful people treats everyone the same—with respect. They never, ever act like they are better than you. They're smart enough to realize that having more money or being president of a company doesn't make you better, or happier. The ones who think they're successful because of all their material possessions, and treat others poorly, are failures in life. These mean, self-absorbed people are really poor, misguided souls with so much yet to learn. I saw a sign in front of a church the other day that read: "Don't let possessions possess you." You can gain a lot of wisdom from those church signs.

- **So Be a Nice Person**. I know, sometimes that's really, really hard. Especially when someone isn't nice to you. But always remember, when people act like that, it has little or nothing to do with you. They're just miserable human beings (in more ways than one) and you actually should feel sorry for them, pray for them, because they probably like themselves even less than you like them. So be nice. To your neighbor. Your co-worker. The restaurant hostess or server of your food. To the maintenance man. The garbage collector. The telephone solicitor . . . you get the idea. And do what you can to make other people's lives a little easier. You may not think some little act of kindness is a big deal. But just ask that handicapped person you opened the door for. Or that lonely child you sat on the floor and played with. Or those coupons you left on the grocer shelf where that struggling single mother was thrilled to find. And when you go to a parking lot, park far away. Leave open spots for those who really could use a closer one (Besides, walking is good for you). Be kind to animals, babies, children, and old people. Because they deserve it.

- **Cut People Some Slack.** Never assume anything. You never really know what other people are going through. Maybe they're having a bad day, or year, or life. If you have an issue with someone, talk directly to that person, not to everyone except that person. People do that all the time. They want to avoid confrontation. But communication saves a whole lot of hassle and misunderstandings. Remember what I say: You will be a happier person being an open, honest and *nice* person, and doing nice things for others. Trust me on that one.

- **If You Become a Mother, Be The Best One You Can Be.** Want a better world? Raise good people. Children really are the future of the world. Jacqueline Kennedy had it right when she said, "If I fail at raising my children properly, then I have failed at life." I simply can't top that one.

- **Don't Ever Lose Your Sense of Humor.** Even God has

that (just look at the giraffe, the aardvark, Richard Simmons). There are humorous situations in even a bad day. Don't take everything so seriously, especially yourself. Lighten up. Laugh at yourself. Be a little silly.

- **If You're Not Happy** - Then you're not doing what God wants you to do. Go a different direction. Make some changes in your life. Meet new people.

- **Hug a tree**. Yeah, yeah, I know, it sounds really corny. But trust me (again). It's amazing how wonderful that feels. Here's how: Find a big old tree in your yard, or during that hike in the park. Stand in front of it and spread your arms wide. Then lean forward and press your face (gently, that bark's a bit coarse) against it, and wrap your arms around it. Close your eyes and stay there for awhile. Breathe in and out. Feel the strength, oh the tremendous strength, from that tree. This simple great act reminds us how minuscule we are in this world and we can draw strength—literally—from that big oak. Then go about your merry way. You'll find yourself smiling.

- Now here's an old favorite: **When Life Hands You Lemons, By All Means, Make Lemonade**. It does you no good to pout and feel sorry for yourself. Get over it. There are lots of people worse off than you. It pains me to say this, but my mother was absolutely right: "The world doesn't revolve around you." Or me. *However*, we are a big part of it, so find ways to produce positive energy. And remember, the unfortunate events in our lives often force us to make changes that ultimately bring triumph.

- **Be True To Yourself.** Honor who you are by never trying to be someone you truly are not. And always listen to that little voice inside you. Feel what your heart is trying to tell you. You have this other sense for a reason. It will save you many times.

- **Go to Church**. Now hold on a minute. I don't mean *my* church. Go to *your* church. Wherever that might be. Right now, you're like your mother, who hated going to church at your age (hopefully, like me, you'll later realize how calming, and beneficial, a real church can be). So go find your own church. It might be the lake, or park, or the sanctuary of your nice quiet bedroom. It really doesn't matter. Just find that place you feel most at peace, more at one with the world. Then say, *Hey God. I need some guidance. And I will listen because I know I'm not done learning yet.* And have a nice long talk, just you and Him. He likes that. Say anything you want. Then at the end, say, *Thanks, God. For everything. I really appreciate it.* Believe me, this goes a long way. I can swear to you, this simple act of thankfulness will make you a happy, appreciative human being. And that's all a mother could want.

Okay, I think I'm done here. Of course there's so much more for you to know. There are things I haven't yet learned myself. So check back with me in about ten years. After I've shed my last few layers.

But for now, I have to go. Oprah's on in five minutes.

Epilogue

*W*hen I was seven or eight, my mother decided I should learn how to swim. She, of course, had no clue that her daughter's fear of water was due to a near-drowning incident when she was five. That was a well-kept secret between her daughter and her favorite sitter. All she knew was that anytime I went to the lake, I would only put my feet in and refused to go further. She thought this might be a disadvantage if I ever found myself in a situation where I needed to know how to stay afloat. She thought I should face my fears (despite the fact, she herself never swam, drove, or flew in an airplane). But she felt everyone (except her) living so close to a lake should know how to swim.

Her son was already a member of the YMCA because they had a program called "Lads Without Dads," for boys with no active male role models. My mother was thrilled to learn of this program, and I believe, relieved, too. It took a bit of the pressure off. The boy needed a good father figure (grandpas don't quite count). The male counselors there took the boys fishing, canoeing, and camping. They taught them how to use a bow and arrow, shoot at tin cans, and how to survive as men. Naturally, I complained about this. Often.

"Why does Dennis get to do all the fun stuff?" I would wait to hear the usual irritatingly lame excuses: "He's older," and of course, "Because he's a boy and you're a girl." But one day she surprised me. I suppose she figured there was a way she could kill two birds with one stone, by letting me have a YMCA activity, and getting me to learn how not to drown.

So I learned the breast stroke, the jellyfish roll, and the back float (which actually felt pretty good, except when water would get in my ears). I even learned how to dive off the diving board. But that took awhile. It was my greatest fear, and biggest challenge. First off, I was afraid of heights. Secondly, I didn't want to do it.

It took the nice counselor lady months to help me drum up the nerve to climb up on that bouncing board, then jump off like a leap frog.

"Please don't let me drown." I looked at her with begging eyes.

"Of course, I won't, honey. You'll do great!" She smiled with more confidence in me than I felt I deserved.

All the other kids had been diving off the board for weeks now and every time I began my ascent up those metal stairs, I'd look down at the deceivingly pretty blue water and feel the bass drum begin in my chest. Then I'd hear the muffled echo of children's laughter through that stupid bathing cap—which was so tight against my ears it was amazing I could hear anything. I took their laughter personally, though no one seemed the least bit interested in my hovering presence above their wet heads. And I would feel the rise of gripping fear that would tighten around me like a straight jacket. Then I'd turn myself around—ever-so-carefully—and climb back down.

I don't know what Counselor Lady said to me that finally got me to go for broke (or maybe it was the simple fact that I was mighty sick and tired of being the kid who couldn't do it), but one glorious day I found myself standing at the edge of that diving board, determined to follow through. To face my ultimate fear in life, and throw my whole body into that aquamarine swirl, and not think of the real possibility of busting my head wide open, or never rising to the surface again. Least I'd go with some dignity. Or would I? Well, I was going to do it anyway, damn it. I was going to stop being such a chicken shit.

I stood on the edge of the board seeing my life pass before me (which quickly switched to an image of my own funeral. "So sad. She was so young. Why the hell did she go jumpin' off that thing anyway?"). I shook my head to rattle away the dark thoughts, raised my arms like I'd been taught to do, and said a prayer, *"Oh God, let me do this and survive."* I took in a deep breath. I squeezed my eyes shut and tried to ignore my pounding heart.

Then I jumped.

I hit the water and went down in like a torpedo. Panic set in, but I remembered what my teacher had taught me. I kicked my ass off. I pushed with my arms wide. And I started to rise. Up and up. I wasn't sinking down like when I was five. I'd learned a few things by then. I knew how to face my fears. I knew how to rise above. I came to the surface and drew in a big breath of delicious air. And in the distance, I heard applause. My teacher was smiling and clapping. I had done it. And survived.

For a brief second, she looked just like my angel lady who

had saved my life in that bathing cap with the floppy yellow-and-pink daisies.

I thanked God. For everything.

After a few more weeks of repeating my success, I made a decision. I'd gone through all the required steps, had made it worth my time and mother's hard-earned money. I became a minnow, then a barracuda, then a swordfish. Then I became a conscientious objector. I realized I had accomplished my goal, overcame my fear (well, sort of) and just didn't want to do it anymore. It wasn't fun for me, like it was for the other kids. I still didn't like to swim. I didn't like getting water in my ears. And it burned my eyes. And I hated that stupid bathing cap. And frankly, swimming took an awful lot of physical effort, which I really wasn't into. I've never been the athletic type. After a bit of persuasion on my part, Mom let me drop the lessons. Because I now knew how to stay afloat. Which would prove handy though some rough times still to come.

There are of course many lessons we learn in life. They come in different forms and degrees. Some storm in, loud and forceful, and smacks you right to the ground in one hard swoop. Others creep in softly, quietly, like a whispered secret. Both are equally effective.

And some lessons don't get learned right away. Some take years, others, a lifetime.

Still, they are always welcomed.

I never thought, in my fifties, I'd still live in the same place where I grew up. I had bigger visions. I saw myself growing and moving—up and out. I thought staying 'stuck' in the same old place where you lived your childhood, would stifle your growth. I used to think it was actually rather sad if you never got out of your own hometown.

After living briefly in other areas, I don't think that anymore.

It's not where you live, it's knowing where you belong.

No matter where we grow up, or what we've been through, or what we believe in (or not believe in), we all want to belong somewhere. And sometimes, it takes most of our lives to realize where that somewhere is. And if we're real lucky, we find ourselves there. Lucky me, I discovered through my life adventures that I actually belong right where I started from in the first place.

Like Dorothy, I was looking for my heart's desire, and through a series of events—good and bad—I found it in my own backyard. Imagine that.

***

There's a saying that goes, "Faith is a journey, not a destination."

And the journey really is the fun part. (Okay, not always fun, but worth the trip.) Still, I always have a destination. Whenever I'm feeling sad. Or happy. Or confused. Or just very grateful, there's a place I go where I feel I belong.

This now-pretty-good Catholic girl goes to church.

Well, most of the time. In summer, I go to Lake Erie. No, I don't swim, but I do get my feet wet. I love being near this great lake—happy just to sit and stare into its blue aura. I go sometimes to watch the sunset. Sometimes to think deep thoughts. Sometimes to pray.

Because it seems like just the place where God would hang out.

Photo by Jeff Adams

Deanna Adams is a freelance writer, essayist, and author. Her articles and essays have been published in a variety of publications, including the Cleveland *Plain Dealer*, *Northern Ohio Live, Ohio Magazine,* and *Lake Erie Living* magazine. Her first book, *Rock 'n' Roll and the Cleveland Connection,* published by Kent State University Press, was named a 2003 finalist for the Ohioana Award for nonfiction, and for excellence in research for the 2003 ARSC Awards (Association for Recorded Sound Collections). Deanna is an instructor at Lakeland Community College, The Lit Center in Cleveland, and is director/founder of the Women Writers' Winter Retreat. Her website is www.deannaadams.com